D1118587

# Split Self/
# Split Object

Paul A. Alkin, Ph.D.
311 B Street
Davis, CA 95616

# Split Self/ Split Object

## Understanding and Treating Borderline, Narcissistic, and Schizoid Disorders

Philip Manfield, Ph.D.

JASON ARONSON INC.
*Northvale, New Jersey*
*London*

Production Editor: Judith D. Cohen

This book was set in 11/13 Baskerville by Lind Graphics of Upper Saddle River, New Jersey. It was printed and bound by Haddon Craftsmen of Scranton, Pennsylvania.



10 9 8 7 6 5 4 3 2 1



**Library of Congress Cataloging-in-Publication Data**

Manfield, Philip
Split Self/Split Object : Understanding and Treating Borderline, Narcissistic, and Schizoid Disorders / by Philip Manfield.
p. cm.
Includes bibliographical references and index.
ISBN 0-87668-460-6
1. Personality disorders—Treatment. 2. Borderline personality disorder—Treatment. 3. Narcissism—Treatment. 4. Schizoid personality—Treatment. 5. Psychotherapy. I. Title.
[DNLM: 1.Borderline Personality Disorder—therapy.
2. Narcissism. 3. Psychoanalytic Therapy. 4. Schizoid Personality
Disorder—therapy. WM 190 M276e]
RC554.M26 1992
616.85 85'—dc20
DNLM/DLC
for Library of Congress 91-44052

Manufactured in the United States of America. Jason Aronson Inc. offers books and cassettes. For information and catalog write to Jason Aronson Inc., 230 Livingston Street, Northvale, New Jersey 07647

To My Dad

# Contents

## Part II

## Part III

# Acknowledgments

It is a long-awaited privilege to be able to sit down to write about how this book came to be written and to acknowledge all the many people who contributed to it and to whom I am so very grateful. Although the acknowledgments appear first in a book, they are written last. I began writing this book nearly five years ago and I have looked forward to writing this final section for a long time.

The book began in November of 1986 on a visit with my brother David Manfield, a clinical psychologist in Portland, Oregon. I had been taking training at the time with the Masterson Institute, and I was very excited about the diagnostic process I was learning and about some of the clinical ideas. David and I had been discussing these ideas and applying them with good results to our cases. Frustrated at the lack of resources available to learn more about the material we had been discussing, David suggested, "Why don't you write a book?" By that evening, the two of us had worked out a rough outline for this book. He has continued to support me throughout its writing, reading each chapter as it was written and offering professional suggestions and brotherly encouragement, for which I am deeply appreciative.

During the first several years of writing, I did not know if a publisher would be interested in the book. I had written no journal articles and had no professional recognition outside of the communities in which I practiced. I never doubted that I would finish writing the book, but I was not sure whether anyone besides my students, my colleagues, and my friends would ever read it.

During this period, I was very fortunate to have the support of many colleagues and students who read chapters from the unfinished work, provided me with valuable feedback, and never seemed to doubt that the finished book would be published and widely appreciated. In addition to my students my thanks go to Andrea Rechtin, Shirley Issel, Barbara Short, Patricia Padgett, Duncan Bennett, Karen Hoyt, and Larry Metzger, who took the time to read early chapters and make extensive and very helpful comments.

Special thanks to Elise Miller, who generously contributed her expertise in writing combined with her familiarity with the material to help me refine the shape of the book and improve its organization. Special thanks also to Larry Metzger and Marilynn Martin for consulting with me on the section on treatment of alcohol abuse.

My thanks to Jason Aronson, my publisher, for his support, his openness, and the professional and human way he has gone about the business of publishing the manuscript. It has been a pleasure to work with a publisher who appreciates, as Dr. Aronson does, the attributes of the book that I too most value.

I am truly indebted to James Masterson and his associates, not only for developing the ideas that originally motivated me to write this book, but for establishing a training program in the San Francisco area that made his ideas accessible to me. My special thanks to Ralph Klein for the clinical perspectives that he offered me, especially with respect to his approach to working with schizoid disorders.

My deeply felt thanks to Linda Harrison, Bill Robbins, and Ken Seider for not only contributing enormously to the final quality of this book, but for helping to make the writing of it a pleasurable and exciting experience. I have sometimes heard people describe writing as an isolating endeavor; for me, however, writing this book has been the opposite experience. It has been the source of many fascinating and enriching conversations; it has provided endless opportunities to confer with colleagues, to exchange ideas, to sharpen our understanding, and to engage in many pleasant hours of honest sharing about our clinical experiences.

Linda Harrison has been a valued friend and colleague for many years. We share an office and meet weekly to consult with each other about cases and to refine our treatment approaches. She has read each chapter as it was written, often reading several drafts of a chapter and offering her extensive thoughts, suggestions, and editorial notes about each. She has been willing to tell me very directly what she liked and what she didn't like, and she has always offered useful ideas for improvement. During the course of the writing, she has helped me to sharpen many of the ideas that went into the book.

Bill Robbins has been extremely encouraging of my writing from the very beginning. I have appreciated his support as a friend as well as his contributions as a professional. He has read each chapter enthusiastically and has always offered extensive and helpful comments. His objections and suggestions for improvement were always valuable and thought provoking. His assessments of strengths and weaknesses were always frank, usually accurate, occasionally painful, and always very helpful.

Ken Seider has been a valued colleague, consultant, and friend throughout the writing. His scholarly understanding of a broad range of systems and analytic approaches, combined with his clinical acuity, has led to many interesting discussions between us of the proposed content of the book, discussions that have been extremely enjoyable as well as stimulating and informative for me. His input has helped to enrich this book and to make it a more learned and professional treatise.

My warm appreciation to my secretary, Meg Kilday, for her help in converting many of my notes and lecture tapes from chicken scratch into text, for her calm, cheerful presence, and for her willingness to pitch in and be on my team. I have been consistently amazed that as my personal shorthand has evolved and become more and more obscure, she has had the willingness and talent to continue to decipher it.

My deepest gratitude to my wife, Janet, who has patiently shared me with the computer throughout this seemingly endless process of writing. She has also provided the voice of moderation when my priorities lost their clarity and the book crowded out other important aspects of life. She has read each chapter, sometimes before it reached the printer, and offered feedback as a wife and as a psychotherapist. She has been an ally, an adviser, and a source of great support.

My son Mark was born during chapter three. He has grown up with the book. Along with his mother, he has been a reminder of my priorities. In the beginning, his way of letting me know that I was spending too much time with my computer was to shut off the power switch. I am very grateful to him for being himself and for constantly reminding me what life is about.

December 1991

# Introduction

A personality disorder is a disruption of the psyche at the most basic level, distorting a person's perception of himself, others, and relationships, preventing the person from achieving genuine satisfaction in love, work, or play. These distortions naturally extend to the relationships patients[1] with personality disorders form with their therapists, making these patients particularly difficult to treat, especially when the treatment approach used is oriented toward neurotic patients. For the most part, however, patients with personality disorders are treatable. The purpose of this book is to present the personality disorder from a clinical perspective, with a minimum of discussion about theory and a clear emphasis on practical problems a therapist encounters when conducting treatment with these patients. The book presents a way of understanding the inner dynamics of patients with personality disorders that explains many otherwise confusing clinical phenomena. It describes a diagnostic process that is useful to any clinician, regardless of clinical orientation, because of the insight it provides into the

[1] I prefer the word *client* over the word *patient* to refer to the person who receives the services of a psychotherapist because it puts less emphasis on pathology. Some emphasis on pathology is appropriate; however, too much interferes with the therapist's ability to attune to the patient. The word *patient* has been used, however, throughout this book because it is the word traditionally used in books of this type.

patient's inner thoughts and feeling states. It presents a way of tracking clinical events that makes them understandable in the context of the personality disorder, and it offers a variety of useful forms of intervention.

This book began as a class outline for a graduate course in diagnosis and treatment of personality disorders. In preparation for teaching the course, I spoke to students about their scholastic backgrounds and what they felt were the biggest gaps in their training. Consistently they said that they were having difficulty translating theory into clinical practice, and that the concept of diagnosis was confusing to them because it did not seem to contribute very much to the selection of treatment methodology. As the course proceeded, the students' questions helped me to identify further the areas where the interface between theory and practice was least clear; these questions played an important role in shaping the content of this book.

It will be clear from reading any portion of this book that it is written in a style that is unusual for a professional book of this type. I have tried to address the reader and the reader's practical needs directly. As much as possible, I have attempted to focus on the clinician's actual experience when treating these patients. The book is written in relatively nontechnical language with many clinical transcripts to illustrate the practical application of the concepts. The transcripts that are presented are nearly verbatim and usually represent a significant portion of a session so that they convey the flavor of how the patient appears in treatment, the context of the therapist's interventions, and how the patient responds to the various interventions.

## SPLITTING

The process of *splitting,* referred to in the title *Split Self/Split Object*, characterizes people with personality disorders. It will be discussed throughout this book. The essential characteristic of splitting is that the person who is splitting has a distorted view of reality and in particular of relationships. He views himself and others (objects) in essentially all positive or all negative terms, black or white without grays. As a primary way that he relates to the world, it limits and distorts his experience of himself and his emotions, making his experience of the world very different from that of other people, who commonly misunderstand the meaning of what the person with a personality disorder says and does. In the context of psychotherapy, a misunderstanding of this type on the part of a therapist is likely to result in misattunement and ineffective treatment.

Some therapists would say that after all the theoretical smoke clears, what the psychotherapist really has to rely upon when he is seeing a patient is himself. His personal resources include his self-awareness, his unconditional positive regard for the patient, and his ability to be authentic and empathic. These therapists might say that beyond these skills, there is nothing really for a psychotherapist to know. With respect to treating personality disorders, I disagree. A therapist's capacity to comprehend and be empathic with a patient's inner feeling states is limited by the therapist's ability to understand the meaning of the patient's comments and behavior. Patients with personality disorders speak a foreign language; they use familiar words but in some instances with meanings uniquely shaped by the peculiar way these patients experience the world. The therapist's fluency in that language will substantially improve his understanding of what he is hearing. In order to learn how to translate, the clinician needs to study the language of the personality disorder. This book is designed for that purpose.

## THE UNSEEN SELF

In general, with any patient, a therapist will be unable to observe the patient's inner pain. A patient, for instance, comes into a therapist's office distraught about having been deserted by her husband, as she had been by her father as well when she was young. To the therapist, the nature of the patient's pain might seem obvious, but what is the patient really experiencing? What do these desertions really mean to her? Does she feel primarily worthlessness, failure, guilt, vulnerability, exposure, loss, abandonment, fear, isolation, or some other feeling? Initially, if the therapist believes that he knows what the patient is experiencing, he is probably projecting, assuming that she is feeling what he himself would be likely to feel in this same situation. All that the therapist can observe directly of the patient's pain is her affective expression and her defenses.

Unlike the characteristics of *DSM-III-R* personality disorders, the characteristics used in this book to define personality disorders are not directly observable. To treat a personality disorder, a psychotherapist must try to identify the underlying intrapsychic dynamics so that he can more fully understand and empathize with the patient. The most common use of the term *personality disorder*, however, refers to the eleven personality disorders described and defined in the *DSM-III-R*, which omits any discussion of internal nonobservable dynamics; these descriptions are limited to observable behavioral characteristics. To minimize confusion, in this book terms like *borderline personality disorder* will be used for references to the *DSM-III-R* definitions, while terms like *borderline disorder*, omitting the word *personality*, will be used to refer to the entire clinical picture, including internal dynamics and external manifestations. In contrast to the eleven categories listed in the *DSM-III-R*, the personality disorders will be divided here into three categories: borderline disorders, narcissistic disorders, and schizoid disorders, each with a distinct pattern of internal psychic organization. A possible fourth category, the antisocial disorder, is not addressed in this book because of the lack of an effective treatment method for these patients. Although typical behavioral characteristics do exist for each category, they do not define the category. All three categories have in common the patient's difficulty in connecting to his own inner self, impairing his ability to reference his own values, preferences, thoughts, and feelings in order to make life choices, develop intimate relationships, and resolve tensions and conflicts. Heinz Kohut (1978) aptly applied to these disorders the term *disorders of the self.*

For example, a patient enters treatment complaining of a job situation in which he is underpaid, his skills are vastly underutilized, and his boss has been unresponsive to his attempts to rectify the situation. When questioned about why he stays with such a job, he says that if he were to take another job he knows that his boss would be upset, but the patient says that it is clear that he needs to begin looking for another job. As time goes on, however, the stories of how the boss takes advantage of him continue, and it appears to the therapist that the patient will put off looking for another job indefinitely. In this case, the avoidance of looking for another job is a defense and indicates to the therapist that the patient is protecting himself from some kind of emotional pain, but the nature of the pain is unclear.

The patient's unique configuration of behaviors and defenses, when observed, can indicate the presence of a personality disorder, but intrapsychic organization remains hidden. In the example just given, the patient may perceive himself as lovable only when he complies, and bad when he acts autonomously. The prospect of looking for a new job is an autonomous step that brings up so much anxiety that he would rather stay where he is (borderline). Alternatively, the patient may be unable to perceive his relationships in other than a "master/slave" form, so that although he feels controlled and exploited by his boss, the patient feels that this is the best that he can hope for (schizoid). Another possibility is that the patient is trying to preserve an inflated view of his own importance, a view that shields him from an alternate self-perception of worthlessness and inadequacy; he may perceive the process of looking for a job as demeaning, which would put him in touch with that sense of worthlessness and be so humiliating for him that he finds it preferable to stay in the present situation and complain about being undervalued (narcissist). Each of these possibilities applies to a different personality disorder, a distortion in the patient's view of himself, others, and relationships, which significantly impairs his ability to function. If the therapist is able to understand the patient's personality disorder, the meaning of the patient's apparently irrational behavior becomes clear so that the therapist can develop a fuller empathy for the patient's struggle and will be better able to help the patient.

Since the inner dynamics of the personality disorder are not readily observable, the process of learning about them in depth is difficult. The best way for a clinician to study personality disorders is to listen to patients talk about themselves; however, even the most sensitive of therapists will have difficulty grasping the meaning of the patient's comments when these comments reflect a level of distorted perception that is ambiguous and beyond the therapist's own experience. In addition, before a patient is willing to disclose and explore deep feelings about his sense of himself, he must feel understood and accepted by his therapist, so the therapist must be adequately attuned initially to allow the patient to feel sufficiently understood. It is helpful for a therapist to begin with a general understanding of the typical inner feelings and struggles of a personality disorder so that it will be easier for her to grasp the subtle significance of some of the comments and behaviors of these patients. The therapist will then be more able to recognize comments and behaviors that are particularly laden with meaning, and will be better able to establish a therapeutic rapport with the patient. The best way to obtain an initial understanding of the personality disorder is through ongoing case consultation. However, for those who do not choose this route, this book will provide a start.

## IMPORTANCE OF DIAGNOSIS

Regardless of the particular treatment approach used, the additional information produced by the diagnostic process proposed here should be extremely useful to the clinician. The diagnostic categories are not intended to be complete or discrete; some patients will appear to straddle two categories or migrate between them during the course of treatment. Diagnosis, as it is conceived of here, is a careful way of listening to the patient; it is an ongoing process that begins when the patient enters treatment and continues until the treatment is terminated. Once a diagnostic impression has been established the therapist can continually check the patient's comments for consistency with the diagnosis. If a comment seems inconsistent, either the therapist's diagnostic impression is inaccurate or the therapist has misunderstood the intended meaning of the patient's comment.

One of the primary objections of many therapists to the practice of diagnosis is that it tends to confine the therapist's perception of the patient to a narrow set of attributes, causing the clinician to miss those qualities of the patient that are not addressed in the diagnostic process. They describe this process as dehumanizing, claiming that the patient is not seen as whole person but as a collection of narrowly defined traits.[2] I believe that this objection is important. It is difficult, when looking for particular characteristics or behaviors, to be open to seeing the whole person. I think diagnosis, like any attempt at organizing information into patterns, tends to relegate to a status of secondary importance those bits of data that do not fit into the patterns. Furthermore, there is a danger, when using diagnostic information, of getting ahead of the patient. The clinician can easily frighten patients by making comments that indicate a knowledge of them that is significantly deeper than they intended him to have or than they themselves might be aware of. It is challenging for a therapist both to diagnostically organize the information that the patient presents and at the same time to remain open to experiencing and relating to the

[2]To support this position, they point to books like this one that will sometimes refer to people as narcissists or borderlines, characterizing them entirely by their pathology. In this book there is an attempt to refer to people as narcissistic patients or borderline adults. However this terminology can become cumbersome when used over and over in a paragraph, so the shorthand terms of *narcissist* or *borderline* are sometimes used. This is not intended to obscure the breadth of a person's humanity who happens to meet the criteria of one of these diagnostic categories.

patient as a whole person at the level that the patient presents himself. This tends to be a problem whenever a clinician learns something new about treatment. At first the new information or skills are not fully integrated in the clinician and his genuineness and spontaneity suffer. I believe that once the diagnostic process and the additional information it offers are integrated, they will not interfere with the mature clinician's ability to be present with his patients. In fact, because of the additional sensitivity this process affords the clinician, its ultimate impact should be to enhance that ability.

One difficulty in understanding patients with personality disorders is that they use the same language as other patients, but the meaning of the words they use is usually quite different. Basic words like *love, depression, feel, need,* and *help* have different meanings when used by patients with personality disorders than when used by more neurotic patients. Whole patterns of behavior have different motivations and different meanings. In addition, these meanings can vary widely with the different types of personality disorders. Many of the inner thoughts and feelings of a patient with a personality disorder are so painful that in most cases they are neither discussed nor even internally acknowledged, adding to the clinician's difficulties in understanding these patients. Diagnosis is useful in helping the clinician clarify all these ambiguities and fill in the blanks left by the patient's own lack of awareness.

Diagnosis is also important because a patient in each of the three categories of disorders described in this book will have a characteristically different way of viewing the therapist and of responding to various types of interventions. Whereas for one an interpretation might be helpful, for the other it might feel invasive. For one, a request of the therapist for advice would be a sign of progress as an indication of deepening trust; for another it might be indicative of a regressive response to the treatment. Patients from one category might feel that the therapist is uncaring if he does not address the patient's destructive behavior patterns; patients from another might feel criticized, betrayed, or wounded if the therapist does address the patient's destructive behavior patterns. An accurate diagnosis facilitates the therapist in attuning to the patient.

Each of the three categories suggests some distinct guidelines for treatment. It is useful for the clinician to arrive at a probable diagnosis when selecting a treatment approach because it allows the clinician to tailor his treatment approach to the patient's condition, it enables the clinician to construct a diagnostic hypothesis that can then be tested against the treatment results obtained, and it forces the clinician to consider carefully the different possible meanings of everything the patient says and does. As treatment progresses, the selected approach will naturally be modified as the clinician better understands the patient.

The ability to differentiate among the three categories is useful throughout treatment. In general, the most difficult stage of treatment with these patients is the initial one, because there is not an established rapport or trust between therapist and patient. During this period, if the therapist makes wrong choices about the type of intervention that the patient can tolerate and respond to, the treatment can be severely hampered or aborted. The diagnostic process presented in this book is especially helpful in informing the therapist's choices during this period. As the treatment progresses, the clinician has more information about the patient, making the choice of interventions easier. Most errors in clinical judgment made during later stages of treatment can be fairly easily repaired so that the choice of interventions becomes less critical. However, during these later stages, the ongoing diagnostic process facilitates the clinician's understanding of what the patient is intending to communicate, how the patient is tending to process the events that occur in treatment, and how the patient is likely to respond.

The diagnostic approach presented in this book is an ongoing process that helps the clinician, regardless of his psychotherapeutic orientation, to continually question and interpret to himself the deeper meanings of the patient's comments and actions. It helps the clinician understand what the patient is saying about his inner feelings and about how he perceives himself.

## APPROACH TO TREATMENT

Unfortunately, it is easier to present clinical problems in a transcript than it is to present true clinical successes, because the successes are subtle and build gradually over time. So-called breakthroughs are likely to be meaningful to the observer only when taken in the context of a lengthy treatment process preceding them. Consequently, the transcripts presented in this book are more instructive in the insight they give about how a personality disorder presents clinically than they are instructive in effective treatment technique. Included with each transcript is a commentary that carefully evaluates the impact of the various interventions and suggests improvements.

The treatment orientation presented in many of the transcript commentaries is analytic, with the therapist intervening minimally. The idea behind this orientation is that patients with personality disorders need to work out issues concerning autonomy, individuation, separation, and separateness; when the patients seem to be exploring their own concerns without external direction, intervention by the therapist is unnecessary and in fact often sidetracks their work. In most cases, there are strong therapeutic reasons for the therapist to avoid becoming overly active in the treatment process; on some occasions the commentaries in this book caution against too much activity on the part of the therapist. In general, however, rather than point out the problems with a particular style of treatment, the book will present aspects of treatment that will be useful to most clinicians, regardless of their therapeutic orientation.

Another characteristic of the treatment approach presented here is a careful attention to the patient's defenses as an indication of the presence of underlying dysphoric feeling states. By closely tracking the occurrence of defenses in the patient's comments and behavior, the therapist is able to understand with exquisite clarity the meaning of many otherwise confusing clinical events. Complementing the attention to defenses is an attention to emotions, spontaneity, and genuine attempts at self-exploration. The patient's subtle dance between these complementary phenomena is described and illustrated, a dance which, when observed, elucidates the patient's inner struggles.

## ORIGINATORS OF THE APPROACH PRESENTED IN THIS BOOK

During my sixteen years in practice I have constantly been involved in various types of training, ranging from family systems and humanistic approaches to analytic approaches. In the analytic area, I most recently trained for four years with the Masterson Institute in the treatment approach developed by James Masterson. Although I found that my clinical skills improved enormously during this training, I have continued to have strong reservations about aspects of Masterson's approach. I think that the primary benefits I received from this training were an improved understanding of patients with personality disorders and a greatly expanded awareness of clinical phenomena that typically occur with these patients.

I believe that because many clinicians find certain aspects of Masterson's approach to treatment unacceptable, they reject some of the valuable and useful aspects of his contributions as well. In particular, Masterson's diagnostic breakdown of the personality disorders, his method of tracking defenses, and his identification of borderline, narcissist, and schizoid triads (the concept of a *triad* is explained in detail in Chapters 3, 4, and 5) are extremely useful and can be combined effectively with most clinical orientations. They form the core of the material presented in this book. In addition, the chapter on the treatment of narcissistic disorders presents ideas developed by Kohut and Kernberg, and the chapter on the treatment of schizoid disorders presents some of the contributions of Guntrip and Ralph Klein. Many of the clinical transcripts reflect aspects of Masterson's approach; in the transcript commentaries, the impact of these is evaluated.

This book diverges from Masterson's approach in many important ways. I think that Masterson's narrow focus on tracking defenses, although very powerful, leads to an overemphasis on pathology; it does not give adequate attention to the patient's human attempts at connecting to the therapist or the positive motivation for the patient's behavior. He takes the position that the patient's defenses must be tenaciously pursued by the therapist. In some cases I believe that this aggressive treatment provokes more defense in the patient. In the area of diagnosis, Masterson recommends that the clinician arrive at a probable diagnosis early on in treatment and then pursue a treatment strategy consistent with that diagnosis until the events of treatment prove that this diagnosis is incorrect. I believe that the clinician's diagnosis should always be considered tentative, more of a heuristic tool for understanding than a prescription for treatment. Masterson insists on the discreteness of each of the three diagnostic categories. In my experience, most personality disordered patients seem to fit well into one of the three categories, but some patients do not. The aberrant ones seem to straddle two categories without fitting into either, or they may alternate between two categories. Sometimes the patient's diagnosis appears to change well into the treatment process. I believe that the category of borderline disorder that Masterson describes is considerably less populated than he suggests. For instance, Masterson (1989) recommends thinking of most of the eleven *DSM-III-R* axis II categories as borderline. I believe that many of these categories are at least partially populated with narcissistic disorders and one, the *avoidant*, should be thought of as high level schizoid. Finally, central to Masterson's approach is his adherence to the goal of the patient working through deep-seated abandonment depression. I do not place nearly the importance on working through that he does; I think there is a wide range of ways in which a patient can benefit from treatment.

## THE TRANSCRIPTS

The transcripts used in this book are based upon actual sessions, slightly shortened and edited to conceal the identity of the patient. In all cases an attempt was made to preserve the personal qualities of the original transcript so that the reader can get a sense of how the therapist and patient interacted. In addition to my own, transcripts for this book were contributed by colleagues and student interns. In the interest of the patients' anonymity, contributors are not specifically named.

## CONCLUSION

This book is intended to help clinicians to recognize personality disorders, to understand patients' experiences of these disorders, and to use this information in selecting effective treatment approaches. It presents a way of understanding patients with personality disorders, some useful guidelines to treatment of the various personality disorders, a variety of interventions, and a useful diagnostic process. It is written from a clinical perspective with a minimum of theory. All of the concepts presented are illustrated using clinical transcripts.

The book is divided into seven chapters. The first contrasts some fundamental characteristics of a personality disorder to those of a neurosis. A series of short transcripts of an ongoing treatment is used to illustrate the points that are made. The second chapter discusses defenses, a phenomenon of universally acknowledged importance but one that is not usually given careful attention in psychotherapy texts. Since defenses play a prominent role in both identification and treatment of personality disorders, this chapter provides a foundation for the next three chapters, which focus in turn on the individual categories of borderline, narcissistic, and schizoid disorders. Each of these three chapters concentrates on one disorder and addresses intrapsychic dynamics, typical behavioral characteristics, etiology, clinical presentation, countertransference, and treatment. Each of these chapters also contains at least two clinical transcripts that serve as concrete examples for how these patients present themselves in treatment and how they respond to both appropriate and inappropriate interventions. The sixth chapter talks about differential diagnosis in practical terms, and the final chapter discusses a variety of intervention possibilities and the situations that call for each.

# Part I

# 1

# Personality Disorders

A neurotic patient is preoccupied with conflict: "Why do I do what I do? What is driving me?" He struggles with guilt: guilt for committing forbidden acts, for entertaining forbidden thoughts, for surviving where others did not, and for experiencing forbidden pleasure. Generally, the neurotic patient's problem is in finding release from a harsh, judgmental, controlling, internal observer. Psychotherapy of the neurotic patient is designed to uncover deep unconscious motives for questionable thoughts and behavior.

In contrast to the neurotic patient with typically overdeveloped and restrictive values and standards that constrain him, there is the patient with a personality disorder whose values and standards have been borrowed from parents and others. The term *personality disorder*, also called a *disorder of the self*, refers to a lack of a genuine sense of "self" and a consequent impairment of self-regulating abilities.[1] Instead of looking within themselves to locate feeling or make decisions, patients with personality disorders look outside themselves for evaluations, directions, rules, or opinions to guide them. While a neurotic patient is struggling with feeling repressed and overcontrolled, the patient with a personality disorder struggles with the opposite problem; without a

[1]The term *disorder of the self* was introduced by Kohut and Wolf (1978) and later adopted by Masterson (1989).

strong internal monitor of his thoughts and actions, he finds it difficult to maintain self-control. He often acts impulsively in ways that interfere with his ability to relate intimately to others, to successfully pursue a career, or to obtain satisfaction in life. The treatment of a personality disorder focuses initially on helping the patient to actively observe, evaluate, and control his behavior in order to improve his functioning and stabilize his life. Then it facilitates the patient in restoring his sense of self.

The dichotomy between neurosis and personality disorder is not as clear-cut as it may appear. There probably are no purely neurotic patients; people who appear to be neurotic in most respects probably have areas of themselves that they have closed off, causing them occasionally to function more like people with a personality disorder than like neurotics. There can, however, be unfortunate consequences if a therapist mistakes a patient with an extensive personality disorder for neurotic. If this should happen, the therapist will probably focus on loosening up the self-control of the patient, whose self-control is already marginal. The patient is then likely to become increasingly dependent upon the therapist to provide an external supplement of structure, support, and control. As the patient depends more on the therapist for these functions, the therapist will probably feel increasingly responsible for the patient, and will be in less and less of a position to intervene neutrally and therapeutically.

The purpose of the present chapter is to illustrate as clearly as possible the differences between neurotic conditions and personality disorders, and to explain why it is essential that clinicians be able to distinguish one from the other.

## THE NATURE OF A PERSONALITY DISORDER

The term *disorder of the self* is descriptive of a personality disorder because these patients are out of touch with themselves. They identify themselves with a facade, a false defensive self that they have developed to adapt to a world that they perceive as hostile. Typically, when they were young, they needed to adapt to one or more parents whom they perceived of at times as hostile, withholding, absent, attacking, or devaluing. To protect themselves from this environment, they relied on relatively primitive defenses. In particular, they tended to reduce their views of people and relationships to black and white.

Even a parent who was sadistically cruel much of the time could be seen at other times as supportive and loving. To people whose childhood was dominated by abuse, engulfment, or neglect, this mechanism, referred to as *splitting*, allowed them to preserve an internal image of a loving environment that could be insulated from painful reality.

Although this polarized way of viewing the world is normally used by toddlers to preserve their image of the all-loving parent upon whom their survival depends, those who develop personality disorders never relinquish this defense as a primary protective mechanism. They develop into one-dimensional adults who view the world as either positive or negative, with very little in between. Although their views can shift back and forth between black and white, bad and good, they have great difficulty seeing combinations of partly black and partly white or shades of gray. Their relationships are shallow because of their limited ability to see people realistically. From the perspective of observable behavior, a patient with a personality disorder as described in this book is likely to fall into one of the categories defined by *DSM-III-R* as a personality disorder. Conversely, from an intrapsychic perspective, at the heart of every *DSM-III-R* personality disorder is an impairment in the person's experience of his self. This limitation naturally restricts their ability to relate to a psychotherapist as a multifaceted person, and prevents them from developing mature transference relationships. Without the ability to develop transference, they have been considered unanalyzable by some traditional psychoanalysts. Therapists using more humanistic approaches have also been frustrated in attempting to get through the "false self" of these patients to their true inner selves because these patients are unable accurately to perceive and respond to the therapist. Object relations theory provides a therapist with a way to understand these patients so that the therapist can help them to shed their false selves and allow their true selves to emerge.

## Splitting

In one sense patients with personality disorders are easily identified. Their characteristic ability to suddenly reverse their view of a therapist is not common in neurotics. Some patients with personality disorders might view the work of their therapist as skillful and inspired, and then a few minutes later question whether there is anything of value occurring in the treatment. Some personality-disordered patients vacillate wildly in their opinion of the therapist's level of concern and caring about them. At one moment, the patient views the therapist as sensitive and caring, and the next moment as unfeeling, withholding, and critical. When a neurotic patient's assessment of the therapist changes dramatically, the patient usually observes that such a dramatic change is unusual and wonders what it represents. In contrast, the patient with a personality disorder does not tend to be curious about his rapidly changing view of the world. Whatever his current point of view, he takes it as reality and rarely questions it.

To the uninformed observer, such swings in mood and opinion may appear to be simply an eccentricity. The observer assumes that anyone who holds such contradictory points of view in such a short span of time must be somewhat uncomfortable with the degree to which the two points of view clash. To the neurotic observer, it is beyond the realm of his normal experience that antithetical points of view might coexist in a person's mind without influencing one another, but for the person with a personality disorder, these points of view do not influence each other because they are not held at the same time. When one is held as true, the other is "split off," and simply not considered. All people use splitting at times to some degree. A negative measure of a patient's psychological health is the degree to which he relies on splitting to manage internal conflict.

### False Self

Similarly, an alertness to the characteristics of the personality disorder is almost essential in order to fully identify the facade, or false self, that is presented, and to see beyond it to the frightened, isolated, angry, or hurt feelings that it shields. A personality-disordered patient's false self facade can take many forms: the cooperative patient who cares more that the therapist like him than he does about the success of his treatment; the charming patient who is so afraid of criticism that he attempts perfection and control in everything he does; the self-confident patient whose brittle exterior can tolerate no expression of individuality or difference from other people; the intelligent patient who desperately seeks a relationship, but is terrified when any real contact occurs between himself and another; the helpful patient who seems to be concerned about everybody else in his life except himself; or the helpless patient who secretly believes that to support his own efforts would result in rejection and isolation. These are only a few.

When a person is able to express himself both outwardly and inwardly without tailoring his expression in a defensive way to the expectations or demands of others, he is able to pursue his own genuine interests and aspirations; he can express his real self. The term *real self* is used in a wide variety of ways with subtle differences of meaning by various theorists. In this book, along with *real self*, the terms *inner self*, *true self*, and *self* are also used at times to refer to a person's ingenuous core that gradually reveals itself to the patient as well as the therapist as the layers of false self fall away.

### Difficulties with Self-Regulation

Because they are out of contact with their inner selves, people with personality disorders have a limited ability to use their inner resources to soothe themselves when painful affect arises. This ability seems to be available naturally to neurotics and other people without such an impairment of the self. In addition, people with personality disorders have difficulty with many other self-regulating functions that healthier people seem automatically to be capable of. These include impulse control, limit setting for one's self, self-affirming, self-comforting, self-empathy, and self-soothing. One of the important roles of the therapist who treats these patients is to provide an external substitute for these functions that are lacking internally until patients can learn to provide them for themselves.

## DIFFERENCES BETWEEN A PERSONALITY DISORDER AND A NEUROSIS

To illustrate some of the many differences between neurotic patients and those with personality disorders, consider the characteristics of the following neurotic patient and which of these characteristics would probably be different if this patient had a personality disorder:

### Dr. Berger's Most Famous (and only) Case

The patient is presented here through partial transcripts of a series of five treatment sessions. He enters outpatient treatment at age 17 in the mid-nineteen seventies after a suicide attempt followed by a month of inpatient psychiatric treatment.

**Session #1**

**T:** Hi. Did you have trouble finding the place?
**P:** No. (The patient's affect is flat.)
**T:** Good. How long since you've been out of the hospital?
**P:** A month and a half.
**T:** Feeling depressed?
**P:** No.
**T:** On stage?
**P:** Pardon me?
**T:** People nervous, treating you like you're a dangerous character.
**P:** Yes, I guess a little.
**T:** Are you?
**P:** I don't know.
**T:** How long were you in the hospital?
**P:** Four months.
**T:** What did you do?
**P:** I tried to off myself. (irritated/excited) Isn't it down there?
**T:** (calmly) It doesn't say what your method was.
**P:** Double edge—super blue.
**T:** Oh. (nods) So how does it feel being home? Everybody glad to see you?
**P:** (flat affect) Yeah.
**T:** Friends?
**P:** Yeah.
**T:** You're back in school?
**P:** Yeah.
**T:** Everything okay in school, teachers?
**P:** Yeah.
**T:** No problems?
**P:** Hmhmm.
**T:** So why are you here?
**P:** Oh, I'd like to be more in control.
**T:** Why?
**P:** So people can quit worrying about me.
**T:** Who's worried about you?
**P:** Oh, my father mostly, this is his idea.
**T:** What about your mother, isn't she worried about you too?
**P:** I don't know. If you're a friend of Dr. Crawford I guess you're probably all right, but I'll be straight with you. I don't like this already.
**T:** Well, as long as you're straight.
**P:** What do you know about me? Have you talked to Crawford?
**T:** Yes, he called me on the phone and he told me to look for you. He said you had a brother who died. Boating accident was it? Do you want to tell

me about it? (silence) Well, I suppose you talked this over with Crawford at the hospital, right?

**P:** Right.

**T:** Good. How did that go?

**P:** It didn't change anything.

**T:** What did you want it to change?

**P:** (irritated) I told you. I'd like to be more in control.

**T:** Why?

**P:** (irritated) I told you so some people can quit worrying about me.

**T:** (calmly) Well, I'll tell you something. I'll be straight with you, okay? I'm not big on control. But it's your money.

**P:** So to speak.

**T:** So to speak. Okay, how's Tuesdays and Fridays same time?

**P:** Twice a week?

**T:** (matter-of-factly) Well, control's a tough nut.

**P:** I've got swim practice every night.

**T:** Well that's a problem. How do we solve that?

**P:** I guess I have to skip practice twice a week and come here.

**T:** Well, that's up to you.

**P:** I don't like being here. I've got to tell you. I don't like being here at all.

**T:** Umhumm.

*Commentary for Session #1*

If the preceding dialogue seems familiar, it is because it is taken from the 1980 motion picture, *Ordinary People*.[2] Originally published as a novel in 1976, this fictionalized account portrays the treatment of Conrad, a teenage boy played by Tim Hutton, who is treated by Dr. Berger, a psychiatrist played by Judd Hirsch, after a suicide attempt and depression related to the drowning death of Conrad's older brother. Berger helps Conrad to identify repressed emotional trauma related to the drowning incident and to work out Conrad's confused and painful feelings about his parents. While Berger's style of treatment is unorthodox by most current standards, the transcripted interactions have a quality of authenticity to them. Judging from the popular reception of the movie, one can conclude that most viewers had little difficulty believing that these therapist–patient interactions might actually have occurred and might have had a therapeutic effect.

The fact that this account of psychotherapy is fictional does not

[2]Excerpt(s) from ORDINARY PEOPLE copyright 1980 by Paramount Pictures. 

detract from its credibility as an illustration of clinical phenomena. The characters in *Ordinary People* are realistically portrayed, as evidenced by their ready acceptance and believability by so many viewers. The inclusion of popularized fictional characters for the purpose of illustrating psychotherapeutic concepts has many precedents in psychotherapeutic literature. Jung is well known for using characters from popular mythology to represent character types. Freud, himself, (1916), in his writing used characters from the works of Homer, Shakespeare, Ibsen, and others in order to present and discuss various character types. He thought of these characters as skillfully crafted out of the author's subconscious awareness of the human mind.

The portion of the first session presented above provides a flavor of Dr. Berger's style—blunt, perhaps even cocky. Comments like "So why are you here?" and "I'm not big on control" border on sarcastic, not typical of most psychotherapists. However, these comments do also have an honest, down-to-earth quality to them. Although not indicated in the text of the transcript, Dr. Berger's facial expressions and general presentation convey a sense of genuine interest in Conrad. Although Berger plays a very active role in the session, asking many questions, it is unclear whether his high level of activity is a response to Conrad's adolescent reticence or if it is a typical aspect of his treatment style in a first interview.

It is also unclear in this first session if Conrad's brief responses in the session are evidence of depression, or if they are indications of a difficulty he has in determining his own genuine interests in this situation. The former would be common for a neurotic who is depressed, and the latter would be typical of a personality disorder. Conrad's lack of affect is probably a result of depression. Many patients with personality disorders appear to have little emotional affect because they defend against their deep emotions by distancing from superficial as well as deeper emotions. This possibility does not seem to apply to Conrad because he demonstrates the accessibility of his emotions when he becomes spontaneously irritated several times, and then returns to his flat affect.

### *Defensive Avoidance*

Conrad is fairly direct about telling the therapist what he doesn't like. However, when the subject of his mother comes up, he is indirect, defensively changing the subject to avoid his feelings about her. Avoidance is a defensive process that is typical of, but not limited to, patients who have personality disorders. It is not a typical defense of a neurotic; however it is not entirely out of character for a neurotic to use it.[3]

**Session #2**

**P:** Well, what do I do, tell you my dreams?
**T:** I don't put much stock in dreams.
**P:** What kind of psychiatrist are you? They are all interested in dreams.
**T:** Really, what's happening? What's going on?
**P:** I just feel so (pause)
**T:** What?
**P:** Jumpy. (pause)
**T:** Look, kiddo, I lied. I do believe in dreams; but sometimes I want to know what's happening when you're awake. Now come on. Tell me. Something's bugging you, making you nervous. You're making me nervous.
**P:** Maybe I need a tranquilizer, you know.
**T:** Tranquilizer?
**P:** Yeah, what do you think?
**T:** I think you came in here looking like something out of *The Body Snatchers*. It is not my opinion that you need a tranquilizer.
**P:** (turns clock toward himself) What is this?
**T:** A clock.
**P:** Oh, I see, you get to tell the time but I can't. Is that it?
**T:** Hmhmm.
**P:** So you know when the hour's up?
**T:** Right.
**P:** Fifty minutes, 55 minutes, what is it? (silence) Maybe I don't want to swim any more. I mean my timing's for shit. He's got two guys who swim

---

[3]Since this is one of the rare instances in which Conrad's character appears to be inconsistent from a psychological point of view, it is interesting to note that this inconsistency was not present in the original book, *Ordinary People*, but was introduced into the screenplay. In the book, several exchanges take place after the subject of Conrad's mother is brought up. Then Conrad becomes irritated with the barrage of questions coming from Berger, and Conrad stops talking. Berger asks him what is going on, and Conrad responds with the line that appears in the movie version in which he says that he doesn't like Berger. As it arises in the book, this line is a natural response to irritation over Berger's intrusiveness, and not an avoidance of the subject of Conrad's mother; it is a response that would be expected of a neurotic.

the 50 who are better than me, and, Jeez, they're a bunch of boring-assed jocks. And him, I can't stand him. He's a tight-assed SOB.

**T:** Have you thought about quitting?
**P:** Are you telling me to?
**T:** No.
**P:** It wouldn't look good.
**T:** Forget about how it looks. How does it feel?
**P:** How does it feel? How does it feel?
**T:** Yes, how does it feel?
**P:** (shrugs) Same thing that happened last year. It's the same damned thing I did last year.
**T:** Are you the same person you were last year?
**P:** I don't know.
**T:** That's why you need a tranquilizer?
**P:** You tell me.
**T:** No, it's up to you.
**P:** Fifty bucks an hour. Can't you decide if I should have a pill or not? You're a doctor. I'm supposed to feel better, right?
**T:** (wryly) Not necessarily. (pause) How is it with your friends? Is it getting any easier?
**P:** No.
**T:** Is any place easy?
**P:** The hospital was.
**T:** It was. Why?
**P:** Because nobody hid anything there.
**T:** Was there anyone there you could talk to, I mean besides Dr. Crawford?

*Commentary for Session #2*

The second session begins with Conrad wanting Berger to tell him what to do in the session. This could be the natural response of a neurotic patient trying to adjust to a new and uncomfortable situation or the response of a patient whose personality disorder makes it very difficult for him to initiate anything that would require him to check inside himself for direction. In particular, the process of determining for himself what is important to talk about in a session is difficult and produces anxiety for a patient with a personality disorder.

Berger responds to Conrad's reticence by asking him, "What's happening? What's going on?" Then he says, "Now come on. Tell me. Something's bugging you, making you nervous. You're making me nervous." The implications of this intervention are several. Most importantly, Berger believes that Conrad knows he is feeling something and furthermore that Conrad knows what that feeling is. If Conrad had a personality disorder, it is very possible that neither belief would be true. Secondly, Berger is apparently not afraid that Conrad might feel criticized by the comment "You're making me nervous." Patients with personality disorders have great difficulty maintaining clear boundaries between themselves and others; to such a patient, "You're making me nervous" would be a very upsetting comment.

While neurotic patients struggle to control and express their painful feelings, personality-disordered patients tend to protect themselves by channeling their attention away from painful feelings before they can be experienced. This shifting of attention away from the experience of feelings can take many forms including avoidance, denial, and acting out. All are automatic defensive responses, rather than considered choices. While the neurotic patient might choose to set a painful subject aside for the moment in order to address a demanding situation at hand and then pick that subject up later, the patient with a personality disorder is likely to sidestep the subject so quickly and automatically that he is usually entirely unaware of the painful or scary feelings engendered by the subject. Consequently, he will not have reason to go back and pick up the subject at a future time. If he is asked what he felt before he changed the subject, he might remember, or he might respond, "Nothing." If Dr. Berger had urged a patient with a personality disorder, "Tell me what's bugging you," the patient might have felt frustrated or criticized, unable to comply even if he wanted to.

Because a patient with a personality disorder is out of touch with his insides, he will have a shaky self-image, and will depend on other people's opinions for a sense of himself. Consequently this patient will be very sensitive to other people's comments and attitudes about him, and will have a tendency to be strongly influenced by other people's evaluations of him. If Berger had said, "You're making me nervous," to a patient with a personality disorder, the patient would have been likely to feel criticized, bad, violated, or offended. In the above transcript, Conrad does seem to interpret Berger's comment as somewhat critical, because he suggests that the problem of his nervousness might be solved by a tranquilizer, a suggestion to which Berger responds in his characteristically frank style, telling Conrad that he does not believe a tranquilizer would be helpful to someone who came in looking like something out of *The Body Snatchers*. Berger does not seem to be particularly concerned about offending Conrad.

**Session #3**

**T:** What are you thinking?
**P:** That I jack off a lot.
**T:** Does it help?
**P:** Sometimes.
**T:** What are you thinking about now?
**P:** John Boy.
**T:** Who?
**P:** You know, the Waltons, John Boy.
**T:** Yeah, what about him?
**P:** My father came into my room that day and he didn't know what to say. This was right after Buck died. And he came over and sat on the bed next to me and put his arm around my shoulders. And he just sat there, and I remember I was watching his feet and I was—because his foot was turned on its side—and I was thinking "he's so uptight." Just back off. And I know I should have felt something, but I didn't know what to feel. I keep thinking about the stuff they say on TV, like "Oh, my God." I didn't say that because I didn't feel sad so much as . . . . (pause)
**T:** So much as what?
**P:** I don't know. I kept thinking that John Boy would have said something about the way he felt.
**T:** What would John Boy have said? (pause) Come on—oh, come on.
**P:** Come on what?
**T:** Don't hold back.

*Commentary for Session #3*

Again, Berger assumes that Conrad's pause is an indication that he is holding back, conflicted about whether to say what he is thinking. Internal conflict is a theme for neurotic patients. They wonder whether to talk about things, whether to take various actions, even whether it's okay to be thinking what they're thinking. Personality disorders, on the other hand, avoid conflict. They avoid even thinking about subjects that involve conflict. Whereas the neurotic has a strong internal observer, an observing ego that creates internal conflict by noting the neurotic's discomfort with many of his impulsive desires for gratification, the patient with a personality disorder has a weak observing ego, if any.

By the end of the third session, the intensely interactive character of Berger's style of treatment has not abated. Conrad does not seem to be thrown off by Berger's active involvement, except for the fact that

Conrad does not tend to initiate discussion of areas of his own interest. He does, however, freely respond to Berger's direction. When Berger asks what he is thinking, Conrad reveals that he has been thinking to himself about an apparently significant memory. With little encouragement he describes the memory of an incident and his present concerns about how he reacted at the time of the incident. He interrupts himself after saying, "I didn't feel sad so much as . . . ." He is conflicted about whether to finish his sentence. Again, Conrad's conflict does not arise as much from a difficulty in determining what he feels, as it does out of an internal conflict over whether to describe his feeling to Berger. It is important to note also that Conrad's concerns are about whether he should have been feeling something different than he actually did, and whether he can accept what he did feel. To him, other people's opinions about what he felt are of secondary importance.

Patients with personality disorders would have reacted very differently than Conrad to the therapeutic treatment just described. Because they are disconnected from their insides, they have great difficulty in generating their own directions based upon a sense of what is right for themselves. In therapy sessions, they struggle with the problem of deciding what to talk about. If the therapist suggests a subject to discuss, even if the subject is not central to the patient's concerns, the patient with a personality disorder will commonly use the therapist's suggestion as an opportunity to bypass the problem of identifying the patient's own inner direction. The patient will either launch into a long lifeless monologue on the subject or give a relatively short factual answer and then sit back and wait for the therapist's next direction. Instead, Conrad responds to "What are you thinking?" by making a spontaneous association and proceeding to address meaningful material. Conrad's difficulty does not appear to be in generating this spontaneous material so much as in communicating about it.

If a therapist were as active in treating a personality disorder as Berger appears to be in these sessions, the patient would probably avoid initiating significant exploration. Although "What are you thinking?" is not a particularly directive question, it can nevertheless interfere with a personality-disordered patient's work. It focuses the patient on thinking rather than feeling, and it conveys an expectation that when nothing is being said, the patient can rely on the therapist to fill the silence. While these two implications may seem subtle, they do not escape the fine sensitivity of the patient with a personality disorder.

This patient's response to the above intervention is likely to be an increase in passive behavior, causing the patient to depend more heavily on the therapist in the future to fill silences and suggest directions for exploration.

Patients with personality disorders would also be very unlikely to explore silently a memory involving emotional conflict like the one described by Conrad. Instead, they would distract themselves and think about something else, in order to avoid emotional conflict. If they were to interrupt themselves, it would probably not be because they are unsure about whether to talk about something, but because they are uncomfortable thinking about something. In addition, they would not have had the degree of observing ego demonstrated by Conrad. Conrad thinks about what happened during the incident involving his father, notices that he did not feel anything, and wonders what he *should* have felt, his primary concern being whether he can accept his own response to the situation. Because they are out of touch with themselves, patients with personality disorders are very poorly equipped to observe and evaluate their own behavior. Instead, when they evaluate their behavior, their primary concern about how they responded to the situation is what other people will think.

**Session #4**

(Conrad has decided to quit the swim team.)

**T:** What does your dad say about it?

**P:** I haven't told him yet.

**T:** How come?

**P:** I don't know. He'd worry about it.

**T:** Did you tell your mother?

**P:** My mother. My mother and I don't connect. Don't you remember? I told you that. What do people have in common with mothers anyway? It's all surface crap. You know. "Brush your teeth. Get good grades." I don't know. (looks at clock) Two o'clock. I'm just wasting your time. I'm not going to feel anything, all right; I'm sorry.

**T:** No, "sorry" is out. Come on, something's on your mind. Come on, come on. Remember the contract? Well maybe there's some connection between control and a lack of feeling.

**P:** I don't know what you mean.

**T:** Think about it.

**P:** What do you want?

**T:** I'll tell you what I want. I want you to leave "I don't know" out there with the magazines.

**P:** So if I don't have an answer, you want me to make one up.
**T:** Yeah, make one up right now about there's no feelings in there.
**P:** I said I had feelings.
**T:** Oh, now you have them, now you don't. Get it together, Jarrett.
**P:** Why are you hassling me? You're trying to make me mad, right?
**T:** Are you mad?
**P:** (emphatically) No!
**T:** Oh, cut the shit. You're mad. You're mad as hell. You don't like being pushed so why don't you do something about it.
**P:** (agitated) What?
**T:** Tell me to fuck off. I don't know.
**P:** (impulsively) Fuck off. No.
**T:** Why not?
**P:** Uh uh. It takes too much energy to get mad.
**T:** Do you realize how much energy it takes to hold it back?
**P:** When I let myself feel, all I feel is lousy.
**T:** Oh, I beg your pardon. I never promised you a rose garden.
**P:** Oh, fuck you, Berger.
**T:** What fuck you?
**P:** What about you? What do you feel? Do you jack off or jerk off or whatever you call it?
**T:** What do you think?
**P:** I think you married a fat lady, and you go home and you fuck the living daylights out of her.
**T:** Sounds good to me. A little advice about feeling, kiddo. Don't expect it to always tickle.

*Commentary for Session #4*

Conrad again avoids talking about his mother when the subject comes up. He focuses instead on the clock and pleads hopelessness, saying that he is not going to feel anything and that he is wasting Berger's time. Apparently, he intends to act out his hopelessness by stopping the therapeutic work of that session, but Berger urges him to continue, saying, "Come on, something is on your mind." In general, neurotic patients tend to work with the therapist to try to understand themselves, while personality-disordered patients in the initial stages of therapy tend to be unable to participate in this therapeutic alliance. So, patients with personality disorders are far more likely to avoid a sensitive subject than neurotic patients. In this case, however, Conrad demonstrates the fact that neurotic patients sometimes also become resistant and avoid sensitive subjects.

Avoidance is a primitive defense because it is a defense that is utilized in early childhood and is normally given up as a person grows and matures emotionally. If not relinquished, the avoidance defense can be an extremely destructive one; taken to the extreme, it can cause havoc in a person's life. Bills can get shoved in drawers and left unpaid, jobs can be lost because people procrastinate about difficult important tasks, classes can be skipped to avoid having to take an exam or make a presentation, and generally the business of life does not get handled.

Primitive defenses tend to be used by patients with personality disorders to protect themselves, while neurotic patients are able to use more mature defenses that are less destructive. Whereas the neurotic patient uses defenses like repression, reaction formation, and rationalization to protect his ability to function by keeping painful memories and feelings out of consciousness, the personality-disordered patient's defenses often impair his ability to function. Patients with personality disorders use defenses like splitting, avoidance, denial, projection, projective identification, primitive idealization, and devaluation[4] to protect themselves from painful memories and affect, but these defenses actually interfere with, rather than enhance, functioning. This difference accounts for the fact that while the level of functioning of neurotic patients may improve as a result of a therapy that focuses them directly on painful historical material, the level of functioning of patients with personality disorders might decrease under the same conditions because the patient is forced to rely more heavily on his defenses which are maladaptive. In some cases the personality-disordered patient's level of functioning goes from adequate at the outset of such a therapy to poor soon after the painful memories and affect begin to flood into consciousness.

The harassing or "hassling" that Berger does in session four would overwhelm most patients with a personality disorder. Comments like "Why don't you do something about it?" would be experienced as very forceful by such patients. Conrad, however, stands his ground, continues to maintain his attitude that Berger is a well-intentioned person, and tries to understand why such a person would become so aggressive suddenly. Conrad says "You're trying to make me mad, right?" It would be very difficult for patients with a personality disorder to observe the apparently hostile behavior of Berger and at the same time think of Berger as well intentioned. They might become

[4]These defenses are defined and discussed in Chapter 2.

self-critical, think that they were bad and had done something wrong, and respond by compliantly attempting to "be good." On the other hand, they might perceive Berger as threatening, and either withdraw or devalue him.

Focusing intensely on the transference can tend to undermine the therapy of patients with a personality disorder.[5] When brought to their attention in the early stages of treatment, they would either deny having feelings about the therapist, or the intensity of the therapeutic relationship would frighten them, especially when negative aspects of the intense transference feelings are emphasized. More superficial comments like pointing out when a patient seems hurt or withdrawn from the therapist are universally recommended because they heighten the patient's awareness of his resistances and defenses, as long as these interventions are not so intense as to bring up feelings strong enough as to be likely to overwhelm the patient. Since neurotic patients can view relationships in more mature and complex ways than those with personality disorders, neurotics like Conrad can understand that they can become angry at the therapist without necessarily suffering dire consequences.

### Session #5

**T:** Tuesday worked out great. You had a Christmas tree and everything was hunky-dory okay.

**P:** You're the doctor.

**T:** Don't take refuge in one liners like "You're the doctor," okay, 'cause that pisses me off. So everything was fine until you had this fight with your mother. Then you felt lousy.

**P:** Yes, but I don't blame her; she's got her reasons. It's impossible after all the shit I pulled.

**T:** What shit have you pulled? Remember, I'm talking proportions here. Now, what shit have you pulled? Come on, you must be able to come up with at least one example, and don't give me "I tried to kill myself" because that's old turkey. What have you done lately?

**P:** Lately, come on, I'm never going to be forgiven for that. You can't get it out. All the blood on her towels and rugs. Everything had to be pitched. Even the tile in the bathroom had to be regrouted. She fired the

[5]For certain types of personality disorders, however, both Kernberg and Kohut do recommend focusing intensely on the transference.

goddamned maid because she couldn't dust the living room right. You think I'm going to forgive—she's going to forgive me? (pause)

**T:** What? (soft music)

**P:** I think I just figured something out.

**T:** What?

**P:** Who it is who can't forgive who. . . .

*Commentary for Session #5*

Again Berger's interactions with Conrad are quite aggressive. He tells Conrad, "Don't take refuge in one liners, . . . 'cause that pisses me off," and asks Conrad, "What shit have you pulled? . . . and don't give me 'I tried to kill myself,' because that's old turkey." To a neurotic, these intense comments may be taken as a congruent expression of the therapist's frustration and strong conviction. Conrad does not appear to be offended by them. Personality-disordered patients, however, are intensely sensitive to each nuance of the therapist's expression. Strong comments from the therapist would be extremely upsetting to these patients, probably causing them to protect themselves vigorously from further anticipated assault. Instead, Conrad continues to explore his attitudes toward his mother, and eventually makes progress, in realizing that he has not been able to forgive her.

Even with a neurotic patient, Berger's cockiness, which sometimes borders on aggression, is not a typically recommended form of therapeutic demeanor. However, cockiness combined with aggressive limit-setting are occasionally used to cultivate an idealizing attitude in certain patients with personality disorders who would otherwise be likely to aggressively devalue the therapist and then leave treatment. One can imagine that cockiness might also have a similar effect on some relatively healthy teenagers with typical adolescent narcissism.

## Personal History

Although the transcript of Conrad's treatment seems to support a diagnosis of "neurotic," Conrad's history with his mother, as presented in the movie, does not so clearly suggest such a diagnosis. She is portrayed as a cold and unfeeling woman who tolerates no conflict and demands complete control over her immaculate environment. As the movie progresses it becomes clear that there is no emotional bond between Conrad and his mother. She tolerates his imperfections grudgingly, and is seemingly incapable of maternal affection. One would expect that Conrad would have long ago given up any hope of connection to his mother, but in the movie he gives it another try, only to be rebuffed again.

For a person to be able to engage in an intimate relationship with another, he must have trust, a basic belief that the relationship will be reasonably safe and satisfying. This belief can only arise from a firsthand experience of such a relationship. The healthy adult usually relies on his experience as an infant and later as a child relating to a caring adult, usually his mother. If, as in the movie, the child is unable to bond with his mother, he is deprived of the opportunity to develop this trust with her, and will tend to look to other adults for emotional nurturing. Empirically it appears that different children with very similar resources have differing degrees of success in compensating for deficiencies in the primary caretaking they receive. Probably the degree of genetic endowment of the child is the critical factor in determining how well these children are able to compensate.

## Trust

In the movie, Conrad's father seems emotionally available and capable of bonding with his son, and one must assume that Conrad related to his father fairly intensely as a young child in order to obtain the emotional supplies that Conrad was not receiving from his mother. As a teenager, Conrad seems connected to his father, and he seems to be able to open up to Dr. Berger with surprisingly little difficulty. He develops a relationship with a female classmate in which he is able to be vulnerable, and, although he expects rejection, he is able to be open with her and to maintain the relationship. Each of these three relationships suggest an ability for intimate relating that would not be expected in a person with a personality disorder.

Unlike Conrad, the person with a personality disorder is unlikely to be able to trust and be vulnerable in a relationship. He will feel loved and accepted in a relationship for a relatively short period of time until some event inevitably occurs to injure him or make him feel disappointed or rejected. At that point his feelings can suddenly reverse, becoming intensely negative. To be open about himself, his insecurities, and his lack of a sense of self would be too risky for the person with a personality disorder.

## Difficulty of a Neurotic Therapist Treating a Personality Disorder

Often, the therapist treating people with personality disorders is neurotic. A common problem arising from this situation is that the neurotic therapist assumes capabilities on the part of these patients that they have not developed. Because the therapist is neurotic, he has never experienced a deprivation of those capacities and does not recognize or empathize with these patients' limitations. He is likely to use methods of treatment that have in the past achieved successful results in the treatment of neurotic patients. Perhaps even in his own personal therapy the therapist may have found these methods to be successful. The patient with a personality disorder, however, is unable to benefit from these methods.

This confusion on the part of the therapist is compounded by the patient's use of neurotic-sounding words. A patient with a personality disorder will talk about himself, his wants, or his feelings; however the patient will mean something different from a neurotic patient who says the same things. A person with a personality disorder is unable to identify his own inner wants; what he says he wants is what he thinks will support his defensive facade or what someone else has suggested to him. Before getting treatment a patient with a personality disorder who says "I feel depressed" usually means a state of relative detachment from feeling. Even if he displays his "depression" through dramatic emotional outbursts, these tend to serve a defensive distracting function, rather than being deeply felt. A neurotic patient, on the other hand, would be referring to a state of intensified feelings of sadness and hopelessness. A patient with a personality disorder who talks about feeling hopeless is usually simply excusing himself for acting helpless, not attempting to grapple with his problems or feelings. A neurotic patient who says the same thing may be feeling frustrated and fearful. A personality-disordered patient who says "I love" means "I am dependent upon," "I feel passion for," "I am approved of and cared for by," "I feel safe with," or "I feel understood and appreciated by." None of these meanings includes the sense of mutual respect and support of individual exploration, self-expression, and growth that is included in the neurotic's meaning of "love."

Just as neurotic therapists find it difficult to appraise the limitations of a patient with a personality disorder, therapist interns who are neurotic are often skeptical toward the concept of personality disorders. With each new patient they begin treating, they try to convince their clinical supervisor that the patient is neurotic. They find themselves identifying with some of their patients and project onto the patients' problems the kind of internal conflict that such problems might produce in a neurotic. The interns make interventions based on these projections and often interpret the patient's compliant response as a successful integration of the interventions. As the supervisor repeatedly points out specific patient comments and behaviors that are atypical of a neurotic patient and asks how the intern explains these in terms of the intern's understanding of the patient, the intern becomes confused. Ultimately, the intern becomes open to accepting the supervisor's explanation because it successfully explains the clinical phenomena.

### Personality Disorder's Inability to Process Transference

When a neurotic patient is experiencing feelings toward the therapist, the patient is also usually observing what aspects of those feelings are irrational and probably derive from historical relationships of emotional importance. These feelings become useful to the treatment process because the neurotic patient is able to observe, experience, and try to understand them. When the patient with a personality disorder experiences feelings toward the therapist, the patient is usually splitting, and the feelings the patient experiences are directed toward only a split part of his internal representation of the therapist, rather than the whole person. Unlike the neurotic patient, the patient with a personality disorder is often unable to separate which of his feelings are appropriate to the reality of his relationship with the therapist and which are derived from the patient's personal history. Because these feelings often cannot be evaluated realistically by the patient, they act more as a hindrance to the process of the patient's self-exploration than as a path toward greater understanding. In order to be effective with a personality-disordered patient, a therapist must understand that with respect to the therapist, the patient is often unable to separate reality from projected fantasy. I have heard Masterson whimsically describe this phenomenon: "The neurotic patient thinks of the therapist as helping the patient to look at the patient's problem; a patient with a borderline personality disorder thinks the therapist *is* the patient's problem."

## FOUR CATEGORIES OF PERSONALITY DISORDER

As with most new developments in psychotherapeutic theory, there is a wide range of theorists with divergent points of view who characterize themselves as having an object relations orientation. Many theorists divide personality disorders into four categories: narcissistic disorders, borderline disorders, schizoid disorders, and antisocial disorders, each encompassing several *DSM-III-R* categories of personality disorders. Theorists do not, however, agree upon what these four terms mean. One theorist may view a patient's problem as a narcissistic disorder while another may view the same problem as a borderline disorder.[6]

Kohut looks at two independent developmental lines in evaluating a person's maturational progress. On one line is the movement toward creative self-expression, and on the other is the movement toward separation from emotional dependency upon others for a stable sense of self. Creative self-expression is central to a satisfying and productive life, both at work and at play, and an independently stable sense of self is necessary for mature object relations (satisfying and enduring intimate relationships with others). Kohut thought of patients as belonging somewhere on a continuum defined by these two lines of development.

With respect to creative self-expression, it is informative to examine patients' motives for achievement. The neurotic patient seeks achievement in order to gain personal satisfaction; it is linked to anxiety only in the form of a fear of failure. The borderline patient also views achievement as a source of personal satisfaction, but for this patient, success *increases* anxiety. Narcissistic, schizoid, and antisocial patients seek achievement in order to reduce anxiety. For the narcissistic patient, it is a way to feel excited and inflated instead of inadequate and anxious. For the schizoid, achievement means self-sufficiency, a protection against dependency and vulnerability. For the antisocial personality disorder, achievement means power, control, and survival.

The second line of development can be calibrated by the type of love

[6]In this book the terms will be used similarly to the way Masterson uses them. This usage is somewhat similar to Kernberg's, with some differences. The term *narcissistic personality disorder* or *narcissistic self disorder* will be used where Kernberg would indicate *borderline personality organization with narcissistic defenses*.

relationship a person in each category would seek. A neurotic person seeks a relationship in which each partner supports the other in being himself or herself, in growing and changing, and in his or her creative self-expression. Because of the splitting off phenomenon described earlier, people with personality disorders are unable to relate to a partner as a whole person, making their experience of love relationships limited at best. The borderline personality thinks of a love relationship as one in which he derives comfort and relief by being taken care of by his partner. In exchange for this dependence, the borderline person compliantly subordinates his own needs to those of his partner, sacrificing creative self-expression. The narcissist cannot permit himself the kind of dependency sought by the borderline, because the vulnerability it would expose him to would be unbearable. Consequently, narcissists pride themselves on being self-sufficient and emotionally independent. Rather than seeking emotional support from a relationship, they seek fuel for their narcissistic grandiosity: beauty, power, money, fame, and perfection. The schizoid personality yearns for emotional closeness in a relationship, but cannot tolerate it; for him, the vulnerability associated with closeness is even more threatening than for the narcissist. The schizoid is not only independent and self-sufficient, but self-contained. Where the borderline seeks emotional dependence upon a partner and the narcissist seeks from a partner support for his own grandiosity, the schizoid often seeks no partner at all. Despite the schizoid's yearning for connectedness, the emotional danger posed by a relationship often prevents the schizoid from even attempting to form one. If he does enter into a relationship, it is as a slave to a master, believing that if he is completely servile he might be safe from attack. The antisocial personality represents the furthest point in this continuum of nonrelatedness. Although the antisocial personality appears to engage in relationships, none of his partners has any value or meaning to him except in their potential for helping him to achieve his concrete goals. Whereas the other personality disorders all are interested in some form of love, the antisocial personality has no interest in love; for him, it is too risky even to let another person matter. For this reason there is wide agreement that the antisocial personality cannot be successfully treated through verbal psychodynamic psychotherapy, and so will rarely be mentioned in this book.

It is interesting that among the various personality disorders, patients' abilities to function successfully in the world seem to vary inversely with the degree of their quest for creative self-expression. The borderline appears to be the lowest functioning of the four. She seeks achievement as a source of personal satisfaction. However, personal achievement brings a sense of anxiety or isolation which she defends against by sabotaging her accomplishments and acting dependent, so her successes are short lived. The narcissist, on the other hand, does not use achievement for personal satisfaction as much as for support of a grandiose self-image, which is used to keep from experiencing inner feelings of defectiveness and worthlessness. While success for the borderline increases emotional stress, for the narcissist, success strengthens defense and consequently reduces emotional stress. In addition, the narcissist's sense of entitlement, her fascination with her own creations, her intense external goal orientation, and her ready access to aggressive energy enable her often to appear impressively successful.

The schizoid, like the narcissist, is often successful in the world, although not in as dramatic, public, or grandiose a fashion. Even more than the narcissist, the schizoid concentrates on controlling himself and his environment. Whereas the narcissist's successes are in the service of his grandiose defense, the schizoid's successes are in the service of his distancing defense. If the schizoid can control his environment, he is safe; the issue of safety is foremost for the schizoid. In addition, schizoids tend to mentally process information and experiences intensely. They tend to excel at jobs that require a level of mental activity that would feel alienating to most people, but to the schizoid, this intense mental activity provides a welcome refuge from the world of people and relationships. Although many schizoids find occupations that make it unnecessary for them to interact with other people, the more successful schizoids tend to be the ones who can tolerate superficial social interaction.

Of all the personality disorders, the most successful by some standards may be the antisocial disorder. His single-mindedness, his disregard for emotional entanglements except as a vehicle to achieve his goals, his lack of conscience, and his skill at manipulation, charm, and deception enable him to perform in ways that other people cannot. So, of the four personality disorders, the one that shows the lowest level of success in functioning, the borderline, is also the only one that actually attempts to achieve success for personal satisfaction and is the one most capable of a meaningful relationship to another person.

## ROLE OF MALADAPTIVE DEFENSES IN THERAPY

### Patient's Reliance on Maladaptive Defenses

There is a strong correlation between personality disorders and the use of primitive defenses (Vaillant and Drake 1985). The more mature the defenses of a person, the less likely he is to have a personality disorder. Conversely, the more disturbed the person is psychologically, the less mature (more maladaptive) will be his defenses. As you might expect, the use of more mature defenses tends to correlate with higher levels of functioning careerwise and more satisfying and stable personal relationships.

In general it is the defenses of the person with a personality disorder that appear most dysfunctional to an observer. The inner feelings of pain, worthlessness, self-hatred, despair, depression, and isolation are usually only partially experienced by the person before they are defended against; the observer only sees the defenses. The defenses used are usually maladaptive in that they are mechanisms to achieve a temporary reprieve from dysphoric affect in exchange for an undermining of self-esteem and functioning. To the observer, these defenses appear to be self-defeating. To the person with the personality disorder, they actually appear to operate in his own self-interest; they seem ego-syntonic.

One of the early tasks of treatment after a working relationship has been established between therapist and patient is to convince the patient with a personality disorder that his maladaptive defenses do not support his self-interest, but instead undermine it. Until the patient sees this, his functioning in his private and work life will be impaired, creating an environment that is not sufficiently safe or stable for the patient to explore deeply his troubling feelings. As long as the patient acts automatically to dissipate his dysphoric affect, the affect is not available for observation and exploration.

### Supportive Contrasted with Reconstructive Psychotherapies

The two psychotherapy objectives that seem to be most often recommended for various patients with personality disorders are control of destructive defensive behaviors and repair of psychological deficiencies. The process of repairing deficiencies resembles more closely the treatment of neurotic patients. The conditions necessary to permit repair are a source of some controversy among various theorists. Most believe that repair can only occur after the destructive defensive behaviors have been understood and reasonably controlled by the patient, when the personality-disordered patient's behavior approaches that of a neurotic. A patient can be helped to control his defenses in a variety of ways, including directly pointing out to him his defenses and their impacts, so that he becomes aware of which of his defenses are destructive. This process of supportive psychotherapy directly helps the patient to increase his level of functioning.

In this book, emphasis is placed on supportive psychotherapy leading to control of maladaptive defenses rather than repair of psychological deficiencies for two reasons. First, it is assumed that most readers of this book rarely, if ever, conduct intensive psychotherapy with patients that involves seeing them three or four times a week over many years. Most theorists agree that this kind of intensity is necessary in order to repair the deep psychological deficiencies of most personality disorders. The readers of this book as well as their patients are likely to have more modest goals, and achievement of these goals will necessitate the modification of defenses.

The second reason is the strong arguments in favor of the point of view that the control of destructive defensive behavior is a prerequisite for any deeper work with patients with personality disorders. The destructive defenses that these patients use interfere with productive functioning. Transference feelings that are the central focus of intensive psychotherapy are not available to patients with personality disorders. Instead of experiencing and exploring transference feelings, these patients defend against feelings before they can be experienced or explored. Until this defensive process is controlled, relevant feelings and memories will generally not be available to the patient.

Patients with personality disorders who attempt reparative reconstructive psychotherapy before their defenses are controlled ultimately bypass the most central issue, their inability to feel and express their own inner selves. Since these patients defend against spontaneous feelings and do not have access to their real selves, they cannot genuinely explore their real selves. Until these patients can control their defenses there can at best only be the facade of such an exploration. Control of defenses can be achieved through a combination of helping the patient feel understood and safe, so that he feels less of a need to defend, and helping him recognize his defenses and understand their function. These processes are central to supportive psychotherapy, and will be the central focus of this book.

## CONCLUSION

A neurotic patient will respond vastly differently to therapeutic interventions than will a patient with a personality disorder. The failure of a therapist to assess accurately the capabilities of a patient with respect to this distinction can lead to ineffective and inappropriate treatment. The focus of this book will be on the process of assessing patients and establishing a treatment plan that will address their specific needs and developmental levels. Because an understanding of defenses is essential to both diagnosis and treatment, a chapter focusing on defenses appears next.

# 2

# Defenses

Defenses play a central role in the treatment of any patient. However they are even more prominent in the treatment of personality disorders. Not only do these patients exhibit defenses within the therapy hour as described by psychoanalytic writers from Freud[1] to Greenson,[2] but they also use defenses outside the therapy hour in ways that interfere with treatment. Personality-disordered patients have a very low tolerance for internal conflict and dysphoric affect. As a result, they engage in defenses far more frequently than do higher functioning patients; they tend to act impulsively to rid themselves of dysphoric affect rather than to endure the affect long enough to explore their situation and take constructive action. In addition to

[1]When Freud first wrote about defenses in 1894 ("The Neuro-Psychoses of Defence" [*Standard Edition* 3:43-68] and Breuer and S. Freud [1893-1895], "Studies on Hysteria" [*Standard Edition* 2:268-270]) he was interested in what subsequently became known as *repression*. Later he broadened its meaning, while still restricting it to resistance within the treatment hour to the analytic process. In 1925, in "Inhibitions, Symptoms and Anxiety," Freud defines *defense* to include all procedures that have the purpose of "the protection of the ego against instinctual demands" (*Standard Edition* 20:164).

[2]As late as 1967, in *The Technique and Practice of Psychoanalysis*, Greenson restates the traditional analytic focus on defenses as a resistance to the analysis. He writes, "Resistance is in essence a counterforce in the patient, operating against the progress of the analysis, the analyst, and the analytic procedures and processes" (p. 60).

making their lives chaotic, this behavior dissipates meaningful affect and makes the affect unavailable for exploration in treatment.

The almost continuous activation of the personality disorder's defenses, together with the destructive nature of his defenses, makes an understanding of defenses essential for the treatment of these patients, so much so that any meaningful discussion of treatment without first discussing defenses would be difficult. The present chapter will describe a broad range of defenses, provide clinical examples to demonstrate each defense, and show how a therapist might address it. It will also describe how a treatment approach that is defense-oriented would use this information. The chapters that follow will discuss specifically the treatment of each of the various disorders.

## RESISTANCE TO TREATMENT

Defenses are patterns of behavior or thought that people use to protect themselves from emotional pain or discomfort arising from present life situations usually linked to painful childhood memories. A particular behavior may or may not be defensive, depending upon whether its intent is to protect. A smile, for example, can be an expression of amusement, an expression of affection, or a defensive attempt to avoid conflict or hide discomfort.

In any careful psychotherapy, the success of the treatment is dependent upon the patient's successfully overcoming his resistances to treatment. At first, the patient enters treatment with the expectation that treatment will make him feel better. Ironically, it does not take long before the patient realizes that treatment may bring up dysphoric affect and make him feel worse, or at least less comfortable. The patient responds automatically by protecting himself, drawing from the same arsenal of defenses that he uses outside of treatment to blunt the impact of painful events and mental associations. By bringing these resistances to the attention of the patient and clarifying the role they play, the therapist helps him to gain control over them so that the patient can explore the protected feeling and associated memories.

Attempts on the part of a therapist to deepen the feelings of a patient with a personality disorder prematurely often cause the patient to become either overwhelmed or emotionally closed down. If these patients respond to the therapist's efforts by exploring deeper feelings, they may become overwhelmed and rely increasingly on defenses that are destructive. For patients who do not experience their feelings, attempts to elicit feelings may result in confusion and frustration. In addition, when asked about their feelings, these patients may feel pressured, humiliated, or misunderstood.

The traditional principle of focusing treatment first on the patient's resistances is especially important with personality disorders. It is equally important that the therapist not provoke more extensive defensive behavior by making the patient feel threatened. Especially in the initial stages of therapy, the therapist must strike a balance between heightening the patient's awareness of defenses that interfere with the progress of treatment and allowing the patient to establish a pace for himself that allows him to feel safe, so that he can voluntarily let go of defenses. In doing this the therapist must prioritize defenses in terms of their relative adaptive and maladaptive impacts, and then decide which defenses the patient inaccurately views as self-supporting and is therefore unlikely to give up until their maladaptive aspects have become apparent.

### Defensive Acting Out

In general, personality-disordered people see their problems as originating outside of themselves, so they look outside of themselves for the solutions. People feeling insecure and afraid in the world might attempt to resolve these feelings by trying to get other people to like them or they might go to the opposite extreme by buying weapons and literally converting their homes into armed fortresses. People feeling helpless might attempt to find someone to take care of them. Those who feel insecure might ask someone for reassurance. These are all ways to attempt to deal with internal dysphoric feeling by taking external action, rather than processing the feelings and the conflicts related to them internally and resolving them in that way. In *Ordinary People*, when Conrad suggests that he be given tranquilizers, he is looking for an alternative to exploring his feelings in treatment.

Attempting to resolve the discomfort caused by a feeling through action or avoidance rather than through introspection and reflection is called *acting out*. Acting out brings immediate relief by dissipating feeling, but the feeling is never explored or the original precipitating problem resolved. The opposite of acting out is *containment*. Only through containment of related feelings can a problem be explored long enough to arrive at a solution. The defenses used by personality disorders tend to be forms of external acting out, in contrast to the defenses usually used by neurotics, which tend more toward internal ones, like repression, reaction formation, and rationalization. The neurotic defense of sublimation, although it ends with the taking of action, begins with the internal transformation of anxiety into a creative constructive drive.

The painful emotions acted out by personality disorders may include depression, envy, shame, helpless dependency, hopelessness, rage, fear, panic, guilt, humiliation, emptiness, and/or abandonment. Commonly, patients defend so well against this pain that the pain is never consciously experienced, and they are unaware that it exists until something happens to interrupt their defenses against it. They may, however, consciously experience a hint of the pain in the form of a nonspecific feeling of anxiety, a general feeling of malaise, unexplained somatic complaints, or a chronic lethargy.

The function of acting out is well illustrated by the experience of Masterson, when he was called upon to help control a hospital ward full of acting-out adolescents. The hospital was concerned because of the damage that the adolescents were causing to the facility. When Masterson was able to train the hospital staff to control the adolescents, he noticed a curious phenomenon; when the adolescents stopped acting out, they became depressed.

Defenses are undoubtedly indispensable for everyone, healthy or disturbed. They can make it easier for a person to function from day to day, but if they are maladaptive, they can make it harder, hampering job performance, relationships, and self-esteem. Vaillant (1977), in his unusual thirty-five year longitudinal study of ninety-eight healthy college men, developed a hierarchy of defenses ranging from mature defenses typically used by neurotics to maladaptive defenses most often used by personality disorders and more disturbed people. He then correlated the men's mental health statuses and degrees of life success to their use of defenses. He found that the men who used more mature defenses tended to be psychologically healthier and were more highly functional. Haan, in a separate study (1964), showed that mature defenses lead to increased intelligence and social status. In his book, *From Denial to Recovery*, Metzger (1988) traces the relationship between the twelve steps of recovery in the Alcoholics Anonymous program and the movement toward progressively more mature defenses. He also indicates that a downward movement on the hierarchy of defenses is associated with the path of addiction.

The defenses described in this chapter are some of the ones on the maladaptive end of the hierarchy. They are used by patients who are not personality disordered as well as those who are. However, personality-disordered patients will rely primarily upon these defenses, while neurotic patients may use these defenses secondarily to other more mature defenses. Patients with personality disorders will tend to be unaware of their use of these defenses and will have more difficulty controlling these defenses than will neurotic patients.

The defenses described here are divided into three categories: clinging defenses, distancing defenses, and narcissistic defenses. Clinging defenses are common for object-oriented patients, for whom the quality of their relationship to another person is very important. Because these defenses bind the patient to other people, including the therapist, they tend to stabilize the therapeutic relationship, making them relatively easy to address directly by a therapist. Conversely, distancing defenses are more delicate to address because their nature makes the relationship between the therapist and patient relatively less secure. Narcissistic defenses tend also to be relatively delicate to address because they are often activated as a protection against injuries that have occurred within the treatment itself so that the therapeutic relationship has to be repaired before the defense is explored. Furthermore, the mere exploration of the use of a defense often leads to a narcissistic injury followed by narcissistic defense.

The examples that follow illustrate the defenses, along with typical clinical interactions in which the therapist points out the maladaptive nature of the defense using an interpretive or confrontive intervention. For the purpose of illustrating more clearly the maladaptive aspects of these defenses, the therapist's responses in the examples are often more explicit than would normally be necessary, so they may seem to the reader to be somewhat heavy-handed or even harsh.

## CLINGING DEFENSES

### Transference Acting Out and Externalization

In the transference phenomenon, the patient projects onto someone around him or her the traits and significance of a historical figure like a mother or father. The patient then attributes to that person's actions meanings that would be appropriate to the historical figure's actions, and experiences the accompanying historically based feelings, like rejection, helplessness, or anger. These feelings might actually be appropriate to the present situation, but their intensity is likely to be more appropriate to the historical situation than the present. The patient is unaware of the historical contribution to the feelings he experiences, thinking that his entire response is to the present situation. An example of this is a patient's anger at his therapist's unwillingness to give advice. The patient is reminded of his mother who was withholding and nonnurturing. On the strength of his historical feelings of hurt and isolation, the patient becomes very upset, interpreting the therapist's behavior as intentionally withholding and mean-spirited.

In transference acting out, the patient attempts to deal with these painful feelings by taking action, as if the painful feelings were a product of the patient's environment, rather than a product of his psyche. This acting out of the feeling often takes the form of attempting to alter the present situation, which the patient believes to be the sole source of the feelings. Since the feelings are in part historically based, this attempt at resolving them by changing the situation will at best be only partially effective. For instance, in the above example, the patient tries to get the therapist to give some advice, as if the advice would reduce the patient's historically based feeling of being unloved. Another example is a person who attempts to get an adversary to apologize after a disagreement, as if the seething anger that the person feels inside as a result of years of parental abuse would then be resolved. This sort of acting out of transference material is referred to as *externalization* when it happens outside of a therapy setting. When it occurs within the therapist–patient relationship, it is referred to as *transference acting out*.[3]

When a person attempts to resolve his painful feelings through this form of acting out, he never achieves what he seeks; the historical pain remains intact. In addition, the person believes that the resolution of his internal feelings must come from someone else's actions, rather than from within himself. The price the person pays for this defense is

[3]James Masterson (1976) has used the term *transference acting out* in a very specific way, which will be discussed in detail in Chapter 3. He points out that since personality disordered patients are not able to perceive the therapist as a whole object, they are not capable of experiencing stable transference. Instead they engage in transference acting out as a defense against the feelings arising in the therapist–patient relationship.

intense feelings of frustration and helplessness, a sense of being unable to control his own life. His behavior reinforces his belief that someone else generates and therefore controls his deepest feelings. While he waits for this external relief, his internal conflicts go unresolved, and his relationships become a series of repetitions of painful childhood patterns.

*Example of Transference Acting Out of Helplessness*

**P:** My boss is coming up on Thursday to go over my territory with me. I hate when he comes up. He always makes me feel like a kid. He treats me like I just graduated from kindergarten. He even tries to tell me how to get to places in my own territory. I mean, I've been driving the area for three years now, and he thinks I need directions how to get to places. Do you have any suggestions of how I can get him to treat me with more respect?

**T:** What have you thought of trying yourself?

**P:** I thought maybe you could hypnotize me or something.

**T:** Well, have you thought of any approaches that you could try that might change his attitude toward you?

**P:** No, I can't think of anything. You know. You're the guy with all the training. You must have some ideas about what I can do.

**T:** You are very concerned about being seen as a child, yet when faced with the problem of how to deal with your boss, you seem to want to be related to as a child; you act helpless and ask me to take over and do it for you. How do you reconcile these two positions?

**P:** Yes, I am doing that, I guess. I feel like no matter how I think about it, it won't be right. That's how I felt with my father too. I tried my best, but he never valued anything I did. It was never good enough for him. It was as though I was just a kid, and when I became competent at things, he would never acknowledge it. I guess after a while I just stopped trying.

In the above example, the patient's defensive transference acting out of helplessness with the therapist takes the form of an attempt to get the therapist to do his thinking and solve his problem. This is similar to the dynamic that he complains about with respect to his boss. He indicates that he does not like to be treated like a kid, complaining that his boss makes him feel like a kid by taking over for him. But in the therapy hour, rather than trying to think through his own problem, he attempts to get the therapist to treat him like a kid and do his thinking for him. Predictably, this patient has a history of conflict with a parent about the parent's unwillingness to treat him as an adult.

As shown in this example, the transference acting-out defense often shows up in sessions as transference acting out of helplessness or hopelessness. Typically the patient will say, "I don't know" or "That's about it," and pause to wait for the therapist to take over and ask a question or indicate a subject for the patient to talk about. The patient's fantasy is that if the therapist takes over, the patient will no longer feel bad. In reality, however, if the therapist takes over for the patient, the patient's feelings of dependency on the therapist increase, and the patient's feelings of strength and self-sufficiency diminish, leading to increased feelings of helplessness and hopelessness. Another way helplessness is often acted out is through asking the therapist a question or falling passively silent and waiting. This passive silence is, of course, quite different from a pensive silence or an angry silence. In most cases the therapist need not address the helplessness at all. Simply by remaining silent and waiting, the therapist conveys the message, "I think you are capable of making this decision for yourself." Of course, some patients do not have the psychic capacity to look internally for direction; the impairment to the self is too great.

*Example of Transference Acting Out of Helplessness*

**P:** Driving over here today, I tried to think of what I wanted to talk about, and I couldn't think of anything. I couldn't remember what we left off with last week either, but I think it was pretty interesting. What was it? I just don't remember. Do you remember what it was?

**T:** Do you know what you felt right before asking me that question?

**P:** Well, I was trying to remember, and I couldn't so I thought maybe you would know. (Silence.) Oh yes, I remember; it had to do with my getting up the nerve to talk to my boss. You know, Thursday, I realized something about that situation. (Silence. The therapist is tempted to ask about the patient's realization, but doesn't!) You're awfully quiet. Were you about to say something?

**T:** You interrupted yourself. How come?

**P:** I don't know. I was waiting for you to ask about what I realized.

**T:** It's interesting to me. You had a hard time getting started today, but you were able to decide what you wanted to talk about. Then you stopped and turned to me as if you needed my encouragement in order to continue.

**P:** Well, I know I don't need you telling me to finish my thought. I don't know why I do that. It's nice to get encouragement sometimes, but I guess it doesn't make sense that I stop in my tracks if I don't get it. Anyway, I realized that I'm always expecting my boss to come down on me, so I don't ask for what I want. I really owe it to myself to talk to him, and tell him why I think I should go back on the day shift. I know that there are some potential problems. I don't know how he would react. (long pause—pensive silence) Well, even if he doesn't like it, he's not going to fire me. (pause) All this makes sense when I say it, but I know I'll never do it. I can get up the nerve sometimes, but I just can't make myself do it.

**T:** This is the same difficulty you have here with me. You decide to talk about something, and then you stop.

**P:** Yes, for some reason I need encouragement. I get anxious. I think you really don't want to hear what I have to say. I guess that's the same as with my boss.

Silences play important and varied roles in therapy sessions. Sometimes they are used by patients to create distance from the therapist and other times to express helplessness. Sometimes they are intended to punish the therapist. At other times, they allow the patient to think through and integrate some material that has just come up. These last might be called "deepening silences" because when the patient finally breaks these silences, he or she usually begins addressing the material on a deeper level than before the silence began.

In the example above, the first two silences and the patient's question are all minor examples of transference acting out of helplessness. The first silence was an expression of dependency, an attempt to get the therapist to help out, so that the patient will not have to think back and try to remember. When the therapist does not comply, the patient recalls the information himself. In the second silence, the patient again attempts to get the therapist to take a more active role in the therapy. The patient says, "I realized something," and then waits for the therapist to ask about the realization. If the patient has a personality disorder, this silence probably arises out of a feeling of anxiety produced in the patient by the autonomous behavior of conducting his own exploration of his thoughts about talking to his boss. For most personality disorders, independent exploration produces discomfort of one sort or another. If the therapist obligingly responds to the invitation to step in, the patient feels reassured, his anxiety disappears, and he assumes a more passive role in treatment; the patient's current exploration of material is interrupted. The last silence comes as a result of the patient's thinking through his situation with his boss and becoming anxious about the possibility of his boss responding negatively. Sometimes this sort of silence is an unconscious response by the patient to his having touched upon uncomfortable feelings. In this transcript, the patient contains the anxiety and continues to think through the situation. The therapist apparently assumes that the patient is capable of pursuing the treatment fairly independently. Although the patient would prefer to be reassured and soothed by the therapist, the therapist believes that the patient's history of destructively dependent relationships would be reenacted in the treatment if the therapist cooperates with the patient's preference for reassurance over the more uncomfortable task of self-exploration. The therapist's attitude is based on the assumption that the patient is capable of this uncomfortable self-exploration without ongoing soothing support. If the therapist believed that the patient were not capable of this degree of autonomous behavior or would not tolerate this degree of therapeutic pressure, he would doubtlessly handle the interaction very differently. For instance, if the patient's turning to the therapist were not seen by the therapist as defensive but rather as arising out of an internal structural deficiency, the interaction might have gone more like the following one.

### *Alternative Example— Therapeutic Response to Structural Deficit*

**P:** Driving over here today, I tried to think of what I wanted to talk about, and I couldn't think of anything. I couldn't remember what we left off with last week either, but I think it was pretty interesting. What was it? I just don't remember. Do you remember what it was?

**T:** Do you know what you felt right before asking me that question?

**P:** Well, I was trying to remember, and I couldn't so I thought maybe you would know. (Silence.) Oh yes, I remember; it had to do with my getting up the nerve to talk to my boss. You know, Thursday, I realized something about that situation. (Silence. The therapist is tempted to ask about the patient's realization, but doesn't!) You're awfully quiet. Aren't you going to say something?

**T:** You are waiting for me to ask you about what you realized. You are hesitant to talk about your realization unless you know that I am interested in what you have to say.

**P:** Yes, that's true. What I realized is that I'm always expecting my boss to come down on me, so I don't ask for what I want. I really owe it to myself to talk to him and tell him why I think I should go back on the day shift. I know that there are some potential problems. I don't know how he would react. (long pause–pensive silence) Well, even if he doesn't like it, he's not going to fire me. (pause) All this makes sense when I say it, but I know I'll never do it. Sometimes I know what I need to do but I just can't make myself do it.

**T:** What you are describing with your boss is similar to what you experienced as a child and what happened here a moment ago. You are naturally reluctant to express yourself when you don't expect to be heard, and you question whether you will be heard because you were constantly frustrated when you were young in your attempts to be heard by your parents. So you protect yourself by pulling back and waiting for encouragement.

**P:** Yes, I need encouragement. I get anxious. I think people really don't want to hear what I have to say, even you. As irrational as it is, that really is how I think about it.

The differences between these two patterns of intervention are manifest. In the first, the therapist assumes that the patient has the structural capacity to observe his own behavior and to modify it when it runs counter to his own interests. The therapist simply points out the patient's maladaptive pattern of behavior and relies on the patient to do the rest. In the second, the therapist believes that the patient's level of internal psychic structure is more seriously impaired, that the patient's apparent helplessness is really an attempt to borrow from the therapist's strengths in order to overcome fears or anxieties about the therapeutic task of looking inside himself. The therapist believes that simply to point out the patient's defenses would be experienced by the patient as so critical and injuring to him that he would not be able to make productive use of the information and he might be driven to withdraw emotionally away from treatment in order to protect himself. Therefore, the therapist attempts to normalize the patient's pulling back and waiting for reassurance while at the same time noting the self-protective (defensive) nature of it.

*Example of Externalization*

**P:** I feel stuck. I feel bad because my boyfriend and I had a really bad fight last night. I just drove him crazy and I can see what happens. I go into complete boredom when he's not around much and I can't focus on him, complete boredom, which leads to fighting, which lasts a couple of days. When we're not fighting, I'm bored, and I feel nothing; I feel nothing for him. The only way I'll feel something is if we fight. It's really unhealthy. When I get him really mad, the boredom feeling goes away and I feel more passion for him. I turn myself into this bitch, this nag, then I'm just this ugly person. Last night, Bob came home at 8:30. He'd said he was going to be home by 8:00. It got to be 8:15 and no Bob. I started to get concerned. I mean who knows. Maybe he'd been in an auto accident, or maybe his car had broken down and he was standing at the side of some road. I even thought of calling the highway patrol to see if there'd been any accidents. Anyway, by the time he came waltzing in at 8:30, I was pretty upset. He said he'd been late getting out of the office. I said, "Well, haven't you ever heard of the telephone?" He just shrugged, and started to walk away. Over his shoulder, he muttered, "Next time I'll call." I probably should have let it go at that point, but when he turns his back on me like that, it drives me crazy. I said, "Wait a second, what do you mean 'next time?' Are you planning a next time? Come back here and talk to me." Well, that did it for him. We went at it for a good thirty minutes, and finally he left, saying, "I've got to get out of here for a couple of hours." After he left, I felt utterly alone. I thought of all the things I should have said, and I couldn't stand waiting until he got home. I got in the car and went looking for him. I was very upset; I almost got into an accident. . . .

**T:** What exactly upset you so much that you felt compelled to chase after him?

**P:** Well, I just hated sitting home alone and waiting for him. I had to do something.

**T:** How come?

**P:** I don't know. I just know that I had to get out of there.

**T:** You are aware that you hated being home alone, but you don't know why. We've talked in the past about how you act impulsively before you have a chance to explore what you are experiencing. You immediately try to escape whatever you are feeling by distracting yourself, but you know that the feeling keeps coming back. You've come to therapy to work on your feelings of boredom and depression. How can you hope to get a handle on them if you don't give yourself the chance to experience them and try to understand them?

In the above example the patient acts out her feelings of deadness and boredom by fighting with her boyfriend. In the specific incident she describes, she acts out her anxiety about his lateness by becoming aggressive. Then, unable or unwilling to contain the feelings of abandonment stimulated by his turning his back on her, she acts these feelings out by again using aggression in a futile attempt to get him to comply. Her fantasy is that if he complies, she will no longer feel alone. Their ensuing fight and his subsequent leaving stimulate further feelings of abandonment. Rather than try to contain her feelings while waiting for him to get home, she acts them out by going out and looking for him. This repeated pattern of attempting to escape her feelings of abandonment by trying to obtain gratification from the people around her will predictably be reflected in treatment by attempts to obtain gratification from her therapist that have the effect of interrupting therapeutic exploration.

In the previous example, implicit in the therapist's intervention is the assumption that this impulsive behavior is something that the patient has the capacity to control if made aware of the destructive and pervasive nature of it. Since her tactics do serve to distract her momentarily from her pain, she is not likely to give them up easily. However, until she can calm down long enough to look at what is going on inside her, she will not work in therapy. The therapist responds therefore with a particularly confrontive intervention. The therapist apparently believes if the patient is aware of the price she pays for the luxury of impulsively acting in lieu of feeling, then she will have enough will power to control her impulse to act and will allow herself to experience her feelings, calm down, and think about what is happening inside her.

For a patient who does not have the capacity to control this behavior, this intervention would not make sense. However, in this case, the therapist apparently believes that the patient does have the necessary capacity. The patient says about the incident with her boyfriend, "I don't know. I just hated sitting home alone and waiting for him. I had to do something." She is saying that she had no choice but to act. In this comment she is also saying the same thing through her behavior in response to the therapist's question. She is saying, "I don't know and I don't intend to try to explore it." This is what the therapist points out in his intervention, asking how she hopes to understand herself if she does not stop and look at her inner experience. Similar interventions will undoubtedly have to be repeated many times in various forms before this patient begins to see her behavior as self-destructive and to control it.

If the therapist had believed that the patient were not able to stop, observe herself, and explore what was going on inside her, the therapist would have attempted himself to explain to her what was going on inside her rather than point out the destructive consequences of her inability to explore this question for herself. For instance he might have said, "You describe how you use your boyfriend as a distraction from your painful feelings of boredom and deadness. When your boyfriend left, you felt alone and helpless. Having to manage your feelings by yourself was so painful that you felt you had to do something to again distract yourself from them, so you chased after him."

The problem with a patient like this who externalizes is that she does not realize that there is anything relevant going on inside herself to look at, nor does she consider the negative consequences of acting out her impulses. She will react to the therapist just as she does her boyfriend; she will try to get immediate gratification from him so that she does not have to feel her feelings. If the therapist gratifies her demand, he implicitly validates the reasonableness of the demand, strengthening the patient's belief that the problem really is outside of herself. On the other hand, if the therapist is actually distant or critical in his delivery, the patient will rightly feel attacked. Thus the therapist needs to take care to be as emotionally neutral as possible in describing the patient's behavior.

In this transcript, the patient begins by pointing out (no doubt as a result of treatment) how she focuses on her boyfriend, but then goes into a lengthy description of the incident that occurred with her boyfriend. This description essentially reenacts in the session her focus on the boyfriend; the only reference to her own experience in this description is the initial comment about boredom and the use of the vague phrase "it drives me crazy." This pattern in treatment of keeping the discussion focused on other people and away from the patient's own experience and feelings is common for patients who externalize. If the therapist actively participates in maintaining the focus of the discussion outside of the patient, even if part of the discussion includes things the patient did and said but not how she processed these events internally, the patient's belief that outside events are her problem will again be validated.

## Clinging Defenses

Many people, when feeling depressed or alone, will often turn to another person for companionship to soften their depression while they work it out. Some people turn to others to distract themselves from the depressed feelings and never work the feelings out. With these people, the depression is never addressed; the feelings of loneliness and depression are always present under the surface and so the need for nurturing or companionship can never be satisfied. They will frequently remain in a destructive relationship in order to avoid the experience of being on their own, or they will have affairs and jump from one relationship to another. As patients, they commonly cling to their therapist and use the therapy relationship to help them to break off another relationship to which they may have been clinging. They usually have difficulty being by themselves, so they will call people on the telephone or visit with people to avoid being alone. Faced with the need to make a decision or take action, they will attempt to give the responsibility to someone else, or at least dilute the responsibility by obtaining other people's agreement before making any move.

Although clinging is one of the more commonly used defenses, it is usually one that a therapist will want to hold off in addressing until the therapeutic relationship is fairly strongly established. If a patient enters the therapy relationship with a tendency to cling, this tendency will provide the initial glue to bond patient to therapist. It is therefore unwise for the therapist to start off by challenging the clinging defense unless the clinging is to such a degree as to hinder other therapeutic work. It is equally imprudent and usually counterproductive for the therapist to encourage the patient to cling, because this discourages development of the patient's own sense of self and recreates the environment that was probably the original source of the clinging, a parent who discouraged separation and individuation.[4] But to simply allow patients to continue to cling during the initial stages of the therapy is often essential in establishing the relationship. They may know no other way of being in a relationship other than clinging. They may have no experience entering into a relationship as an autonomous adult, so if they were not able to cling they would have no other way to relate to the therapist.

*Example of Clinging*

**P:** They treat me terribly. . . . The other day they were in town and they didn't even call me. They could have the courtesy to stop in or at least call.

**T:** You've just spoken at length about how terribly these people treat you. Now you seem to be upset that they don't pay you a visit. Do you have any thoughts about that?

**P:** Sometimes he's mean and sometimes he's not. (tears) I guess I'm crying because I'm attached to these people who aren't so wonderful. When they're nice I feel good, and when they're mean, I don't feel good. I try to be good to them, but they can either be caring or mean.

---

[4]*Separation and individuation* is used here in the sense that Mahler uses it. It will be discussed in detail in Chapter 3.

Within the therapy session, a common form that clinging takes is talking or thinking about a nurturing and approving figure, rather than dealing with an anxiety-producing problem at hand. In the following example, a young woman faced with the problem of taking an independent step reassures herself by thinking of her confident sister. Rather than experience the anxiety of thinking her problem through, this woman adopts the attitude that she can always call her sister. In the process, she sacrifices the opportunity to explore the nature of the anxiety or to think through the move she is about to make and plan to provide for her needs.

*Example of Clinging*

**P:** I can't stand living with my parents one more month. I know I need to move out, but I've never lived on my own before. Where would I go? My sister moved out when she was 18. She says I'll be just fine. I guess she's right. She says if I get scared, I can always call her. I think I'll be all right.

**T:** Is it more reassuring for you to think that your sister says you'll be fine than it is for you to think the situation through and satisfy yourself that you do in fact have acceptable alternatives to choose from?

**P:** What do you mean? (pause) Oh, "Where would I go?" I did sort of drop that didn't I? I don't know what I'd do. (thinks) I guess I could answer a "roommate wanted" ad, and live with a couple of other women until I can afford my own place. . . .

The above are examples of relatively mild clinging. Clinging, however, can become very intense. The presenting issue for many patients is that their spouse has left them, and they are having difficulty with the loss. Some believe that they will not be able to survive the loss. They say they would do anything to get the spouse to come back. Externalization of helplessness is a form of clinging. From the point of view of the treatment, it is not necessary to make a distinction. These patients undermine their own self-esteem by acting helpless, as if their spouse's coming back would influence how they feel internally about themselves. Naturally the focus in treatment needs to be on how these patients feel inside rather than on what their spouse is going to do.

## Compliance

The compliance defense is sometimes one of the harder ones to spot. It is a form of externalization, in that the patient attempts to please those around him in order to avoid facing the painful feelings associated with acting independently. The patient is more involved with the reactions of others then he is with his own thoughts and feelings. A patient can appear to be making progress, when actually he is producing the "therapeutic" material that he thinks the therapist is looking for. A common scenario is one in which the therapist addresses the patient's maladaptive behavior. Rather than understand and integrate the therapeutic intervention, the patient converts it into a message from the therapist that this behavior is "bad." The patient, in an effort to be "good," changes the behavior. The result can appear to be therapeutically beneficial, but actually there has been no internal change in the patient; the patient has learned nothing about himself.

With patients who have been in therapy for many years, this defense is more common and usually more subtle. By then, patients have become so sensitive to the nuances of their therapists' responses that their compliant behavior can appear to be quite spontaneous. There are many clues that can alert the therapist to the possibility that the patient's therapeutic work may be in the service of compliance. The affect produced may not move the therapist emotionally to the degree that spontaneous affect does. The patient may describe life events in which he or she has avoided conflict or confrontation by giving in to other people. Therapy may seem to be going well but not producing movement in the patient's life. The patient may be coming to therapy but does not appear to think of it as a priority; the therapist may have more of a stake in the therapy than the patient. The patient may be experimenting with behaviors that are new and difficult and that would be expected to bring up anxiety, yet no anxiety appears. He or she may come to sessions reporting thoughts, feelings, and discoveries experienced outside of the therapy session, but within the session does not seem to be struggling with a real life problem. If there is a problem, it is more of a conceptual sort of problem, like, "How can I get more impulse control?" rather than, "I eat too much and it is endangering my marriage and my health." While none of these clues point exclusively to compliance, each of them suggests the possibility of compliance. The key factor is whether the question being examined by the patient is genuinely the patient's own concern, and whether the patient is earnestly attempting to find an answer to the question.

Compliance is a defense that cannot be described easily in a short interaction within a session. It can be identified when described as an interaction outside the session, or as a pattern over time within sessions in which the patient responds to other people's needs at the expense of his or her own. It is, however, usually accompanied by other defenses, and these may be more easily identifiable. What follows is an example of clinging and compliance defenses.

*Example of Compliance/Clinging*

**P:** (Beginning of a session after a three week break in treatment) Well, I've decided I want to stop coming to therapy because I don't feel that I'm getting much. I need somebody who will give me feedback or ask questions. I feel like I'm wasting my time and money. All the insights I get, I get outside of these sessions. I keep saying to myself that I should be getting what you are trying to get across. This is very hard for me. The last time I was here, you asked me if there might be any other reason why I was coming late. I'm annoyed that you don't give me more feedback. I come here and talk and cry, and I'm getting more feedback from my family and friends. I feel like I've been coming here mostly out of a sense of obligation or loyalty to you. If people won't help me pinpoint the problem, then they're of no use to me. . . . It reminds me of when I came in here and said I was getting overwhelmed with the BigCo contract, because they were asking for more and more from me. I expected you to say that they were being unreasonable, but you didn't say anything either way. My friend Tom agreed with me when I told him about it. He's a good friend. He helped me and you didn't.

**T:** Why did you need me or Tom to say it when you already knew it yourself? You knew BigCo was asking for too much, yet you seem to feel that unless the thought comes from somebody else, you can't trust it.

**P:** I don't know. I just don't seem to believe it when I say it. People keep pushing me. Like with BigCo, they kept wanting more from me, and all I wanted to do was get them off my back. I'm afraid to say no to people; I wanted to please BigCo. I was afraid that somehow I was going to get into trouble with them. I knew their request was unreasonable, but I didn't trust myself.

The above patient's compliance defense is apparent from her coming to therapy out of a sense of obligation or loyalty to the therapist, and her difficulty setting limits with BigCo. Her clinging defense is indicated in her inability to face a decision without turning to a friend or the therapist for reassurance. The therapist's intervention addresses only the clinging defense.

Commonly, when facing the issue of dependency and their difficulty in making their own decisions, compliant patients may come into a session and announce that they have thought it over and they have decided to terminate therapy. They will explain that it is a scary thing for them to do but that they have decided to rely on their own judgment about what is best for them. They repeat the therapist's words that it doesn't make sense for them to be coming to therapy just for the sake of the therapist. This places the therapist in a bit of a bind, needing to confront the patient's destructive behavior without opposing the principle involved. In actuality, the patient is usually involved in acting out any of a variety of feelings. She may be frightened by something that has occurred in treatment and uses the therapist's words as a way to leave therapy without appearing to be making an autonomous decision. What frightens her could be the sudden realization that the therapy or therapist has become more important to her than she can be comfortable with or it could be some other affect that is beginning to surface as a result of treatment. She may believe that the therapist's comments actually reflected his secret desire to rid himself of her and that she is really acting in accordance with his wishes. The therapist can respond to this situation by pointing to the patient's struggle with the issue of autonomy and the function of the treatment in supporting her attempts at autonomy. It does not make sense why, with so many other areas of dependency that concern the patient, she would choose to begin her self-assertion by pulling away from therapy, the place where she derives support for being autonomous. The therapist might ask the patient how she thinks about that.

## Projection

Projection refers to the process of attributing to someone else feelings that are really one's own. Patients use projection as a way to place their uncomfortable thoughts and feelings outside themselves so that they can disown and disavow them. A common feeling that is projected is anger. People who have internal prohibitions against feeling anger might instead see the object of their anger as being the one who is angry. Another common use of projection is to avoid evaluating the propriety or consequences of one's actions. In the following example, an adolescent woman attempts to avoid examining how she feels about some of her actions by projecting these feelings onto the therapist.

*Example of Projection*

**P:** I had two tests to take on Monday, and I'd agreed to play doubles in tennis with Jason on Sunday, so I didn't really have time to study for them. I studied a little bit for one, but the other one would have been a real bust. I decided it would be better to miss the class completely than to get an F, so I spent fifth period in the cafeteria. I don't know what's going to happen with that class. I'm not doing too well in it. You probably think I'm a real flake, huh?

**T:** What you think about yourself is more important.

**P:** Well I don't feel too good about what I did. My mom keeps saying that I'll never get into a good school the way I'm going. I don't see what's so important about a good school anyway. I think if a person can't accept me the way I am, why should I care what they think? I hate when you just sit there and don't say anything. I feel like you're sitting there judging me. Sometimes I wonder why I come here and pay good money to be judged. You do think I did the wrong thing by cutting, don't you? You think I'm this poor rich kid who hides behind her parents' money, but can't make it on her own.

**T:** I've noticed that twice now in the past few minutes you have begun to talk about how you feel about what you're doing in school, and both times you shifted your attention instead to what I think. You are acting as though your own thoughts and feelings don't count. You are treating yourself as though you're someone who "can't make it on her own."

The patient herself, in the previous example, thinks she's "a real flake." Rather than ask herself why she would agree to play tennis when she needs to study for two tests, she projects her own judgments about her behavior onto the therapist. When the therapist focuses the attention back onto what the patient thinks, the patient projects that the therapist thinks she's "hiding behind her parents' money," again an idea that she does not wish to realistically own and examine. The important thing about these projections is that they serve to distract the patient from the difficult task of examining her own thoughts and feelings, which is what the therapist points out to her. Implicit in the therapist's final comment is the belief that the patient does have the capacity to make it on her own.

## DISTANCING DEFENSES

Distancing defenses tend to be less object-oriented. However, in some cases, they can still be handled by the therapist directly, pointing out the price one pays when one uses them.

## Avoidance

Avoidance has been included as a defense in both of the case examples that will be given in this chapter because it is a common defense and one that often must be addressed early on in treatment. If a patient avoids meaningful issues in treatment because they are uncomfortable or painful, the treatment will falter unless they are taken up. Avoidance will take many forms. Outside of the therapy session it takes the form of sidestepping uncomfortable issues like finances, conflicts, and decisions. In therapy sessions, the most obvious forms may be frequent subject changes, lateness to sessions, canceling sessions, missing sessions, and ultimately dropping out of therapy entirely. By the time the patient drops out of therapy, obviously it is too late to begin addressing this defense. If, however, avoidance has already been established as a maladaptive defense that the patient commonly uses, then the therapist may be able to help the patient to understand the desire to quit therapy in the context of this defense. The therapist can then remind the patient that this strategy for dealing with problems has not been effective in the past and has in fact contributed to the situation that brought the patient into therapy in the first place. If the process of avoiding problems has already come to be viewed as destructive (ego-alien) by the patient, he or she may reconsider the decision to discontinue therapy.

## Denial

Denial is similar to avoidance, except that with avoidance, a feeling or situation is consciously being avoided; the person knows he is avoiding it. With denial, the person is not fully consciously aware of the feeling or situation that is unpleasant. It is a term commonly used in describing substance abusers and their partners. The person creates an alternate reality so as to not have to face the true situation. An alcoholic, for instance, might say, "I can drink beer; it's the hard stuff that always gets me in trouble. I really don't have a problem with beer." A patient cannot learn to deal with problems whose existence he is denying. Problems that are denied will not be addressed and are likely to get worse. Despite the unconscious component of denial, the person who denies is often given ample evidence pointing to whatever it is he is denying. If the therapist makes a patient aware of the pattern of denial, the patient can begin to recognize situations in which the state of the outside world seems to be inconsistent with the patient's own beliefs or expectations. The patient can recognize that these situations are likely to be ones involving denial.

In the following example, a woman attempts to deny the implications of her husband's alcoholism. She tries to convince herself that it is not going to be a problem. When the therapist draws her attention to this, she again denies the serious nature of the problem by proposing that the problem might solve itself. When this is again pointed out to her by the therapist, she recognizes the seriousness of the problem. At this point, unable to continue her denial, she turns to avoidance as a defense against taking a realistic look at her problem.

*Example of Avoidance/Denial*

**P:** I know I talk about Joe and little Joey a lot, but it all comes back to how I feel about myself inside. For example, Joe's boss was fired and replaced suddenly a month ago. Since then he has been under a lot of stress and our communication has tended to drift once in a while. Last night the only talking we did was ten minutes before going to bed. I was upset about how little attention I get from him. Also, our regular child care person moved to Sacramento yesterday, so I was feeling tense even before he got home. I don't understand how he can spend two hours in a bar with his friends, and all he has time for with me is ten minutes. (continues with five minutes of stories about Joe's drinking.) The other day, Joe had had a few beers, and he tripped over one of Joey's toy airplanes. He got angry at Joey, and began screaming at him. I felt sorry for Joey. He's not big enough to understand.

**T:** You indicated a while back that you were going to give an example that illustrates how you feel about yourself. I'm aware that you're talking about Joe again, rather than how you feel about yourself. I'm not clear about your purpose in turning the discussion to Joe.

**P:** Well, I keep trying to convince myself that it's not going to be a problem.

**T:** Why would you want to convince yourself of something that you don't necessarily believe is true?

**P:** Well, I see certain things happening and I get scared. (teary) I guess I'm still frustrated. I don't know which direction to go. I think that maybe if I just accept the way he is and take a positive attitude about it not happening again, maybe it won't.

**T:** Are you saying that if you look the other way, it might correct itself on its own?

**P:** Well, sort of.

After the patient's denial of the seriousness of her husband's drinking problem was called to her awareness by the therapist, she began to shift toward avoidance. At the same time, she continued to deny by minimizing the seriousness of the problem. The therapist's second intervention addressed both defenses. In the next bit of transcript the therapist continues with this patient by focusing directly on the avoidance.

**T:** It hasn't happened that way for you in the past. (Therapist lists several other situations that deteriorated while the patient avoided addressing them.) Why would you expect this problem to work itself out if you ignore it?

**P:** I don't like thinking about where it's going with Joe. I don't think that he's ever going to stop drinking. I don't know if he would physically hurt me again. My brother is coming in next week for a visit, and I hope that Joe and he get along. My brother and he have had fights before, not physical ones, but loud. He doesn't like the way Joe has treated me. Whenever he comes for a visit, I get nervous. They can get like two stags fighting for turf. I hope this visit is better than the last one. The last time my brother came. . . .

**T:** Are you aware what just happened? You were talking about not liking to think about where the situation with Joe is going, whether you thought Joe would become abusive with you again, and then you changed the subject to your brother's visit. You didn't like thinking about it, so you changed the subject. This is another example of what we just talked about. You cannot solve your difficult problems if you don't think about them.

**P:** Well, deep down inside, I feel it is going to happen again, and I feel that this is a main concern in my life right now. I couldn't live with myself if I kept letting him do that to me. Things around me do not seem to be changing, so I am going to need to deal with it myself somehow. I have a friend who let her boyfriend keep beating her up, and I lost all respect for her. I have to do something. . . .

The last intervention in this example pointed out the patient's use of avoidance within the therapy session. This can be particularly meaningful to the patient because the experience is fresh, and the patient may be able to look at what happened for her at the time she avoided. From her response in this example, it appears that she did not integrate the therapist's intervention. She did not seriously consider the price she pays for avoiding thinking about her life problems. Instead, she took the therapist's intervention as a directive to go back to the subject that she was avoiding. The goal of this kind of intervention is to render the avoidance defense ego alien, rather than to induce the patient to return compliantly to the subject matter being avoided. If the patient takes these interventions as directives instead of considering their meaning, she will passively talk about the subject areas she believes the therapist to be directing her toward, and there will be no progress in the therapy. The therapist will need to clarify for the patient how she misinterprets the intention of these interventions and if possible tie her compliance into a broader pattern of compliance that has created other problems in her life.

Another feature of this series of interventions is the therapist's tenacity. Patients who are actively avoiding never immediately integrate the therapist's intervention. If the intervention makes sense to them, they may think about it, but then they go back to avoiding. If the therapist permits the subsequent avoidance to go unchallenged, the impact of the initial intervention is lost. It is only through consistent challenging of the avoidance that the patient recognizes the pervasive and destructive nature of this defense. This could take weeks or months and requires great patience on the part of the therapist. As with all defenses, if the patient does not currently have the capacity to handle the underlying affect, the therapist must be careful about challenging the defense.

It is not entirely coincidental that this transcript illustrating denial and avoidance is one involving alcoholism. In general, denial is usually the central defense of alcoholics, followed closely in centricity by avoidance. These defenses are often also central for codependents; however externalization is usually even more central for them. In the previous transcript the initial issue that the therapist takes up with this codependent patient is the continual focus of her attention on her husband, to the exclusion of her own thoughts and feelings.

*Another Example of Avoidance*

**P:** I've felt for some time that I'm really not accomplishing anything here; my real therapy work has happened outside of this room as a result of my conversations with friends and family. Lately therapy is just me coming in here and doing a monologue. I update you on all the news in my life. Then I pay you and leave.

**T:** Yes, I've noticed the same thing. Why do you spend your time here in that way?

**P:** I don't know. I don't really have anything to work on, so I give you news reports.

**T:** I think you do have things to work on. I've noticed that several times in today's session you brought up important questions but haven't pursued them. For example, you wondered whether you should still be working for your parents. As soon as that question got a little sticky, you moved on to something else.

**P:** That's a tough question.

**T:** Yes, it is.

**P:** (pause) I know I brought it up myself. I'm not sure why I let it drop. I guess I feel that if it happens that I get another offer, that will be fine with me, but if not, I don't think I want to pursue it. I really don't want to upset what I've got now. I can't explore other options without risking my relationship with my parents. That's probably why I let that question drop.

**T:** What you decide to do about your situation will of course affect your relationship with your parents, and I can understand your caution about taking action. But you avoid thinking about the question entirely. If you don't think about it, you can't hope to find a satisfying resolution.

**P:** I've always had so many different feelings about my relationship with my parents and about my job. The job is very important to me, and our relationship is very important. It would be very hard for me to be away from them. I think I'm afraid to look at it too closely, because if I really think about being on my own, I could just get depressed and not want to work at all. I know there are aspects of my work situation that are very restrictive for me, but I haven't until now made myself look at the alternatives.

As patients continue in treatment, they should demonstrate an increasingly more mature overall level of functioning and defenses, although one can expect temporary setbacks and relapses. Compared to the previous patient, the above patient's relatively higher level of functioning is evidenced by her acknowledgment of the point the therapist is making. Unlike the previous patient, she does not compliantly begin to talk about the subject matter that was dropped. Instead, she acknowledges that she raised the issue of what to do about her job situation, and wonders why she then dropped it. Although she does not immediately explore why she dropped it, she does think later about why she dropped it, realizing that she is afraid that thinking about it will make her depressed.

### Intellectualization

Intellectualization is a common defense and often one of the more benign ones. In this defense the patient relies on intellectual exploration of his situation, devoid of emotional content, often taking the form of reading pop psychology books and conjecturing about childhood experiences, rather than focusing on where he is presently emotionally blocked. In therapy sessions, intellectualization often takes the form of painstaking unspontaneous dredging up of historical material. In the early stages of therapy, it is rarely necessary for the therapist to comment on this defense at all because there are almost always more maladaptive defenses to address, and because patients who utilize intellectualization will often tend to move past it on their own and begin more meaningful work. Since many patients, especially narcissists, have no sense of what they are feeling, to address the defensive intellectualization runs the risk of wounding the patient by making him feel inadequate. The therapist can, however, test the patient's sensitivity to this issue by occasionally asking what he feels, especially if the patient appears to be experiencing some affect. Only when the disavowal of affect is extremely pronounced and poses an obstacle to productive work in therapy might the therapist choose to address it more aggressively.

*Example of Intellectualization*

**P:** I read an article in the *Times* this weekend about children of alcoholics. My parents weren't alcoholics, but they sound just like the parents in the article in every other way. They didn't support me in the things I tried to do. I think they were probably threatened when I did well at something. You know, neither one of them feel like they've ever accomplished a whole lot. Anyway, I was thinking how different I'd probably be now if they had supported me. I would probably still be happily married, for one thing. Barbara never supported me either, and I think I took what she dished out because I didn't know any better. If I'd gotten support from her or my parents, I think I would have done better in my career, and she probably wouldn't have left me. I think they just didn't have it in them to give. They didn't know any different. Their parents weren't physical with them, so they weren't physical with me. Their parents didn't give them a lot of encouragement, so they didn't give it to me. For that matter, I guess I don't give it to David either.

**T:** How is that for you?

**P:** Well, what happened back then can't be changed. There's no use getting worked up about it. The only thing I can do is try and understand how it happened. Now with David, that's different. I think I need to take a look at how I treat him. I think I could be more supportive of him. I read that children who spend fifteen minutes a day going over their homework with one of their parents do twice as well in school—it was the results of a study that someone did. I guess that my relationship with David is a lot like my other relationships. I don't get down in the trenches with him. I keep a safe distance. We go to scout meetings together and I help out with his soccer practices, but we never have man-to-man talks. I think he's doing OK.

**T:** You talk about not getting down into the trenches in your relationships, and I wonder if that isn't also happening here with me. Probably because it's so hard for you to know exactly what you're feeling, you tend to share your thoughts and insights without sharing your feelings. Is that what you mean by not getting down into the trenches?

**P:** Well, yes, I guess I do that with you too, don't I? I don't really know how to do anything else. No wonder David doesn't tell me how he's doing; I never talk to him about me either. Barbara used to say I was like a stranger. It's not that I don't want them to know what I feel, I just have never had words for my feelings.

*Example of Intellectualization/Avoidance*

**P:** I hate waiting for the answer. Is Al going to stay with me or not? I want to know one way or the other. It's like taking an exam and waiting for your grade. Except with a test at least you know when you're going to get the results. With this I just don't know what to expect. I wonder if my doubts are some self-fulfilling prophecy—if he's going to think I hang on too much and get turned off by that. I wonder if I'm attractive enough for him, and then I wonder why it's so important to me that he does stay. Half the time we're together we fight anyway. I think it's my experience growing up with an alcoholic mother that makes me so unsure of myself, always expecting to be rejected. I think it makes you feel that you must have done something wrong, because otherwise why would this person be so mean to you. I never knew how my mother was going to treat me the next time I saw her. So naturally I'm going to feel insecure in relationships. I've been reading a book about children of alcoholics. They give five personality types. I wonder which one I am. I think I'm the one who hides and tries not to be noticed. But if Al doesn't notice me, then I worry that he's not going to stay interested in me. So I work extra hard to please him. So I'm not sure that's the type I am. . . .

**T:** You are jumping so quickly from topic to topic that I'm losing track of what you're trying to get across. I know you asked a question a moment ago that sounded important, but that doesn't seem to be what you're talking about now.

**P:** (pause) You mean about why it's so important to me that Al stay? I didn't answer it, did I? I've been with him for so long. I don't remember. . . .

The above patient's work can be misleading, appearing to be deeper than it actually is. Although she thinks about herself and produces insights, she avoids trying to answer the hard questions about her life, and her work lacks affect. She talks about wanting to know where she stands with Al. Then she wonders out loud about several things, and questions why it's so important to her that he stays. She posits that it might have to do with her being the child of an alcoholic, and then talks about what she read in a book on ACAs. Although her discussion of ACA issues is a response to her question about why it is so important to her that Al stay, her discussion of the book is purely intellectual, and she uses it to escape really looking at that question. As is often the case, intellectualization is used here in the service of avoidance and distancing.

## Projective Identification

Projective identification is the only defense that requires the participation of the therapist. It is projection with a twist. The patient projects onto the therapist the part of himself that is either too painful or threatening to keep in himself, or is too precious and needs to be placed with the therapist for safekeeping.[5] The therapist unwittingly takes on the projected feelings, usually because the patient unconsciously exerts pressure on the therapist to accept them, largely by assuming the parental role that brought these feelings about in the patient originally. For instance, the patient might cast off the part of himself that feels helpless or inadequate by projecting that part onto the therapist and then assuming the role of the critical, demanding, attacking, or devaluing parent. This aggressive role probably feels better to the patient than the helpless inadequate role, and it tends to influence the therapist by making her feel inadequate, the feeling that is being projected. The therapist, however, reacts to these feelings in his own unique way. He processes the feelings using his own coping abilities and responds to the patient's projected feelings in a somewhat different and presumably more mature way than the patient. By

[5]The idea of projective identification regarding a "precious" part of a person is a novel one that is explained in greater detail in Ogden's 1979 article, "On Projective Identification." An example might be the idealizing transference of a "closet" narcissist. The closet narcissist feels threatened to display his grandiose feelings so he projects them onto the therapist, idealizing the therapist, who in turn feels an inflated sense of himself.

observing how the therapist handles these feelings, the patient can discover a relatively mature way to handle his own problems. Some theorists believe that this process is the most important healing component of psychotherapy (Ogden 1979).

Subjectively, the therapist at first experiences the patient's projection as originating within himself. If the projection that the therapist has accepted is foreign to the way he normally thinks and feels about himself, the quality of foreignness acts as a signal to alert the therapist that there is countertransference or projective identification involved. If the accepted projection happens to conform approximately to feelings and thoughts that the therapist commonly holds himself, the projective identification is far more difficult for him to identify. Sometimes it takes months or years before the therapist is fully aware of it.

A valuable clue that will usually appear is when the therapist notices that he is modifying the frame, that is he is straying from the fundamental rules that he has set for himself about the conduct of treatment. These include the fee charged, the beginning and ending time of sessions, the cancellation policy, and so on. When one of these rules is set aside by the therapist, he may have a therapeutically sound reason for doing so or he may be responding to subtle unacknowledged pressures that arise as a result of countertransference or projective identification. Careful consideration by the therapist of his motives for modifying the frame can be extremely enlightening.

In order to protect himself from accepting patients' projections, a therapist sometimes maintains an emotional wall between himself and his patients. Such a wall interferes with his ability to be empathic and consequently limits his effectiveness in conducting treatment. It can be argued that a therapist who is emotionally receptive to his patient's emotional communications will inevitably allow some of the patient's projections to be experienced as his own thoughts and feelings; the many subtle pressures exerted by patients cannot all be consciously recognized and processed by the therapist. Hopefully, however, at some point the therapist will recognize the projection as coming from the patient and will be able to use his experience of the patient's projection to help him to deal with the part of herself that the patient is projecting.

*Example of Projective Identification*

**P:** I've been coming to you now for four years. When I began coming I had a pretty good job; now, my job is the pits. When I began coming I was on good terms with my family; now they're not speaking to me. Since I started coming, my husband has left me, and other men don't seem to be showing much interest. I'm not sure that this therapy is helping me. Maybe I'm just not good therapy material. Maybe my problems are beyond the scope of what therapy can handle. Maybe I need some other kind of therapy. I don't know. Every time I ask you for help, you ask me a question. I mean, I know you can't go out and find me a man, but I'm not sure if there really is anything you can do for me. I come here week after week, pay good money for the privilege, and I feel worse than I did when I started. Maybe I should take the money and spend it on myself. At least that might make me feel good.

**T:** In listening to you I am reminded of how you have described your mother, and I think I am understanding more clearly how you must have felt as a child, constantly criticized by her and told that you were worthless. No matter what you did, she was upset with you. You must have felt very frustrated and hopeless.

The foregoing example is grossly oversimplified. Psychotherapy would be so much simpler if projective identification were so easily identified and addressed. Normally, the therapist goes through weeks or months of perceiving a mysterious impasse in the treatment before the projective identification becomes clear. In general, it is not necessary or possible for the therapist to produce the perfect interpretation of the patient's behavior involving this subtle process of projective identification. The therapist is faced with projected feelings and a projected self-representation that the patient has spent a lifetime struggling with without success. Such struggles are usually not easy ones. Over time, the therapist's careful attempts to maintain his own sense of himself as he responds to the patient's projections offer a model to the patient of how she can prevail in her own struggle. If the therapist is able to contain his countertransference and respond appropriately to the patient, projective identification can offer an opportunity for the patient to make significant gains in her treatment.

## Withdrawal

Withdrawal is one of the more primitive defenses. The patient feels hurt or overwhelmed and protects himself by pulling back behind his wall and raising up the drawbridge. Unlike avoidance, where the patient is trying to escape looking at a particular issue or problem, withdrawal is a more general pulling back and shutting down. It can be in response to feeling threatened or a response to the vulnerability of feeling too close to other people.

In a patient's life, withdrawal is acted out by staying at home, not calling people, not receiving calls, quitting jobs, or being generally uncommunicative. In therapy sessions, it can take the form of missing sessions, coming late to sessions, or periods of silence during sessions. For some patients it is a response to feeling that the therapist has gotten too close, violating what feels like a safe distance. There may be a fear of being smothered or overwhelmed by the therapist. For other patients, withdrawal is a reaction to some specific thing the therapist did that felt injurious. Perhaps the therapist said something that sounded critical or that demonstrated to the patient the therapist's lack of an adequate understanding. The therapist may not have said anything at all; she may have taken a vacation, canceled a session, or been late for a session, and the patient felt either slighted or rejected.

What the therapist needs to do in these instances depends upon the patient's motivation for the withdrawal. If the withdrawal is a result of the patient's feeling wounded or slighted, it is usually adequate for the therapist to indicate an understanding of what occurred, specifically what was hurtful to the patient. If the therapist has made a "mistake" that has wounded the patient, it is usually helpful for the therapist to acknowledge the mistake. If, on the other hand, the patient's withdrawal is a response to feeling rejected or alone, the therapist can acknowledge the source of the hurt, and in addition gently point out how ironically the withdrawal defense intensifies the patient's isolation. Sometimes, withdrawal is a result of the therapist's having gotten too close to the patient or of the patient having come in contact with memories or feelings that were more than the patient was willing to tolerate. Then, the therapist might acknowledge the patient's pulling back, and in some cases might interpret the reason for the patient's withdrawal.

### *Example of Withdrawal*

**P:** (animated discussion of the unpleasant aspects of being alone, after breaking up with his wife the previous month) . . . So, I really want to be in a relationship, but sometimes I question why. At least now I don't have some of the problems that I did when Audrey was there. The other day, I came home from work, and I didn't feel like eating. "Monday Night Football" was on, and I took a couple of beers from the fridge and stretched out in front of the TV. And I think that's okay. Sometimes a guy needs that.

**T:** Are you saying that if you were in a relationship, you might not have gotten to do that?

**P:** Well, it's been that way with Audrey. There were times that I would come home, and she was there and had dinner waiting, and she hadn't done anything all day except wait for me to get home. It was like from the moment I got home I had to make up to her for having been gone. That's an easy one though; I can always arrange in advance to take that time. Yes, just because I'm in a relationship it doesn't mean that I can't have that time to myself (two minutes of silence).

After an extended animated discussion, the above patient becomes silent. The therapist must evaluate what the silence means. In this particular case, the therapist knows that the patient has established a pattern of becoming silent after narcissistic wounds. The therapist therefore begins to wonder during the silence what might have been wounding to the patient. It occurs to the therapist that the patient may have felt that the therapist's comment implied an inability on the part of the patient to work out a problem: how a guy can stand up for himself sufficiently to take a little time for himself. The patient may have felt that the therapist thought that this was a relatively trivial problem, and so the patient felt belittled in the eyes of the therapist. In response to this wound, the patient defended himself by saying that taking time for himself is really a rather simple matter with a simple solution, and then withdrew into silence. The therapist can now correct the problem by acknowledging the injury and letting the patient know that it is understandable that the patient would have difficulty with this aspect of a relationship. It is not uncommon for a patient to deny that an injury occurred, but privately to appreciate the therapist's acknowledgment of it.

**T:** I wonder if that sounded like I was implying that I thought this was a simple problem to handle.

**P:** Well, not exactly. I mean it's not the world's most difficult problem.

**T:** What might be easy for one person can be difficult for another, because of their special psychological makeup. I'm reminded of your story of how you stayed after school one day to participate in a gymnastics contest, and instead of being proud that you entered and won, your mother scolded you for not leaving yourself enough time to finish your homework before dinner. I should think it would be hard for you in a relationship to take time for yourself, because, even though you feel it's a healthy thing for you to do, if your partner doesn't think so she might be critical of you. Knowing how painful criticism is for you, even if it is unreasonable, I can understand why you would protect yourself from that kind of exposure by reining yourself in and trying to be beyond the possibility of criticism.

**P:** (apparently relieved) Yes, it's not like if I were analyzing somebody else's relationship, I couldn't give them good advice about taking space and the value of doing that. (laughs) That brings up a good point, the last evening I spent with Audrey. . . . (goes on with further animated discussion)

By acknowledging the patient's feelings about the therapist's comment, the therapist helps the patient to feel understood; the patient again feels safe with the therapist and goes on with further discussion.

## NARCISSISTIC DEFENSES

The term *narcissistic defenses* refers here to a set of defenses common to but by no means exclusive to narcissists. Most of these defenses are present to some degree in almost all people. Depending upon the actual diagnosis, narcissistic defenses tend to lend themselves best to interpretation.

### Grandiose Defense

The above interaction also demonstrates the grandiose defense. The patient perceived the therapist as implying an inadequacy on the part of the patient in not being able to solve this problem, so the patient responded by saying that the problem was actually quite easy to solve. The patient's acting as though the problem is beneath him is a grandiose defense against the perceived injury. The function of the defense is to restore the patient's inflated perception of himself.

Normally, when used, the grandiose defense is a pervasive one. Patients who need to defend themselves against an underlying feeling of utter inferiority, emptiness, and powerlessness often do so by presenting a front to themselves and the world of wonderfulness and omnipotence. As will be explained in detail further on, either overt or covert grandiosity is a defense employed by all narcissistic disorders. If something or someone should puncture their grandiosity by saying something that interferes with their inflated view of themselves, these patients experience a narcissistic injury, and often respond by expanding their grandiosity, thus shoring up and reinflating their self representation.

## Devaluation

The example of projective identification presented earlier in this chapter contained devaluative comments. The message was, "I'm stuck, because you haven't helped me" or "I'm miserable, and you're not helping." The devaluation defense is different from devaluation in projective identification in that it is not necessary for the therapist to have a countertransferential response of feeling bad about herself. This defense is usually used by a patient who feels wounded by someone. The devaluing message can be direct or subtle. It is an attempt to hurt the person back and to prop up the wounded ego with a feeling of superiority by putting the other person down. This defense can also be an attempt by the patient to distance himself from someone with whom he has felt a kinship but who has recently disappointed him and proved herself unworthy of any close association. The therapist can respond to devaluation of this type by acknowledging it and by suggesting why the patient might feel wounded. In the following example, the object of devaluation is the therapist.

*Example of Devaluation*

**P:** Where would you like to begin today? I thought, on the way up here, where are we going to go from here, after the last couple of times? I really couldn't come up with any direction. I want to see this through, but I'm uncomfortable with where we go from here. I'm not looking for "the answer." I ask questions because I'm curious. I look at you as the expert, full of thoughts and ideas. You have the background. This is your field. I would expect you to have answers for me, the same way as I expect people to ask me questions about my field. I don't expect a sudden brilliant flash, and then the answer, but it would be kind of nice to throw out a question once in a while and get some real help. Sometimes it seems like I'd be better off keeping my money and talking to a wall instead of coming here.

**T:** You sound very disappointed with me. Is there anything in particular that you can think of from our last session that you were disappointed with?

**P:** No. I can't think of anything. (pause) Well, there might have been one small thing. I did feel you interrupted me in the middle of my sentence to tell me that we were out of time. I thought that was a little tacky. I was in the middle of a sentence, and you didn't even bother to wait until the end of it.

**T:** I understand your irritation at feeling cut off and not heard out. I don't intend to interrupt you in mid-sentence, but sometimes my timing may not be just right. Perhaps your irritation is one of the reasons you seem especially impatient with me this week.

**P:** Well, now that you mention it, that could be. I didn't say to myself, "I'm pissed at him," but I did feel sort of slighted, like "whatever you have to say, it can wait."

## Self-sufficiency Defense

Self-sufficiency is in itself a healthy quality, unless it is used in the service of avoidance of the vulnerability that comes from interrelatedness. In that case, it is not true self-sufficiency; it is the pretense of not needing another person, and it leads to isolation. In therapy sessions, it appears as a continuous theme. There are usually other more maladaptive defenses for the therapist to focus on initially. However, the therapist can lay a foundation for future exploration by acknowledging the patient's need to protect himself from becoming dependent on another person. In the case of narcissists and schizoid patients, the difficulty with vulnerability and dependence is an important theme in their treatment. This acknowledgment helps the patient to understand why it is so difficult for him to trust the therapist.

In the following example, a female patient is defending against painful affect associated with her therapist's comment. Either she feels separation stress due to his announcement that the customary appointment schedule will be interrupted, or she feels a narcissistic wound associated with her inference that he is offering to reschedule because he assumes that she might need him.

### *Example of Self-sufficiency Defense*

**T:** I'm going to be away next Wednesday, but if you want to reschedule I do have a time next Thursday.

**P:** No, thanks, I think I can survive a week by myself.

**T:** It sounds like you heard me imply that you needed the session, and that offended you.

**P:** I knew you didn't mean that; I was just making a little joke.

**T:** Whenever you talk about making an appointment, you seem a little ambivalent. You have always prided yourself on being self-sufficient. I imagine that for you coming to therapy is like an admission that there is something wrong with you, something that you can't handle yourself.

### Manic Defense

The manic defense is used by most people at one time or another as a defense against underlying feelings that are uncomfortable. When these feelings surface, instead of feeling them, the person gets busy, takes on new projects, and generally immerses himself or herself so completely in activity that there is no time to feel the feelings. This defense is distinguished from the avoidance defense of the workaholic in that the manic defense can occur in spurts and be only somewhat maladaptive, while the workaholic's avoidance defenses tend to be chronic, and are consequently more maladaptive. Since a mild manic defense is relatively benign, this is a defense that would rarely be addressed by a therapist in the initial phase of treatment unless it was in conjunction with avoidance defenses.

## RELATIONSHIP BETWEEN SYMPTOMS AND DEFENSES

In medicine, symptoms are the observable conditions a patient exhibits that direct the physician to the underlying pathological condition. In psychotherapy, symptoms are the behaviors that a person displays that suggest to the therapist an underlying emotional imbalance. Some typical symptoms for depression, for instance, are melancholia, lethargy, anxiety, changes in eating patterns, changes in sleep patterns, difficulty concentrating, sudden outbursts of tears, loss of interest, and hopelessness. Generally, a patient goes to a doctor or a patient goes to a psychotherapist to control or eliminate symptoms. A depressed person with a personality disorder might seek psychotherapy, for instance, out of concern about his difficulty sleeping or his difficulty concentrating at work, surface manifestations of an underlying depression.

Patients with personality disorders usually have difficulty functioning in many areas of their lives, so they complain of multiple symptoms. Typically, the therapist feels like he or she is constantly helping them to put out brush fires, while unable to attend to the forest fire. Their symptoms are often actually the problems created by their maladaptive defenses—for instance, the patient who compulsively eats to defend against feeling alone, or the woman who can't decide whether to stay with her husband because she does not trust her own ability to make decisions, a defense against the frightening feelings associated with standing on her own. Even the term *depression*, which the personality-disordered patient might use to describe anxiety, extreme boredom, lethargy, or the inability to activate, may be a symptom of the patient's defensive suppression of affect. The symptom of inability to hold onto a job can result from a variety of defenses including avoidance, clinging, devaluation, or grandiosity. High school truancy, on the other hand, can also be a symptom arising from a variety of defenses or it may itself be a specific example of avoidance.

If a symptom results from a particular maladaptive defense, a therapist must address that defense, rather than the symptom. Otherwise, if the defense remains active, it will produce new symptoms, and the therapist will face an unending string of symptoms. For instance the person who avoids feeling unloved by escaping to romantic movies and novels might switch to watching television, smoking cigarettes, and daydreaming at work. If this is curtailed, she might shift to overeating or substance abuse. This curtailed, the same patient might begin to arrive late to treatment sessions or cancel them entirely, saying she is too depressed to even get out of bed. All of these are examples of avoidance. In each case the patient engages in a symptom-producing behavior in order to avoid addressing unpleasant affect or issues.

## Case Example—Depression Resulting from Avoidance

Avoidance can produce a wide range of symptoms. Take Mr. A., a 21-year-old man who enters therapy with a presenting problem of poor performance at school, excessive sleep, and depression. By depression, Mr. A. means a negative self-image and a lack of interest in life. Although excessive sleeping can be viewed as a component of a vegetative depression, in this case it is a form of defensive avoidance. Mr. A. describes it as a way to put off facing the problems of the day. Similarly, Mr. A.'s failure at school is a result of avoidance of stress-producing situations like homework and tests. The depression is actually a sense of hopelessness, failure, and disappointment that Mr.

A. feels as a result of repeatedly letting himself down, doing things that undermine his own productive efforts.

A principle that lies at the base of this discussion is that when people let themselves down, they feel bad. If they do it repeatedly, they develop a negative self-image, which is, in a sense, reality based. Although people who come to therapy complaining of depression and low self-esteem usually have emotionally deprived histories, they make themselves feel worse when they treat themselves badly, when they fail to support their own efforts at expressing themselves and managing their lives.

Suppose that when Mr. A. begins in treatment, the therapist addresses his presenting problem by pointing out that the reason he is failing is that when he is faced with a difficult problem to solve, he procrastinates or sleeps, so that he ends up being unable to address the problem properly. Mr. A. is able to see this, and alters his behavior, resulting in greater successes at school. While these successes are satisfying to Mr. A., he begins to feel anxious. It will be explained more fully in later chapters that Mr. A.'s is a typical borderline response to personal success. To manage his anxiety, Mr. A. finds himself drinking increasing quantities of alcohol, which again impairs his performance. The therapist, unaware of this increase in alcohol consumption, encourages Mr. A. to explore the reasons for his poor performance. Four months pass with no progress. During this time, Mr. A. discusses a wide range of topics in therapy, tending to jump from one topic to another. The therapist comments on this process of frequent subject changes, indicating that it prevents him from concentrating on the problem at hand, namely figuring out why he is doing poorly in school. Eventually, Mr. A.'s work in therapy becomes more focused, the drinking problem is identified and addressed, and his performance at school improves. Then, Mr. A. reports one day that his financial situation has gotten so bad that he will not be able to continue therapy. The therapist asks how long Mr. A. has been aware that there was a financial problem, and he says that he has seen his savings dwindling for the past year, but could not see a solution.

In this example the therapist has identified many of Mr. A.'s problematic behaviors but new ones continued to appear. What is lacking in Mr. A.'s treatment is a unifying principle. Underlying all these behaviors is Mr. A.'s belief that it feels better to avoid an uncomfortable situation than to meet it head on. This is displayed in his procrastination with school work, his tendency to sleep or drink rather than address his problems, and his avoidance of his developing financial problems. In sessions, it is displayed by his tendency to jump from topic to topic, not remaining with any one topic sufficiently long to grapple with the problems involved. As is frequently the case with personality disorders, it is Mr. A.'s defensive behavior outside of the treatment room that ultimately defeats the treatment.

A solution to this unpleasant scenario is for the therapist to use a defense-oriented approach to treatment. To prevent the appearance of an unending procession of self-defeating avoidant behaviors, the therapist would repeatedly point out the pattern of avoidance, making sure that Mr. A. can see its consequences, until Mr. A. is convinced that the feelings of defectiveness and low self-esteem that his failures produce are ultimately far more painful than the discomfort of confronting a difficult situation head on. The therapist would repeatedly show Mr. A. how each of these avoidant behaviors comes at a time when he is finally beginning to make progress in his life. The excessive drinking began when he started to face stressful situations at school, and the jumping from topic to topic began when he finally began to grapple with the problem of his school performance.

Whenever possible, the therapist would point out how Mr. A.'s behavior within the therapy hour is an example of avoidance. When Mr. A. jumps to a new subject to avoid exploring a question he himself has raised, the therapist would point this out. If Mr. A. persists, the therapist would become more direct, asking him how he hopes to answer the questions he raises if he does not even try to puzzle them out. Each symptom would be linked in this way to a unifying theme; they are all examples of the same defense, in this case avoidance. As each example of avoidance becomes apparent, hopefully Mr. A. would realize the costly price in self-esteem that he pays for the ephemeral comfort afforded by the avoidance. Eventually he would come to understand this principle and see his avoidance as self-defeating. He would learn to independently recognize the emergence of new avoidant behaviors when they arise and begin to curtail them. As he gained control over his defenses, the underlying painful affect that he has been defending against would begin to surface.

This approach, in treating individuals, is similar in some ways to the systems approach used by humanistic therapists in treating couples and families. Traditionally, systems-oriented therapists have viewed symptoms as serving a purpose, perhaps a call for help, a diversion of attention, or an acting out of a parent's unspoken wish. Systems-oriented therapists have recognized that when one symptom disappears, it generally is replaced by another. The new symptom serves the purpose formerly served by the old one. Patients can appear to make progress in therapy because their symptoms disappear, but if these symptoms are replaced by others, the perceived progress is questionable. So systems-oriented therapists have concluded that it is important to understand the function of a symptom, and to find a way to render that function unnecessary.

When a patient views a defense as helpful and relies on it heavily for comfort, she is unlikely to be receptive to letting go of it. If a therapist wishes to challenge the relative benefit to the patient of the defense, the therapist must first bring the defense into clear focus by establishing repeatedly how it works, so that the patient recognizes its presence. Then, if the patient does not already see them, the therapist can begin to point out the unwelcome consequences of the defense. Whereas all of Mr. A.'s symptoms were related to a single defense, avoidance, most patients utilize a variety of defenses. To focus on several defenses simultaneously might confuse the patient and make her unreceptive to any of the therapist's input, so usually the therapist must choose the defense that appears to be the most destructive and concentrate on that defense until it has been brought under control. Then, the therapist can shift the focus to another defense. The exception to this principle is when the patient rapidly shifts from one defense to another, in which case all of the defenses must be looked at together.

### Case Example—Variations on a Theme

Miss B. is an example of a patient with multiple defenses. She is a woman in her early twenties who comes to therapy because her life is "a mess," and she is depressed. She does not get along with her mother, but feels close to her brother, upon whom she depends heavily for support. She repeatedly attempts to go to college, but ends up skipping classes and dropping out. She has a job that does not pay her enough of a wage to cover food and lodging, and that utilizes only a small portion of her intellect and skills. Based on this description of symptoms, her active defenses appear to be avoidance and clinging. Splitting is suggested in her negative attitude toward her mother and her positive attitude toward her brother, to whom she clings.

Suppose her therapist plays the role of a supportive parent. The therapist is openly pleased when Miss B. asks her boss for a raise, encourages her in her efforts to reconnect to her mother, and shows interest when Miss B. talks about the class she is taking. When Miss B. eventually is unable to complete the course, the therapist reassures her, pointing out that she lasted longer in that class than in any of the other classes she has taken recently.

This treatment encourages Miss B. to be compliant, possibly successful in some things, but ultimately unchanged. Perhaps Miss B. succeeds in reconnecting to her mother and in so doing is able to decrease her dependency on her brother. She nevertheless lacks self-sufficiency and a sense of adult autonomy; she very possibly goes from being dependent on her brother to being dependent on her mother and on her therapist. Her clinging behavior is not addressed. She obtains a raise, which gratifies her, but she is unmotivated to seek employment that will challenge and satisfy her. She learns more acceptable excuses for dropping out of school; with the additional motivation of pleasing her therapist, she is able to persist longer in a class before dropping out, but is still unable to commit to taking a course and following through with it.

Dependency is a central theme for Miss B. She clings to her brother and to an inappropriate job. She does not support herself in the things that she attempts to accomplish, like the classes she takes, and so feels depressed. Like Mr. A.'s, Miss B.'s depression is a result of seeing herself repeatedly letting herself down. In therapy sessions, Miss B. seems to have very little to say. She cancels appointments and makes no effort to remember what was talked about in the previous session, all further examples of her unwillingness to support herself, her pursuit of the fantasy that someone else will do it for her.

Often she will say something like, "I don't know what else to say," or "That's about it," followed by an uncomfortable silence. The therapist might be tempted at these times to ask a question, but should realize that the issue here is whether this patient will learn to support her own efforts, or whether she will become dependent on the therapist, as she has on other people in her life, by acting helpless, unable to think of anything to talk about that is relevant to her own life struggles.

The therapist must ask himself the question, "What is the principle maladaptive defense the patient uses to manage the uncomfortable feelings that arise when she attempts to grapple with a problem?" In Miss B.'s case, when she tries to break away from the people to whom she regressively clings, she feels bad and alone. For example, she reports that her brother invited her to come to his home for dinner on an evening that she had planned to read a book that she needed to complete for a class. Faced with the unpleasant prospect of disappointing her brother, she puts off doing the reading she has planned. The next day, rather than go to class unprepared and possibly feel embarrassed, she decides to have lunch with a friend. Her defenses in this example were clinging (to her brother), compliance (deferring to her brother's needs over her own), and avoidance (putting off the reading and skipping class because she was unprepared). In all three instances, she undermines her own efforts at furthering her education.

## A Congruent Response to Self-destructive Behavior

What is the appropriate response for a therapist who sees a patient shooting himself in the foot? If the patient is capable of handling direct feedback, the appropriate response is to observe out loud that it is indeed the patient's own foot that he is shooting, and to question why he would want to do that. A therapist who is simply supportive and understanding toward such a patient inadvertently conveys the message that this behavior is within the realm of reasonableness. In addition, if the patient is aware of the destructiveness of what he is doing, the therapist's understanding response leaves the patient wondering why the therapist has not questioned this behavior, and so conveys the additional message that either the therapist does not care or the therapist believes that this patient is capable of no better.

The term *confrontation* in psychotherapy refers to any intervention in which the therapist observes something about the patient (Hamilton 1988), usually a behavior or aspect of a behavior of which the patient has been unaware or in denial. Unfortunately, the word "confrontation" has an aggressive connotation that does not apply to its use as a term in psychotherapy. A confrontation can be as simple as bringing the patient's attention to a minor discrepancy between two things she has said or might consist of pointing out a connection between the patient's presenting problem and the way the patient is behaving toward the therapist. Confrontation will be discussed in detail in Chapter 7.

In the case of Miss B. and all patients, the therapist who uses a defense-oriented approach must observe Miss B.'s defenses until he can determine which defense is most detrimental to her. Then the therapist needs to focus on that one pattern of defense repeatedly until Miss B. becomes aware of when she does it and the price she pays for doing it. Eventually, she will learn to catch herself as new examples of that defense emerge. Then the therapist can move on to Miss B.'s next most maladaptive defense. Since avoidance is an especially destructive defense and can also lead to the premature termination of treatment, the therapist should probably focus on Miss B.'s avoidance defense first. The therapist might take up with Miss B. how she thinks about her pattern of quitting undertakings when she becomes uncomfortable; he might ask her how she thinks this pattern affects her life.

But if this question is asked of Miss B., will she be able to stop and try to answer it? With some patients, a question of this sort will be heard purely as critical: "You're saying that I'm doing something wrong." The response will range from, "Why should I come here and pay good money to be put down by you?" to "What can I do to make you like me again?" Other patients will say to themselves, "I hate hearing that, but it's something I've known all along that I have to look at. It's about time I did."

Naturally, then, in order to decide how to respond to the patient, the therapist has to be able to distinguish between those who can benefit from a direct questioning of their destructive defenses, and those who cannot. This is one of the things that is assessed during differential diagnosis, when one differentiates between a borderline, a schizoid, and a narcissist. A borderline patient can handle this directness, whereas a schizoid or a narcissist cannot. In general, it works better to interpret a narcissist's defensive behavior rather than confront it because a narcissist has a less developed observing ego with which to process the confrontation. The schizoid patient will take confrontation as a thinly veiled command that must be obeyed.

If no diagnosis has been made, a simple working criterion will serve in most cases: to what degree is the patient object oriented? Object-oriented patients look to relationships as sources of soothing and support. Object-oriented patients with personality disorders look to relationships to give them a sense of being lovable. They seek reassurance, advice, and fulfillment of general dependency needs entirely by another person. These patients will tend to attach themselves to a therapist more easily than those who pride themselves on their independence and who see others as interchangeable providers of needed interpersonal functions. The more interrelated the patient is willing to become with the therapist, the stronger the bond will be, and the more likely the patient will be able to tolerate and utilize disagreement and direct confrontation from the therapist. In addition, object-oriented patients tend to be emotionally stronger than patients who are so threatened by intimacy that they avoid meaningful relating. Object-oriented patients are generally more capable of taking in confrontive feedback and considering it, without automatically characterizing the therapist as attacking and diverting their attention to the therapist instead of themselves.

## HIERARCHY OF DEFENSES

In this chapter, a variety of defenses have been discussed, and it has been indicated that some are more maladaptive than others. A therapist must choose the most maladaptive one displayed by a particular patient and concentrate on that defense until it is handled. If, for example, the patient displays a variety of clinging and distancing defenses, as well as grandiosity, the therapist would focus on the distancing first because it is most likely to interfere with treatment, and on the grandiosity last because in moderate amounts it may represent some of the glue that holds the patient together and gives her the strength to look at other aspects of herself. On the other hand, the clinging or the grandiosity may need to be addressed earlier if it is so intense that it prevents the patient from tolerating the discomfort necessarily involved in looking at herself. If the therapist does not remain focused in this process or uses the shotgun technique of simultaneously addressing every defense that is identified, the patient will be overwhelmed, unable to integrate any of the information the therapist is conveying, and likely to feel criticized and attacked by the therapist.

Before making an assessment of maladaptive defenses, it is necessary to be sure that patients are functioning on a level that will permit them to begin to look at their defenses. For instance, extremely low-functioning patients may be experiencing so much difficulty structuring their lives that they cannot possibly generate the organization of thought necessary for integrating additional information. Such patients are likely to require a counseling approach in which the therapist helps them to structure their lives in an attempt to create some order. These patients have incompetent defenses that are unable to protect them from their painful underlying affect, which consequently presses toward the surface, precipitating irrational defensive behavior that makes it difficult for these patients to maintain a rudimentary organization to their lives.

In Vaillant's (1977) hierarchy of defenses, he labels the most primitive defenses as *psychotic* defenses and the most mature sets of defenses as *neurotic* and *healthy* defenses. In between are the defenses commonly used by personality disorders. The defenses that Vaillant categorizes as *psychotic* defenses are denial of external reality, distortion, and delusional projection. The relatively healthy defenses include intellectualization (isolation, obsessive behavior, undoing, rationalization), repression, reaction formation, displacement (conversion, phobias, wit), and neurotic denial. The most mature defenses are sublimation, altruism, suppression, anticipation, and humor. As defenses commonly used by personality disorders, Vaillant includes fantasy (schizoid withdrawal, denial through fantasy), projection, hypochondriasis, passive-aggressive behavior (masochism, turning against self), and acting out. To this last list might be added splitting, clinging, distancing, projective identification, denial, avoidance, and grandiosity (including devaluation). The first phase of the treatment of personality-disordered patients may be viewed as a process of helping them to recognize and discard immature defenses in favor of relatively healthy ones.

## Order of Treatment

There is also a natural hierarchy indicating which defenses make sense to be addressed early on in the therapy and which can wait. The defenses requiring most immediate attention are those that might make the patient a danger to himself or others, or might cause an abrupt and inappropriate termination of treatment. Less destructive but nevertheless also requiring early attention are extreme forms of transference acting out, because while they are actively pursued, there can be no serious work done in therapy. If the patient is acting out transferentially, he will do this instead of integrating the therapist's interventions. For the compliant patient, for instance, the patient is primarily concerned with convincing the therapist that the patient is being "good," rather than understanding the true implications of what the therapist is saying.

The next most important defense, after transference acting out, is any other defense that directly interferes with the conduct of the therapy. This includes distortions of the therapeutic contract or frame violations. Then come avoidance and the more destructive defenses. Toward the end of the list generally come clinging and finally relatively benign defenses like intellectualization and the manic defense if in fact these defenses are being used in a relatively benign way.

## CONCLUSION

Observation of defenses can provide useful information about the nature and function of symptoms. It can help in diagnosis and contribute information about the level at which the patient functions. This chapter has discussed a large variety of defenses, has given examples of each of these defenses as they are likely to appear in a therapy session, and has offered interventions that the therapist might have made in each of these examples. It has also discussed how a defense-oriented treatment approach would treat these defenses. The next three chapters will discuss the various personality disorders and an effective method of treatment for each.

# Part II

# 3

# Borderline Disorders

A young woman patient who has been in treatment for several months comes to a session depressed, saying, "I can't bring myself to wean my daughter from the breast. I know it's necessary and important for her; she is 14 months old, and her need for my breast is very confining for both of us. But every time I withhold my breast, she cries and sucks her thumb. It makes me feel like I'm torturing the poor girl, so I give in. It concerns me that I'm not doing what I think I should be doing." In many ways, this patient is summarizing the borderline conflict and also the difficulty a clinician encounters in treating a borderline patient.

Until an infant is weaned, her only source of nourishment is her mother; her mother is indispensable. Weaning represents a mother's letting go of an infant's dependency on her and encouraging the infant's independence. According to Masterson, the encouragement of independence and self-exploration is what the borderline patient missed as an infant. Instead of encouragement, the infant experienced either a withdrawal of maternal supplies or increased maternal clinging in response to movement away from dependence on the mother. Consequently, the borderline patient does not feel comfortable being self-reliant. She is uncomfortable asserting herself, acting independently, or even thinking independently, and she does not feel comfortable being separate, because all of these represent being cut off from maternal supplies (nurturing). The borderline adult either clings to nurturing figures, or fears maternal smothering and distances from nurturing figures; she generally alternates between clinging to other people and distancing from them.

Treatment, then, for the borderline resembles a reenactment of the process of separation and individuation (Mahler 1975) from the mother that failed to take place during infancy, except that in the treatment context the nurturer is a therapist who is willing to support autonomy in the patient by letting go. The patient, like the infant, feels deprived when the symbolic breast of the therapist is withheld, and may complain bitterly. Without some degree of withholding, however, the patient cannot be weaned and will not mature into a fully functioning adult. The above woman dramatizes the maternal struggle that can lead to the development of a borderline child, and at the same time she dramatizes an adult borderline's struggle. Just as this woman finds it difficult to do what she knows is in her own best interest and in the interest of her child, the borderline patient is typically unable to act on her own behalf if such action entails uncomfortable feelings of separateness or isolation. Often, in order to avoid dysphoric feelings, the borderline patient takes actions that provide immediate comfort but that are harmful to her.

## BORDERLINE SPLITTING

Masterson might liken the borderline adult to a frightened child who has never grown up, an adult child searching for the "good" mother whom he never really had. The good mother is loving, warm, nurturing, kind, and supportive. The borderline adult tries to be good, helpless, and cooperative, even submissive, in order to maintain the affection of the good mothers he is able to find. Nevertheless, he constantly fears that if he is too independent, too competent, too confident, or too capable, his good mothers will suddenly turn away and abandon him. Life becomes a subtle conflict between the inner ("real") self of the borderline that wants to grow up and become an independent and confident adult, and the defensive self that feels anxious whenever he does anything self-supportive, because such behavior is linked to a fear of the loss of the good mother. Without the love of the good mother, the borderline's euphoria turns to dysphoria, and his self-image changes from that of a good person to that of a bad person. Instead of praise, he expects criticism and attack from the bad mother, and he feels lonely, unloved, angry, or guilty for the "trouble" he has apparently caused.

The borderline manages simultaneously to hold to these two mutually contradictory realities, the good world and the bad, by paying attention to only one at a given time. He is conscious of both realities. However, the reality that is split off occupies a dormant status, holding no emotional immediacy. The ability to juggle these two mutually contradictory realities in this way is known as the *borderline split*.

As practiced by an infant, the splitting defense represents a healthy attempt to protect the internal image of the "good" mother upon whom the infant's survival is dependent. The negative aspects of the caretaker are split off and literally thought of as belonging to someone else. Mahler (1975) describes as an example of this a 2 1/2-year-old boy who is feeling angry and deserted by his mother who has been away from him several days in a hospital. In the morning, when the mother calls the boy on the telephone, he clings to her, unwilling to hang up for forty-five minutes. He denies, however, that the person to whom he is talking is his mother, saying he is talking to a "nice lady." In so doing he protects his image of the "nice lady" to whom he clings from the angry feelings he feels toward his mother. Another example is offered by one of my colleagues whose 3-year-old son had gotten into a struggle with his mother. After a temper tantrum the son turned to my colleague, who was innocently standing by, and said reproachfully, "Bad daddy!" His angry feelings toward his mother, the "good" object, were transferred to his father, allowing the child to keep his anger segregated from his positive feelings toward his mother.

## CHARACTERISTICS OF BORDERLINE DISORDERS

### Behavioral Characteristics

While no behavioral characteristics are common to all borderline adults, many characteristics are typical of the borderline condition. A borderline has difficulty in making decisions that involve her own self-interest. Such decisions require her to think of herself as a separate person and to ask herself what she wants, a task that produces great anxiety. Instead, she puts off making decisions. The borderline adult often has little difficulty making friends. She either plays the role of a helper to them, or manipulates them to take care of her by playing the role of the helpless child. Her friendships, however, tend to be short-lived because she is always afraid that she might be deserted by a friend; at the first sign of discord, she may end a friendship in an attempt to avoid being deserted herself. On the other hand, she may cling to relationships and accept blatant abuse in order to avoid being deserted.

Similarly, the borderline adult usually has a spotty work record. Job satisfaction is rare, because jobs are not chosen on the basis of what produces the greatest personal satisfaction; they are chosen on the basis of external standards like other people's approval. In addition, the borderline's tendency toward avoidance and lack of initiative and independence often lead to poor job performance. At the first sign of disapproval from a boss, the borderline may attempt to avoid the feelings of abandonment that accompany being fired by prematurely looking for a new job. The borderline adult often works at a series of jobs for relatively short periods of time. These jobs are often well below her skill level, because they enable her to feel secure that she will not be fired, and they entail few anxiety-producing challenges or responsibilities.

## Case Example—A Codependent Patient

Because of their difficulties with self-regulation, their tendency to seek out magical cures for anxiety and discomfort, and their resistance to facing unpleasant situations, borderline patients are often involved in substance abuse or have substance abusers in their families, adding to the complexity of their treatment. Mrs. C., a fictitious woman in her mid-twenties, provides an example of how such a patient can easily receive inadequate treatment.

She was married to a man who abused alcohol and periodically became physically violent with her. She had been with him under these conditions for four years. When asked why she stayed with him, she explained that when he wasn't drinking, he was very nice to her. She would further explain that he always felt very sorry for what he'd done to her, and he always promised that it would never happen again.

She came to therapy because she was depressed and she wanted help in dealing with her husband's problems. She also had a 6-year-old child by a previous marriage, and she wanted help in handling him as well. Her tendency in the sessions was to talk about either her husband or her son, and very little about herself. When the therapist would ask her to talk about herself, she would talk about how frustrated she felt with her husband or son and then describe some particular situation that she found especially frustrating. The emphasis would be on what they did, rather than on how she felt about it. The situations she described did indeed sound frustrating to the therapist, and he sympathized with her plight. He himself could not see any simple solutions other than for her to get out of the marriage, and he found himself often feeling helpless.

There are many possible endings for this story about Mrs. C. In one version, after her husband has been dry for four months, Mrs. C. decides that her therapy has been successful. She is no longer depressed and she is happy with her relationship with her husband. Her husband has expressed concern about the expense of the therapy, and Mrs. C. has decided that the financially responsible thing to do is to stop therapy for now. She knows that she can always come back "if things get bad again."

In another version of Mrs. C.'s story, she stays in therapy for years. Periodically she decides that her only choice is to leave her husband, but each time she makes this decision, her husband makes a new commitment that he will never take another drink, and Mrs. C.'s relationship with him improves. Her clarity of thinking disappears with the hope that this time he can really change. As her hope increases, her work in therapy becomes a series of descriptions of the progress that he has made. If pressed, she will talk about areas of the relationship that are still problems, but these do not appear significant in the context of her reborn relationship. Eventually, Mrs. C. and her husband begin marital counseling, and Mrs. C. decides that she cannot afford both therapies, so it will be necessary for her to sacrifice her individual therapy. Marital counseling ultimately ends and all is calm until Mrs. C.'s husband decides that he can handle an occasional drink. The occasional drink is uneventful for a while until his drinking becomes out of control again, and Mrs. C. finds herself in the same situation she was in when she started therapy.

In still another version, Mrs. C. finally gets to the point that she cannot stand the continual disappointments of her life with her husband, or his abuse becomes intolerable to her, or the relationship between her husband and her son deteriorates to the point that she is forced to choose between them. She leaves him and cannot financially afford to continue in therapy. She also believes that therapy has accomplished its purpose, so she quits.

In each variation, the theme is the same. Mrs. C., a codependent, comes to therapy and focuses on her husband and son. While doing this, she does not learn about herself. From a therapeutic point of view, she does not identify and learn to handle her problems. She does not know or trust her own thoughts and feelings. When painful feelings of her own do surface, she avoids exploring them by focusing again on her family. She would like to believe that the source of her unhappiness is outside of herself. With this attitude, there seems to be nothing that can be resolved in therapy since the culprit is not present, so she attempts to use the therapist as a support person. If she succeeds in using therapy in this way, the therapy goes nowhere. Often a patient like Mrs. C. manages to use therapy to support her in divorcing one alcoholic spouse, and then leaves therapy and marries another alcoholic.

Like Mrs. C., borderline patients use relationships to avoid looking inside themselves. They have low self-esteem and attempt to fight their underlying feelings of isolation and depression by clinging to lovers, family members, teachers, friends, and anyone else who is willing to comfort them. They see their therapist as another person to cling to. For their therapy to be successful, they must learn to value their own thoughts and feelings.

If the therapist allows himself to become involved in focusing on the codependent patient's story, the story will go on and on without end, and the therapist will begin to feel as hopeless about the patient's situation as the patient does. The therapist should remind himself that the patient's unending story of abuse is a defense against thinking about and talking about herself; it is an avoidance of painful internal feelings. Avoidance and denial are the two defenses that usually show up first with codependent or substance-dependent borderlines, as they do with all codependents and substance abusers. These defenses are usually so ingrained that they must be identified over and over again before the patient is willing to address them.

## Case Example—The "Good" Patient

Another example of a typical borderline patient who can easily receive inadequate treatment is the one who is so good at pleasing everyone around him that his therapist may be lulled into a false belief that the patient is making progress. Eventually the therapist may begin to suspect a problem when the therapy process seems to go on and on, never coming to a natural ending point. The therapist begins to wonder why such an apparently successful therapeutic experience does not lead eventually to the patient's feeling an increasing sense of autonomy and a desire to leave therapy. The reason these patients never seem to finish their therapy process may be that their central problem, dependency, has not been properly addressed. They are successful at producing the type of behavior that the therapist is looking for, but in the process they continue to forfeit their own self-esteem and sense of individuality.

Take the case of Mr. D., a young man in his mid-twenties who came to therapy because he could not decide what to do professionally. In addition, he was somewhat depressed and resentful, feeling that he had had more than his share of bad luck. He had majored in French in college and graduated with good grades. Since then, he had held four different jobs, none of which satisfied him. In each of the jobs, he had felt resentful about being underpaid and being taken advantage of by his employer. There was some reality to his perceptions of inequity since he worked many extra hours in order to be sure that his employer would be pleased with him. If his employer wanted him to come to work nights or weekends, he would do that too.

In therapy, Mr. D. appeared to do very well. He expressed feelings, explored historical material, and made changes in his life. During sessions, he recalled painful memories from his childhood accompanied by appropriate affect. He realized that his parents had shown interest in him only when he performed for them, and that as an adult he was still working hard at getting other people's approval. When he realized that many of the painful aspects of his relationship with his parents were reflected in his relationship with his boss, he began looking for a new job. He found and secured one that was appropriate to his skills, and eventually received several raises. He still resented his employers, but he was able to manage his resentment so that it did not affect his job performance.

Although Mr. D. had made changes in his life, he still displayed many of the same patterns that he had had when he began therapy. He still depended on other people's approval in order to feel that he'd done a good job, and he was still unable to set clear enough limits for people so that he would not feel he was being taken advantage of. Mr. D.'s insights about his need for approval had not influenced his behavior. In fact, the therapist soon learned that even Mr. D.'s career decisions had been largely influenced by his hopes of impressing his father and the therapist. It was no more healthy or self-fulfilling for Mr. D. to advance in his career in an attempt to gain the therapist's approval than it had been for him to work nights and weekends in an attempt to get his boss's approval. Mr. D. had been so skillful at generating the therapeutic material and the behavior that his therapist was looking for that his therapist had missed the compliant nature of the behavior, and had perceived Mr. D. as working hard and succeeding in therapy.

Mr. D.'s case exemplifies an important therapeutic dynamic: when a patient recalls painful childhood memories, and associated painful affect, the patient usually appears to be working in therapy, especially when the affect is genuine and intense. This is because such memories and affect usually do appear when a patient is genuinely working. In Mr. D.'s case, however, the memories and feelings that he had generated in sessions had served no therapeutic purpose. Early in his therapy Mr. D. had recalled a period of his childhood that was quite painful. This memory had been accompanied by sadness and tears. The crying had felt cathartic to him, and from his therapist's reactions, he had probably concluded that the emotion was therapeutically useful as well. Subsequently, in his effort to be a good patient, perhaps Mr. D. had focused on whatever painful childhood memories he could remember. With the recall of these memories, he could emote feelings, and both Mr. D. and his therapist had believed that Mr. D. was doing therapeutic work.

When a patient grapples with a problem and breaks through a resistance, memories and associated affect will appear spontaneously; the work is likely to be therapeutically productive. Memories and affect that are generated, however, by the patient's attempt to produce "therapeutic" material do not in fact lead to growth. In Mr. D.'s case, for example, there was major internal conflict between his wanting to please others and his desire to attend to his own needs. He had touched on this conflict early in his therapy, and from then on had bypassed it. If he had struggled with it further, he would have identified many situations, including the therapy itself, in which he chooses to take care of others' needs to the exclusion of his own.

The price borderline patients like Mr. D. pay for their compliance is that in their excessive concern over other people's opinions, they are devaluing their own thoughts and feelings. They have lost confidence in their own judgment and are hesitant to even formulate their own opinions. Their self-esteem suffers accordingly. Attempts at breaking this pattern bring up anxiety and conflict, so these patients give up the struggle to address their problems.

Borderline compliance may be hard to spot, especially when accompanied by other defenses, like avoidance. A compliant patient can appear to be working hard in treatment while avoiding his most difficult issues or continuing extensive acting out. Even if the therapist is not directive or self-disclosing, the patient can often guess accurately at the therapist's expectations for successful psychotherapy. If the therapist is somewhat directive or disclosing, the problem is that much worse. Any suggestion the therapist might have made or preference she might have indicated, however subtly, can be enough to cause a patient like Mr. D. to veer off the course of paying attention to his sense of his own needs. A therapist needs to learn to follow these patients' therapeutic journeys from a safe distance, maintaining a neutral stance requiring the patient to choose his own direction and find his own standards for success and failure.

When a therapist observes a pattern of compliant behavior on the part of the patient, it is not always prudent to address it immediately. In the early stages of treatment with a borderline, clinging can be the glue that holds the patient in therapy. To address compliance at that time might introduce instability into the therapist–patient relationship. It is usually therapeutically productive if the therapist begins by focusing on other defenses, like denial and avoidance, and later addresses compliance. By that point it would be well established how the patient undermines himself by focusing on the object instead of the self, by interrupting self-exploration, by aborting attempts at life accomplishments right after progress has been made, and by clinging to destructive relationships. Once this is established, it is relatively easy for the therapist to point out how compliance represents another way in which the patient considers others' needs to the exclusion of his own. When he becomes curious about why he does this, he will either defend in another way or he will begin to explore the feelings he associates with activation, possibly spontaneously recalling associated memory and affect. If, however, when the therapist begins by addressing other defenses, the patient responds by trying to give the therapist what the therapist wants without integrating any of the therapeutic work, this aspect of the patient's compliance will need to be taken up. It *can* be useful for a patient whose life is chaotic to respond compliantly to the therapist and in so doing bring a reasonable degree of order to his life.

However, until the compliance is addressed there will be little progress for the patient in getting in touch with his real self.

### The Helpless Patient

Mr. D. used his therapist to help him maintain his destructive patterns by focusing on pleasing her rather than examining his own thoughts and feelings. Other borderline patients for whom it is painful to follow their own thoughts and feelings find different ways to use the therapist to help them maintain their destructive patterns. One of the most common ways, for instance, is to become helpless and hopeless when faced with a situation requiring independent thought or action. Since helplessness and hopelessness are uncomfortable feelings for everybody, including therapists, beginning therapists sometimes try to help their patients get past these feelings by suggesting solutions to the patients' problems. For instance, if the patient is unable to think of what to talk about, the inexperienced therapist might suggest subject areas the patient might want to explore in therapy.

The helpless patient is looking for someone to cling to who will take care of her. When this patient enters treatment, she may be complaining of depression or isolation arising from the need to end a present relationship to which she clings, or arising from the recent loss of a relationship to which she has been clinging. Far from intending to explore the uncomfortable feelings of separateness from which she protects herself by clinging, this patient intends to obtain comfort from the therapist by manipulating the therapist into a caretaking role in which the patient's individuality is lost. As long as the therapist is successfully used by the patient as a barrier against the experience of separation and individuation, the patient will not address anxiety-producing issues relating to autonomous functioning and therapeutic progress is likely to be stalled.

For instance, the beginnings of sessions tend to be difficult; the patient, feeling anxious about deciding for herself what is important to talk about, turns to the therapist for help. The patient cannot remember what has taken place in previous sessions, and does not know what she wants to talk about. Because she has not been thinking about therapy between sessions, she has no thoughts, insights, or dreams that she wants to discuss. "Well, I really don't have anything this week," she might say, or she might begin a story about how she has visited her brother, and what her brother told her. There is little introspection because independent thinking interferes with the comfortable dependency that the patient is attempting to maintain.

If the helpless patient is able to find a new prospective caretaker in her life, she will talk about her encounters with this person and what various friends and relatives say about the new prospect. If the prospective caretaker turns out to meet the patient's expectations, the patient is likely to consider the work of treatment to be successfully completed, and terminate treatment. The patient will not, however, have made progress; she still clings to others to make her decisions for her, and still feels incapable of autonomously conducting her own affairs. To the casual observer, she might appear to have benefited from therapy because she came to therapy feeling depressed and left feeling euphoric, but the therapy has failed to address her real problems; her newly acquired feeling of well-being does not come from within, but from the ephemeral fantasy of being loved in her new relationship. As with Mr. D., it is essential that the therapy of these patients addresses their patterns of clinging and dependency.

Noteworthy here is the fact that with his predominantly clinging defenses, Mr. D. is fairly relationship oriented; he is still looking for love. He is a *high level* borderline patient, meaning that he functions relatively well and has relatively mature defenses that tend to be more clinging than distancing. This is not to be confused with a generally neurotic patient who is very high level and for the most part does not have a personality disorder. In general, borderline patients tend to oscillate back and forth between clinging defenses, when the good self and object representations are active, and distancing defenses, when the bad self and object representations are active. Poorer functioning patients with more severe pathological patterns are referred to as *low level*; they tend to view relationships less positively, predominantly feeling bad or unloved by an object they view as bad and defending themselves by distancing. High level patients tend to have less severe pathology and view relationships more positively, spending more of their time feeling loved and defending against dysphoric affect by clinging to the good object. It takes more of a negative stimulus to cause them to switch from the positive split in which they view objects positively to the negative split. In terms of the *DSM-III-R*, the low level borderline disorder would be more like the borderline personality disorder and the high level borderline would be more like the dependent personality disorder. When histrionic personality disorders arise from borderline personality disorders, they tend to be higher level. Passive aggressive personality disorders, when arising from a borderline personality disorder, can be higher or lower level.

## TREATMENT OF THE BORDERLINE DISORDER

### The Triad

Masterson has developed an exceptionally valuable concept for understanding and predicting the behavior of borderline patients. He watches for what he has termed *self-activation* on the part of the borderline patient. Self-activation is the adult equivalent of Mahler's separation and individuation. It includes any activity that requires the patient to think for himself, express his own thoughts or feelings, or take action on his own behalf. According to Masterson, activation brings up for the borderline adult the painful feelings that were associated with childhood separation and individuation. This dysphoric feeling is then followed by defense against the feeling. He calls this sequence the *borderline triad*.

For instance, a patient reports standing up to his wife in a conflict in which she was unreasonably demanding that he go along with her plans. He then relates that he became concerned that perhaps she was right in her claims that he was just being selfish and that he really had no right to withhold agreement from her, so he felt guilty, anxious, and "bad." To stop her accusations, he then reversed himself and gave in to some of her demands. In the context of the previous discussion, this patient self-activated by standing up for himself, then became afraid that he had been "bad," and attempted to avoid this feeling by appeasing his wife. He bought emotional tranquility at the price of his own self-respect; he failed to support himself.

The borderline triad is also a useful concept in understanding the borderline patient's behavior in the treatment session. For instance, after struggling to find a suitable subject to discuss in a session, a female patient who has come to treatment to overcome indecisiveness begins to talk about her fear that her husband might be having an affair; she wonders if perhaps she is not sufficiently attentive to him. Without further exploring this subject, or the feelings she has about it, she asks the therapist why a man would seek out women solely for sexual gratification. By choosing a topic of discussion and by touching a subject involving anxiety and concern, the patient has activated herself. Activation brought up her fear that she might be inadequately attentive ("bad"), and she defended against this feeling by avoiding any further independent exploration and acting out helplessness in the treatment. She turned to the therapist and asked him to take over for her and speculate about possible causes for the problem. In other words, after beginning to support her own self-exploration (in treatment), she became afraid that she had not been dependent enough (with the therapist as well as her husband) and she defended against this fear by acting out dependency with her therapist. In so doing, she undermined her attempt at self-exploration in treatment, and reinforced her negative self-image as a person who can only be loved as an appendage of another person. Armed with this understanding of the patient, the therapist can now understand more fully the patient's dependent behavior. The concept of the triad is a fairly simple one to grasp. However, the process of identifying triads as they occur in treatment can be subtle. The value to the clinician of identifying self-activation as well as dysphoric affect and defense is enormous. There will be further examples of triads in the transcripts that follow in this chapter.

## Acting Out

The concept of *acting out* is critical to the formulation of a treatment approach for borderline patients, since most theorists seem to agree that acting out by the patient must be dealt with in treatment before other meaningful work can be done. Unfortunately, as with so many other terms, theorists do not agree on what the term acting out means. Some theorists (Freud 1914) refer to it as a patient's taking action in response to internal conflict rather than examining the conflict in treatment sessions. Other theorists use the term to refer to destructive or mischievous behavior. Still others (Hamilton 1988), use it only to refer to action that symbolically represents unconscious material that has been brought up in treatment.

For the purposes of this discussion, acting out will mean the taking of action in response to internal conflict rather than examining the conflict in treatment sessions. It is essential that a therapist take this behavior up in treatment until the behavior is eventually curtailed, because through acting out, the patient dissipates the tension and the feelings that he would otherwise be exploring in treatment. In other words, while the patient continues to act out, his feelings are not available for examination, and therapeutic progress stops.

The concept of acting out is particularly important in the treatment of borderline disorders because during the initial stages of a borderline's treatment there is little else but acting out (Masterson 1976). Since the therapy situation itself presents the borderline with the question of what is important for him to talk about, he is constantly faced with the need to self-activate and decide what issue to address. Even this decision produces internal conflict to which he is likely to respond with some form of defensive acting out. Therefore, in the initial stages of the treatment of a borderline patient, the therapist must repeatedly identify and address the patient's acting out.

## Confrontation

There is some disagreement among theorists about what is the most effective therapeutic intervention for the borderline patient who is acting in ways that either undermine his effective functioning in life or interfere with the effectiveness of treatment. All agree that some intervention is required. Some therapists would attempt to interpret the patient's behavior. In the case vignette of the woman who turned to the therapist after describing how she was afraid her husband was having an affair, these therapists might interpret to the patient that the fear of abandonment by her husband leads her to try to protect herself from any possible abandonment by her therapist by engaging him in a dependent relationship in which he is needed to answer her questions. This type of interpretation is actually a combination of mirroring of the patient's fear of abandonment and interpreting her reason for clinging to her therapist. This process interpretation is distinct from a genetic interpretation, which attempts to explain the patient's behavior in terms of the patient's history rather than in terms of the current feelings against which he may be defending. The process interpretation just given would be a genetic interpretation if the therapist added a comparison to the way the patient historically avoided abandonment from her father. Other theorists would recommend confronting the acting-out borderline patient, which is the point of view that Masterson takes. Again, however, few theorists seem to agree about what form the confrontation should take.

Greenson (1967), in his classical text, describes confrontation as a technique that is necessary, along with clarification, to make a patient aware of a particular resistance or transference phenomenon and how or when it occurs. Although the defenses Greenson describes are those that are common to neurotics, his description of the function of confrontation is consistent with other authors who write about it. He says that confrontation is a process of bringing a phenomenon to a patient's awareness, and clarification explains more about the phenomenon, when and how it occurs. For him, the purpose of confronting the patient is to establish an area of agreement between therapist and patient about the patient's behavior so that they can examine this behavior and it can then be interpreted by the therapist.

Some theorists, such as Hamilton in *Self and Others* (1988) define confrontation very broadly as any intervention that makes explicit to the patient something about herself. This includes a simple acknowledgment of the effect of one of the patient's behaviors or pointing out a contradiction between the patient's words and her behavior. Like Greenson, they see confrontation primarily as a tool to bring material to the point where it can be effectively interpreted. They claim (Hamilton 1988) that acting out is usually the result of negative transference, and that if it is confronted, it can then be properly interpreted. Presumably this will lead to a cessation of the acting-out behavior. Apparently, the confrontation itself, in this view, does not lead to the behavior change.

In applying this last approach to the borderline patient who comes into treatment already seriously acting out, it would appear that this patient needs to be confronted until she becomes aware of the acting-out behavior and why she does it, and the patient should then be able to bring the behavior under control. Masterson would disagree, believing that in many cases of extensive acting out the therapist must directly call the patient's attention to the negative consequences of the behavior before the patient will be sufficiently motivated to bring the behavior under control. He argues that until the acting-out behavior becomes ego dystonic to the borderline patient, the patient is not interested in changing the behavior so she will not be receptive to an interpretation. For the active alcoholic, for instance, until her denial is effectively confronted she will minimize the seriousness of her drinking and will continue to act out in this way.

Another point of view (Cashdan 1988), is that confrontation is a form of limit setting, saying "no" to the patient. Since the sources of the borderline patient's poor object relations lie primarily in nonverbal interactions between the patient as an infant and the infant's caretakers, the repair of object relations must occur on a nonverbal level through the patient's relationship with the therapist. From this perspective, when the patient makes a request of the therapist that is of a defensive nature, an adequate confrontation would be to simply not gratify the patient's request; to respond to the above patient's question about men would encourage her maladaptive dependency and promote intellectualization on her part, leading the patient away from her deeper feelings.

According to this viewpoint, the therapist's limit setting would serve a therapeutic purpose by ultimately forcing the patient to look at her feelings of frustration and the object relations assumptions that underlie her demands. Any attempt on the part of the therapist to soften the impact of his refusal to gratify the patient's verbal and nonverbal demands diminishes the patient's frustration, undermining the effectiveness of the treatment. For the therapist to huddle together with the patient and attempt to understand the patient's motives would soften the therapeutic impact of the therapist's refusal to gratify the patient's demand. From this point of view, the therapist might respond in the above case vignette by pointing out that the answer to the patient's question is one that the patient is as qualified to speculate about as is the therapist.

Masterson (1976) makes a convincing argument against the use of interpretation with borderline patients who are acting out. He uses a concept he calls an *object relations unit* in explaining his approach. When the borderline splits, her affect, self-image, and object-image are all related. He thinks of each of the two halves of the split as object relations units, one containing the fantasied good mother (caretaker), a euphoric affect, and a self-image of a person who is loved and accepted for being helpless and passive. The other borderline object relations unit contains the fantasied bad caretaker, a dysphoric affect, and a self-image of a person who is unloved and unlovable.[1]

[1]Masterson refers to the first of these two units as the *Rewarding Object Relations Unit* (or *RORU*) and the second as the *Withdrawing Object Relations Unit* (or *WORU*). The good object in the RORU is nurturing, loving, giving, praising, and always present. The euphoric affect includes feeling good, comfortable, childlike, worryless, or lovable. The self representation in the RORU is of a loved, compliant, helpless, cooperative, or dependent person. The object representation in the WORU is of an attacking, critical, withdrawing, withholding, or unloving person. The dysphoric affect includes feeling bad, uncomfortable, angry, sad, alone, or unlovable. The self representation of the WORU is one of an unloved, bad, isolated, despicable, uncooperative, or argumentative person.

Masterson reasons that for the therapist to cooperate or resonate with either of these units would be to reinforce the borderline patient's process of splitting, seeing the world as black or white. When the patient acts dependent and makes an implied demand that the therapist take care of her, Masterson argues that an interpretation on the part of the therapist would represent partial gratification of the patient's demand, since in an interpretation the therapist explains for the patient the patient's behavior instead of requiring the patient to attempt to do that for herself. In gratifying the patient's demand, the therapist would be inadvertently playing the role of the fantasied good (rewarding) caretaker and reinforcing the patient's object splitting. Furthermore, since the unit of the good caretaker contains a self-image of passivity and helplessness, the patient is likely to respond to the interpreting therapist as to the good caretaker and become increasingly passive, further interfering with treatment. Masterson's term for this gratifying behavior on the part of the therapist is *rewarding*. I believe that the applicability of this argument varies from patient to patient and must be evaluated for any particular patient by observing how the patient responds to the type of interpretation that Masterson would characterize as rewarding.

Masterson offers a different type of confrontation than those previously described. Using the triad concept, he might suggest that the therapist point out the two most apparent parts of the triad, the activation and the defense. When these two aspects of the triad are linked, the patient often spontaneously provides the third aspect, the dysphoric affect. For example, in the case vignette of the woman who was afraid her husband was having an affair, the therapist might reflect back to the patient that she was just beginning to explore a topic that she considered important when she interrupted herself by turning to the therapist. In Masterson's terms, she had activated by beginning the exploration, become anxious about this independent behavior, and defended against her anxiety by clinging to the therapist.

If after a number of this type of interventions the patient is unable to see for herself why turning to the therapist in this way is contrary to her own interest, the therapist using this approach might become more explicit, pointing out that this behavior is consistent with the patient's pattern of turning to other people for answers (clinging, acting out of helplessness), rather than exploring her own thoughts and feelings. The therapist might point out that as a result the patient remains confused about her own feelings and is unable to make decisions (her presenting problem). If this intervention were not effective and the pattern of turning to others were to be repeated often, Masterson might recommend that the therapist ask the patient how she hopes to understand herself enough to make decisions, when she repeatedly turns to others rather than exploring her own thoughts and feelings. Ideally, in this way, the patient comes to see how her defense interferes with her adult functioning and perhaps leads to the very problems for which she first entered treatment.

## CLINICAL EXAMPLE—RUNAWAY TREATMENT

### Confrontation of Acting Out

The range of behavior that is considered by a therapist to constitute acting out can vary significantly from one therapist to another. On one end of the spectrum are those therapists who view acting out solely as overt destructive or mischievous behavior, and on the other are those therapists who view all maladaptive defensive behavior as examples of acting out. The relevant question is whether the behavior in question, if not effectively addressed, would interfere with treatment. To facilitate the reader's consideration of this question, this book will attempt to identify the widest range of behavior that might qualify as acting out.

As indicated earlier, if one views acting out in its broadest definition, the behavior of a borderline patient in the initial sessions of treatment may consist of little else but acting-out defenses. This can most easily be illustrated by examining a few actual transcripts of borderline patients in treatment. Two transcripts of borderline patients will be presented, the first with a therapist who does not address the patient's defenses and the second with a therapist who does. The numerals in parentheses are referenced in the discussion that parallels or follows each transcript.

When reading the first transcript, the reader might find himself feeling restless or bored. This feeling may remind him of some of his own sessions with borderline patients, when for one reason or another the patient was presenting an impenetrable defensive facade. The therapist in the transcript is aware that the patient is not addressing her feelings. To bring the patient back to her feelings, the therapist repeatedly asks or comments about them. As you will see, this approach proves ineffective.

**Mrs. E.—(Session #10)—**

**T:** How are you today?
**P:** Okay. (shakes head)
**T:** You're shaking your head.
**P:** Christmas Eve didn't go so well.
**T:** Why not?
**P:** (1)Because before dinner was even on the table, my parents were both swashed. I knew I shouldn't have let my brother invite them over. I should have said, "It's them or me."
**T:** They drink a lot?
**P:** (2)Well, my dad definitely overdoes it, and I guess my mom drinks, but usually not too much. This was unusual. She couldn't talk or walk straight. I was upset, and I didn't hide it well. I'm sure she knew how I felt.
**T:** (3)What was it like for you?
**P:** Well, it reminded me of my mom's parents. I can't remember a single Christmas when they weren't bombed. I just wanted to get out of there. I didn't want my daughter subjected to the same thing I was.
**T:** You wanted to protect her.
**P:** (4)Of course! It was getting worse. My brother can drink too much sometimes too, and he was getting started when I said, "Adios." He could become an alcoholic. The whole scene was a mess.
**T:** (5)You were upset that your daughter saw it.
**P:** Yeah.
**T:** What were your specific concerns?
**P:** I don't know. (6)They were smashed. Their behavior was disgusting.
**T:** You have strong feelings about this.(7)
**P:** I kept trying to avoid them. They would go into one room, and I'd leave that room and go into another. There was no way I could carry on a conversation with them. It just brought up too many ugly memories. (8)My grandfather used to drink until he couldn't stand up. Then he'd drop into his chair and be out of it.
**T:** (9)How did that feel for you?
**P:** (pause) To be honest. I liked it when he passed out because then he wouldn't be trying to kiss me, and be slobbering all over me. (pause) So (pause).
**T:** (10)That sounds like a lot for a little girl to have to deal with.
**P:** (long pause) I used to seethe inside. "Merry" Christmas! It made me so angry. I would swear that next Christmas I would stay away from them.

Grandpa used to follow me around with the mistletoe. Everyone thought it was real funny. I just kept moving.

**T:** It wasn't funny to you. (11)It must have been very painful.

**P:** (long pause—teary) (12)Mom and Dad weren't much better last week. Dad didn't chase me around, but when he talked to me, he would lean toward me, and his breath was unbearable. (She goes on to talk more about her father's and mother's drinking and tells several anecdotes from Christmas Eve.) I've never done it before, but this time I just went over to Brian and said, "I don't want to stay any longer." Then I said, " Sara, honey, we're leaving."

**T:** How come you were able to do that this time; what was different?

**P:** Because I'll be damned if Sara is going to go through the same shit that I did. I don't want her around anyone who's been drinking, not even me. If I drink, it's after she's gone to bed. Then maybe I'll have a couple of beers. I kept looking over at her and thinking what it must have been like for her, and I didn't want her to think that this is normal behavior.

**T:** You were concerned about her, and you took care of her.

**P:** (silence)

**T:** You wanted her to know that this behavior is unacceptable.

**P:** Yeah. It just won't fly in my book. (She goes on talking about how "gross" her parents can become when they have been drinking.) Sometimes I wonder how they could have loved me and treated me that way. As an adult I sometimes feel as though they're strangers to me. I wonder if I maybe got married just to get away from them. (She talks about her husband,(13) how she used to feel he would protect her but that he never does.) Just one time I'd like to see him take the liquor away from them and say, "I think that's enough drinking for one night." He's probably afraid of them. He can't even stand up to his employees at work.

**T:** You were talking about how your parents sometimes feel like strangers to you. (14)I was surprised that there wasn't more feeling when you talked about that.

At this point the therapist is well aware that most of the patient's comments have been about other people or a narration of events that have occurred (1, 2, 4, 6, 8, 12, and 13), despite the therapist's attempts to bring her back to focusing on herself (3, 5, 7, 9, 10, and 11). If the therapist continues in a similar vein, the treatment will continue to stagnate. The therapist now becomes more confrontive, but without clarity or conviction. He had available to him many choices of possible areas of confrontation. He could have addressed her helplessness by asking, "You seem to feel that you need to wait for your husband to set appropriate limits on your parents for you. Why do you feel that you can't do that for yourself?" He could have focused on her avoidance by pointing out, "You had just begun to talk about feeling like a stranger toward your parents when you changed the subject. Do you remember why you did that?" or simply, "You just interrupted yourself. Do you know why you changed the subject?" He could have taken up the patient's pattern of focusing on the object by commenting, "Notice how you just began talking about yourself and then shifted the subject away from yourself to your husband." Rather than adopt any of these approaches, however, the therapist opts to highlight Mrs. E.'s lack of affect by reminding her of what she had said about feeling like a stranger with her parents and pointing out her incongruous lack of feeling when she said it. A confrontation of this type might be effective for a patient who defends against feelings by intellectualizing, but it is not the best confrontation for Mrs. E.

**Neutrality**

The issue of therapeutic neutrality in this situation may seem unclear. Each of the five possible confrontations indicated above can be interpreted by the patient as an implied directive. However, the one that the therapist actually chose is the one that most violates therapeutic neutrality. Avoidance and acting out of helplessness are themes of this patient's defenses. Focusing on the object is a form of avoidance, and in this particular session it is repeatedly used as a defense. Each of the four alternative confrontations offered above calls Mrs. E.'s attention to one of her defensive themes. If she were to respond to any of these confrontations by compliantly returning to the subject of her feelings toward her parents, the confrontation would not have accomplished its primary purpose of making her aware of her defense. If she were to consistently respond to such confrontations in this compliant way, the therapist would need to address her compliance as a form of defensive transference acting out. Rather than directively changing a patient's behavior, these four confrontations are intended to heighten the patient's self-awareness, which is, of course, likely to lead to change. Unfortunately, even the most astute clinician cannot always identify when a patient is responding compliantly, so that this type of confrontation can lead to prolonged compliance. The confrontation actually chosen by the therapist in this transcript addresses the patient's suppression of feeling, which is not one of her significant defensive themes. Rather than talk about a painful subject without feeling, she tends to avoid talking about the tender area entirely, defending against painful feelings by changing the subject, by focusing on other people's feelings, and by helpless dependency. There is no purpose served by the chosen confrontation other than to remind Mrs. E. of what she had been talking about and to invite her to talk about her feelings about that subject. Her reason for changing the subject in the first place is not addressed. As Greenson (1967) puts it (in the particular context of a patient's resistance to talking about sex), "We first have to analyze his resistance to talking on sexual matters before we can effectively analyze his sexual problems. Furthermore, he will not be able to present a clear picture of his sexual problems until he is able to communicate effectively on (his resistance to talking about sex)" (p. 106). Before it is useful for Mrs. E. to explore her feelings, she will need to examine her resistance to focusing on herself.

The pitfalls traditionally associated with violations of neutrality in general psychodynamic psychotherapy apply especially to the treatment of borderline patients. If the therapist becomes directive or nurturing, the borderline patient will perceive the therapist as the good object, and will attempt to be "good" by complying with whatever the patient perceives as the therapist's agenda. The patient's pursuit of separation and individuation will be replaced by a pursuit of the therapist's approval. If the borderline patient is able to make successful life changes with the help of the therapist's direction, the patient will not come away with a sense of satisfaction and well-being, but with a sense of dependency upon the therapist.

This problem is especially serious in clinics where therapists' tenures are often only a few years. If the therapist has not been neutral, the patient can view the relationship between therapist and patient as a real relationship in which the therapist acts somewhat as a friend. The patient views his progress as a function of the particular therapist. When the therapist leaves the clinic and is forced to terminate the patient's treatment, the patient feels abandoned, and perceives all his gains from therapy as being lost with the loss of that therapeutic relationship. He believes that he must now start over from the beginning with a new therapist. Although it is natural for a patient to feel the loss of a therapist, the disruption in the patient's treatment can be substantially reduced if the patient has perceived himself as being the primary resource in his own treatment and if, as a result of treatment, the patient has learned improved coping skills and increased autonomy. This will be more likely to happen if the therapist remains neutral, facilitates the patient's awareness of defenses, and does not encourage regressive exploration of affect to the degree that it overwhelms the patient's defenses.

In the next section of transcript, the therapist continues to confront Mrs. E. His confrontive stance, however, is inconsistent and Mrs. E.'s defenses are unaffected. This patient is like a steamroller that the therapist tries to slow down by erecting Tinkertoy barriers; the result is chaotic treatment. Since the therapist has chosen a course of confrontation that has not been hitting the mark, a broad confrontation is called for here followed by persistent follow-up confrontations if the patient does not respond. For instance, the therapist might point out that the patient seems unwilling to remain focused on any of her own feelings. Rather than explore her problems, she focuses on other people and jumps from topic to topic. How can she hope to resolve her problems if she does not explore them? Normally, it would not be necessary to spell out the consequences of the patient's behavior so fully because the patient can figure this out herself, but this patient is particularly resistant to looking at what she is doing to herself.

**T:** You were talking about how your parents sometimes feel like strangers to you. I was surprised that there wasn't more feeling when you talked about that.

**P:** Oh there's feeling. If I started telling you about all the shit they've pulled, I'd keep you here all night. It's not all their fault. You know, they say alcohol is like a disease. My folks keep trying to stop but it doesn't work. I don't think they're ever going to stop.

The therapist misses many opportunities to point out this pattern of the patient focusing outside herself. Mrs. E. begins to become upset at her parents' behavior and then reverses herself and tries to defend them. This is another example of her shifting the focus to the object at the expense of her own feelings.

**T:** I'm not saying that you don't have feelings; I'm saying that you don't talk about them.

**P:** I know, because I don't like to get upset. It's the same with my husband. I don't like a lot of things he does, but I don't usually say anything because it would only hurt his feelings, and we'd both end up feeling bad. When I mar-

She then declares that it makes no sense to her to express her concerns to her parents or to her husband because she doesn't like to get upset and because everyone will "end up feeling bad." The therapist might inquire why she places "hurting their feelings" above her own concerns, and why his becoming upset means that she must then feel bad. Alterna-

ried him, I thought he was real together emotionally. He ran his own company and had people working for him and he always seemed to know how to handle situations. Now it seems like he lets people push him around a lot. I don't know if he's changed or what.

tively, if the therapist holds off a sentence or two, he could point out that she is again changing the focus to her husband instead of exploring her own feelings about telling people what upsets her.

**T:** Do you know what I mean when I say you don't talk about what you feel?
**P:** Not exactly.

When the therapist follows with a weak inquiry over whether the patient understands that she is not talking about her feelings, she responds "Not exactly."

**T:** Well, you've been talking about things that sound very upsetting, but you're just telling me the story. You're not talking about your feeling of upset.
**P:** Well, all this has been very upsetting to me. When I left with Sara on Christmas Eve I was almost in tears. I told her that we had to go because she looked tired and she needed sleep; I didn't say it was because of the drinking because I didn't want to upset her any more than she already was. I can't always tell when she's upset because she's already pretty good at hiding it, but there was no way that she wasn't upset that night. Anyway, (she goes on talking about Sara) so I'm between a rock and a hard place. If I tell her about the drinking, I'm afraid she won't feel like she can love them anymore; it would be like she doesn't have grandparents. If I don't tell her, she'll think all this garbage is normal. There's really no way

The therapist responds to this passive answer by taking over for her and explaining again what he means. Instead, he could have asked her what she does understand the therapist to mean. In this way he discourages passive dependence by putting the problem back in her lap. Finally, a few sentences later the patient again changes the subject from her feelings on Christmas Eve to a narration of how she dealt with the daughter on that evening. This change of focus could have been confronted, or the therapist might have pointed out how the patient seems preoccupied with her daughter's feelings to the exclusion of her own. The patient goes on to permanently shift the focus to her daughter, again inviting confrontation from the therapist.

out. (pause) She's really so delicate, so sensitive. I'd hate to see her be hurt in any way. Last month Brian had to go out of town, and whenever he goes away he brings her a little toy when he comes back; she really likes that. Anyway, last month when he got back, the toy had gotten broken on the plane, and she was real upset. It was just a little five dollar ceramic doll, but she was really upset. In a way, she's fragile too, just like the doll.

## CLINICAL EXAMPLE – CONFRONTATION WITH A HIGH-LEVEL BORDERLINE DISORDER

The transcript that follows is approximately two thirds of a session with a thirty-year-old woman in her third session of ongoing weekly outpatient treatment. It is an example of persistent confrontation applied to a patient who avoids looking at her problems.

In this transcript, the patient wants to address the difficult question of what she can do about her marital dissatisfaction, but she is unwilling to focus on this question long enough to explore it. One can assume that the process of focusing clearly upon a difficult question and grappling with it is a threatening act of individuation for her. Instead, she defends by shifting her focus from herself to her husband, by avoiding her feelings about the question, and by acting as if she is helpless and needs a rescuer. After the therapist repeatedly points out her defenses, the patient finally begins to explore her question.

From the Masterson perspective, this is a good example of a borderline patient's response to both appropriate and inappropriate confrontation of defenses. At first she accepts the confrontations intellectually but does not integrate them; she continues her avoidant behavior with respect to the question that she has come into treatment to explore. The therapist at first repeatedly points out the defense, but without adequately relating empathically to the patient's struggle. A confrontation without empathy would feel critical even to the healthiest of neurotics. This pattern was probably present in the previous session, because the patient begins this session by apologizing, "I'm sorry." Eventually the therapist becomes more empathic, without abandoning his confrontive stance, and the patient becomes more genuinely introspective, looks at her use of the defense, and sees that the defense is inhibiting her progress. The patient attempts to control the defense and engages in some therapeutic exploration of her issues.

**Mrs. F., 3rd Session**

**P:** (laughs) I'm sorry. I had to do that.

Patient Focuses On the Object

**T:** What's that?

**P:** I don't know. I was really tense coming in here today so I had to laugh. Maybe I'm just a little punchy. My three-year-old was up most of last night with a fever so I didn't get too much sleep. It was a tough night. I guess I am a little punchy today. Well, what would you like me to start with?

In the beginning of the session the patient turns to the therapist for direction. Borderline patients often ask what the therapist would like them to begin talking about. In doing so they are acting out several feelings. Faced with the need to activate and choose a subject to explore, they feel as if they are on their own, so to bypass the feeling of separateness that this situation precipitates, they invite the therapist to take over for them. When Mrs. F. did this she also implied that anything she might talk about would be for the benefit of the therapist; she asks him what he would like her to start with.

**T:** Well, I think where we left off is with your difficulty in making decisions for yourself, in deciding what is important to you. So, that's a good place to start—by deciding what is important for you today.

The therapist responds by pointing out a connection between her presenting problem of difficulty with decision making and her current difficulty in deciding what to begin talking about. Furthermore, he addresses her confusion over whom the treatment is for by emphasizing that the patient must decide what is important to her.

**P:** Oh. I think I know what is important but it is something which is very, very difficult for me to address. I do know that decisions

From the patient's response, it is apparent that she understands the significance of the therapist's comment; she herself points out that her

have to be made. Sometimes decisions are made for me and these are the ones I can deal with. I would just as soon go around it as have to face it. I pretty much know that. I guess that's why I'm here. I need to do that and that is very hard. Some decisions, some things I have to deal with.

I already know I have to deal with my relationship with my husband, my relationship with my father, and most importantly with how I'm feeling inside—really taking a good look at that and deciding how I'm going to handle it. Communication seems to be the key. I just don't want to hurt anyone's feelings when I sit down with them and say, "Look, I want to talk to you. This is how I'm feeling." I'm just afraid the whole thing is going to blow up in front of me. I don't like to see people hurt. Sometimes it's more comfortable to just accept the way things are than to have to face it. I did that this summer with my husband. I had been exercising quite a bit and doing a lot of thinking; I was feeling a lot of internal energy and confidence and feeling that I could handle that. When I did tell him how I was feeling it was such a surprise to him when all along I don't think that I had not hinted that something was wrong here. I'm not sure. If I am communicating maybe I'm not being direct enough or my husband doesn't want to listen to me. He's choosing not to hear what he's

attempt to induce the therapist to make her decision is connected to a pattern in her life of trying to get other people to make decisions for her.

Triad—Activation Followed by Affect Followed by Defense

The patient now begins to explore a meaningful subject, her relationship with her husband. She discusses some of the history of the situation and alludes to some of her present feelings. Finally, when she says "I'm really afraid," she makes her first really clear statement of the feeling she is struggling with.

During this period the therapist has said nothing. The patient is working on bringing her internal struggle into focus. Without help from the therapist, she is able to shift her focus from her husband to herself. The therapist's self-restraint in not intervening is a vote of confidence in the patient, that she can self-activate and identify for herself her own concerns.

hearing. Or he doesn't know what I'm saying. He listens to me but he doesn't hear what I say. That's important to me. Sometimes I'm not clear. The times when I am clear with him it's really frightening because he is so volatile. He can't believe what he's hearing and suddenly there's a rage. That frightens me. I don't think he would physically hurt me. When it comes to sitting down and discussing why I feel this way it's very one-sided. It all goes back to, "Well, you're the one that's changing because of all this stuff you're doing. It would never have happened if you hadn't started reading all those pop-psych books." That's what he calls them. So it's hard. I know I have to deal with that. I just choose not to right now. It's easier. I think it's time to face it and I'm really afraid. (pause)

I'm just really afraid. For the most part I know my husband loves me. He loves me a lot. Even though he is not real physical with his emotions toward me, I do know that. He has told me many times that he does. I'm just not happy in the relationship. He doesn't see it himself. To say the things I need to say to him will really hurt him. I'm not the type of person to go around hurting people. And I feel tomorrow will be different. I saw him get real excited this week. He was offered a lateral promotion at work. The pay wasn't much more but it was in a whole new area that he's been

As is often the case, the pause that follows her comment about what she is feeling represents the beginning of an internal conflict in the patient about whether to pursue this painful subject. Her next response is equally common for a borderline patient; she immediately acts out her fear by shifting the focus of her exploration from herself to her husband, avoiding further exploration of her painful affect. Consistent with her focus on him, she eventually says that she thought perhaps it was his job dissatisfaction that is making her so unhappy in the relationship. She describes "hanging on" to a hope that the solution to her problem might come from him.

interested in. It would give him the opportunity to do something he has always wanted to do which is a philosophy I have. If you're not happy doing what you're doing you should work toward doing something else. Suddenly he got excited. When he was told he got it, he came home and said, "that's what I want to do." I saw him so vibrant and so alive for a moment. I thought that maybe his negativity about his job is what is making me so unhappy in our relationship. I thought maybe there's hope. Maybe there's something there I can hang on to.

He was talking about the things he wanted to do. After a long weekend we were talking about it again this morning and now he's not sure that's what he wants to do. He's afraid of changes as well; he doesn't know if he will be successful in this new area. I'm back to being as down about our relationship today as I was a week ago. I don't think things can change. For the most part I guess I would like to tell him it's just too hard and I need some things to change. I don't know how he would handle that. I'm afraid he would shut me out completely. "OK, this is your decision. That's it. You stay or you get out." I've heard him make those ultimatums to me before and that frightens me.

**T:** The permanence of it.

**P:** Yeah. Sometimes I hope that I can get all those feelings back. I enjoy my family life.

Mrs. F. continues to focus on her husband and gradually shifts her focus to what she would like to do. At the point that she talks about being frightened by her husband's ultimatums, the therapist makes an ill-timed mirroring remark. His motive for this remark is unclear. Perhaps he is identifying with the husband when he hears the patient say how unsatisfied she is with the relationship (with her husband), remarks that may have also been referring to the therapeutic relationship. Perhaps the therapist could not sit still any longer while the patient did her work independently of him. In that case he would be reenacting the borderline patient's history of being discouraged from being independent. It should be noted here that the patient has just moved from a fairly intellectualized discussion to a more down-to-earth focus on her feelings of fear of abandonment. It is unfortunate that the therapist chooses as an intervention the very point where the patient's work is deepening and she is beginning to explore her dysphoric feelings. Perhaps he is uncomfortable with the affect that may be surfacing. Whatever the reason for the intervention, the impact of his comment is clear from the transcript; she stops working, and attempts to restore an upbeat outlook on her life. It is difficult enough for a patient to begin to explore dysphoric affect that has been avoided; when the therapist interrupts this exploration, the patient is likely to discontinue it.

**T:** When you say you hope you get the feelings back you mean you hope they will come back. You are not planning on doing anything to try to get them back. Is that right?

Repeated Confrontation of Acting Out of Avoidance

The therapist observes that the patient has been focusing outside herself, in particular that she is waiting for a solution to be presented to her without actively exploring the problem herself. There is an abrupt quality to this intervention.

**P:** Yeah I guess that's what I'm saying. I've never really thought about that. I'm really not doing anything about it. I'm just waiting for a change to happen. I'll admit that. I know that's a weakness. It wouldn't be the first time.

The patient responds by acknowledging what the therapist has said, however there is no affect in the patient's response, and it is reasonable to suspect that the patient is merely being compliant when she is actually either angry at the therapist or at least distrustful of him. She admits the "weakness" that he has pointed out; in other words, she feels criticized or attacked.

**T:** When you say that, I'm not sure how conscious you are of the implications of what you're saying. You mentioned several situations last week from your past when you were faced with the need to make a meaningful deci-

In response to the patient's apparent willingness to accept her avoidance as a fact of life, and her resistance to considering the cost to herself of her avoidance, the therapist now confronts the same issue again, this time citing additional examples from

sion and take action, and you became afraid or nervous so you put off making the decision by doing something that you later regretted. In one instance, you dropped out of school when faced with having to choose a major. In another, you were faced with an important career decision, and instead decided impulsively to get married. It's a pattern. You let things happen rather than face something that scares you. Then you feel bad about yourself afterwards when you have to face the consequences.

**P:** Okay. That's what I said last week. That's true. (pause) It's harder. I don't want to be that type of person. I would like to be the type of person that could make the decisions and stand by them and be responsible for them.

That's something I learned recently. I'm responsible for everything that happens in my life. I've created the situations and allowed them to continue. I'm not blaming anyone but I'm not sure how I go about changing the decisions I've made already.

**T:** You're not talking just about decisions you've made. You're talking about continuing in the same process of not facing your decisions that are there to make now.

the session before, so that it becomes more difficult for the patient to avoid the therapist's intended conclusion.

In this confrontation, the therapist describes the triad; Mrs. F. is faced with a decision (activation) that makes her feel nervous or afraid (depression) so she avoids facing these feelings by letting things happen or acting impulsively instead of making a meaningful decision (avoidance defense). *Demonstrating to the patient in one intervention the repeated occurrence of the same triad can be very effective in helping the patient to be able to recognize a pattern of self-defeating behavior.*

Her response is to talk about her defensive avoidance in a manner that acknowledges that this behavior is not in her own best interest (ego-dystonic). It is unclear how much of her comment is intended to appease the therapist, and how much is an honest expression of her thoughts.

She now retreats again to her intellectualized manner of thinking about herself, and indicates even more clearly than before that she views the situation as a fact of life, saying that her decisions are "already made" and "what can be done now?" Again, she is attempting to dissipate the discomfort she feels at facing the destructive consequences of a deeply ingrained pattern of avoidance that has until this point been ego-syntonic.

The therapist again points out the present reality that the patient is actively avoiding.

If the therapist had wished to continue his line of confrontation, it would probably have been more effective at this time if he had pointed out how Mrs. F.'s last comment was in fact an example of the kind of avoidance that she was just saying that she was uncomfortable with. By acting as though her avoidance of decisions is all in the past, she avoids looking at the decisions that are presently before her. It would probably have been better for him to consider why there seems to be so much difficulty in reaching this patient. The patient is probably angry at the therapist and feels criticized. If this session were being conducted after several months of treatment, there would already be an established relationship between therapist and patient. However, in this third session there appears to be a severe weakness in the relationship, a lack of rapport and trust. Additional confrontation of defenses at this point, however accurate, seems to cause the relationship to degenerate further. An alternative to confrontation might be to ask the patient how she is responding to the therapist's style of intervention, giving the patient an invitation to come out from behind her shield of compliance and tell the therapist honestly how she is experiencing the session.

**P:** Right. (pause) Yeah, that's what I need to do. It's a nasty pattern to break. I've already done it several times. I really hope I can learn something, change something. I feel like I'm a pretty together person on the outside. I'd like to be together on the inside too. I'm not sure I know how to go about it. (long pause) Well, where do you want to start?

Now, the patient appears to momentarily consider what the therapist is pointing out, and then returns to her acting out attempts to induce the therapist to take over for her. This time the therapist comments on the present acting out.

**T:** In a sense you are doing the same thing right now by asking me that question because you are faced now with a decision—where to start, what to explore.

**P:** (pause) I guess I just heard what you said but . . . I'm here for counseling to figure out how to do this on my own but I'm sitting here looking at you with long pauses and silence and I'm wondering if I'm supposed to be saying something, if I'm supposed to be thinking about something. I'm not sure what I'm supposed to do at this point. I feel . . . I'm not sure.

**T:** You are saying you are not sure what happens in therapy.

**P:** Yeah.

**T:** Well, it's a place for you to understand yourself, to explore yourself and hopefully be able to make changes. One of the hardest parts for you is starting a session because you need to decide what is important to you.

She responds by saying that she does not understand how treatment works. The therapist is unable at this point in treatment to be certain whether Mrs. F.'s question is a further escalation of acting out of helplessness that occurred in the previous two sessions in an attempt to get him to take over for her or a genuine expression of her confusion about treatment. He responds to the question at face value by giving her the information she requests. This represents a turning point in the course of this treatment hour.

**P:** Okay, so I choose something I need to explore right now. Do I need to continue therapy to figure this out or . . . ? I realize I have to do this on my own. I'm supposed to. It's not going to get done unless I do it on my own. Are you saying that I don't need to come because I can do this on my own?

**T:** Not at all. I'm saying that here you are in this situation in which you are here to explore. You recreate the problem by inviting me to tell you where to start,

Withholding Therapist/Unlovable Patient

At this point the patient is probably feeling annoyed at being turned down in her bid for direction from the therapist, and is experiencing the therapist as withholding and rejecting. There may also be some reality to this perception, as the therapist's confrontations have had a somewhat rigid and unempathic quality that may or may not be entirely apparent from the written transcript. The self representation that accompanies the object relations unit that contains

because how can you explore what is important to you if you have me direct you? I have no way of knowing what is important to you.

angry affect and a withholding object representation is one of a bad, unlovable person. Consistent with this self representation, she asks the therapist if he wants her to stop coming to treatment. This question may also be intended to manipulate the therapist into expressing a positive feeling about the patient or it may be an angry projection of the patient's desire to stop coming to treatment. Rather than take up the meaning of the question, the therapist chooses to simply answer her directly, focusing again on her difficulty in finding her own direction. This confrontation, however, is delivered more softly than previous confrontations, and it is more understanding in tone than confrontational, conveying to Mrs. F. that he appreciates how difficult it is for her to do this.

**P:** I'm used to a lot of structure in my life and this is somewhat unstructured. It is difficult for me. That's what I'm also trying to say.

**T:** I understand that. You have been happiest at school and at work where there is a lot of structure.

**P:** Exactly.

**T:** In a way I think that is why you have come here, because you have felt good when you didn't have to struggle with your insides, when the structure came from outside. You are in a situation now where you realize you are not happy and you are wanting to make changes, but there is no outside structure bringing about change. You would like to initiate it yourself, but first you must decide what

Integration of Confrontation

Now the patient begins to examine for herself why she needs the therapist to direct her, and she explains that she is used to having structure in her life. This is another way of saying that she has been out of touch with her insides so that the only way she has been able to function effectively has been when she was in a highly structured environment in which she was told what to do. She tells him that this "is difficult for me," and follows this by saying "that's what I'm also trying to say." There is a sense from this last comment that the patient is now starting to feel understood by the therapist, and she wants him to further understand how difficult this process is for her.

The therapist acknowledges her

you want, what's right for you, and for that you must find out who you are inside. That is hard for you. You don't have experience doing that.

difficulty and relates it to earlier experiences in her life. She feels further understood, and responds, "Exactly." Now the therapist empathically relates her difficulty with inner directedness to her present unhappiness and to her difficulty in treatment, pointing out again that she cannot solve her problems until she looks at herself.

**P:** (thoughtful) That's right, I don't. (somber) I can't even say I have made any attempts at it before. I realize that now. (pause)

Triad—Introspection, Affect, Avoidance (Focusing Outside Herself)

Now Mrs. F. makes a lengthy statement in which she reiterates her problem in greater detail. This statement illustrates beautifully the way the triad is subtly repeated over and over as the borderline patient struggles to confront her problems. She begins by considering what the therapist has said, acknowledging that she does not attempt to solve her problems by looking inside. She becomes momentarily somber, and immediately defends against this affect, saying, "I realize that now." There is a sense that this comment is really meant for the therapist, and indicates a momentary shift in the patient away from the introspection that has brought on her somber feeling.

Right now the most important thing is that I have to feel better. I don't like this feeling of indecision and not knowing what is going to happen next. I'm unsure of what I do or say next, of what will happen after that. It's fear of the unknown. I do know that those things that bother us most,

Triad—meaningful exploration, fear, intellectualization

In the pause that follows, she returns to her thoughtful introspection. Her comments become gradually more focused on her feeling until she says,"It's fear of the unknown." In response to the dysphoric feeling brought on by the thought of facing

we should address first. Do something about it, make a change, or rearrange until that feeling goes away. I've been going on for too many years feeling that I know I have to do something about it but won't do anything about it. I have a whole library of books at home. Self-help books. You name it I've got it. I've probably read 3/4 of them and I still can't find the answer.

the "unknown," she begins to intellectualize, reciting rules about life. Without help from the therapist, she quickly becomes aware of her intellectualization, commenting that she has a whole library of self-help books that have not helped her; she is mocking her attempts to intellectualize her problems.

In a lot of ways I already have the answers. I already know what I need to do. I just have to find the strength to do it. (long pause) When I think about knowing what I have to do I get very sad. Which is what I'm feeling right now. That confuses me too. If I think I know the things I need to do or what I need to say, why shouldn't there be a feeling of comfort that comes with it, but it's not. It's not comfortable. (long pause) Sitting here at this moment is very uncomfortable. I guess I need to really think about what I need to do. Or make an attempt to make some choices. At the same time I'm not sure I know what I want. Security is very important to me. Security of home and other things that go along with that. I'm unsure. I know what you're saying and what you've said is true. I haven't figured it out up until now. I want to be secure and yet in order to make changes it involves going into the unknown. Sometimes I feel I'm too middle-class Amer-

From this point until the last sentence of the transcript, Mrs. F. does her most meaningful (least defensive) work of the session. She feels spontaneously sad as she thoughtfully explores the reasons on both sides of her decision whether or not to stay with her husband. She sustains her affect and her focus on this difficult question for an impressive length of time. Finally, she pauses and again completes the triad by interrupting this extended activation and defending against the self-deprecating affect it stimulates; she changes her focus from herself to the therapist by asking him for reassurance, "So I guess I'm right, huh?"

The genuineness of Mrs. F.'s self-directedness in exploring her decision about the future of her marriage is emphasized by the spontaneous affect it inspires. While Mrs. F.'s investigation at the end of this transcript might appear trivial when compared to the typical therapeutic work of a neurotic, the significance to Mrs. F. of self-exploration of this type should not be underestimated. Borderline patients do not normally take it upon

ica. Just growing up knowing, having a nice house, car and kids and a husband is what most people want in life. Giving that up might mean that I'm not part of the people around me. (pause) Sometimes when I try to think through it, like all the things that have angered me with my husband, his drinking and his way of disciplining the children and things like that, I wonder if those are just coverups or if they are finally the excuse I need. I have thought about that. Maybe it isn't those things that really anger me. Those are excuses for my anger. The anger is probably really directed at myself for not being strong enough to make choices on my own. (pause) So I guess I'm right, huh?

themselves in the early stage of treatment to explore carefully the vicissitudes of a problem; to do this would represent a degree of autonomy and individuation that would be threatening to them and would lead to defense.

This transcript is an example of the use of persistent confrontation to address defensive acting out of helplessness, intellectualization, and avoidance. In addition, it demonstrates the need for empathy as an essential element in effective confrontation. When the acting out is finally contained for a brief period of time, the patient engages in some meaningful self-exploration. Masterson's perspective is that through confrontation, the borderline patient learns to control his acting out so that he can organize his life, improve his functioning, and sustain further introspective exploration.

Considering the fact that the transcript of Mrs. F. represents the third hour of treatment, it should be remembered that the borderline diagnosis is tentative. Although most of Mrs. F.'s responses seem to be consistent with that diagnosis, many of them are also consistent with a diagnosis of "closet narcissist," as defined by Masterson (1981), especially her sensitivity to criticism; her response, when she feels injured, of questioning whether she needs to come for treatment; and her comparisons of herself to other people as a way to evaluate her life. The "closet narcissist" diagnosis will be discussed in the next chapter.

## COMPARISON OF TWO APPROACHES TO TREATMENT

The diagnosis and the primarily confrontive treatment approach demonstrated in the previous transcript are most representative of Masterson's approach. Kohut, the originator of self psychology, would adopt a very different approach. Like Masterson, Kohut would view Mrs. F. as personality disordered; however Kohut would treat her as a narcissist and would not use confrontation.

### Masterson

Masterson views the first goal of treatment of the borderline disorder as the control of destructive acting-out behavior with the ultimate goal of working through deep abandonment depression, historically based dysphoric affect against which the patient has been defending. Masterson uses confrontations to make a patient aware of her acting-out defenses and their destructive or pathological nature so that she will control them. According to his model of treatment, when the defenses have been inhibited the underlying dysphoric affect will begin to surface, and with it the associated historical material. According to Masterson, the therapist's providing the patient with a soothing alternative to self-activation can be construed by the patient as conveying a message that she can be taken care of without needing to separate and individuate, and would interfere with the therapeutic process.

### Kohut and Self Psychology

Kohut (1977) viewed the goal of treatment as the strengthening of compensatory ego functions in the patient to enable him to live a relatively functional life, despite ego deficits. This goal is considerably more limited than Masterson's goal of working through.[2] Kohut viewed change as occurring in these patients through "transmuting internalizations," a process by which the patient develops adaptive ego functions through the overcoming of manageable frustrations ("optimal frustrations"). Kohut described the role of the therapist as one of lending his mature ego functions to the patient in order to help reduce

[2]All but the lowest level patients referred to by Masterson as *borderline*, Kohut referred to as *narcissists*.

life's frustrations to manageable ones. According to Kohut, the origins of these patients' ego deficits historically have to do with overwhelmingly frustrating conditions in childhood that did not permit the child to develop internal strength. What the child needed was parental help that would reduce the frustrations to "optimal" ones, just as the patient needs to borrow the therapist's mature ego functions to organize his frustrations into "optimal" ones. One of Kohut's primary interventions was interpretation, helping the patient to understand himself and his behavior. He also used mirroring interventions that help the patient to feel seen, understood, and appreciated by the therapist. An intervention that is soothing to the patient is considered by self psychologists to be helpful if it helps the patient to maintain his internal organization or cohesion. Rather than challenge the patient's maladaptive defenses, the self psychologist takes the point of view that the patient naturally yearns to find his true inner self, so that if the patient feels safe enough in treatment his defenses will become unnecessary and he will abandon them in favor of relatively open exploration of his self.

### Differences between These Approaches

At the core of the differences between Masterson and the self psychologists concerning the treatment of high level borderline personalities is a disagreement over the capacity of the patient. Masterson does not consider internal cohesion to be a problem for the borderline patient; he assumes she can provide the necessary cohesive functions for herself unless this assumption is proven wrong by a particular patient's clinical performance. He asserts that the borderline's developmental arrest comes during Mahler's "rapprochement" subphase, after the "practicing subphase" in which those cohesive functions are first developed. Borderline patients therefore have a more cohesive self than narcissistic patients but struggle with their fear of abandonment or punishment by a caretaker who wants to maintain their infantile dependency and rejects them for separating and individuating. He asserts that the borderline patient views her defensive structure as ego syntonic, so that she will not be likely to let go of it as long as she receives the caretaking that she is looking for. Masterson does not use interpretation with these patients because he claims that they will respond to it as a form of caretaking that reinforces their belief that clinging defenses will obtain the caretaking they think they need.

Kohut, on the other hand, classified Masterson's high level borderlines as narcissists and said that these patients have an internal structural deficit that makes it impossible for them to perform certain self-cohesive functions without the help of an external object (therapist, spouse, parent, etc.), because the structure for these functions has not yet been internalized. To assume that the patient can take over these functions for himself would therefore be a repetition of the childhood experience of subjecting the patient to overwhelming frustration, rather than the optimal frustrations that are necessary for the building of internal structure.[3] In addition the self psychologist views these patients as capable of recognizing and responding to a supportive therapeutic atmosphere established by the therapist. Self psychologists take the point of view that the characteristics identified by Masterson as high level borderline are actually iatrogenic, artifacts of Masterson's confrontive treatment approach, and that these patients are simply narcissists who have been incorrectly understood and improperly treated.

Masterson describes the curative process of the confrontive treatment of the borderline patient as one in which the patient borrows the therapist's healthy ego functions and gradually develops his own. This is very similar to the self psychologists' view of the patient's experience of the therapist as a "selfobject,"[4] an object that provides a cohesive function for the patient that the primitively organized self can otherwise not provide for itself, and that enables the patient to experience his own self more fully. The patient eventually develops the ability to draw upon selfobject experiences that rely less directly upon actual caretaking figures. The apparent difference between the two approaches lies in what can reasonably be expected of the patient (how great is the patient's structural deficit) and consequently how much frustration is optimal and will lead to the most rapid development of internal structure.

## Treatment of Defenses

When the patient uses destructive defenses, including clinging, outside of the treatment hour, both approaches would recommend some sort

[3]See Chapter 4 for an explanation of Kohut's theory of self psychology in which the process of transmuting internalization is seen to build internal structure as a result of optimal frustrations from the caregivers from whom that structure is being borrowed.

[4]Selfobjects are discussed in some detail in the next chapter.

of intervention that would call the patient's attention to the destructiveness of the defense. However, when the patient turns to the therapist for direction within the session, the two approaches differ sharply over the appropriate therapeutic response. The self psychologist typically sees this as the narcissist's expression of the need for the cohesive selfobject function of the therapist to compensate for the patient's internal structural deficits. In other words, the patient is seen as unable to organize himself, and the therapist provides that organization by making interpretations or other nonconfrontive interventions. Alternatively, the self psychologist might view this as a reasonable attempt to obtain reassurance from the therapist, a recharging of the patient's psychic batteries from the therapist. It is apparently uncommon for a self psychologist to view such behavior as a defense, a patient acting helpless in order to avoid separation or individuation.

Masterson would view this behavior as defensive. His approach to this patient when she turns to him for direction would probably be to reflect upon her request by wondering out loud why she is turning to him for help at this time. In other words, he would explore the meaning to the patient of her request for direction rather than going ahead and reacting to the request at face value. He might point out the triad involved, asking why, when the patient has just begun to support herself, she would interrupt that process by turning to him. Alternatively, he might point out several examples of how in the past she has been able to provide for herself the function that she is now asking the therapist to provide. He might ask why she is now giving herself a vote of no confidence. By continually taking the position that the patient is capable of supporting herself, Masterson encourages this patient to face the feelings of abandonment, anger, fear, and hopelessness that accompany separation and individuation. Masterson would not expect the patient to respond to the first confrontation of a particular defense by integrating the confrontation so that the defense becomes ego-dystonic; however, Masterson would continue to use confrontation to make the patient aware of the defensive function of this process of turning to the therapist. The most common initial patient responses are to attempt to comply or to feel criticized. A particular confrontation is not perceived by Masterson to be integrated until the patient takes over for himself the therapist's confrontive function. The patient borrows and then internalizes the therapist's healthy ego function. It is, however, not always clear when this has occurred.

## Criticism of Kohut's Approach

Although the Kohutian therapist does not see himself as gratifying the patient's request for direction when he interprets the source of the patient's need for direction, he is nevertheless providing the organizing function for which the patient is asking. If, as Masterson claims, this patient is capable of individuating or providing that organizing function for herself, then the therapist's gratifying response may recreate the patient's childhood experience by reinforcing the patient's dependency and consequently discouraging separation and individuation. It is apparent, however, from the numbers of talented and effective clinicians who practice self psychology that there are many patients who are able to respond in a therapeutic way to interpretation of their need for direction from the therapist.

A possible conclusion from this is that high-level borderlines have enough of an ability to view their interactions objectively that they are often able to accept a certain amount of gratification without severely regressing by becoming more dependent. Another way of thinking about this is that the therapist's interpretive response gratifies to a small enough degree that it does not pose a significant obstacle to most borderline patients' attempts at individuation, although it may slow down the patients' progress. Another possible conclusion is that these patients are the ones with whom self psychologists tend to be less successful. Less successful in this case could mean that the therapeutic progress is not sustained after termination of treatment, or the patient's defenses are strengthened; they make progress in their careers and get along better with people but do not achieve a deeper degree of intimacy in their relationships.

## Criticism of Masterson's Approach

There is evidence that indicates that Masterson's approach is effective with many patients of this type. Although Masterson's formal research was limited to adolescent patients, there is ample anecdotal evidence of replication of these results with adults. From the Kohutian standpoint, Masterson's apparent effectiveness is understandable because his confrontations do, in fact, provide a selfobject function for the patient. These confrontations are analogous to the parent who says to the 9-year-old, "If you watch television now, when are you going to do your homework?" Self psychologists would say that the reason

Masterson might be successful is that eventually a strong selfobject transference develops in which the therapist nonverbally provides an empathic mirroring function and a realistic limit-setting selfobject function. From the self psychology perspective, each confrontation helps the patient to organize himself and set limits. The patient does not have the capacity to internalize the confrontation; however the patient complies with the therapist's implied wish. As the confrontations continue to focus on a particular theme, the patient becomes increasingly conscious of the therapist's healthy ego function represented by the series of confrontations. Eventually this ego function is internalized.

The Kohutians would add, however, that Masterson's approach would be more effective if he were more accepting of the patient's real limitations in the area of self-activation. They would say that Masterson interferes with the formation of a stable selfobject transference by rejecting the patient's request for help; that he causes the patient initially to attempt to comply, thereby clinging more to the therapist; and that he ultimately causes the patient to act more regressed (act out) as a result of the unstable selfobject transference. Masterson would reply that if the patient portrays himself as helpless when he is actually capable of far more than he admits, the therapist who takes this helplessness at face value, rather than challenging it, encourages regression. This would seem to apply more to the borderline personality-disordered patient who roughly fits the description of a dependent personality disorder.

Some Kohutians might see Masterson's confrontations as similar to saying to a 3-year-old, "Now you act like a big girl and behave yourself while Mommy goes to the store," asking the patient to do something that is beyond her developmental ability, and encouraging her to pretend that she is a "big girl" and comply. They would argue this lack of attunement to the patient's capacities is likely to provoke the feelings of abandonment that Masterson claims the patient is defending against; in other words these therapists would argue that the phenomenon that Masterson points to as a validation for his theory is iatrogenic.

To evaluate this argument, it might be helpful to examine a particular Masterson confrontation and ask whether it is likely to produce overwhelming frustration for the patient. For example, these patients often interrupt themselves by turning to the therapist as they struggle to think through an issue about which they are in conflict.

They might ask the therapist to say something, which, in Masterson's approach, would usually be interpreted as the patient's attempt to avoid feeling the feelings of abandonment that accompany self-activation. If the therapist focuses the patient back upon the fact that the patient is interrupting his own efforts to solve a problem, the patient may begin to be aware of affect, affect that Masterson's theory would indicate has been defended against. This may not be optimal frustration according to some observers, but it is not likely to be seen as overwhelming frustration either, unless it is viewed as part of a larger frustration produced by a continual pattern of confrontation. The argument can be made that this affect can be partially the result of rejection and abandonment feelings toward the therapist that result directly from the confrontations.

The self psychologist would probably be most concerned about the patient who seems to respond compliantly to the confrontation by becoming a "well behaved patient." Some Kohutians would assert that Masterson's confrontations correspond to the parent telling the 3-year-old, "If you don't put on a jacket before you go outside, you'll catch a cold." They see these confrontations as directions, providing a structure that is only required by very poorly functioning patients and that simply invites the patient to comply. Masterson would claim that he sees himself saying this to a more developed person who is mature enough to learn from it. Again the primary difference seems to be in the assessment of the patient's capacity.

A self psychologist might compare the therapy process to the process of learning to ride a bicycle. As long as the rider senses the presence of the parent behind him holding on to the seat, the rider is not afraid. Whether the parent is actually present or not, the rider's sense of his connection to the parent allows him to maintain his balance. However, if he suddenly becomes aware that the parent has fallen back and is no longer holding on to the seat, he panics and falls. This process is analogous to the fragmentation experienced by the narcissist in treatment when there is an interruption to the selfobject transference (see Chapter 4). If the stabilizing parent figure is withdrawn, but is still near at hand when the child discovers that it is missing, the child attempts to maintain his balance until the parent's influence is restored; this is an optimal frustration and will eventually result in the child's learning to maintain his balance for increasingly longer periods of time until this skill has been fully learned. Sadly, we sometimes hear a patient describe how he learned to ride by himself without being taught; he was eventually successful only after many falls and bruises. When Masterson confronts the borderline patient's turning to the therapist, he is letting go of the rider's seat. Kohutians would say he lets go too much, inhibiting the patient's learning; if the patient learns, the process is more painful than is necessary. Masterson would say that he is letting go just enough so that the patient can see that he is able to balance himself.

### A Compromise Position

Further investigation is necessary to clarify these points. However, my belief is that both sides are partially correct. I believe that many of the patients classified by Masterson as borderline are able to tolerate minimal gratification in the form of interpretation without regressing, while some of them cannot, and those will represent the group of cases that do not respond well to the self psychology approach. In *DSM-III-R* terminology, the group that would probably require Masterson's approach (confrontation) are particularly the Dependent Personality Disorders. These patients view dependency as a positive experience in which they are successful in obtaining the nurturing that they seek. It is extremely difficult for the therapist who is interpretive and soothing with these patients to avoid reenacting the original parental pattern in which the patient sees herself as dependent, making successful treatment unlikely. On the other hand, I believe that the self psychologists are correct with respect to many other patients that Masterson would diagnose as borderline, but whose response to confrontation will be compliance. I think these patients will display an inordinate sense of being "bad" because they perceive the therapist as critical, and will try to be "good" so that the therapist will stop criticizing them. They will probably benefit from complying with the therapist's confrontations of their destructive behavior patterns in that their lives will become less chaotic. However, they will perceive the therapist as potentially hurtful and will continue to hide their real selves.

## PHASES OF TREATMENT

As with all personality disorders, the borderline patient comes to treatment believing that his problem lies outside of himself. Usually this belief is demonstrated by the patient's insistence upon talking about other people and situations that the patient believes create his problem. While the patient can acknowledge his own complicity in the problem, this acknowledgment is rarely more than an intellectual understanding; it does not translate into action. For instance, the patient may say, "I know I am too dependent on him. How could I want to be with someone like that?" At the same time, she continues her clinging behavior and complains about the lack of adequate attention that she gets from her boyfriend; she still believes that the solution to her problem is for her boyfriend to be more reassuring. The therapist's first task after establishing rapport with the patient is to help her to understand that she must look inside herself for solutions.

The primary task of the therapist is to understand the patient and to help him to understand and experience himself. For the therapist who uses confrontation to treat a borderline patient, this involves much more than reflecting back to the patient what the patient has said; it involves exercising the therapist's own presumably healthy observing ego to ask the questions that the patient's inadequate observing ego is not asking of himself. "Why do you do this?" "What is it that is painful for you about this?" "Are you aware that you seem to do this whenever that happens? What are your thoughts about that?" Understanding the patient involves understanding the beliefs and feelings that motivate the patient's behaviors. The therapist points out and wonders why the patient focuses on other people in the treatment hour to the exclusion of himself. The therapist points out how the patient denies the implications of his behavior or avoids dealing with uncomfortable situations, and the therapist is curious about why the patient continues to do this, especially since the patient believes that this behavior is contrary to his own well-being.

For the therapist who prefers interpretation, the initial task with the borderline is to help him to begin to explore himself, his beliefs, feelings, and behaviors. The borderline patient, however, is likely to resist introspection, especially when it involves dysphoric affect. One way for the therapist to help the patient to turn inward is to use the frame, the parameters of treatment. When the patient pressures the therapist to take care of him by making special arrangements with respect to appointment times, fee payments, punctuality, therapist self-disclosures, or any of the myriad of requests for special treatment that these patients predictably make, the therapist can, without being unreasonable, maintain the frame and refuse to gratify the patient. When the patient responds by feeling judged, scolded, or deprived, the therapist can explore and interpret to the patient the meaning of this experience, tying it in to the patient's original reason for entering treatment. For instance:

**P:** I get the feeling that you're judging me—that you really don't approve of how I'm going about this. I asked you to tell me if at least I am on the right track and you still put it all on me. If you could at least just nod your head a little more, anything like that, I'd feel a lot better.

**T:** You'd feel better? What are you feeling?

**P:** Well, I'm anxious, upset. I just need a little reassurance that you don't think I'm a terrible bore.

**T:** I understand how upsetting it must be for you to come here with the hope of resolving your anxiety about the possibility of your boyfriend falling out of love with you and leaving you, and then to find yourself feeling similar feelings here, anxious that you're not saying the right things and that I don't like you. Do these feelings come up in other areas of your life?

**P:** Well, now that you mention it, the same type of thing is happening with my boss. (The patient goes on to elaborate.)

**T:** I imagine that this pattern of expectations might have something to do with how you feel inside about yourself.

## Testing Phase

It is especially important with borderline patients that the therapist address the patient's major defenses, whether they occur within or outside of the treatment hour. With almost all treatment models, the therapist looks for indications of the patient's resistance to the treatment, and attempts to address them. The stronger the resistance, the greater it will interfere with treatment. With a neurotic patient one looks for silences, meaningless or lifeless exploration of material, lack of affect, drowsiness, lateness to sessions, and other frame violations as indications of resistance (Greenson 1967). Acting out on the part of neurotics is minimal, so the patient's feelings and memories are relatively available for exploration in the treatment session unless the patient is resisting. The borderline patient, however, acts out her feelings often, sometimes continually. Her acting out occurs both in and out of sessions and dissipates her feelings so that they are not available to be examined in treatment. It is not uncommon, for instance, for a borderline patient to call the therapist between sessions in a panic demanding that the therapist rescue her and then the following session to claim that everything is fine and that she cannot think of anything to discuss in the session; the feeling was acted out in the helpless telephone call so that there is nothing left to explore. Because the borderline patient's acting out often occurs outside of the treatment hour, and the borderline is unlikely to address her acting out as a subject that must be explored, the therapist must point it out or interpret its function. It is common for some significant acting out on the part of the borderline to go unnoticed by a therapist, causing the treatment to stall for months or even years until this acting out is addressed. Substance abuse, for instance, may not be reported to the therapist or may be directly denied by the patient, but until this issue is successfully addressed, progress in treatment will be severely limited.

The initial phase of treatment with the borderline patient has been called the *testing phase* (Masterson 1981) because it is a period in which the patient tests the therapist to see if the therapist will conform to the patient's model of object relations. In other words, the patient relates to the therapist as the "good" parent and assumes that the therapist will play his part appropriately; then, if the therapist does not play the expected role of the "good" parent, the patient perceives the therapist as the "bad" parent and expects the therapist to play that role. If the therapist does not cooperate in playing either of these polarized parent roles, the patient is likely to continue to attempt to view the therapist in one of these roles. Eventually, if the therapist is consistent, it will become increasingly hard for the patient to see the therapist in either polarity and the patient will become anxious and try to understand what is happening. The borderline either attaches to a "good" object at the cost of his own individuality or distances emotionally from a bad parent; to him there is no such thing as a relationship in which he can be himself without cutting off the relationship. The patient feels anxiety at being unable to relate to the therapist in either of these familiar roles. The anxiety increases as the patient tries to relate to the therapist as a nonpolarized object, and the patient renews his attempts to bring the therapist into conformance with one of the expected roles. The test is whether the therapist can succeed in remaining real, neither "good" nor "bad."

## Working Phase

According to Masterson, the testing phase is completed when the patient becomes convinced that she will be unable to induce the therapist to take one of the familiar object roles. When this happens, the patient can no longer blame the therapist for the enormous anxiety that she is experiencing, and she must ask herself what it is within her that is causing it. This begins a period of self-examination in which the patient views the therapist as someone who is accompanying her in her self-exploration; there is a beginning *therapeutic alliance*. The patient enters a working through phase.

This schema, however, appears simpler than it is. In fact there are windows of working through throughout the testing phase and almost all patients terminate without completely working through. If the working through phase is reached, there nevertheless continue to be periods of testing. For the patient who comes to treatment once a week during the testing phase, it is perhaps easier to think of a *working phase* that occurs between the testing phase and the working through phase. The working phase begins approximately when the patient gains enough control over his acting-out defenses that he is able to work therapeutically with little confrontation from the therapist. During this phase there are sustained periods within sessions in which the patient works, exploring dysphoric affect and associated memories. Although the patient is working, the low frequency of sessions limits the depth of material that he can explore and work through. During this phase, he also continues to identify counterproductive defenses and attempts to replace them with more benign ones. Often in sessions during this phase, the patient becomes aware without help that he is defending, and controls the defense. The therapist raises questions and makes interpretations to help the patient to understand more fully what he is exploring (Masterson 1976).

The therapist, however, must continually monitor the patient's responses to determine if the patient is slipping back into further testing of the therapist. The boundary between these two phases is not at all a sharp one, and the patient will go back and forth between the two many times, often several times within one session. Genetic interpretations must be attempted only with care. They can not only renew the patient's fantasy of the "good" nurturing therapist, thus leading the patient back into further testing, but, if not properly timed, they can induce deep painful feeling in the patient which the patient is ill-equipped to handle, so he defends, interfering with his therapeutic work.

### Working Through Phase

The working phase ends at the point that the patient's defenses are relatively healthy and enable him to lead a relatively smooth functioning life. At this point, the patient must make a decision about treatment. If the patient stops treatment, he will be a recovering borderline, in the same sense that an alcoholic who stops drinking is a recovering alcoholic, independent of the number of years since his last drink. The borderline in recovery will always be sensitive to certain kinds of stresses. He will need to be vigilant, for instance, to identify separation stress in his life, and to be sure that when he defends against his abandonment feelings, he does so in a relatively adaptive way.

It is only minimally productive at the end of the working phase for the patient to continue in treatment without an increase in the frequency of sessions. With his maladaptive defenses in check, he will increasingly be exploring in treatment the painful feelings and memories that his defenses have been shielding him from. These feelings and memories will naturally lead to deeper feelings and more memories, and the patient will need additional support from treatment to sustain this exploration without returning to dependence on his old defenses. Two, three, or four sessions a week are typically necessary to provide the patient with adequate support. This intense phase is termed the *working through phase* because the feelings and memories that give rise to the way the patient views and reacts to the world are unearthed. Theoretically, when the patient has worked these memories and feelings through he will have a different experience of himself, others, and relationships. When feelings arise for him in daily life, they will usually be feelings that are familiar to him. Whereas once these same feelings may have been unconsciously associated to feelings or memories that he has disavowed, split off, or repressed, they are now likely to be associated with feelings that he has learned through treatment to tolerate. These associated feelings will be accompanied by a context and perspective that allow him to experience them to a degree that is appropriate to the situation in which they currently arise.

## Separation Phase

Where the working through phase ends is subjective. I don't believe that anyone fully works through, so that the working through phase is never completed. As it proceeds, the process of working through enables the patient to experience himself more and more fully as he recalls and reexperiences deeper memories and affect. Once he has explored those areas that relate most closely to his present life limitations, the process reaches a point of diminishing returns. The area of abandonment, however, cannot be fully explored while treatment continues, because the soothing effect of the therapeutic relationship itself offers too convenient an escape from the feelings of isolation and abandonment. These feelings only appear fully when the termination of the therapeutic relationship becomes a realistic possibility. Normally, neither the patient nor the therapist is eager to introduce this subject.

At some point it becomes apparent that the reason termination is not being discussed is to avoid the accompanying feelings of loss; to continue to skirt the subject, however, is countertherapeutic. Termination and the associated feelings of loss now become the focus of treatment, and what Masterson has called the *separation phase* begins. This is a delicate period, especially for the borderline patient. Since the borderline patient's core issues have to do with separation and abandonment, the process of termination inevitably brings up the deepest and most painful feelings. Even patients who have undergone otherwise successful treatment often abort this final phase, as evidenced by many published descriptions of "successful" analysis in which the patient terminates by getting married and moving to another city, accepting a prestigious job in another city, or going through other life changes that make it logistically or financially difficult to continue treatment. In other words, the patient avoids exploring the pain of leaving her therapist by creating a necessity for cutting the final phase of treatment short. It is worth noting here that even very successfully treated patients may later undergo some trauma in their lives that cause them to seek a brief period of additional treatment.

## COUNTERTRANSFERENCE

There is a theme to the countertransference typically experienced by therapists treating borderline patients. Just as the weaning mother at the beginning of this chapter felt like she was depriving her infant, even though she was doing what she thought was in her baby's best interest, the therapist working with borderline patients often feels withholding when he refuses to respond to the patients' spoken and unspoken demands to be taken care of. With many borderline patients this demand is incessant. Since the borderline patient can see objects only as either all good or all bad, the therapist who appears to be denying nurturing to the patient will be seen as withholding and perhaps critical. Even if the patient can see that the therapist's behavior is necessary and useful to the therapy process, these awarenesses become split off and vanish when the patient is seeing the therapist as the "bad" object. The patient may withdraw from the therapist in response to this negative splitting, the patient may become increasingly helpless in an attempt to draw the therapist into the desired caretaking role, or the patient may attack the therapist for being unfeeling, uncaring, withholding, or uninterested.

Especially if the therapist has any borderline characteristics himself, this withdrawal or criticism is likely to activate his own "bad" self representation, and the patient's complaints and accusations will ring true to the therapist. Under the sway of this pressure, therapists often automatically begin to attempt to gratify the patient's demand, or they begin to question themselves and their approach to the treatment of this patient. They ask themselves, "Have I perhaps been withholding?" or "I think I'm annoyed with the patient; I wonder if I'm acting that out by being critical." As the therapist wavers, the patient can become relentless, and the therapist often does begin to feel annoyed and withholding toward the patient. Projective identification commonly occurs as the therapist takes on the self representation of the inept "bad" person and the patient is left to act out the role of the critical, attacking, rejecting parent.

All this can occur very subtly. The patient begins to talk about her mother and how she was ungiving and unnurturing. As the gruesome details unfold, the therapist says to himself, "What a terrible person. I certainly would never be someone like that." The therapist feels barely perceptibly anxious and begins to feel an impulse to say something reassuring to the patient as if to compensate in some small way for the deficiencies of this terrible mother. Without much thought, a nurturing comment pops out of the therapist's mouth. The therapist's anxiety now disappears as the patient gives the therapist a grateful smile of relief as if to say, "You really do care about me, don't you?" and the therapist smiles back, feeling comfortable at being appreciated in this helping role. The patient stops talking about her terrible mother and begins to talk about her boyfriend, who just bought her a terrific birthday present.

### Use of the Frame

Frame issues are important with all patients, but with personality disorders they are even more important. When a neurotic patient projects onto the therapist, the patient often has a sense that there is something about the projection that isn't right. Then, the therapist and patient can work out the meaning of the projection to the patient. When a patient with a personality disorder projects onto the therapist, the patient sometimes does not have even a hint that it is a projection. For instance the patient cancels an appointment and gives notice that is less by only a half hour than the agreed upon cancellation notice. The therapist explains that the patient will need to pay for the canceled session, and the patient cannot understand why. Certain that the therapist is unreasonable, tight, and punitive, the patient asks what difference a mere half hour makes. If the therapist is in the throes of the projective identification described earlier, he might begin to wonder if perhaps the patient is being reasonable on this issue and the therapist unnecessarily rigid. Since the therapist is not conscious of the projective identification that is occurring, it is extremely difficult for him to grasp what is taking place.

The frame, however, is the key. The frame is a set of mutually understood rules by which the treatment proceeds. There is no reason spontaneously to distort the frame once it has been established. If the therapist finds himself impulsively about to distort the frame, he can be alerted that there is a high likelihood that this impulse is a form of countertransference acting out. With his awareness thus focused, the therapist may now be able to analyze and understand his countertransference.

## CONCLUSION

The therapist who treats borderline patients must resolve the same conflict as the weaning mother described at the beginning of this chapter. If the therapist does not offer the symbolic breast, the borderline patient will complain that the therapist is withholding and unnurturing. If the therapist is to feel good about herself, this good feeling is not going to come from the complaining patient; the patient will not say, "I know this hurts you more than this hurts me." The therapist's good feeling must come from within, from the confidence that the unpopular position that she is taking is necessary if the treatment is to be effective. In order for the patient to learn to rely on his own internal feelings for well-being and self-esteem, the therapist must be able to do the same.

4

# Narcissistic Disorders

"I want to see *Sesame Street*."

"*Sesame Street* won't be on for another hour."

"But I want to see it now."

"Well, I'm sorry; there's nothing I can do."

"I want to see *Sesame Street*, now!"

It is self-evident that the above conversation would not be expected to take place between two adults. The degree to which the first speaker feels entitled to watch the *Sesame Street* television show immediately, without regard to practical limitations, reflects a view of the universe in which he is the center, and it is unacceptable that his needs will not be gratified. It is for most of us a fact of life that we are not the center of the universe and that our demands for gratification often go unmet.

Our learning about our limitations and our acceptance of the many small disappointments in our attempts to make the world respond exactly as we wish have been essential parts of our healthy development into mature adults. According to Kohut (1971), as a person gradually faces the reality that other people cannot provide perfect "mirroring" of her wants and needs and that the idealized omnipotent object lacks certain idealized aspects, she develops internal psychic structure to compensate for what cannot be obtained externally. Through a process of transmuting internalization, a person gradually develops an internal sense of her self. As she lets go of the fantasy of an omnipotent other who is perfect, she develops a sense of her own power. Through this developmental process, the blind, unrealistic narcissism of childhood is converted to a mature adult narcissism that permits the adult to face and overcome challenges, and to value her own creations.

Kohut (1966) tells a story about Winston Churchill to illustrate healthy youthful narcissism. As a boy, Churchill was being chased by two playmates. Finding himself cornered on a bridge over a ravine, with a pursuer at either end, Churchill dove off the bridge, calculating that the young fir trees below would break his fall. They did, and many of his body parts as well; it was three days before he regained consciousness. Kohut appreciates Churchill's youthful boldness. To jump was a creative way to escape, and one might admire Churchill's ability to think quickly under pressure, to devise a plan, to confidently convert his plan into action, and to courageously take the leap. This same decisiveness, creativity, fearlessness, and positive attitude later matured and served Churchill well as a statesman and leader. Fortunately, Churchill did not make a habit of this particular form of creative thinking.

The gradual development of internal structure through transmuting internalization does not occur if the failures and disappointments that the child experiences are so great as to overwhelm him. If, for instance, the caretaker is consistently unresponsive to the child or will only respond if the child behaves in a prescribed manner, the child feels unacceptable and is ashamed of his spontaneity and uniqueness; there is not enough external support for the child to build the internal structure necessary to restore his sense of self-worth. If the adult caretaker, who is supposed to provide the child with a sense of safety and strength, is himself or herself impaired, perhaps as a result of substance abuse, mental illness, or disease, the child cannot hope to compensate for the parent's huge deficits, and feels exposed, vulnerable, and helpless to protect himself.

According to Kohut (1971, 1977), the child whose attempts at development of healthy narcissistic structure are thwarted by an unsupportive environment does not develop the internal structure necessary for healthy adult narcissism. His development is arrested and remains characteristically infantile even into adulthood. He acts in many respects the part of the child who expects the world to revolve around him, the child who feels omnipotent and invulnerable, who cannot imagine harm coming to him. He insulates himself from his true feelings of emptiness, shame, and isolation by building a shield of grandiosity that protects him from those feelings. The two poles of feeling, deflation and grandiosity, remain insulated from each other in his mind. At one moment he can be feeling defective, fragmented, vulnerable, worthless, and painfully deflated; in the next moment he can reinflate himself with grandiose fantasies, and be entirely emotionally disengaged from the feelings of a moment before. His shield wards off intimate contact with others that would involve being himself, because any experience of his real self would involve the painful experience of feeling unlovable and worthless. He relates to others primarily through identification, seeing them as an extension or reflection of himself. He maintains his grandiosity by continually feeding it, making himself feel superior to others by devaluing them, striving for perfection in all things, and blaming his imperfections and failures on others. He seeks power, sex, money, beauty, and the admiration of others to further inflate his grandiosity and convince himself of his own adequacy.

## BEHAVIORAL CHARACTERISTICS OF THE NARCISSISTIC DISORDER

In *Ordinary People*, Conrad's mother displays some of the typical characteristics of a narcissistic disorder. She is cold and unfeeling. She demands love in the form of agreement and adulation. To disagree with her or to express dissatisfaction with her behavior is taken by her as criticism. She is self-satisfied, believing that her attitudes and behavior are perfect. She presents a facade to the world that she probably confuses with her self. When that facade is challenged, she is deeply injured. When her husband, in the movie, tearfully shares with her his unhappiness with their relationship, she responds without feeling. She is wounded. To protect herself from further injury, she coldly retreats to her bedroom, packs her bags, and leaves. This behavior demonstrates the extreme brittleness of the narcissist. Despite the seemingly impenetrable wall surrounding the narcissist, she is easily offended and extremely vulnerable to injury.

When a narcissist is of the type who displays his grandiosity, he generally feels on top of the world; he can do no wrong, and certainly feels no need for psychotherapy. As in the case of James Bond (agent 007), narcissists can display remarkable talent, be quite charming and likable, and achieve dazzling successes in certain types of relationships. Although they are unable to sustain an emotionally intimate relationship with another person, they do not miss it. They strive for precision, control, and order in their lives, and constantly work to expose and defeat Chaos.[1] Their inability to self-soothe makes them susceptible to boredom, so they strive to obtain excitement through external forms of stimulation like risk taking, sexual conquest, intense involvement in work, or involvement in grandiose projects. Often they are very successful in these endeavors because their lack of emotionality enables them to effectively manipulate other people. In fact, it is rare for exhibitionistic narcissists to seek treatment when they perceive their lives as exemplary. Only when faced with undeniable failure in their lives do they entertain the possibility that they might be flawed in some way and might benefit from psychotherapy. Even then, they initially seek therapy only as a means to restore their perfection, rather than to explore their inner selves. Their prognosis in treatment is often poor because of their tendency to compensate for the failure or injury that produced their presenting problem by finding a way to restore their grandiosity with an inflating experience or fantasy, thus losing their motivation for being in treatment.

## EXHIBITIONISTIC AND CLOSET NARCISSISTIC DISORDERS

### The Exhibitionistic Narcissist

If a child is supported in his grandiosity by an environment that tells him he is superior, but that ignores his individuality, personal feelings, and interests, he develops into an adult who attempts to restore his belief in himself by coercing his adult environment into supporting his grandiose claims of superiority and perfection. If, for instance, the parents are narcissistic and continue to encourage and even require the child to display grandiosity as a reflection of themselves, a chip off the old block,

[1]"Chaos" is a reference to K.A.O.S., the evil empire in *Get Smart*, a television spoof of James Bond.

the child grows into an adult who believes that the only way that he can be lovable is to continue to be perfect.

Rather than hide his grandiose feelings, he flaunts them, continually striving to prove his superiority and perfection. He feels entitled to special treatment commensurate with his own specialness and superiority, and is offended when treated as ordinary. He is likely to become abusive of service personnel who do not treat him in the manner he expects and demands, and he is prone to feelings of outrage concerning the imperfectness of others. As a person who considers himself perfect, he is usually offended when anyone offers him suggestions for improvement, which he interprets as criticisms, attempts to tear him down. This type of narcissist is variously referred to as an *exhibitionistic*, *exhibiting*, *displaying*, *grandiose*, or *phallic* narcissist.

### The Closet Narcissist

Alternatively, if the child's grandiosity is considered threatening and is consequently disapproved of or forbidden by the parent, the child grows into an adult who secretly believes in her own superiority but does not feel safe to allow anyone else to see her grandiosity. If the parents, for instance, are narcissistic personalities, they will expect the child to be an extension of themselves; the child will not be acknowledged for her own uniqueness. If the parents expect from the child a perfect reflection of their own specialness in the form of adulation, and the child has her own feelings of grandiosity and omnipotence, she quickly learns that for her to display those feelings would be far from the adulation that the parents seek and would result in disappointment and probably attack from the parents. The child learns to keep her own grandiosity to herself (in the closet). She can be charming, witty, efficient, thorough, and extremely cooperative, often to the point of obsequiousness. She can even appear self-effacing and meek. Her secret feelings of grandiosity, entitlement, and superiority are revealed very carefully and only when she is convinced that such revelations will be safe. However, they are reflected in her obsessive concerns about perfection and her hypersensitivity to criticism.

In the treatment context, the level of security necessary for the narcissistic patient to be able to display her grandiosity often takes years to establish. Instead of superiority, she commonly claims feelings of inferiority. Upon close examination she is usually willing to admit that the inferiority is how she has been characterized by others, but that she herself does not believe she is actually inferior. This type of person may be referred to as a *closet* (Masterson 1981), *covert*, or *false self* narcissist. The following interaction would not be atypical for a closet narcissist:

**P:** I'm such a screw-up!
**T:** Do you actually believe you are a screw up or is that something that's been *said about you* that you go along with?
**P:** No, I know I'm not a screw-up, but that's what people have been telling me all my life. I guess I've just gotten in the habit of saying it myself.

The line between the closet and the exhibitionistic narcissist is a fuzzy one. It can be said that beneath his grandiosity every exhibitionistic narcissist is a closet narcissist at heart; as treatment progresses, the exhibitionistic narcissist reveals that he has displayed only part of his true feelings of grandiosity. It can also be said that every closet narcissist, given enough encouragement and support, can become an exhibitionistic narcissist; during the course of treatment, the closet narcissist reveals his secret grandiosity.

With this grandiosity can come greater confidence and achievement of greater successes, which further bolster the narcissist's grandiosity. This phenomenon can be problematic for treatment because the unwary therapist may mistakenly take this external show of accomplishment as a sign of health and therapeutic progress. The therapist must keep in mind the distinction between success in the service of bolstering the narcissist's grandiose defense, and success in achieving self-actualizing goals.

## SELFOBJECT TRANSFERENCES

Kohut identified two types of positive transference-like phenomena that the narcissist typically develops with the therapist, the *idealizing* transference and the *mirror* transference. Often a mirror transference will develop and gradually be supplanted by an idealizing transference. Strictly speaking, these are not actual transferences because the patient experiences the impact of these relationships directly, rather than purely as a result of their symbolic meaning with respect to historical parental relationships. In addition, the patient is not able to view the therapist realistically enough to make a traditional transference relationship possible; the observing ego[2] necessary to explore the true meaning of transference feelings is not sufficiently developed.

The primitive or low level narcissistic patient has no clear experience of herself as separate from the object; she experiences the two as blurred together. She sees the object as an extension of her self. With the higher level narcissistic disorder, not to be confused with a neurotic with narcissistic defenses who is very high level, the degree of distortion through the fantasy of merger is not as severe. She is, however, unable to turn inward to see herself, so that she must see herself through the object's eyes.

Kohut (1971, 1977) called these various mergers of self and object a *selfobject* and he used the term *selfobject transference* to refer to the two transference-like phenomena that he identified. The idealizing transference involves the patient maintaining an idealized view of the object. By elevating her opinion of the object to whom she feels connected, the patient is able to enhance her view of herself and to bask in the glow of the object. She borrows from the object the strength necessary to maintain an internal sense of cohesion that enables her to tolerate frustration. If in treatment she idealizes the therapist, she is by association uplifting herself. Another way for the patient to feel good about herself is through the admiration of others, which Kohut compared to the gleam in the mother's eye when she observes and appreciates her young child's play. In treatment, the patient might attempt to impress the therapist so that the therapist reflects back the patient's accomplishments and grandeur; the patient's sense of well-being and internal cohesion is maintained by continually eliciting admiration from others. Kohut (1971) called this a *mirror transference*.

More specifically, he considered the idealizing transference to be a replication of the child's experience of the father, who is perceived as omnipotent. Through the relationship with the omnipotent object the child draws strength, ideals, values, goals, and ambition. Kohut considered the mirror transference to be a replication of the child's experience of the mother. Through the mother's validation of the child's experiences of excitement, discovery, pleasure, and pride, the child develops a strong sense of self-esteem. Without that validation, the child concludes that there is something wrong with his feelings, and

[2]*Observing ego* was discussed in Chapter 3. It is the patient's ability to observe and evaluate his own thoughts, feelings, and behavior as they occur.

he feels ashamed of them. He learns to disavow his affect and comes to be unaware of them.

### Mirror Transferences

Kohut (1968) divided the mirror transference phenomenon into three types, each corresponding to a different level of developmental arrest. The more primitive the narcissist's condition, the more limited will be her ability to recognize separation between herself and objects. The least mature of the mirror transferences is the merger transference in which the patient views the therapist as a virtual extension of herself, recognizing no separation between self and object, no evidence of separateness between therapist and patient. The patient expects the therapist to be perfectly resonant to her, as if an actual part of her. For the therapist to act in a discordant manner would be experienced by the patient as if one hand were trying to act independently from the rest of her body. If the therapist fails to show a perfect understanding of the patient or expresses a slightly different point of view from hers, the patient experiences a painful breach in the cohesive selfobject function provided by the therapist. In response, the patient is likely to feel criticized or betrayed, and will withdraw or become devaluing. For a particularly primitive narcissist a more mature mirror transference is unlikely because it requires some acknowledgment of a separation between self and object. As Stern (1985) indicates, this merged perception of self and object never actually occurs in normal infancy; most therapists agree that it is pathological in both children and adults.

The second level of mirror transference, *alter-ego* or *twinship* transference, is one in which the patient thinks of the therapist as like himself, of similar psychological makeup, a twin, separate but alike. For the twinship transference, there must be a sense of two separate people of like mind existing in tandem. It is a very common form of selfobject transference.

The third mirror transference, the least archaic, was simply referred to by Kohut as the *mirror* transference. The patient experiences the object as separate from herself but is unable to care about and appreciate the object as a unique and separate person. The patient with this transference is interested in a therapist only for the function that the therapist can serve in reflecting the patient's grandiosity or in validating the patient's positive experience of himself and his achievements, not as a real person. Kohut (1968) states that "the transference, however, functions as a specific therapeutic buffer. . . . In the twinship and merger, the analogous protection is provided by the long-term deployment of the narcissistic cathexes upon the therapist, who now is the carrier of the patient's infantile greatness and exhibitionism" (p. 98).

From a clinical point of view, the significance of these three levels of mirror transferences is that a therapist who is alert to them can more accurately assess the kinds of interventions that will be soothing to the patient and the kind that will be wounding. Of equal importance is the fact that the therapist who is sensitive to the level of the patient's need for mirroring can respond to the patient with the amount of mirroring that is minimally necessary without overly encouraging the patient's regressive fantasies and demands. For example, a vignette will be presented later in this chapter of a patient requesting that the therapist come to the window and admire the patient's new used car. For an extremely primitive narcissist who has been unable to acknowledge that he cares what the therapist thinks, this gesture might be perceived of as progress; it might be seen as the beginning of a shift from a devaluing to an idealizing transference, or alternatively it might be seen as the beginning of the patient's willingness to expose his grandiosity. In the context of a higher level of mirror transference or an idealizing transference, this request might be seen as defensive, a request for gratification of the patient's need for external validation. Alternatively, as suggested by the authors of the book from which this vignette was taken, it might be viewed as the patient's attempt to genuinely share his realistic pride in an accomplishment, that of purchasing a new vehicle. In the context of a very high level of transference that would be likely to occur during the process of working through, this request might be a healthy attempt by the patient to share with the therapist a genuine interest that the patient has recognized through his newly acquired ability to introspect, in other words an expression of the patient's "real self."

### *Archaic Relationships Reflected in Transferences*

According to Kohut, the different narcissistic selfobject transferences reflect different aspects of the relationship between the infant and the caregiver. Recently, followers of Kohut have expanded his concepts of the mirror transference to a broader category of relating that corresponds to what Stern describes as *affective attunement*; the caregiver mirrors in movement, affect, shape, texture, and intensity the expression of the infant, validating the infant's expression and creating a sense of security and trust in the infant. From Stern's perspective, the selfobject might be called a *self-regulating other*. The primitive narcissist requires this exquisite attunement from the therapist in order to recognize and accept his internal affective states. Kohut believed that mirroring provides a function of helping the infant to value himself. He likens mirroring to the gleam that the infant sees in the mother's eye when she observes him succeed in his efforts. "Look, Mom, no hands!" For the exhibitionistic narcissist, the primary function of his display of grandiosity is to impress those around him and, through their admiration, to receive the mirroring that he craves in order to stabilize his own sense of himself.

The idealizing transference corresponds to the infant's belief in the omnipotence of the caregiver,[3] which contributes to the infant a sense of confidence, power, and well-being. For the adult narcissist, the idealized selfobject transference similarly provides a sense of potency and well-being. So important is this function to the narcissist that the idealizing narcissist will often choose to fault himself rather than recognize a defect in the object. For instance, in the following transcript excerpt the therapist disappoints the patient and the patient blames himself in order to preserve his idealization of the therapist.

The patient has just described at length some physical sensations that his wife has been feeling in the past few weeks.

**T:** My sense as you were describing your wife's condition is that, in addition to your concern about your wife, you were hoping to demonstrate to me your technical command of the various medical phenomena involved. This is your professional area of expertise, isn't it?

The therapist is unable to understand the relevance of the patient's lengthy description, but eventually realizes that the patient is showing off his knowledge of medicine. The therapist acknowledges the patient's expertise. Although this comment is intended to acknowledge the patient's request for collegial recognition from the therapist, it is taken by the patient as a criticism of his showing off.

[3]More specifically, Kohut associated mirroring with the mother's role and idealization with the father's role.

**P:** Well, yes that's true. I wanted to impress you. I guess I did go a little bit overboard with technical detail in my description, didn't I?

The patient criticizes himself saying that he went "a little bit overboard."

**T:** I didn't intend that comment as a criticism. It was not until you were finishing your description that it occurred to me that part of the reason you were giving so much technical information is that it is important to you to feel a collegial relationship with me as well as a therapeutic one. You've talked about how demeaning it feels for you to be in treatment. I know you are proud of your medical competence; it represents an accomplishment that was the result of a lot of hard work. I understand that you would want recognition from me, especially since it was so hard for you to obtain recognition as a child for your accomplishments. I was just asleep at the switch.

Recognizing that the patient feels criticized, the therapist attempts to normalize the patient's wound by acknowledging that the patient did not get encouragement as a child for his genuine areas of interest and competency, and so it is natural for him to seek this from the therapist. By his comment, "I was just asleep at the switch," the therapist indirectly acknowledges that his failure to be impressed by the patient's expertise was injuring to the patient.

**P:** Of course you're right. That recognition is so important to me, and when I didn't think I was getting it from you I was disappointed and went into more and more detail so that you could not help but notice how thoroughly I understand this area. The real problem is that I can't seem to learn to ask for what I want; if I could I wouldn't get into these long-winded lectures.

The patient responds by ignoring the therapist's comment about being asleep at the switch. Instead he acknowledges that he does indeed seek this recognition, and that it was painful for him when the therapist did not admire his expertise, but that the real problem was how he, the patient, is unable to ask for recognition. In so identifying the problem, the patient protects his idealization of the therapist by denying the importance of the therapist's role in causing the injury and instead blaming himself.

If the therapist does not interfere, the closet narcissist will generally form an idealizing transference with the therapist. The therapist's position of authority, his title of "doctor," his neutrality and relative silence allow the patient to see in him whatever qualities of power and wisdom that the patient wishes. It is extremely common for the closet narcissist to report improvement soon after beginning treatment. This is usually not traceable to any significant therapeutic event, but to the stabilizing effect of the idealized selfobject. This apparent progress will, of course, disappear if treatment is prematurely interrupted.

Although exhibitionistic and closet narcissists can develop any of the selfobject transferences, the idealizing transference seems to be a more mature transference than the mirror transference, since it requires of the patient that he be able to accept a certain amount of separateness from the therapist. When a mirror transference is generated in treatment, it is likely to be succeeded by an idealizing transference. If the patient's internal structure is too weak to permit an idealization of the therapist, the patient is likely to develop a mirror transference. It is normally not necessary for the therapist to cultivate this transference by mirroring the patient. If he is sincerely empathic and understanding of the patient and makes a few accurate, albeit superficial, interpretations the patient is likely to feel understood, leading to a feeling of kinship with the therapist and a mirror transference. When mirroring is used, it is usually possible to combine mirroring effectively with simple interpretation.

## AN EXHIBITIONISTIC NARCISSISTIC DISORDER

### Insight without Change

Because of the stabilizing effect of the transference, narcissistic patients often appear almost magically to make progress in therapy. The therapist sometimes sees dramatic change in the behavior that the patient reports as taking place outside of treatment, but cannot trace the changes back specifically to the treatment. In the treatment hour, perhaps this patient conceptualizes about himself rather than experiences himself, and there is no significant observable change. Despite the therapist's uncertainty about her own effectiveness, the patient may be effusive in his praise for the therapist and her clinical skills.

### Case Example—Mr. H.

Patients like these often do not benefit in the long run from their treatment, although they are not commonly identified as therapeutic failures. Mr. H., a 43-year-old sales manager for a medium-sized corporation, is a hypothetical example of such a patient. He came to therapy because he was dissatisfied with his marriage of twenty years, and was considering leaving his wife for another woman. He could see both advantages and disadvantages to doing this. He thought his wife had been a good wife and had tried very hard to please him, but he found her unexciting. There was a missing piece to his life that he felt he could find in the excitement and euphoria that accompanied this new relationship. He wondered, however, whether he might eventually feel about the new relationship like he does about his marriage.

On the face of it, Mr. H. appeared to be a reasonable, likable, and highly competent man, although the emotional distance with which he spoke of his wife was apparent, and his overall ability to relate to his feelings seemed limited. As a result, his work in therapy remained primarily on an intellectual level. He began most sessions by asking his therapist a question that he read from a list of concerns that had occurred to him during the week before the session. Most of the questions centered around his relationships at home and at work. The therapist answered Mr. H.'s questions by carefully pointing out the patterns Mr. H. seemed to repeat in his relationships. Mr. H. would respond to these explanations with interest, the way a manager might be interested in a report he received from an employee. Occasionally, Mr. H. might comment that the answer was "right on the nose." However, more often he would counter with an explanation about why the therapist's answer only applied in certain situations, or how the answer failed to explain certain factors. He appeared to be very intelligent and was insightful in his attempts to make sense out of the information and concepts that arose during the course of treatment.

As months went by, Mr. H. became less dependent upon his list of questions during the therapy hour, and he talked more about himself. He explored his limited memories of his childhood, some of the dynamics between him and his wife, and his ambivalence about starting over again with a new woman, all with very limited affect. He appeared pleased when his therapist showed understanding of what he was saying, but was quick to correct the therapist if she paraphrased his remarks using a word that did not have exactly the meaning that Mr. H. intended. The therapist found it easier simply to use Mr. H.'s own words when reflecting back what Mr. H. seemed to be saying. Mr. H. traveled often in his job, so there were many occasions when his session needed to be rescheduled. In addition, Mr. H. canceled or came late to many more sessions than most patients, and was very difficult to usher out the door when the session was over. There was always one last question, or a last minute need to reschedule the next appointment.

Mr. H. eventually decided to leave his wife, but never felt able to recover the missing piece to his life. He also suffered a major setback at work when a promotion he felt deserving of was given to somebody else. He became depressed. Feeling that his life was suddenly unraveling, he decided that he had made a terrible mistake in leaving his wife. Finally, after a year and a half of therapy, he cried for the first time in a session, wondering if he would ever have a successful relationship with a woman. His therapist was pleased with the session, and felt that they were finally making progress. However, this session proved to be their last. Mr. H. called the following week to say that he did not feel the therapy was helping him and that he would not be coming back.

**Avoidance of Intimacy**

Narcissistic personalities surround themselves with an impenetrable wall that protects them from the vulnerability that comes with forming relationships with and caring about other people. They are extremely sensitive to devaluation and will react to the slightest intimation of a fault in their character. They seek perfection in the things they do, since any imperfection might expose them to painful criticism. Even insight is often wounding for these patients because it underscores their failure to understand themselves perfectly. It is also wounding in that it usually implies to them that there is a way of handling their situations that is better than the way they have been doing it.

Since these patients feel so threatened by intimate relationships, they form functional ones with people they perceive as equal in perfection to themselves. In a functional relationship, people are valued only for what they can do, for the functional role they can play. In a mature caring relationship, there is an emotional bond; people are valued as unique whole beings. Functional relationships are safer than caring ones in that one can avoid emotional attachments. For Mr. H., after many years of marriage, the question of whether or not to stay with his wife was primarily a practical one. He thought she was attractive, a good homemaker, and a good mother, so there were significant reasons to stay. Also, he was concerned about whether his friends and family would judge him for leaving her and about the financial implications of such a move. On the other hand, she was no longer exciting to him, and he felt he deserved to be with a woman whom he found exciting. Sentiment was significantly missing as a factor in his decision. Particularly striking was his lack of concern about the effect of his actions on his children and his relationship to them.

The narcissistic patient's message to his therapist is, "I want you to understand me, not cure me!" The narcissistic personality often does not believe that there is anything about him to cure, despite the fact that he has engaged a psychotherapist. He sees his problems as a product of his environment, and he engages the therapist in the same manner that he might engage an accountant to audit and certify his books. He does not seek an emotional bond; in fact he does not experience a mature emotional bond with anyone. He thinks of other people in terms of their functional value. Especially for the more primitive narcissist, the closest he comes to caring about others is when he feels bonded to them, a state in which the boundaries between him and them are blurred in his mind so that there is a perceived merger. If this fantasy of merger or connectedness is disturbed, he experiences a loss of the relationship, which translates to him as a loss of part of himself. The clinical implications of this phenomenon are vitally important to the treatment of these patients, and will be discussed at length later in this chapter.

## NARCISSISTIC SPLITTING

### Impaired Self

Mr. H.'s presenting problem had deeper roots than may at first have been apparent. His complaint was that he was unable to decide whether to leave his wife in favor of another woman. It was clear that this problem was directly related to his lack of emotional connection to other people, but it also represented another problem that is characteristic of narcissistic personalities; he was in a situation in which he was forced to rely upon his own insides in order to choose a major life direction. Because narcissistic personalities are out of touch with their insides, they find situations in which they must identify their own inner direction to be painful, exposing, and often humiliating.

Narcissists are almost always busy advancing in one direction or another (usually what they consider to be upwards); they seem to know exactly where they are going. It should be remembered, however, that their goals probably have little relationship to their inner selves. On the contrary, narcissists look for external direction and goals from society, authorities, or idealized others, and then strive to obtain those goals. These goals, often including wealth, power, and fame, are devoid of inner meaning. The narcissistic personality strives toward attainment of them in order to prove his superiority and to support his grandiose view of himself, which in turn protects him from experiencing feelings of defectiveness and worthlessness.

Although he learns over and over that achievement of these goals does not bring satisfaction or happiness, he rarely faces this reality; instead he repeatedly attempts to soothe his internal emptiness through symbolic successes. Although Mr. H. initially characterized his reason for treatment as solely related to his decision about his marriage, he probably entered treatment because he felt lost. He did not know what he wanted out of life or who he was. He had attained most of the goals he once thought would bring him happiness, and they had not. The decision he was faced with about his marriage symbolized his position in life. How could he find the satisfaction that he lacked? As is common of narcissistic personalities, he believed that the solution to this internal problem could be found by making the right external choices.

## The Narcissistic Split

It may seem confusing to read a description of the narcissistic personality as defending against feelings of worthlessness and isolation, and a moment later to read a description of him as believing that there is nothing about him in need of cure. The narcissist himself is not confused by this apparent contradiction. For him, the phenomenon described earlier as *splitting* is at work. The narcissistic personality may be aware of both parts of the split; however, affectively he only experiences one at a time. In the *fragmented* object relations unit containing the (part) self representation of being worthless, incompetent, empty, and unlovable, there is a representation of a (part) object that is punitive, critical, and attacking, and an accompanying affect of emptiness, self-loathing, hopelessness, shame, and isolation. In the *grandiose* object relations unit containing the (part) self representation of superiority, omnipotence, and perfection there is a representation of the (part) object as special, omnipotent, and perfect. The affect accompanying this unit is one of feeling elevated, unique, and special. Similar to other types of splitting, while either unit is active, the other is emotionally disavowed.

## Defenses of Grandiosity and Distancing

Mr. H.'s primary defenses were his grandiosity and his distancing, both physical and emotional. He made little effort to hide his grandiosity. He insisted that everyone around him support him in his inflated opinion of himself. Although through treatment he learned to talk about his feelings, he was not actually feeling them. Like a good student, he learned the jargon of therapy and diligently explored memories of his early childhood, producing interesting insights devoid of affect.

The people with whom he chose to form relationships would idealize him and feed his grandiosity, but they would expect him to take care of them. Such choices are common for this type of patient. In romantic relationships these patients confuse excitement, passion, and euphoria for love. As the partner becomes more insistent upon empathic caretaking, people like Mr. H. switch from a positive to a negative view of the partner (splitting), feel criticized, and respond by devaluing the partner and pulling back. Eventually these patients often withdraw from the relationship entirely.

The intellectual way in which Mr. H. distanced from his therapist allowed him to feel safe with her. For him, feelings represented a part of himself of which he was ashamed. When he broke through to his feelings during a session, his therapist thought of it as progress, while to Mr. H. it represented unbearable weakness and humiliation. As is characteristic of this type of patient, Mr. H. responded to this humiliation by defending, in this case devaluing his therapist and withdrawing from therapy. Whereas only a week before, he may have been satisfied with his therapy, after a session in which his emotions had been stirred, he could abruptly characterize the therapy as worthless, claiming that nothing was happening in the treatment.

His loyalty to treatment was no greater than his loyalty to his wife. With little warning he could decide to cut off his relationship with his therapist and not give it another thought. This was possible for him because in relationships, although he appears to be relating to another person, in fact he is relating only to the function that the person serves for him as someone who admires him and supports his grandiosity. His frequent rescheduling of sessions, latenesses, and missed sessions were further indications of his tenuous attachment to treatment.

## NARCISSISTIC VULNERABILITY

### Interpretation of Narcissistic Wounds

In general, when a narcissistic patient becomes uncharacteristically emotional in a session, it is important for him to explore his reactions to having displayed his feelings in this way with the therapist. If he does not spontaneously focus on this issue himself, the therapist should take it up with him. If possible, she can do this by looking for and interpreting protective withdrawal on the part of the patient. Had Mr. H.'s therapist done this, his sudden termination of treatment might have been averted.

In addition, she needed to establish early on in the therapy his tendency to defend in the form of devaluation and withdrawal. His many latenesses and cancellations were actually examples of his subtle devaluation of the therapy and his withdrawal response to the subtle hurts he experienced in therapy. These were his ways of protecting himself and letting his therapist know that the treatment she was conducting was not as meaningful to him as she might have believed. These hurts would arise if she failed to understand perfectly or to empathize with him. Perhaps, for instance, he said or did something that he assumed she would understand, or he described something he had done that he hoped she would praise, but she did not. When he did not get the response he was looking for, he would feel silently disappointed or hurt.

If his therapist had been more alert to this process, she might have noticed the subtle frowns or the silences that often accompanied these incidents. She might have been able to recover from these disturbances to the therapeutic relationship by acknowledging Mr. H.'s expectation of her, his disappointment that this expectation was not met, and perhaps his feelings about himself when such a disappointment occurred. This acknowledgment by the therapist can be surprisingly helpful to a patient like Mr. H. It indicates further understanding of the patient, helps the patient to be aware of himself, and reassures him concerning the therapist's expertise. Furthermore, patients like Mr. H. are often unaware that they devalue or withdraw in response to something that they feel. In fact, consistent with their general inability to experience feelings, they are usually unaware that they feel hurt. When it is suggested by the therapist, however, that they might be withdrawing or devaluing as a protection against perceived criticism or injury, they can often recognize how they feel. This recognition constitutes for them a building block in the process of developing an observing ego and of getting in touch with their insides.

Because Mr. H. was so vulnerable to disappointment and criticism, his therapist would have needed to structure her comments to him carefully so that he would not interpret them as critical or judgmental. One way to make interventions more acceptable to the patient is for the therapist to use a positive context to describe the patient's characteristics. This is not difficult to do, since all personality traits have both positive and negative aspects. For example, the therapist can comment on the patient's "exquisite sensitivity" to criticism (inability to hear feedback), the high standards he holds for himself (perfectionism and criticalness), and his self-reliance (isolation and inability to have meaningful relationships).

Without passing judgment, for instance, it would have been helpful for the therapist to point out Mr. H.'s sensitivity to criticism as an explanation for many of his upsets at home and at work. By identifying his sensitivity, the therapist implies that there is a characteristic about Mr. H. that is common to a variety of his upsets with different people. It is surprising how readily patients like Mr. H. are willing to embrace a characterization of themselves as "exquisitely" or "finely" sensitive to criticism; these patients know that they feel criticized constantly and they feel understood when their sensitivity is noticed. They like the specialness implied in a phrase like "exquisite sensitivity"; yet the term is inoffensive in that it does not label them as having a problem. Once Mr. H. recognizes his sensitivity to criticism and the frequency with which it results in upsets, he would eventually conclude that such sensitivity is burdensome.

This awareness might then widen into a greater acknowledgment that much of his experience in life arises from his own psychological orientation rather than from the ineptitude, stupidity, or inferiority of those around him, a concept that he would initially resist because it implies imperfections in his own character. For Mr. H., imperfection represents vulnerability; his own inner feelings are a source of shame.

In treatment, Mr. H. would need to experience himself, including his inner feelings of shame and worthlessness, in order to begin to know who he is and what he wants out of life. The sense of safety and cohesion that he receives from his relationship with his therapist is vital to enable him to explore his feelings about himself, his genuine interests, and his realistic strengths.

**Mirroring**

Some therapists, including control mastery therapists, believe that the reparenting aspects of the therapeutic relationship or the *corrective emotional experience* that it provides are curative in themselves. Self psychologists believe that the selfobject functions that the therapist provides for the patient offer him what he did not receive as a child from his parent or caregiver. These therapists assert that the therapist's recognition and responsiveness to the patient's attempts at self-expression represent a curative departure from the patient's childhood experience and provide a degree of safety, a feeling of being understood, and a feeling of wholeness in the patient that allow him to let go of defenses, take risks, and venture further into a deeper knowing and expressing of himself. One way these therapists may attempt to provide this for the patient is through *mirroring*; the therapist reflects back to the patient the emotional content of what he is saying.

Some theorists believe that this type of intervention reinforces in these patients a regressive fantasy of merger. However, most theorists agree that mirroring of a narcissistic patient's painful feelings helps the patient to recognize them and feel understood. Since the mirroring of feeling is a soothing way for the therapist to call the patient's attention to his experience, mirroring can effectively be used in conjunction with other types of interventions to make them more acceptable to the patient. It serves to make the patient more aware of what he feels and to strengthen the relationship between therapist and patient.

The therapeutic value of mirroring the patient's defensive grandiose feelings, as opposed to his spontaneous euphoric or dysphoric feelings, is commonly questioned. In the case of Mr. H., for instance, a routine was developed in his treatment in which week after week Mr. H. would report about his successes at work, describing in a self-satisfied manner the way he had beaten another salesman to a sale or how he was on the verge of closing a very big deal. His therapist could sense that Mr. H. would be hurt if she did not respond in some way to these reports, so she would make mirroring comments like, "That must be very satisfying for you" or "You must be proud of your accomplishments."

A careful tracking of Mr. H.'s sessions with special attention paid toward the timing of his self-aggrandizing reports reveals that the function for Mr. H. of reporting about his successes is to divert his attention away from feelings of imperfection, failure, or shame, to focus instead on feelings of grandeur and superiority, and to obtain the therapist's admiration in order to further buttress his grandiose feelings about himself. If one agrees that this grandiose inflation functions primarily as a defense against dysphoric affect, one would conclude that it is countertherapeutic for the therapist to mirror the grandiose expansive feelings and consequently collude in the patient's defense, since this defense prevents the patient from experiencing himself. The alternative to mirroring these expansive feelings is to simply not comment on them or to acknowledge the patient's apparent feeling as the therapist did in the previous example involving a physician showing off his medical expertise. If this lack of mirroring response is wounding to the patient, the therapist can then acknowledge and interpret the injury. More to the point, the therapist can acknowledge and perhaps interpret the patient's disappointment and his unmet need for recognition.

### The Search for Spontaneous Feeling

As is characteristic of narcissists, Mr. H. is unable to experience his own feelings. He has a sense that there is a missing piece from his life, but is unable to look inside and find out what it is. Instead, he seeks the admiration of others to convince him that he is worthwhile, and attempts in vain to make up for the wholeness that he lacks. Unless Mr. H. learns in therapy to experience what he feels, the therapy will not have addressed the root problem. The intellectualized process that took place in therapy not only ignored the problem, but it misled Mr. H. into thinking that he was on the right track, that feelings are not necessary for aliveness.

A first step for Mr. H. toward experiencing his inner feelings of worthlessness, inferiority, and emptiness would be to become aware of his vulnerability and the protective mechanisms on which he relies. With enough time and treatment, the impenetrable wall around him could begin to feel confining and could hopefully soften. Mr. H.

would become aware of the way he uses relationships in his life, and eventually he might begin to experience his genuine needs for emotional contact. In doing so he would develop a more realistic view of his therapist, see her as a separate person from himself, and allow himself to feel real feelings toward her. This recognition of separateness would begin subtly, perhaps first appearing in the form of an off-hand comment in which Mr. H. observes an idiosyncratic characteristic of the therapist that is different from himself; he might, for instance, notice for the first time a painting on the wall of her office and comment that he thinks it is interesting. His relationships with his therapist and others in his life would gradually become richer.

## A CLOSET NARCISSISTIC DISORDER

### Case Example—Mr. I.

Mr. I. is another example of a narcissistic patient who maintained an impenetrable wall around himself and his emotions. He was similar to Mr. H. in most respects, but differed in that he tried to hide his grandiose feelings. Patients like Mr. I. are often mistakenly perceived as healthier than they actually are. They are often obsessively thorough and tend to perform well in the business world, but have difficulty in relationships. Unlike Mr. H., whose need for idealization was obvious, patients like Mr. I. conceal their need to be admired, and often seek partners whom they themselves can idealize. Their object relations can appear at first to be fairly healthy because they focus intensely on other people; they are usually pleasant, easy to get along with, and reasonable. Only after closer examination does it become clear that their focus on others arises out of their inability to focus within themselves.

Mr. I. was a 39-year-old lawyer who came to therapy because he was concerned that he had been unsuccessful at finding a woman to whom he felt he could make a commitment. He felt he was getting older, and soon it would be too late to live a normal life, which to him meant marrying and having a family. From his point of view, he had no other problems in life. He did well in his job and received periodic promotions. He had many friends and acquaintances, and he felt he was well liked. For some reason, however, Mr. I. felt that the women he formed relationships with would always end up disappointing him.

He would eventually lose interest in them and begin to look for someone new. The longer a relationship went on, the harder it was for him to feel loving toward the woman. In each case, he could point to shortcomings in the woman that had led to his loss of interest. He did not believe that he was contributing to the failure of these relationships, although he had wondered about that possibility. When difficulties arose in his performance as a manager at work, he was presented with more evidence suggesting that he might have problems in relating to people. He believed that he had approached the job in a logical way, and was confused as to why his co-workers seemed to be having difficulty responding positively to his leadership.

It was clear that Mr. I. was having difficulty in asserting himself. He would choose attractive, aggressive, narcissistic women who would demand of him that he treat them with a deference to which they felt entitled. He would feel that many of their demands were unfair, but to avoid conflict he would nevertheless make an attempt at complying. As his resentment toward the women built, he would inwardly take an increasingly devaluing attitude toward them. Eventually, he would leave them.

As a child, Mr. I. was a model of excellent behavior and high achievement. His father and mother were very proud of him. His father, a surgeon, helped him to excel at sports, and his mother, an amateur photographer, encouraged him in scholastic and artistic endeavors. Both had unrealistically high expectations of Mr. I., however, and on those few occasions when his performance fell short, his parents were bitterly disappointed, acting as though he had betrayed them. Naturally, he obsessed about the possibility of even minor failures, and worked exceedingly hard to avoid disappointing his parents. This childhood pattern was repeated in the relationship Mr. I. developed with his therapist. To Mr. I., it seemed that his therapist could do no wrong. He felt understood and supported by her and was pleased to have her in his corner. He tried to be a model patient.

Mr. I.'s history is relatively mild compared to that of many closet narcissistic disorders. Many have had parents who were viciously attacking and disparaging without apparent reason or were simply absent. Sometimes because one or both of the parents were alcoholic or otherwise emotionally dysfunctional, and sometimes because the parent felt like a failure when compared to the child, the parents were continuously critical of the child. This type of child often grows into an adult who is constantly self-deprecatory and may even marry a spouse who is narcissistic and critical. Many times they claim to be unable to leave the spouse because they believe that leaving the spouse would represent an admission of failure.

Mr. I.'s attempts at being a model patient are similar to Mr. D.'s attempts to please his therapist (Chapter 3); however their motivations were quite different. While Mr. D. sought to remain in his therapist's good graces and avoid the necessity to explore his own thoughts and feelings, Mr. I. sought to uphold what he perceived to be his therapist's lofty standards, to be like his therapist, whom he idealized. While Mr. D. was trying to be "good," receive approval, and be liked, Mr. I. was seeking praise and trying to live up to his therapist's perceived high expectations.

**Differences from the Exhibitionistic Narcissist**

With some important exceptions, Mr. I. was very much like Mr. H., and could have responded well to similar treatment. One important difference between them was that while Mr. H. showed all the outward signs of a person who is commonly considered to be narcissistic, Mr. I. was a gentle, self-effacing type of person who would not fit the common stereotype of a narcissist. Another important difference is in the form of expression taken by their intolerance of separateness. With Mr. H., if the therapist was perceived as different than Mr. H., not perfectly in tune with him, he felt injured. With Mr. I., if the therapist made a remark that demonstrated a faulty understanding of him, Mr. I. tried to rationalize what had happened in a way that did not disturb his idealization of her.

For instance, both Mr. H. and Mr. I. would probably feel slighted if the therapist were to be late for a session. Mr. H. would be more likely to react with some form of acting out; however Mr. I. too might act out. Typically, they might arrive late to their next session, although it is likely that neither would be willing to admit a connection between his lateness and his therapist's. Mr. H.'s lateness would probably be an assertion of his grandiose sense of self-importance in response to the injury he suffered when his therapist treated him as if his time (and he himself) were not important. His lateness would probably also represent his attempt to protect himself from his therapist by withdrawing. For Mr. I., it would also be painful to be kept waiting past the time at which he felt entitled to begin his session, but he would not want to provoke the therapist by being exceptionally late and thereby allowing his grandiosity to leak out, so he would probably by late by only a few minutes. He might attempt to preserve his idealization of her by reasoning, for example, that perhaps her lateness had had to do with an emergency situation that had arisen at the hospital that only she could handle. Asked if he felt hurt or angry about the therapist's lateness, Mr. H. might respond with a devaluation, "Well, it was unprofessional" or, "I really didn't notice. What's a minute or two anyway?" while Mr. I. would be more likely to respond with a rationalization, "Well, I realized that something very important like an emergency must have been keeping you away."

### The Temptation to Confront

With a patient like Mr. I. with an idealizing transference, most interventions seem to work because he tries to find a way to embrace any comment the therapist might make. As a result, this sort of patient can easily be misdiagnosed and consequently inappropriately treated. For instance, Mr. I.'s therapist might mistakenly attribute to him a relatively highly developed capacity for self-evaluation, allowing her to believe it safe to question some of Mr. I.'s behaviors. If she did this, Mr. I. would think that she was being critical of the way he was conducting himself. For instance, she might ask him why he continues to give in to demands that he feels are unfair, pointing out that his lack of self-assertion encourages women to escalate their demands on him. He would take this confrontation to be criticism for the way he is handling the situation and pressure for him to express himself to his girlfriend. Although he might respond by agreeing with the therapist's perception, he would withdraw emotionally. For example, instead of exploring his feelings about this situation or what it might be like for him to express himself to his girlfriend, he is likely to focus attention away from himself by telling more stories about the way that his girlfriend mistreats him, and wondering out loud how anyone could be so crass and insensitive as his girlfriend is being. Privately, he would probably feel that his complaints apply as well to his therapist, that she has criticized him for not standing up to his girlfriend. He experiences the therapist's comments as demands and he becomes reluctant to expose himself to further criticism by sharing with her his insecurities and fears. Instead he tries to stick with subjects that he feels will be more acceptable to her.

## ORIGINS OF THE NARCISSISTIC DISORDER

Theorists disagree about the timing and nature of the origins of the narcissistic disorder.

### Kohut's Theory about Etiology

Kohut characterizes narcissism as a component of everyone's psyche. He sees the characteristics of mature narcissism as useful and positive and considers the maturation of infantile narcissism into adult narcissism to be a lifelong process. He says that like a child, an adult, too, continues to look for other adults to idealize and attempts to find other adults who will confirm her positive sense of herself. At any point during this lifelong process, Kohut believes an arrest can occur. According to him there is a natural process of maturation whereby infantile narcissism develops into mature narcissism through the process of *transmuting internalizations*. This is a process in which a person develops internal structure to compensate for the lack of sufficient external structure. Normally, a person's frustrations are managed through her own internal self-organizing functions and through organizing functions provided by others. If the frustrations with which the person is struggling overwhelm the combination of these organizing functions, the person's internal organization begins to lose cohesion (fall apart) and the person experiences *fragmentation*. If the frustration is only slightly more than the person's normal ability to manage using available internal and external sources, the frustration is considered an *optimal frustration*. Such a frustration requires that the person stretch her own abilities slightly to acquire the necessary capacity to handle the frustration. This stretching takes the form of developing of additional self-organizing functions that are then available in the future to help with other frustrations. In this way, through transmuting internalizations, the person develops an ever greater capacity.

An excellent example of this process is offered when parents attempt to teach infants to sleep through the night. Normally an infant wakes up four or five times a night. If he is unable to soothe himself and put himself back to sleep the infant cries for his parents to soothe him. A process that is currently popular for teaching the baby to go back to sleep without crying for his parents is for the parents to let him cry 3 minutes before going into his room to comfort him. The next time the delay is increased to 5 minutes, and gradually it is increased until the infant learns to put himself back to sleep. Videos of the baby's response to this process show that he gradually develops a way to organize himself and go back to sleep. He may arrange his stuffed animals or his blankets in a particular way or position himself in a comforting way. In other words, the level of frustration is gently increased until it becomes optimal, and the baby then develops his own ability to organize and soothe himself so that he can go back to sleep.

It is clear that when parents respond immediately to the slightest frustration, the baby learns to rely on them and not on himself. If the parents do not respond adequately the baby has a difficult time with trust and other problems are created. Similarly, as a baby grows into a child, if the parent is grossly disruptive to the child's narcissistic fantasies, the resultant hurt and injury may be too large for the child to compensate for internally, so that transmuting internalization does not occur and the maturation of the child's narcissism is impeded. To Kohut, the adult narcissist's condition represents an arrest in a healthy growth process that needs only to be restimulated by the proper supportive environment.

Kohut's views went through significant change during his professional career, from the 1930s to his death in 1981. He ended up with a view of narcissism as developing along two related but independent tracks, or poles. Each pole corresponded to one of the two narcissistic transferences he had identified. The pole involving self-esteem, feelings, and empathy relates to the maternal function of mirroring that the adult narcissist seeks through the mirror transference. The pole involving confidence, values, competency, goals, and ambition relates to idealization, usually tending to involve a paternal function, which the adult narcissist seeks through the idealizing transference. Ultimately, Kohut seemed to abandon the traditional concept of psychotherapy in favor of a process similar in scope to the supportive psychotherapy described in the previous chapter, helping the patient to adapt successfully without necessarily working through. He pointed out that the two poles of the bipolar self can compensate for each other; someone low in self-esteem, for instance, can compensate by becoming more successful and ambitious. On the other hand, a person who has great self-esteem will not feel driven to prove himself through the pursuing of lofty goals. Kohut's treatment process allowed for the reenforcement of one side of the bipolar self to compensate for the other.

## Kernberg's Theory about Etiology

Kernberg uses Mahler's developmental model and posits that pathological narcissism is a form of borderline condition that results from a severe frustration of the infant's attempts at rapprochement, which causes the infant to regress back to the phase of development that Mahler terms the *practicing subphase*.[4] During the rapprochement subphase, the toddler is trying to separate from the mother. If these efforts, however, are severely frustrated, Kernberg claims that the toddler can adapt by "re-fusing," returning to the earlier stage of development of the practicing subphase in which the child feels omnipotent and expects the world to revolve around him. Kernberg believes that the adult narcissist's condition represents not an arrest in the normal maturation of youthful narcissism as Kohut claims, but a fixation, a failure to pass successfully through one of the developmental periods (rapprochement) of early childhood, resulting in a pathological distortion of youthful narcissism and an inability to master the challenges of more mature developmental tasks. The adult narcissist maintains the infantile fantasy of being merged with the object.

## The "Fixation" Argument

Kernberg (1975) presents an interesting argument to support his contention that the narcissist's condition is pathological and results from a fixation early in childhood development. He points to the behavior of the narcissist and that of the two-and-a-half-year-old child and argues that the narcissist's behavior is not an extension of the child's but a pathological distortion. He points out that two-and-a-half-year-olds are not as impervious to reason, as coldly rejecting in their anger, or as uncaring as the adult narcissist.

[4]This is the phase in which the toddler experiences the omnipotent caregiver as his home base. During this phase, the "world is his oyster"; he goes off to conquer the world but constantly looks back to make sure his mother, the source of his omnipotence and well-being, is still there. He looks to her for confirmation and reassuring admiration. He experiences the world as revolving around him, and absolutely expects his needs and wishes to be granted. As he explores and conquers his environment, he is prone to dash off from his caretaker but frequently returns for "refueling." This is in contrast to the rapprochement subphase in which the toddler becomes both more independent and more aware of his dependency. He feels more vulnerable and needs to control the amount of closeness and distance between himself and others.

Kernberg's assessment of two-and-a-half-year-olds is questionable in my opinion and it is not clear why the differences he points out support his conclusions. It is difficult to imagine that someone whose maturation has been arrested at such an early age would not, during the course of adaptation to later life, develop serious personality distortions that would need to be addressed before the normal maturational process could be resumed. These distortions would account for the legitimate differences pointed out by Kernberg between pathological adult narcissism and healthy infantile narcissism.

## Masterson's Theory about Etiology

Masterson, also using Mahler's model, sees the narcissistic disorder as originating during the practicing subphase rather than a regression from rapprochement. The practical impact this difference has on treatment is significant. Masterson sees the narcissist as having a more primitive disorder than the borderline, and suggests a more cautious approach to the treatment of the narcissist than does Kernberg, who views narcissists as having a borderline structure and being able to respond to many of the same techniques of treatment as the borderline disorder. Although disagreeing with Kohut's approach to treatment, Masterson supports the point of view that the narcissistic disorder represents an arrest in the development of healthy narcissism.[5]

## Comparing Apples and Oranges

This discussion of the ways of looking at narcissism is additionally complicated by the fact that the followers of Kohut and the followers of Kernberg use different definitions for borderline and narcissist conditions, so that it is difficult to be certain to which patients their differences in treatment approach actually apply. Furthermore, Kohut and Kernberg worked in radically different clinical settings with very different patient populations. Most of Kohut's experience was gained as a psychiatrist in outpatient private practice, seeing patients who

---

[5]Masterson (1981) writes, "My own opinion is that the narcissistic disorder is a developmental arrest, since in treatment the patient's abandonment depression or fragmentation of self can be precipitated either by his own efforts towards self-expression or self-individuation. It is this latter that suggests a true developmental arrest of individuation has occurred" (p. 26).

represented the healthier end of the patient spectrum. In contrast, Kernberg worked in an inpatient hospital setting with relatively disturbed patients; his patients often appeared to be on the maturity level of antisocial disorders. It is not surprising that Kernberg saw the narcissism of his patients as pathological while Kohut viewed his patients as children whose psychological growing up had been temporarily interrupted.

The difference in treatment conditions may also contribute to the differences in treatment styles. In Kohut's private practice, his patients paid for each session and attended by their own choice. Kohut's style could not be overly offensive to them or they might not come back. In contrast, Kernberg's style had an aggressive quality that might not be tolerated very long by a patient in an outpatient setting. Kernberg did not need to address issues relating to his patients' acting out because the hospital's omnipresent nursing staff served to control patients' acting out behavior. Masterson, working first in a hospital setting and then in private practice, seems to have chosen a compromise style. By addressing patients' defenses, he exerts a significant amount of therapeutic pressure, bringing up dysphoric affect in patients. However, he does this in a gentle way that permits the patient to feel supported and understood by the therapist.

## Clinical Implications

The distinction between these theoretical points of view is important clinically because the one that a therapist accepts will influence the direction of treatment he chooses. Kernberg's style, for instance, seems to reflect his point of view in that he aggressively attacks the narcissist's defenses and interprets what he believes to be the narcissist's pathological negative transference consisting of aggression and envy. Masterson disagrees with Kernberg's theoretical orientation, but he essentially agrees with his approach to treatment of narcissistic disorders[6] in that he emphasizes the importance of addressing narcissists' defenses. His approach seems gentler than Kernberg's, however;

[6]Masterson (1981) writes, "Although I disagree with Kernberg's view of the origins of the narcissistic personality, I share his view of the clinical picture and his psychotherapeutic approach with the reservation that the 'systematic analysis' of the negative transference emphasizes the interpretation of the patient's exquisite need for perfect mirroring or idealizing and his profound disappointment and rage when this need is frustrated by the reality of the therapist" (p. 27).

he attempts to interpret the patient's defenses using a *mirroring interpretation* technique that is intended to help the patient feel understood and safe while his regressive defenses are gradually being dismantled and replaced by more mature ones. Kohut, believing that the condition is an arrest, attempts to create through treatment a situation that would support the patient in taking up anew the maturational process. Using as a model the type of healthy environment that is normally present during the typical successful maturation of an infant's narcissism, he concludes that the patient needs the therapist to play the symbolic role of an omnipotent protector and the supportive role of someone who understands the patient's experience and appreciates his attempts to master the world around him. In general, his attitude toward defenses was that they would fall away naturally as the patient felt understood and safe and no longer felt the need for them during the treatment hour.

## TREATMENT OF THE NARCISSISTIC DISORDER

### Focus on the Self

Most theorists believe that when working with a narcissist, the clinician should focus as much as possible on the patient's experience within the session itself. Comments about external situations that the patient describes can be problematic in many ways. Since the therapist wants to convey to the patient a point of view that favors internal exploration as a strategy to deal with life problems, comments about external situations reinforce the opposite position. In addition, comments about the patient's feelings and behavior in external situations can easily be taken by the narcissistic patient as critical. Even asking a simple informational question like, "What did you say to her?" or "Why do you think she said that?" can be taken as an indication that there is something that the patient did not consider in making the choices that he did, or that the patient could have made a better choice. So the processing of the external behavior of a narcissistic disorder should not be done without good purpose because it can eventually undermine the patient's rapport with the therapist.

Focusing the narcissistic patient on her experience within the session is not often easy. The patient will be pulling to focus the discussion on how other people have wronged her or on why she is righteously correct about the things that she has done. She is unlikely to talk about any dysphoric feelings other than in a possible glancing reference, except if she is fragmenting, in which case she will be feeling like a failure—empty, worthless, and deflated. If the patient has come to therapy because she feels as though her life has fallen apart, she may make repeated references to being a worthless failure with a meaningless life. However, the negative terms that she herself uses should be used only very carefully by the therapist. Because the narcissistic patient refers to herself in negative terms does not give the therapist license to use those same terms with respect to the patient, especially if the patient is suddenly feeling more positive about herself. For instance, it is common for a narcissistic patient who is experiencing the negative part of the narcissistic split to berate herself; in the next session, however, if her grandiosity has been restored, those terms that seemed accurate in the first session would feel alien and deflating.

To focus the discussion on the narcissist's present experience requires a sensitive understanding of what the narcissist actually is experiencing. The therapist needs to be sensitive to the patient's injuries and how the patient defends against hurt, the patient's disappointments and how they are nonverbally expressed, the patient's therapeutic transference and what he expects from the therapist, the patient's attitude toward relationships and what other people's responses mean to him, the patient's reason for being in treatment and whether the present treatment process serves that purpose, the patient's general family-of-origin scripting and how it plays itself out with the therapist, the patient's view of his self, and how this view is expressed in treatment. All of these are aspects of the patient's experience to which the therapist can make reference, offering the patient insight into himself and focusing his attention on his present experience.

Most theorists believe that processing the patient's injuries as they inevitably occur during the treatment hour is an excellent way to address the patient's present experience. In watching for injuries and in interpreting them, it is useful for the therapist to keep in mind the type of transference in which the patient is engaged. With an active idealizing transference, injuries are likely to take the form of disappointments caused by apparent errors or fallibility displayed by the therapist that interfere with the patient's idealization of the therapist. Injuries with a mirroring transference are likely to take the form of minor or major ruptures to the merger fantasy caused by empathic failures on the part of the therapist, instances in which the therapist has improperly understood or reflected the patient's experience. In either case, the patient will probably cover up the actual wound so that the therapist will not notice it; instead, the therapist must look for the patient's distancing and devaluing defenses against the pain produced by an injury, and work backwards from there to discover that an injury has occurred, and what caused it.

Distancing defenses are of course almost always active with narcissists even when there has been no immediate injury. Sometimes distancing can take the form of intellectualization or dutiful compliance in the service of mirroring the therapist's perceived expectations. If there is a consistent lack of affect in the patient's work, the defensive character of the work will be clear. However, sometimes essentially defensive work can appear remarkably genuine, including affect, insights, and memories. To evaluate whether affect-laden work is truly therapeutic, a therapist should look for all of the following qualities:

1. The patient's therapeutic struggle should be motivated by his primary real-life conflict. For instance, if an adult patient is seriously abusing alcohol and is working in therapy on problems relating to his relationship with his mother, unless this is tied into a concern about the alcohol abuse, the entire issue of the mother is probably being used as a further avoidance of the alcohol problem. Similarly if a person is out of work and his finances are in disarray and the work in therapy focuses instead on how other people are not responsive to his needs, no matter how affectively painful this issue seems, it is probably a defensive avoidance of the deeply painful issues involved in making an effort to take care of himself.
2. Sustained work should lead to behavioral changes in the patient's life outside of treatment.
3. If sustained work is genuine, the patient should experience anxiety or depression between sessions. Patients who simply enjoy therapeutic exploration are not experiencing emotional conflict, and are probably experiencing transference gratification instead.
4. As work deepens over time, there should be continuity between sessions both in content and in affect. Some patients make a point of beginning each session with the issue that was being discussed when the last session ended. However, there is no affective continuity; in this case the content continuity is being

used defensively by the patient to avoid having to look internally for direction.

5. If the work includes memories, there should be a natural movement back and forth between present and past, because sustained historical exploration without present affective motivation is not likely to be spontaneous.
6. Sustained affective work should eventually bring up memories, dreams, or other evidence of deepening.

Although all patients tend to begin treatment with some degree of skepticism about whether it can help, narcissists are especially skeptical. They tend to see their problems as originating in their environment rather than in themselves, and they often begin treatment feeling superior to the therapist and questioning whether they themselves are not more capable of solving their problems than the therapist. They also often expect the therapist's attempts at helpful input to take the form of advice, and they doubt whether the therapist can tell them anything they haven't already thought of. What then keeps a narcissist coming back to treatment initially? There are several possibilities, most of which boil down to the relationship between therapist and patient.

**Kohut's Approach**

Kohut viewed treatment as a re-creation of the conditions that are necessary for the development of healthy narcissism. Consequently, as a therapist with a *self psychology* orientation listens to a patient, the therapist tries to fit the patient's comments into a context of childhood development, and then attempts to provide the selfobject functions that this child would have needed from his parent during the appropriate childhood developmental stage. The therapist maintains a neutral stance and looks for the emergence of selfobject transferences. As they emerge, he looks for chance interruptions to the transference. He interprets the patient's experience of these interruptions so that the patient can understand her feelings and how she responds. The therapist's interpretations are often genetic; by referring to the patient's history, the therapist attempts to explain and normalize the patient's behavior and affect.

Kohut did not see the selfobject function that the therapist provides as a curative element as much as an external structure that allows the patient to maintain his internal cohesion. The actual cure comes from the patient's building of his own structure, which happens in small increments during periods when the structure supplied by the therapist is inadvertently interrupted. If the interruptions to the therapist's selfobject function are not so severe as to overwhelm the patient's deficient internal structure, they function as optimal frustrations, and lead to the patient's development of his own internal structure to make up for the interrupted selfobject function.

## Masterson's Approach

Masterson advocates an approach to treating narcissistic personalities that primarily uses mirroring interpretations. Like his approach to treating borderline personalities, he bases his approach upon a careful tracking of the patient's use of defenses. Like his work with borderlines, he looks for a triad consisting of an event that is connected to dysphoric affect, followed by the associated dysphoric affect, followed by defense against the affect. The event in the case of borderline personalities is self-activation that brings on abandonment depression. In the case of narcissistic personalities it is a wound caused by imperfect mirroring (empathic failure) on the part of a significant object (like the therapist), a mistake leading to an interruption in the patient's idealization of a significant object (like the therapist), or by interference with the patient's grandiosity. The resulting wound exposes the patient's feelings of inadequacy or pain and leads to renewed defense. If the injury is so great that it overwhelms the patient's defenses, the patient is likely to fragment.

When a session begins, Masterson does not intervene until he can see evidence of some kind of narcissistic wound. Then he observes how the patient defends against the wound; the defense is usually immediate. Often the patient begins the session in defense, and the therapist listens for clues that can help him piece together the injury that precipitated the defense. When this sequence is clearly established, he makes a mirroring interpretation of the wound, the resulting pain, and the protective mechanism (defense) used by the patient; in mirroring the wound, he tries to focus as much as possible on how the patient feels about himself. For example, "A moment ago, you were indicating some of your concerns about the success of your project at work. You are very upset about the possibility of failing in the project; it makes you feel bad about yourself to even think about it, so you attempted to restore your positive feeling by shifting the subject to one of your successes, the award the company is winning." In the context of the selfobject transference, this patient hopes to feel better about himself by impressing the therapist and gaining the therapist's admiration. As the patient's use of the therapist as a selfobject becomes more clearly elaborated in the treatment through interpretations of the patient's disappointment when the therapist fails to provide that function, the therapist's mirroring interpretations can become more sharply focused.

This type of intervention has much to recommend it. The mirroring component helps the patient to feel understood. At the same time the intervention succeeds in pointing out the patient's defense without sounding critical. Unlike a confrontation that simply points out a defense to the patient, and that the narcissistic patient takes as a negative judgment of his behavior, this intervention seeks to explain why the patient protects himself the way he does, thereby helping the patient to feel understood rather than judged.

Before making a mirroring interpretation, the therapist needs to have identified clearly in the session a dysphoric affect and a defense against it. There are sessions, however, in which the narcissistic patient is grandiose the entire session and does not acknowledge any dysphoric affect or negative situation. Some patients can go on for weeks or even months in this pattern. It is generally unwise for a therapist to puncture a narcissist's grandiosity, because the patient will find it severely wounding and is likely to perceive the therapist as attacking or vicious. This leaves few options for the therapist in those sessions in which the patient continuously mobilizes her grandiose defense.

These sessions require of the therapist particular patience and skill. For example, a female patient in her mid-thirties came into a session feeling elated about having gotten a new job. All she could talk about is how perfect this job was; there was no hint of introspection or of any dysphoric affect. The therapist could find no opening and made no intervention the entire session except to acknowledge the patient's obvious excitement about her new job. Then, as the patient was leaving, the therapist noticed that she had left her eyeglasses on the table. He said, "You forgot your glasses," to which she responded with an expression of surprise and embarrassment saying, "Oh, how clumsy of me." This response presented the therapist with a slight seam in the grandiose armor and offered the opportunity for him to intervene. He commented, "You are so excited about the things that are happening to you that this is all you have been able to think about; in the process you seem to have forgotten a part of yourself." The patient smiled with a mixture of amusement and recognition. In this example, the patient is defending throughout the session and in a moment of surprise she is embarrassed and labels herself "clumsy," giving the therapist the opportunity to interpret the defense (her focus on the excitement of the external world) and how it takes her away from her self.

## COMPARISON OF TWO APPROACHES TO TREATMENT

Masterson's and Kohut's approaches to treatment appear to work at cross-purposes to each other. With most narcissistic disorders, the therapist's mirroring of the patient will encourage a mirror transference; the patient, who openly or secretly maintains his grandiosity and belief in his own superiority, sees the therapist as being a person of like mind. The therapist's mirroring encourages the patient's internal distortion of the relationship; the patient internally blurs the boundaries between patient and therapist and sees the therapist as an extension of himself.[7] According to Masterson, mirroring of the patient is regressive and unnecessary on the part of the therapist; if the therapist encourages this blurring of boundaries, he discourages the development of autonomy and an ability for the narcissistic patient to manage himself using his own internal resources. Kohut's contention is that people are never independent of the need for affirmation and approval from other people, and that through transmuting internalizations the patient will slowly develop internal structure that will enable him to reduce his inordinate dependency on others' admiration to a healthier level.

As a more concrete illustration of these different approaches to treatment of narcissistic personalities, suppose a forty-year-old female narcissistic patient describes to her therapist her difficulties in disciplining her five-year-old daughter. In the characteristic fashion of a narcissistic personality, however, she frames the problem as belonging entirely to her daughter: "She is willful, disrespectful, and rebellious."

[7]Meissner (1959) states, "Kohut uses such terms as merger or symbiosis to describe this extension but reminds us that what is at issue here is not merger with an idealized object, but rather a regressive diffusion of the borders of the self to embrace the analyst who is then experienced as united to the grandiose self" (p. 416).

As an example, the patient explains that her daughter protests whenever the patient makes rules about where her daughter is permitted to ride her bicycle, and then the child ignores the rules, riding her bicycle wherever she pleases, including in the street. It is not uncommon for narcissistic personalities to show extremely poor judgment as parents because they have tremendous difficulties being empathic and sensitive to the experience of the child, because they are unclear about how they feel themselves, because they are extremely uncomfortable with conflict, and because they perceive the child as a miniature copy of themselves. These situations present problems for the therapist, because it is difficult for the therapist to suggest that the patient might have a role in the situation without the patient hearing that suggestion as critical and judgmental.

Some therapists, including some who follow Kohut, will simply avoid addressing the danger inherent in the situation that the patient describes. Their attitude might be that the particular situation is probably only one of many like it and that the patient must be given time to progress in treatment until she gains better parenting skills and judgment. Such a therapist might respond to the above patient by mirroring, "You are upset because she seems to be beyond control" or "You feel so upset when limits are placed on your freedom, perhaps it is upsetting for you to place limits on your daughter." Other therapists might add to this last intervention, "even if they might contribute to her safety." However, for many Kohutians, this addition might be perceived as unempathic and a potential interference to the selfobject transference. Kernberg might focus directly on the patient's aggressive drives and her defenses against them: "You are so afraid of your own rage at your daughter's disregard of your wishes that you avoid confronting her." Masterson might use a mirroring interpretation to address the defense: "It is so painful for you when your daughter accuses you of being unfair, that you protect yourself by not enforcing the rules you make for her."

Some aspects of Kohut's approach may not be as far from those of Masterson and Kernberg as one might think. Although Kohut believed that the therapist must allow the patient's idealization and merger fantasies to develop and grow, he cautioned against artificially cultivating them. He wrote (Kohut 1968), "In the analytic treatment of the ordinary case of narcissistic personality disturbance, however, the active encouragement of idealization is not desirable" (p. 102). Similarly, with respect to the narcissist's needs for mirroring he wrote, "Nongratification of the intensified and distorted need while yet acknowledging appropriateness of its precursor in childhood constitutes optimal frustration for the analysand" (1987, p. 176). He pointed out that as a result of developmental arrest of healthy narcissism, a person will develop defenses that are maladaptive. "The thorough investigation of the various resistances mobilized by the analysand against the reactivation of the old narcissistic needs is, in my view, of greatest importance. . . . They are transference resistances and, as long as they are in the ascendancy, stand in the way of the central working through process of the analysis" (pp. 176–177).

In practice, however, it appears that many therapists who characterize themselves as Kohutians do in fact gratify the patient's distorted need. It is difficult to find published examples of actual transcriptions of Kohutian treatment. Goldberg's *The Psychology of the Self—A Casebook* is an attempt to describe Kohutian treatment as practiced by six prominent Kohutian analysts. Although there is virtually no transcript material in it, the book contains extensive descriptions of therapeutic process, and in places there are detailed enough descriptions of the therapist's interventions to conclude that such gratification is practiced. For instance, in a description of the treatment of a patient with a merger transference, the analyst describes what appears to be an example of the therapist mirroring the patient's grandiosity: "As he calmed down enough to sit, he said that the real hell of feeling this way is that he knows he is childish, but he is unable to prevent it. At the end of the hour, he got up and asked me to come to the window to see his new (i.e., used) jeep. I admired it, and he was pleased" (p. 387). The next paragraph begins, "He wonders about dating my secretary, but decides he is setting a trap for me in that he expects my permission, approval, and guidance. . ." (p. 387).[8] While the book's explanation of the therapist's willingness to admire the patient's jeep is reasonable, I cannot help but believe that the idea of dating the therapist's secretary and expecting the therapist's approval is grandiose and implies that the therapist's response at the end of the previous session did not encourage the patient's grandiosity, in this case a distorted need.

[8]Further on in the text, the significance of this last line is described as follows: "His fantasies of dating the analyst's secretary appear to be motivated by more than simple displacement or revenge out of frustration or guilt; it may be evidence of the desire to demonstrate his ability to manage a better relationship by himself. Here is perhaps a hint of the incipient grandiose self: 'I deserve your secretary: you should help me to obtain her!' Over the course of the next several months' work one might anticipate the further dissolution of the primitive merger transference, and the beginning of a more mature phase of grandiose self" (p. 391).

## Comparison of the Masterson Approach with Self Psychology

To further clarify some of the differences in the way Masterson and the self psychologists do treatment, consider the larger vignette from which the previous quotation was taken:

> As a result of an unavoidable cancellation on my part he became furious, saying, "When you're here, I can act sensibly in my own behalf. Without you I can't think of anything except the immediate, urgent situation of the moment." The next trauma was the cancellation of his scholarship funds for the coming two-month summer session, during which he had planned to be in residence at his former university completing work on his thesis. He came in, threw the letter from Washington in my lap, and confessed to enraged fantasies of "bombing the Capitol," while pacing back and forth. He became more frantic, finally pleading with me, "Doctor, please help me. I am going to explode." I talked to him about how reasonable his disappointment was over having the grant withdrawn after it had been promised, connecting this to previous experiences of disappointment with his mother, when she failed to maintain his self-esteem. As he calmed down enough to sit, he said that the real hell of feeling this way is that he knows he is childish, but he is unable to prevent it. At the end of the hour, he got up and asked me to come to the window to see his new (i.e., used) jeep. I admired it, and he was pleased.
>
> He wonders about dating my secretary, but decides he is setting a trap for me in that he expects my permission, approval, and guidance. He would be outraged and enraged if I were to take over those functions, but disappointed if I didn't. [Goldberg 1978, pp. 387-388]

Kohutian therapists would see this patient as having a structural deficit that makes him incapable of organizing his thoughts without the help of the therapist as selfobject (Stern's self-regulating other). Rather than see his raging and threatening as defensive, they would see it as part of his unsuccessful attempt to organize himself.[9] Indeed, the therapist's interpretation calms the patient down, presumably by

---

[9]Much of the discussion about this section of *The Psychology of the Self—A Casebook* is taken from talks with Marian Tolpin, one of the authors, that took place during the 1989 conference in San Francisco sponsored by the Masterson Institute that attempted to compare Masterson's approach with that of Peter Sifneos and that of self psychology as represented by Tolpin.

normalizing his profound sense of disappointment. The fact that the patient's sense of entitlement leads him to an unreasonable level of outrage over this disappointment is not central when considered in light of his overall difficulty with internal organization; for the therapist to succeed in helping the patient to regain a sense of cohesion is for this patient an achievement. The commentary in the book makes it clear that this patient is viewed as experiencing a "primitive merger transference" (p. 391) that predates the development of "a more mature phase of grandiose self" (p. 391). The Kohutian therapist might compare the patient's raging to the tantrum of a two-year-old who is unable to soothe himself and compensate for a disruption to his sense of self. Just as the parent would attempt to calm the child down out of empathy for him and wanting to help to relieve him of a painful experience, so the therapist has a similar response to a patient with a significant structural deficit. Furthermore, the Kohutian would point out that this patient's ideal is self-reliance. To come to treatment is itself shameful, and to ask the therapist, "Doctor, please help me," must be extraordinarily difficult and shameful to the patient. From the Kohutian therapist's perspective, to respond to this request in any way that might be interpreted as rejecting would make it that much more difficult for the patient to utilize the therapist's selfobject functions in the future. Subsequently, when the patient requests that the therapist come to the window and admire his new car, most Kohutian therapists would say that this is a judgment call. They see it as a minimal request in the context of the intensity of the session, and they are not particularly concerned about promoting a pattern of future demands from the patient for gratification, because if such a pattern were to emerge, it could then be interpreted. Furthermore, from their perspective, the patient's request that the therapist admire his new car is like the two-year-old saying, "Hey, Mom, look at me," asking for the kind of admiration that contributes to the building of self-esteem and healthy grandiosity. The commentary in the book is consistent with this idea, indicating that the patient's subsequent thoughts about dating the therapist's secretary are considered to be evidence of the "incipient grandiose self," positing that the patient is thinking along the line, "I deserve your secretary; you should help me to obtain her!" The primitive merger transference then in place is thought to be about to give way to a "more mature phase of grandiose self" (p. 391).

The Masterson perspective on this vignette would be that the loss of the grant has interfered with the patient's grandiose self representation, injured and temporarily caused him to experience the negative part of his split self representation of emptiness and worthlessness. He is desperately attempting to restore his grandiose self-image by becoming outraged, throwing the letter into the therapist's lap, pacing the floor, and having fantasies of bombing the Capitol. This behavior is considered transference acting out because the patient takes these various actions to discharge rather than feel the painful feelings that have been stimulated by this disappointment. Finally he turns to the therapist, pleading for help before he explodes. When the therapist responds to this request by validating the patient's disappointment without reflecting the meaning of the request or acknowledging the defensive aspect of the outrage, Masterson would say the therapist is engaging in transference gratification, which is then repeated in the therapist's subsequent admiring of the patient's new car. In other words, the therapist is gratifying the patient's request as if it were reality based, ignoring its meaning within the transference.

It should be noted that the above patient did not say, "I deserve your secretary; you should help me to obtain her!" He said that he expects the therapist to approve. Undeniably it would be countertherapeutic gratification for the therapist to actually approve. We must conclude that the therapist's immediately prior action, approving of the car, has led this patient to expect the therapist to gratify him in his fantasy about the therapist's secretary, so the patient sees the therapist's approval in both these instances as having similar meaning.

Whether the patient is exhibitionistic or closet, Masterson would probably have responded with a mirroring interpretation in which he mirrors the patient's pain and points out the defense the patient is using to protect against the pain. In either case, the mirroring interpretation is intended to have the calming effect of a truly empathic mirroring comment as well as the added benefit of helping the patient to be more conscious of the nature of his protective reactions. For instance, assuming previous interpretations have established an acknowledgment of some of the patient's underlying pain, the therapist might say to the closet narcissist, "The withdrawal of your grant has been intensely disappointing. It feels to you like a terrible injustice and it has brought up in you overwhelmingly painful feelings that you are attempting to manage by focusing your attention angrily at Washington, by pacing the floor in my office, and by turning to me for help." The exhibitionistic narcissist is more concerned with entitlement. To him, Masterson might say, "The loss of the grant money to which you feel you are entitled is overwhelmingly disappointing to you; you feel that your value is being ignored, so you turn to me in the hope that I can help you to feel better." The Kohutian therapist's actual response of agreeing with the patient's indignant sense of entitlement constitutes, from the Masterson point of view, a gratification of the patient's defensive demand that the therapist mirror his grandiosity. Although the therapist says that the patient's disappointment is understandable, the degree of the patient's outrage actually represents a distorted perception of reality involving inordinate grandiosity and entitlement. A Kohutian would apparently not think of this behavior as grandiose, and certainly not evidence of pathological grandiosity. Despite Kohut's stated opposition to supporting the patient's fantasies of merger with the therapist, the therapist's response in this vignette suggests that in practice Kohutian therapists may support such a fantasy. This vignette seems at least to be a case of the therapist attempting to cultivate a mirror transference as does the therapist's subsequent gratification of the patient's request that he come to the window and admire the patient's new car.

One of the clearest differences between the Masterson approach and self psychology is that although the two approaches seem to share a fair amount of agreement about the nature of the narcissist's use of other people and external structures to provide direction when this occurs outside of the treatment hour, they have very different perceptions of the meaning of the patient's turning toward the therapist for direction within the treatment hour. The Kohutians see it as a normal attempt to compensate for an internal structural deficit by using the therapist as a selfobject; they normalize it by interpreting to the patient that it is an attempt to fulfill natural needs for attachment, needs to which his parents did not respond adequately during the patient's childhood. Masterson sees this turning toward the therapist as an example of a defensive attempt of the borderline to avoid feelings of separation and separateness, or of the narcissist to avoid feelings of emptiness and worthlessness by obtaining admiration from the therapist. As such, he confronts with a borderline and uses a mirroring interpretation with a narcissist to focus on it as a defense.

A sensible compromise between these two approaches might be to consider the purpose of the patient's turning toward the therapist. If the patient is attempting to use the therapist as a selfobject to help stabilize himself so that he can manage his feelings, this would not be considered defensive, because the patient is using the therapist's selfobject function to help him to experience himself. If, on the other hand, the patient is turning to the therapist in an effort to shift the focus of attention away from himself, this would be considered defensive. For example, in *Ordinary People*, when Conrad suggests that he be given tranquilizers, he is looking for an alternative to exploring his feelings in treatment; his turning to the therapist is defensive.

Both the Masterson approach and self psychology recognize healthy and pathological grandiosity as well as healthy attempts at attachment and pathological clinging. The difference is where they draw the line between healthy and pathological. There is a fair degree of agreement about grandiosity. However, the self psychologists, as demonstrated in the above vignette, would be more likely to view a particular grandiose behavior as healthy than would the Masterson approach.

A criticism by many self psychologists of Kernberg's approach, and Masterson's as well, is that they begin their surgery on the patient before the anesthetic has been applied.[10] Kernberg's approach is fairly extreme, but Masterson's approach also brings up intense discomfort in the patient in the form of depression. The self psychologist would prefer to let the patient discover this depression in the process of trying to contact his real self, rather than as a result of the therapist's targeting of defenses. The borderline patient has more observing ego than the narcissistic patient, and is more capable of maintaining a perspective on the emotional pain uncovered through treatment. The narcissist, however, has more of a tendency to view this pain as having been created by the treatment, and will want to manage the pain by terminating treatment. The stability of the treatment must therefore continually be kept in mind, especially if there is a rupture in the patient's selfobject transference. Masterson advocates repeated interpretation of the narcissistic personality's wish to withdraw as a defense against her painful sense of defectiveness associated with the dysphoric feelings that arise in treatment. The patient's motivation to endure the painful affect that arises as a result of curtailment of defenses can be maximized if the therapist successfully relates these defenses to the

[10]"The rational aims of therapy could not, by themselves, persuade the vulnerable ego of the narcissistically fixated analysand to forego denial and acting out and to face and to examine the needs and claims of the archaic grandiose self. . . . a mirror transference must be established. If it does not develop, the patient's grandiosity remains concentrated upon the grandiose self, the ego's defensive position remains rigid, and ego expansion cannot take place" (Kohut 1968, p. 98).

patient's presenting problems. With the preservation of treatment in mind, Masterson also advises against opening up new areas of exploration immediately preceding a vacation or other interruption in treatment.

## OBSTACLES TO TREATMENT

One significant difficulty in treating a narcissistic disorder is finding a way to keep the patient in treatment. The patient usually comes in because his defenses have been overwhelmed by some major disappointment in life. Although he is attending and paying his money, he usually is very skeptical about whether therapy can help. He believes that his problems have arisen from external situations that are beyond his control. Furthermore, he believes that the solutions to his problems lie in finding a way to change those external situations, not in introspection. It usually doesn't take too long before the narcissist finds a way to change those situations or is able to deny the importance of whatever injury brought him into treatment. Consequently, the therapist often has a fairly small window of opportunity to work with these patients before they have found a way to restore their grandiose protective shield and can no longer see the need for treatment. During that time, if the patient is not able to see the root of his problems as originating within himself, his motivation for introspection will be severely limited.

In the early stages of treatment, the motivations for a narcissistic patient to remain in treatment are that he believes that there is something wrong with him that therapy can fix and he finds his relationship with the therapist to be soothing. The therapist, in her approach to treatment, must strike a balance between these two motivators. If the orientation of treatment is primarily soothing, there is a danger that the patient may remain in treatment for its soothing function alone, and will make little attempt at introspection. Without introspection, the patient will continue to believe that his good feelings are derived from the external environment, in this case the therapy. If the orientation is primarily introspective, there is a danger that the stress produced by the introspection will outweigh for the patient the soothing effects of his relationship with the therapist. The therapist must monitor this balance continually.

## CLINICAL EXAMPLE – COUNTERTRANSFERENCE WITH AN EXHIBITIONISTIC NARCISSISTIC DISORDER

With narcissists in general, and especially with exhibitionistic narcissists, just the act of coming to treatment is wounding because it is an admission that there is something wrong, an imperfection; coming to treatment interferes with the narcissist's grandiose fantasies. This becomes quite clear immediately after the narcissist allows his protective wall temporarily to be lowered enough for him to experience and share some hurtful or vulnerable feelings. In the next session he may react similarly to the way he would to being exposed or wounded, protecting himself by distancing or devaluing or both. His protective wall is reestablished and strengthened. Often he will come late to that session or cancel the session entirely. He may complain that nothing seems to be happening in treatment and that he is considering termination. Even after years of treatment, the therapeutic relationship is often nothing more to a narcissistic patient than a functional arrangement; he can become wounded and suddenly terminate therapy without experiencing the loss of the relationship, only the loss of the therapist's stabilizing function.

In the following transcript, Mrs. J., an exhibitionistic narcissist, begins the session as she has every one of the four sessions since she started treatment, complaining that there is really nothing much wrong with her and whatever the problem is she can handle it herself. This is a common scenario with narcissists in response to the injury inherent in being in treatment.

**T:** I understood from your telephone message that you canceled last week because you felt too tired.

**P:** Yes, I was halfway here and I thought "I'm so tired today; I can't see this doing any good."

**T:** Do you think there was anything about what's been happening here that contributed to your tiredness?

**P:** I don't know. I had the same struggle with coming here today.

Like other narcissists, Mrs. J. believes that she is perfect and that her problems arise from the inadequacy of those around her. Naturally, then, she looks for the solutions to her problems in the world around her. In this case, Mrs. J. thinks that she would be perfectly happy if her husband would only change. Short of that, she sees her alternatives as settling or getting out. She does not consider the possibility that she might be able to understand herself better,

I really don't think it has to do with not wanting to look at myself because I have lunch with my girlfriends and we talk about the same things I talk about here. So I just can't see how anything that happens here is going to fix the situation. The only thing I can hope for is that I can learn to accept my husband the way he is or move on. I don't see how talking about it is going to help me make that decision. And lately I think it's going to be okay with him. The problem is that just when I think everything is okay, my husband gets possessive and then nothing will help.

so to her the idea of therapy seems useless. She both minimizes the circumstances that have brought her into treatment and devalues the therapy and the therapist by claiming that having lunch with her girl friends is a comparable experience to coming to treatment.

**T:** You come here to understand yourself better but it's painful for you to focus inside yourself so you look outside for solutions. You want your husband to change. This is why you're not feeling hopeful about therapy.

**P:** There are a few people I've talked to in that depth. No matter what I know—no matter how much I find out, it doesn't affect my ability to make a decision—I think I've decided to stay with my husband.

**T:** I know that's a difficult decision for you because it means that you will need to stay at home with your kids and not be in the limelight.

**P:** Yes, and then I get bored.

This is an example of a common clinical error with an exhibitionistic narcissist. The patient begins by devaluing the therapy and by extension the therapist. The therapist is apparently annoyed and acts out his irritation by confronting the patient. At first the confrontations are disguised as interpretive comments. The therapist points out that the patient is focusing on her husband because it is painful for her to focus on herself. His comment lacks adequate empathic attunement to how painful this really is to her. She is offended by the comment and responds that at times she focuses inside herself with her friends but that insight is not helpful; only action can help.

Now the therapist manages a mirroring intervention to which the patient responds by elaborating a bit further, an indication that the mirroring intervention was helpful.

Encouraged by this bit of success, the therapist jumps in right away with an elaborate intervention that is intended to be mirroring. There was no reason at this point for the therapist to intervene. The patient had just begun to elaborate on her dysphoric affect. The therapist's comment interrupts this process.

**T:** It's painful for you to feel your own feelings, so you want to be around other people to interact with and get attention from and create excitement with so that you are not left alone with your own feelings.

**P:** I don't agree. I don't get bored with myself. Other day I went shopping. I see people who don't like people as having the problem, not me. I don't know why I get bored. Then I like to go out and my husband doesn't want me to. He's selfish. We each want the other to change. Like yesterday I was jogging with my husband and some friends at the beach. My husband came up to my friend and me and I made a crack about a guy's bod; it was really a quite witty remark, but my husband took it badly, and wouldn't talk with me for a whole day—I couldn't understand why. . . . He took it as sexual. I said, "You're acting jealous and insecure, and I hate that." Maybe there isn't a problem with me—maybe it's him because he doesn't know many people. He's not gregarious like I am. (pause) I don't like insecure men—not because I

The therapist makes an error by pointing out that the boredom Mrs. J. complains about is a result of her not having outside adulation, which she depends upon so that she does not have to focus upon her own feelings. This is experienced as criticism, an injury, and she responds by disagreeing and declaring that she does not have problems, that it is the people who don't like people who have the problem. She has apparently heard the therapist's comment as indicating that there is something wrong with being gregarious. She reiterates that she gets bored and then likes to go out, and then she changes the subject, and focuses away from herself by talking about her husband. The patient is offended by the implication that her boredom is with herself. In a flurry of grandiosity, she restates her position that her unfortunate life situation is the result of other people's problems and inadequacy, not her own. This sort of devaluation and blame is exactly what would be expected of a narcissist who is confronted with a personal failure or defect. The therapist, unable to contain himself, makes an interpretive comment that is superficially understanding, but is really intended to burst her grandiose

need him to be secure so I can feel secure, because I do feel secure. I want a man that other women find attractive. I guess I want my cake and eat it too. I want a secure marriage but I want to be able to go drinking with men. Totally nonsexual. Some men don't think women can have nonsexual relationships with men.

**T:** Last week you talked about wishing Peter was willing to be sexual with you. I wonder if it isn't disappointing for you that he's not, so you're taking the position that you don't want to be sexual.

**P:** Deep down inside I don't really want this person. He fills a facet. I want a man who's good at dance, one who's an exciting lover . . . and then I want a husband. I talked to a man today who had fifteen years of hell in marriage and then it turned around. So it can happen. My husband doesn't want me meeting with other guys, but what he doesn't know won't hurt him. His jealousy makes me want to do it more. If you impose a rule on me, I will find a way to break it. I feel like a little girl who's trying to get away with things. I feel scolded, so I plot with my girlfriend to get around him. That's childish but that's the way they treat us.

**T:** You create excitement so you won't feel bored—empty.

**P:** Not because I feel empty. I'm bored because there's nothing to do at home. Lots of people are

bubble by confronting her with an unpleasant reality she is blatantly ignoring, that she has not been able to interest a desirable man in sleeping with her. Her response to this is to maintain her grandiose stance by insisting that she really isn't interested in sex.

The therapist has not given up his insistence that the patient feels empty inside, something she has alluded to in past sessions. Predictably, she is again offended, declaring that she is not "sick."

bored. I happen to like to socialize. I don't know if that's sick.

**T:** You hear me saying you're sick, that there's something wrong with you.

**P:** Well, it doesn't feel good to be empty inside. . . . I know I'm not empty inside—I have the spirit of God inside. I only feel empty inside when I try to push God out of my life. But when I had my first affair, I just changed because I had to justify what I did. I pushed God out. So I know I'm just not allowing myself to be filled with what I should. I'm not ready yet to ask God to come back because I'm not ready yet to stop seeing men. But God has helped me. I said, "Send Mr. G. on a business trip or something" if you don't want me to see him, and what do you know, he had to go on a business trip.

Another time I said, "Make it so I don't see him" and the meeting got canceled so he didn't come. So I'm being totally "disobedient", see—so much of my life is governed by my religious beliefs. I know it's wrong, what I'm doing. I've decided with Mr. G. to just be friends—I realized he doesn't love me or care about me so I'm seeing him through different eyes.

**T:** What made you change your mind?

**P:** He let it die—he's selfish—it was my birthday and he did nothing for me—I mean anyone who cared would at least do some-

Now the therapist seems to regain some therapeutic neutrality, steps back and simply mirrors the patient's hurt reaction. She appears somewhat mollified but does not directly acknowledge his comment, expanding instead upon her thesis that she does not feel empty inside, that God is within her and intervenes directly to help her to do the right thing. She then acknowledges that she has a negatively critical attitude toward the lover whom she had idealized the week before. In alluding to her change of heart, the therapist risks the possibility that she might resent his pointing out a weakness in her; however, she appears to take his question to arise from simple curiosity, and explains that it is the lover's shortcomings that have led to her change of attitude.

thing. Send a card. Something. Wouldn't you do something?

He's not a good lover any more either—he's selfish—I don't need a man who's not filling my needs. What is he if he's not my friend or lover? My friend Paula says I'm allowing him to treat me like a fool. With Peter, he's a good friend but won't do anything sexually. I'm tired of that. (laughs) I can't get anyone to go to sleep with me. Is that not divine protection?

**T:** Having men seek after you is so important to you because it is a confirmation that you are desirable. When it does not happen you feel hurt and disappointed; you take comfort in thinking of it as divine intervention.

**P:** Well, I'm not really hurt about it.

**T:** You don't like to think of yourself as hurting, because you see that as a failing, a defect.

**P:** I don't like to be down. I rebel against that negativity. I don't allow myself to wear those emotions. That's true. I have to admit that. I had a girlfriend who was always sick. I see it as a weakness. Anything negative, I don't wear well. Yes, so naturally for you to say there's a part of me that doesn't like myself—feel empty—I rebel against that. No, I'm just bored. My best friend is exactly the same way—bored and she gets ten times the attention I get. Since I started being friends with her a year ago I have felt more insecure because she's very attractive—hourglass figure. This

Her subsequent comments touch upon her lack of a satisfying sex partner, which she explains as divine intervention. The patient appears to be quite serious in this notion; however it is more of a grandiose fantasy than a delusion. The therapist points out the injury to her self-image that this lack of male interest represents for her and how she defends against the injury; she denies the injury. The therapist empathically interprets her need to deny the injury, and she responds positively, elaborating on the painful loss of her youthful beauty. These two interventions appear to have been successful in interrupting a defense and focusing the patient on her underlying feeling.

The narcissistic injury that is inherent in the process of aging is a very common theme for narcissistic disorders. When they are young and the world is their oyster, these people see treatment as irrelevant and implying defectiveness. If they do seek treatment, their reason is usually depression that has arisen as a result of some major life failure, like being passed over for a promotion, which has defeated their grandiose defense and uncovered their underlying feelings of defectiveness and emptiness. They may describe themselves as falling apart. Soon, however, they are usually able to reconstitute themselves and restore their grandiosity. At that point they typically declare that the treatment has succeeded; they "feel great" and no longer see

is the first time in my life that I'm not the one who gets the attention. I was almost. . . .

any need for treatment. The underlying depression has again been covered over.

Aging, however, brings defects that are not easily overcome. As they age, most people notice the loss of their youthful beauty; their bodies are not as quick or as strong. They may find that their expectations of greatness have not come to pass, and as time runs out they are forced to face the reality that they will never achieve the heights they'd hoped for. In short, the process of aging confronts people with their mortality. At approximately 40 years of age, it is very common for people with narcissistic disorders to become depressed as a result of the defects that aging has uncovered and to seek treatment. Unlike younger narcissists, older narcissists are not easily able to reconstitute themselves by correcting the defects that precipitated their depression if those defects are associated with aging; their approach to life of attacking whatever might interfere with their grandiose defenses does not generally work. The disappointments of aging are internal and, rather than disappear in time, they tend to get worse. Consequently, narcissists tend to stay in treatment longer and have a better chance for successful treatment when they are older than when they are young.

All of a sudden I don't know who I am anymore. I said jokingly, "Okay, Paula, give me your leftovers." Deep down inside I know I'm lucky they don't want to sleep with me. My husband says why would you want

After describing some of her difficulties in getting attention from men, the patient says, "I don't know who I am anymore." She depends on other people's reactions for her sense of herself. Without the admiration she craves, she feels lost. After further

that kind of attention—wanting to sleep with you? I can't be immodest—I don't want them to be attracted just for sex. My friend Paula, part of me believes she's a bad influence. I wish I could up and move away and start over. So it's not so much that I'm unhappy with me on the inside but now I'm unhappy with me on outside. I look in the mirror and hate it.

description of her difficulties she says, "so it's not so much that I'm unhappy with me on the inside but now I'm unhappy with me on the outside." This is a statement of the attitude toward life of the narcissist: "the origin of my troubles is not within me, but a result of my external situation." Until this belief is altered, the depth of treatment will be limited; the narcissist will continue to attempt to solve his problems by manipulating the world around him, rather than trying to understand himself.

When I didn't have wrinkles and gray hair I had men who would drool over me.

**T:** Their admiration made you feel attractive.

**P:** Maybe it never occurred to me that people like me for my insides. Not that I don't think I'm good on the inside. Now suddenly I have to think, "Would people still love me if I weren't beautiful?" It's something that I just need to work out. I have to live it. I don't know if I want to come next week.

The patient now attempts to restore some of her stature by recalling how men used to "drool" over her. This may have also been a transferential reference to her disappointment at the therapist's lack of sexual interest in her. The therapist comments on her use of other people's admiration to make herself feel good. She does not pick up on this idea, instead shifting the focus to what other people think of her "insides," rather than how she feels about herself. She questions if people would appreciate her internal beauty if they did not recognize her external beauty. By questioning if people would love her she is really questioning whether she is worthy of love. This question makes her very uncomfortable, and she brings up the possibility of not coming to treatment. Consistent with her overall attitude, she is acting as though the dysphoria she feels originates from the treatment rather than from within herself; her solution is to cut back the treatment.

**T:** It is painful for you to think about the loss of other peoples' attention and admiration, so you want to stop talking about it; you question whether you want to come here.

**P:** That's true. I'll probably be here though.

**T:** I don't think you and I have discussed my cancellation policy, so it won't apply to last week's cancellation, but in the future if you schedule an appointment, you will need to pay for it, even if you decide not to come to it. How would that be for you?

**P:** You're right, we hadn't discussed that. Well, I don't think it matters because I don't feel I need to continue to come here because I think I know what the problem is now. I just have to go out and test it.

**T:** To continue to come here would be uncomfortable for you in a number of ways. Coming here in itself feels like a statement that there is something wrong with you; that you are defective. It also represents commitment, which feels to you confining, like your marriage; it represents being commonplace and without excitement.

**P:** You're right, I don't want to be that committed. We've uncovered a lot of my problems. Now I need to fix them.

The therapist comments on this defensive process, and the patient acknowledges it; however, she resists being definite about whether she will attend the next session. The therapist informs her of his cancellation policy and she says that it had not been discussed. His bringing up of the cancellation policy at this point is experienced by her as an injury. On his part, it may be a response to the devaluing nature of her attitude of "maybe I'll be here, maybe I won't." Devaluation, for the narcissist, is the flip side of idealization; a narcissist can switch from one to the other. With a devaluing narcissist, sometimes a clear limit from the therapist can serve as a statement of the therapist's respect for himself, and have the effect of restoring her idealization of him. In this particular situation, for the therapist to have failed to address the patient's testing of the therapeutic frame at this point would have undermined the treatment by abdicating control.

It's not going to do a lot of good now to keep talking about them.

**T:** The decision in treatment is similar to the one you face in your

She responds by questioning whether she needs treatment. He interprets this as an expression of her difficulty with commitment, which she acknowledges without changing

marriage. You want to make a commitment but you question whether you can live with the uncomfortable feelings that will come up. In your marriage you would be trading a sense of doing what you think is right for a sense of loss of attention and specialness. In treatment you would be investing in yourself knowing that for you to turn inward is uncomfortable, unfamiliar, and perhaps painful. I don't know which would be harder, to commit to treatment or to commit to your marriage. The problems are similar—perhaps it would be easier to face them here than in your marriage.

**P:** Can I commit to three weeks?

**T:** Yes, but at some point for the treatment to be effective you will need to make more of a commitment.

**P:** Okay then, I'll see you next week at this same time.

her position with respect to coming to treatment. He comments further upon her difficulties with commitment, again expressing an understanding about how she feels. Her response is positive, indicating that she would like to make a minimal commitment. He accepts her request as reasonable for the beginning of treatment, cautioning her that she will need to make a greater commitment as treatment progresses.

Although some of the therapist's ending comments may appear confrontive, they also contain an explanatory component that gives the patient a feeling of being understood. Whereas a confrontation points out an aspect of the patient's behavior and often raises a question about it, the therapist's interventions towards the end of this transcript are more interpretive, attempting to answer questions about the patient's behavior. Regardless of how the intervention is phrased, however, it will not be heard as supportive if it is not empathic and intended to help the patient to understand herself.

When a narcissist is devaluing, the therapist is alerted to the possibility that the patient feels injured or misunderstood. Despite the therapist's impulse to strike back at the patient, the therapist must instead try to understand the nature of the patient's injury and hopefully the source of it. In the above transcript, the patient has canceled the previous session because she was "tired." This action is a devaluation of the treatment; it says that the treatment is not important enough to attend when the patient feels tired. The therapist attempts to explore with the patient whether the patient feels injured. She says she questions whether treatment can help.

In the above transcript, one can assume that the repeated injuries caused by the therapist's aggressive acting out of countertransference toward the patient would certainly interfere with any mirror transference that might have been established. Narcissistic patients typically respond to this type of loss of selfobject by either withdrawing or devaluing, although in some instances an aggressive or confrontive therapist can cathect in the narcissistic patient an idealizing transference. Since the above patient began the session by defending herself and devaluing the treatment, she is probably responding to the therapist's aggressive acting out from the last session that continues into the present session. It is useful to evaluate the type of transference that the patient seeks in order to determine the most therapeutic stance for the therapist. The patient asserts how wonderful she is and rarely turns to the therapist for confirmation. In the absence of the injuries that have led her to devalue, there would probably be a clearer interest in admiration from the therapist.

In order to develop a mirror transference, the therapist must reflect back to the patient his thoughts and feelings. Since the narcissistic personality blurs the boundaries between himself and other people, he has difficulty with empathizing or putting himself in another person's place and trying to understand the other person's point of view. He feels understood by another person if he is able to see that other person as like himself or even an extension of himself. Consequently, for him to feel understood by the therapist he must feel akin to the therapist. For the primitive narcissistic disorder especially, any appearance of differences of any kind between therapist and patient can cause the patient to feel misunderstood. Consequently, the more primitive the narcissistic disorder, the more precisely the therapist must reflect back the patient's thoughts and feeling states. The narcissistic patient wants a therapist who is exquisitely attuned to him.

In the above transcript, the therapist's interventions not only mirror the patient's hurt feelings but also point out her defenses. When the exhibitionistic narcissist who has just begun treatment says that she does not think treatment can work, she means that she does not experience the treatment as supportive. She wants to be perfectly understood; anything short of that will be accompanied by dysphoric affect. Since the patient does not know what she really wants or why she feels bad, it is the therapist's job to interpret her feelings and to put them into words. For example, without placing emphasis on his own importance, the therapist could have said, "Perhaps you feel misunderstood." This little bit of accurate mirroring may be all the patient needs to restore the therapist's selfobject role and permit the patient to talk about the problem.

In general, when a narcissistic patient responds to an intervention by elaborating on her feeling, the therapist can assume that the intervention was accurate and accepted. When the patient responds with silence, by ignoring the intervention, or by arguing with it, the therapist can assume that the patient was injured.

## CLINICAL EXAMPLE – A HIGHER LEVEL EXHIBITIONISTIC NARCISSISTIC DISORDER

### Negative Transference

This session begins with a verbal handshake after the patient arrives seven minutes late to treatment. Normally such an exchange might be automatic for a therapist; however since Mrs. K. was seven minutes late to this session the patient's opening comment bears a bit more examination. The patient probably has some negative transference, since lateness to sessions is typical for her. If she is seeing the therapist in an authority role, she comes into the session expecting the therapist to be judgmental and possibly irritated about the lateness. A pattern of lateness can feel devaluing to the therapist. Subtle or blatant devaluation is common for the exhibitionistic narcissistic patient. The purpose of the patient's social nicety at the beginning of the session is probably to check in with the therapist and find out if the therapist is irritated. It is a way of assuaging anxiety or guilt about the lateness. By responding the way he does, the therapist takes the pressure off the patient to deal with her anxiety or guilt internally.

**Mrs. K.**

(The patient arrives 7 minutes late.)

**P:** How are you doing?
**T:** Fine.

Countertransference: In this transcript the therapist is almost continually struggling with his countertransference, which leads him to be far more active than he needs to be. For instance, instead of letting the opening comment lead to the patient's uncomfortable feelings about herself, the therapist responds and then continues through most of the session to struggle with his countertransference, which is preventing the patient from exploring her own transference feelings.

**P:** As I was taking a shower before I came over here I was thinking I didn't know what to talk about. I was playing out saying some things in my head but it was all really just filler. It felt like a book of my life was closed and I am not sure what the next book will be.

**T:** What did that mean to you?

**P:** I hadn't really thought of what it meant. On the way over I popped in a tape from April 1983. It was something I had planned sending to my sister and I found it the other day when I was organizing a drawer full of photos. It was about me—my life. Listening to it triggered a bunch of thoughts and emotions. A lot of it had to do with my mother and her recent death. At that time I had thought it was a freeing thing. I was beginning a process of getting to know who I was because until then I had been living out other's people's expectations. The tape was really interesting. As I'm talking about it, I'm wanting to finish listening to the tape. Can I leave now? (smiles)

**T:** I know that was meant as a joke but I imagine there is some kernel of seriousness to it. You seem ambivalent about being here today. You were seven minutes late, you didn't have anything

The patient explains that she did not know what to talk about and jests about preferring to go out to her car and finish listening to a tape that she had been listening to on the way to the session. This patient has been late often and always denied that the lateness had any significance or meaning with respect to feelings about the therapist or treatment. The therapist takes this opportunity to attempt to get the patient to acknowledge her negative transference by pointing out three indications of ambivalence: her lateness, her lack of subject matter to explore, and her jest about wanting to leave the session and listen to the rest of her tape. As in the transcript of Mrs. J., one can assume that Mrs. K.'s therapist seems to be struggling with countertransference toward his patient, because the therapist's first intervention is almost confrontive. It would have been adequate and less wounding to the patient to simply say, "I know that was meant as a joke but I imagine there is some kernel of seriousness to it. You seem ambivalent about being here today." The three examples of the patient's show of ambivalence could have been added later if the patient did not acknowledge her ambivalence or asked what gave the therapist the impression that she was ambivalent. By adding the three examples before the patient

you wanted to talk about, and some part of you thinks you'd get more from listening to your tape.

**P:** Well, I know your work is based on some rigid thing about time, but I really don't think my being late has any special meaning. I'm usually late to things. As a matter of fact, to tell you the truth, so far I think I've done a pretty good job of getting here reasonably on time.

**T:** Did you feel criticized by my comment?

**P:** Well, not really. I understand that your sense is that everything means something. But really, in this case I don't think it does. I just took on one too many things. So I ended up being late.

has had a chance to respond, an element of "I gotcha" is introduced into the intervention.

It is likely that the therapist's behavior in this first section of transcript is an indication of countertransference. Often narcissistic patients can be steadily devaluing of treatment, either through comments or through behavior like lateness. The therapist can easily begin to feel resentful of this devaluation, and without intending it the therapist can subtly strike back at the patient. In this transcript, the therapist does this when he first comments about the patient's lateness; he is a bit confrontive, leading the patient to take offense and become defensive.

In the interchanges that follow, the therapist is quite active. Many of his comments appear to be unnecessary. This activity may represent further acting out of angry countertransference, or it may represent a countertransference response to having ruffled the patient's feathers. Another possibility is that the therapist is using this increased activity to avoid his own discomfort with the patient.

The patient responds to this comment defensively, and the therapist asks her if she feels criticized. As usual, she denies feeling criticized. This is a good example of a common experience that therapists have with narcissistic patients. It is clear from the patient's withdrawal and defensiveness that the patient feels offended or criticized; however, as part of her withdrawal she is unwilling to give anything to the therapist, so she withholds even the acknowledgment of the injury. Also, to acknowledge hurt feelings would expose a vulnerability, which the patient in this defensive state is often unwilling to do. Despite this denial, the therapist's acknowledgment of the injury is important and allows the patient to feel understood.

The next section of transcript is tense. The therapist is gently pulling for the patient to express some of her negative feelings, and the patient first stonewalls and then gradually acknowledges the possibility of some ambivalence towards the treatment. The therapist's high level of activity here again indicates the presence of countertransference material. For instance, instead of the two interventions beginning, "Well, it may not . . ." and "Maybe that . . . ," the therapist could have said nothing.

**T:** Well, it may not mean anything. I have no way of knowing that. My job here is to take what you give me and try to understand what it means, so naturally when you're late I ask what it means.

**P:** I can see that and that makes sense. I'm afraid this time however it's going to be a waste of time to talk about it. Anyway, for what it's worth, I'll accept that I may be ambivalent today about coming because I didn't even have something to talk about.

**T:** Maybe that made you feel that coming today would be a waste of your time.

**P:** No, (smiles) but certainly not a maximal use.

The therapist now continues to pull for the patient to express her negative feelings about the treatment. This particular attempt is successful in that the patient acknowledges that the 50-minute time frame is not optimal for her.

**T:** When you say that my work is based on a rigid 50-minute time frame, you seem to have an opinion about that.

**P:** I would challenge whether that's an optimal way to help people or whether it's really a convenience for professionals.

In mirroring the patient's dissatisfaction with the time structure of the appointments, the therapist is reassuring her that her negative feelings and attitudes are welcome. Similarly, he mirrors her sense that he is judging her and her belief that *he makes her feel crummy*, which he will

**T:** So it hasn't felt optimal for you.

**P:** There are times that I'd like to talk to you when I can't and there are other times when I have an appointment and I don't really have anything to say and I'd just as soon pass. And having to be here at a precise time—I don't like feeling bad when I'm a couple of minutes late. I know being on time is something you look at and it's part of your business to question why people are late and you expect people to be on time but I don't like that I have to feel crummy coming in when I'm a couple of minutes late.

**T:** It sounds like you view me as someone who watches and judges you, like your mother did or your piano teacher. You feel you can't just be yourself with me because if you slip up I will make you feel crummy, hold up your performance to you, and give you a hard time about it.

**P:** (pause) Those are the words Douglas (her ex-husband) would use. He'd give me a hard time about my behavior and before I came here, I did think of therapists as confronting people. Yes, I may be doing that.

**T:** I can understand your reticence to being here if you think of me as being someone who is going to make you feel bad.

**P:** That may be bringing up something unconscious. I don't say to myself, "Oh, this is going to be unpleasant, I want to avoid it." I don't think of you consciously in that way.

**T:** But you do think of me evaluating you.

**P:** There is something about that which I definitely resent.

I should have come in here in the beginning and said, "I really don't feel like being a little late is

later identify as a projection. It is so very common for these patients to blame their dysphoric feelings or feelings of fragmentation on their environment. The therapist needs to help the patient see them as originating within herself.

The therapist's next comment, an attempt to mirror, is really unnecessary. There is no indication that the patient is withdrawing or going into defense. Again this intervention can probably be attributed to countertransference. In fact the therapist's mirroring attempt is inaccurate and causes the patient to become defensive.

The therapist then repairs this minor injury with an accurate mirroring comment, which nevertheless sounds a bit argumentative. The patient now acknowledges resentment over having to be somewhere at a certain time.

something I should be ashamed of." But I wasn't ready to do that right in the beginning. Really, it's probably something bigger for me because I'm always late. I know that people resent it. I usually resent that I agreed to be there at a certain time. I want a lack of accountability.

**T:** What was going on for you when you first came that made you hesitate to tell me how you felt about being late?

The therapist now attempts to focus the discussion back onto the negative transference without success. However, the therapist's comment fortunately does not seem to deter the patient from pursuing further productive exploration of the implications of her general tendency to be late. Here again, it is clear that the therapist's intervention was at best not necessary.

**P:** I probably didn't trust you enough even to admit that I am a person who is late a lot. It is really only lately that I realized the extent that that is true about me. With my son and daughter and with Douglas it has come up. It probably had to do with the standard I grew up with. I was always feeling it was okay to push a little, take 65-minute lunch breaks because I would think, "Well, I work harder when I get back and I produce a higher quality product and I do feel I can take liberties."

I really don't have anyone making me accountable in my life. I really know I'm the one making me feel bad, not you. If I'm late with my son, he doesn't say anything anymore, but I've discovered recently that he doesn't like it. He doesn't say anything because he's given up on me; he just assumes I will be late. When I realized that I thought "Whoa!" I often would tell him one time and then get home at another. Or sometimes I

Now the patient acknowledges that it is she and her lateness, not the therapist, that makes her feel bad. She begins to develop this theme further. Then for the first time she really discusses her lateness as an undesirable trait.

would promise him something and then something else would come up for me and I'd cancel out completely. I should have known it bothered him but I probably just didn't want to know so I didn't think about it. Then last month he told me that it makes him feel like he's an obligation to me when I'm late, like just one more project. That got my attention. I guess I have always been late with him. He probably figured that I wouldn't listen to him if he talked about it with me. Maybe he even tried. I don't know. I think he sees me as pretty stern. Now he pretty much just does his own thing and doesn't talk to me.

**T:** When you came here late today you probably thought I'd be stern and judge you.

The therapist eventually intervenes by again trying to bring out the negative transference, this time with greater success. The therapist's intervention reflects back the patient's concern about judgment from the therapist, which she has acknowledged earlier in the session. Again, the need for this intervention might be questionable. However, the patient seems to go a bit deeper after it, and the intervention does help in setting the stage for the next intervention, a mirroring intervention.

**P:** Probably, because it reflects on my integrity, intention, values, my sense of myself. So that may have had something to do with why I wasn't ready to say anything. When I think about this pattern in terms of my son, it bothers me to think I had a perception that it was okay that I

There is a sense at this point that the therapist and patient are now working together. The patient is looking seriously at herself.

After the patient acknowledges that being late reflects on her integrity and interferes with her treatment, the therapist decides to make a mirroring interpretation of the pa-

would regularly say I'd be home at 5:00 and arrive at 5:30—that I thought it would be okay with him to have that much uncertainty. So I've become more aware of it lately and I've tried to be on time with him when I say I'm going to be home. But for some reason I've resented it more in terms of this time line here than other places. I guess I was holding myself more accountable here than other places, putting more pressure on myself. In truth it doesn't matter—it's only a few minutes. But I should feel uncomfortable because I'm not making choices that allow for something to happen.

**T:** I think those uncomfortable feelings do come up. You've said that being late feels to you like it reflects on your integrity. I think what happens when you question yourself like that and feel bad is that you deflect the bad feeling by thinking of it as coming from me, that I'm pressuring or judging you and then you become angry at me for making you feel bad.

tient's externalization, explaining that the anger that she focused on the therapist served to distract her from the uncomfortable feelings she feels about being late.

The timing of this first mirroring interpretation is important in this transcript. During the initial portion of the session the patient is feeling injured or negative toward the therapist. She would have been less receptive to a mirroring interpretation that highlighted her defensive use of anger and externalization to defend against uncomfortable feelings about herself. Once she has labeled her lateness as ego-dystonic she is far more receptive to the mirroring interpretation.

**P:** I can see that. I feel bad every time I'm late. I do, and I really don't want to break my agreements any more. But I squeak every little minute out of my schedule—I plan one thing on top of another. I set myself up for it by not allowing for something to happen that might slow me down. I think I do associate time, I think, with integrity and agreements. It reminds me of the part

The patient responds with a clear confirmation of the interpretation. "I can see that. I feel bad every time I'm late." This response illustrates a most important and perhaps surprising characteristic of the narcissistic disorder; despite these patients' tendency to become easily offended, they will respond positively to an accurate mirroring interpretation that addresses an issue that they are interested in, even if it points out the

of my life where I haven't kept my agreements and it is pretty sad, when you think about it. I guess that's one of the things that is hardest with Douglas. I'd want to trust him with my feelings. He'd make the kids accountable all day. He'd do it with me too. I'd be angry with him in much the same ways you suggested I was resentful of you. (pause) It almost makes me wonder whether that was a wise choice to tell him about every little thing in my life because he ended up causing me a lot of sadness. (pause) I'll never really figure that one out I don't think. I'm meeting people with dogs and cats and I can understand why they get so attached to them because it's a way of getting affection and it's a lot safer. I've been wondering as I think of having someone to share with in near future, whenever it happens, how I'll deal with something like that.

Sometimes things happen that bring up memories and I get sad—I wonder what I'll do around that. Do I share all that? I'm conflicted about that. *Sometimes it seems like I've got nothing but sadness in my life when I look back on it.* I've been affected by that relationship since the divorce. So far now when I meet men I'm holding back, resisting the urge to spill my guts. So I wonder about that.

patient's defenses, because they feel understood.

The patient continues to focus on herself now. When she brings up Douglas and some of his behavior, she loses some of her clarity of focus. She sees that her anger at him serves a similar function to her anger at the therapist. Then in her next breath she momentarily focuses away from herself by talking about Douglas being the cause of a lot of her sadness. However, she is able to bring her focus back to herself.

**T:** How do you imagine you'd be perceived?

**P:** Well, I guess I'm concerned that I

Unfortunately, the therapist chooses this moment to again interrupt with an unnecessary question.

might meet someone like Douglas who's concerned about being deserted. I was vulnerable and shared everything about myself. He focused on the theme that I was a person who would always do that (leave him for someone else). There must be something about my behavior that made him feel unsafe. I don't know how necessary it is to share so much. What do you think?

This intervention makes no sense in the light of the fact that the patient is working very hard at this point in the session and shows no indication of slowing down. In fact she has just identified a conflict that she is thinking about. There is no potential benefit to intervening at this time and there is a strong risk of interfering with the patient's work, which is in fact what happens. After the therapist's ill-timed question the patient partially shifts her attention away from herself back to Douglas and eventually back to the therapist when she turns to the therapist for help in resolving the conflict.

**T:** I can see that it makes you feel exposed but you are conflicted about it because you think people in relationships should share about themselves. The conflict was uncomfortable for you and you turned to me in the hope that my input would help you resolve it and you would feel reassured.

**P:** I feel uncomfortable. There are things I don't think I want people to know. I still don't tell people I meet that I was married and divorced with Douglas. I'm still bewildered. I wish it hadn't happened, so I am judging myself about that. (Session ends.)

The therapist responds with another mirroring interpretation, mirroring Mrs. K.'s conflict and interpreting her defense of turning to the therapist. There is probably a question in many readers' minds about whether the patient's turning to the therapist in this situation is indeed defensive. It is clear, however, from the transcript that the patient finds the intervention helpful and responds to it by focusing back on herself.

## CLINICAL EXAMPLE—COUNTERTRANSFERENCE CONTROLLED

In the beginning of the session just presented, if the therapist had simply not responded to the patient's initial social nicety, the patient could well have gotten to the same material as she does through a more circuitous route in the actual transcript. For example, the session might have gone like this:

(The patient arrives 7 minutes late.)

**P:** How are you doing? (pause) You're not going to answer, are you? (pause)

**T:** I know people often ask each other that question in polite conversation, but I'm wondering if your asking that here just now doesn't reflect some particular meaning to you.

As before, the patient begins with her social nicety, which this time the therapist does not return. When questioned about this the therapist attempts to suggest that the patient's comment might have some additional meaning.

**P:** God, does everything have to mean something? Can't I just ask you how you are without it having some deep meaning? (pause) You're not going to answer. (pause) Well, anyway, as I was taking a shower before I came over here I was thinking I didn't know what to talk about. I was playing out saying some things in my head but it was all really just filler. It felt like a book of my life was closed and I am not sure what the next book will be. So, in the car on the way over I was listening to this tape I'd made in April of '83. It was something I'd planned sending to my sister back then and I found it the other day when I was organizing a drawer full of photos. It was about me—my life. Listening to it triggered a bunch of thoughts and emotions. A lot of it had to do with my mother and her recent death. At that time I had thought it was a freeing thing. I was beginning a process of getting to know who I was because until then I had been living out

Although the therapist makes this suggestion carefully, attempting to avoid injuring the patient, it is clear from the patient's response that there was some injury. Perhaps this could not have been avoided.

The therapist waits for an appropriate moment to intervene: the patient must make a remark that is a clear indication of defense; it must be apparent what dysphoric affect is being defended against; and, in order to give the interpretation additional weight, it is preferable that a pattern of defense has been exhibited that can be pulled together in the interpretation.

When the therapist does not respond to the patient's argumentative comments, the patient begins to talk about herself in the context of her ride to the therapist's office.

In this version of the session, the therapist does not interrupt the patient.

other people's expectations. The tape was really interesting. As I'm talking about it, I'm wanting to finish listening to the tape.

Can I leave now? (smiles)

**T:** I know that was meant as a joke but I imagine there is some kernel of seriousness to it. My impression when you came in was that you were aware that you didn't have anything you knew you wanted to talk about here. The lack of structure made you feel anxious because you anticipated having to seek inside yourself for direction.

**P:** That's probably true.

**T:** You have talked before about how you feel disappointed with yourself when you put off unpleasant things, and you were probably uncomfortable with having put off being here by allowing yourself to be late. When you asked, "How are you?" you seemed to be trying to manage the feeling of discomfort by shifting the focus of your attention to me so that you could feel reassured by my answer that I am still feeling positively toward you in spite of your being late. When I didn't answer, you became more uncomfortable, and became irritated with me as a way to focus your attention even more intensely on me. When I again didn't answer you began to turn your attention inward. You talked about the tape you listened to and alluded to emotions it stimulated about your mother's death. These emotions are

When the patient finally asks, "Can I leave now?" the therapist sees this jest as clearly defensive, and takes it as an invitation to interpret the patient's difficulty in focusing inward. He does this with a series of mirroring interpretations that describe in a neutral way the patient's struggle with her uncomfortable feelings about herself, and her attempts to manage these feelings by focusing her attention on the therapist in order to distract herself from the dysphoric feeling state.

He begins by mirroring to the patient what she was feeling when she came in and then interprets her question, "How are you?" as an attempt to shift her focus away from her uncomfortable inner feelings. Note that in this instance, as in many instances with narcissistic disorders, the therapist can mirror the patient on a variety of depths. He can comment on her discomfort or guilt about being late, her fear of criticism, or her annoyance with the therapist. It is generally better, however, to mirror the patient's feelings about herself, as this therapist does. He then gives two more similar examples of essentially the same defense. Partly because of the neutral narrative style of the therapist's intervention, but mostly because the intervention accurately describes the patient's behavior and accompanying feeling states, the patient is not injured by the intervention, but instead feels seen and unpainful for you so you again turned your attention to me by asking in jest whether you can leave.

derstood, as evidenced by her response.

**P:** It's true, I was uncomfortable with the idea of being here without knowing what I wanted to talk about. That happens a lot. Really, it's probably something bigger for me because I'm always late—other places too. I know that people resent it. I usually resent that I agreed to be there at a certain time in the first place. I want a lack of accountability. Getting here has felt like even more of a pressure than other places. I should have told you right in the beginning that I'm not someone who gets places on time but I probably didn't trust you enough back then even to admit that I am a person who is late a lot. It is really only lately that I realized the extent that that is true about me. With my son and with Douglas (her ex-husband) it has come up. It probably had to do with. . . .

She responds to this series of interpretations by acknowledging that she does not feel good about herself when she is late, and she begins to explore this issue in greater depth. Her response to the mirroring interpretation is clearly positive, as was her response in the earlier session. However, in this version, the patient gets to this place in the process earlier in the session, and the therapist's countertransference does not interfere with her work.

## CONCLUSION

The treatment of a narcissistic personality requires a special sensitivity to the patient's extreme vulnerability. It can take several directions. A self psychology approach involves establishing a safe, stable environment by allowing the mirroring or idealizing transference to develop; the interpretation of injuries to maintain and restore the selfobject transference when it is interrupted; and the spontaneous occurrence of transmuting internalizations to enable the patient to build internal structure. If the patient is capable of tolerating a fair amount of dysphoric affect without serious acting out, then a treatment can be used that focuses on the patient's painful loss of self and his maladaptive defenses against this pain. If this treatment is attempted, care must be taken to ensure that the painful feelings stimulated by the treatment not overwhelm the patient's limited ability to contain dysphoric affect.

# 5

# Schizoid Disorders

*Eleanor Rigby*
*Picks up the rice*
*In the church where a wedding has been.*
*Lives in a dream.*
*Waits at the window*
*Wearing a face that she*
*Keeps in a jar by the door*
*Who is it for?*

*Eleanor Rigby*
*Died in the church,*
*And was buried along with her name.*
*Nobody came.*

*All the lonely people,*
*Where do they all come from?*
*All the lonely people,*
*Where do they all belong?*[1]

One cannot help but be touched when reminded of Eleanor Rigby's isolated dreamworld existence. The schizoid disorder is in many ways the easiest of the personality disorders to empathize with. The popular stereotype of the schizoid is of a shut-in, a hermit, an ascetic who shuns all society, or a mad scientist who hides away in a garret reading books, formulating theories, and petting his cat, and there is much truth to these characterizations. However, at the same time that the schizoid shuns social contact, he also craves connection with another person; this paradox defines the schizoid dilemma.

As used in this chapter, the term *schizoid* roughly includes the categories of "avoidant," "schizoid," and "schizotypal" as defined in the *DSM-III-R*. Most therapists report that about 10 percent or fewer of the patients in their practice who have personality disorders are schizoid or avoidant. However, I believe that the schizoid condition is far more common than this figure might imply, comprising perhaps as many as 40 percent of all personality disorders.[2] This huge discrepancy is probably largely because someone with a schizoid disorder is less likely to seek treatment than someone with other axis II disorders. In fact, the 40 percent figure may be low because, although people with this condition may be fairly easily diagnosed as having a personality disorder, they often conceal information that would facilitate their diagnosis as schizoid or avoidant.

Schizoids are found far less frequently in psychotherapy than they are in the general population because the nature of their condition makes it unlikely that they would attempt to solve their internal problems by entering into a relationship, especially one with the emotional intensity of psychotherapy. On the contrary, the schizoid seeks safety in emotional and interpersonal distance. Change in interpersonal relationships is extremely threatening to schizoid people so they tend to become tenaciously attached to their existing interpersonal relationships, even if these relationships are abusive. When faced with the possibility of rocking the boat with the apparently remote hope of feeling less isolated, the schizoid person generally chooses to maintain the adaptation that has been keeping him safe. Schizoid

[2] In their 35-year longitudinal study of a fairly random selection of 307 inner-city men who had not necessarily sought treatment, Vaillant and Drake (1985) diagnosed seventy-four of them as personality disorders, having some *DSM-III-R* axis II diagnosis. Just over 40 percent of these were schizoid (eighteen schizoid and twelve avoidant).

people are able to cut off most of their intense feelings of fear, hopelessness, and isolation through workaholism, intellectualization, and other distancing defenses so that they often do not experience themselves as being in great pain. To an observer, they sometimes can appear to be quite successful because their distancing allows them to devote themselves to their work and to make decisions without confusion from emotions. In short, the more effective their adaptation, the less likely they are to want change, and if they do want change, they tend not to view a therapeutic relationship as a safe or likely source of change.

The 40 percent figure quoted above is, in fact, probably low, due to the comparative difficulty in recognizing the schizoid condition. Of the three personality disorders considered in this book, the high-level schizoid is certainly the most difficult to diagnose. Because the dominant issue for the schizoid patient is safety and trust, he will be distrustful of the therapist to the point that he will at least initially be selective about what he feels comfortable allowing the therapist to know about him. He will also withhold information because he does not want to face it. Many therapists familiar with the diagnostic system described in this book find that patients who are originally diagnosed as borderline or narcissistic may appear more and more schizoid as they begin to develop a therapeutic alliance. Many of these therapists report a figure of over 25 percent as the schizoid component of the patients they see.

## CHARACTERISTICS OF THE SCHIZOID PERSONALITY

Unlike the borderline or narcissistic patient, whose behavior patterns and defenses usually give the therapist diagnostic clues, the schizoid may not act out in a characteristically schizoid way. The therapist will see a variety of distancing defenses that may be more in the style of a borderline or narcissist. These commonly include intellectualization, disengagement, suppressed affect, lack of spontaneity, self-reliance, exceptional need to control, and conflict avoidance. There may be additional narcissistic defenses, including some grandiosity, but what defines the schizoid patient is that the underlying self and object representations and the pain against which the patient defends are primarily schizoid. Whereas the borderline's underlying pain is abandonment and the narcissist's underlying pain is worthlessness, the schizoid's underlying pain is isolation and a fear of loss of all connection to humanity.

The diagnostic problem for the therapist with the schizoid patient is that early on in treatment and sometimes fairly well into treatment, the therapist is likely to hear about those representations and that pain only in diluted form because the patient does not trust the therapist with that information and deliberately withholds it. Commonly, a therapist might muddle through a year or several years of treatment with a schizoid patient, believing the patient is either borderline or narcissist. Then, when the therapist finally arrives at the correct diagnosis and becomes more attuned to the patient, the treatment rapidly accelerates; the therapeutic relationship deepens, trust builds, affect appears, and the patient's experience of life eventually changes.

Schizoid patients tend to be extremely loyal in all their relationships, including therapy relationships. The therapeutic relationship means much more to them than they would let on, because it is likely to be the most honest, most meaningful, and sometimes the only relationship of any substance that they have. In fact, one of the clues to a schizoid patient who has been misdiagnosed occurs when the therapist begins to wonder after a long, dry, stagnant period why the patient continues to remain in treatment. Not only has the patient remained in treatment, but most schizoid patients are consistently on time and rarely if ever cancel a session. For the schizoid, the preservation of any stable relationship, regardless of its unpleasant or distant qualities, is literally the *sine qua non* of existence.

The therapist who understands the schizoid's dilemma and can empathize with his struggle usually develops a tender affection for him and in time, as he works in treatment, a deep respect for his courage. The therapist who does not understand the schizoid patient, on the other hand, may experience the sessions as unbearably boring and fruitless. In these cases, probably what has happened is that although the patient loyally attends treatment, he has become emotionally absent. Unaware of the patient's extraordinary vulnerability, the therapist has been insensitive to it and has inadvertently said and done things to injure him, causing him to become even more emotionally distant than he would otherwise be, and giving rise to sessions so dry that almost any therapist who is not attuned to this process will be likely to become helplessly lost, uninvolved, and impatient.

Not all schizoids keep away from people. It is not people that schizoids avoid, but intimacy, self-disclosure, and emotions both positive and negative. In the song "Eleanor Rigby," from which the verses at the beginning of this chapter were taken, there is an additional verse. It is about Father McKenzie who writes "the words of a sermon that no one will hear. No one comes near." The song goes on, "Look at him working. Darning his socks in the night when there's nobody there. What does he care? . . ." Father McKenzie may be an example of a type of schizoid who actually performs or speaks in front of large groups of people, but is extremely uncomfortable with meaningful one-on-one contact. As one patient put it, "I don't mind at all speaking in front of groups; in fact I enjoy it. It's the breaks that kill me. People want to come up and talk to me. I just try to find someplace to hide where no one can find me."

## CLINICAL EXAMPLE—SCHIZOID ADAPTATION

In the following segment of transcript, Mrs. L., a patient one year into treatment, explores her ambivalence about giving up her relatively comfortable adaptation to a life without intimacy, which she says is, in fact, not comfortable but is a way she has found to make the best out of what she views as an impossible life situation. A patient like Mrs. L. would probably not seek treatment at all unless pressured to do so by someone else, in this case her husband. Some higher level schizoid patients also seek treatment when they become aware that without help they will probably never marry and have a family. This commonly occurs when they have begun to feel their age and have had enough experience in life to be able to see a pattern that is unlikely to change without treatment. Usually they are in their mid-thirties to early forties, but this can happen at other stages of their lives. If they are high level, like Mrs. L., they have a stronger yearning for meaningful relationships and have the capacity to enter into a relationship with a therapist. Lower level schizoid patients have more difficulty in seeking psychotherapy as a cure for their problems because they have more fear of relationships. Their adaptation to life is based upon their use of fantasy to feel connected to an imagined object. They might seek treatment if something occurs to interfere with the safety of the tight structure of their lives or of their fantasy lives.

**P:** Last week I said, "I don't really want to change." I don't want to become materially different than I am. I fear the process of change and the consequences of change. Inside all the time I'm saying, "Please leave me alone." At a gut level in my soul I just want to be left alone in my adaptation to life. My husband definitely crowds me toward changing. I feel crowded, pushed, shoved.

This transcript represents the last two-thirds of a session. The patient has felt disturbed by her spontaneous comment of the session before about not wanting to change. Schizoid patients carefully screen the things they say to be sure that they don't say anything that might expose them to attack or rejection or may later be used to pressure or coerce them. When Mrs. L. spontaneously made her comment the previous session, she scared herself; without consciously choosing to, she had let her guard down. This transcript was chosen for inclusion here because in it Mrs. L. expresses beautifully many of the concerns of schizoid people. She is comparatively a very high level schizoid, who in *DSM-III-R* would be considered *avoidant*, and is much more able to tolerate relationships than most schizoid or avoidant personalities. She is relatively satisfied with her life in its present form and is afraid of change. She begins this portion of the session by saying just that; she just wants to be left alone.

**T:** How are you feeling about being here today?

**P:** Today, I feel not at all like being here. For a little while I was anxious to continue, but the last few days I haven't felt like it because I don't want to face any more. I don't want to talk to anyone at more than the level of intimacy I've already reached in these conversations. I don't know what I'm hiding from.

**T:** I wonder if anything happened the last time you were here that

The therapist in the transcript responds by exploring the transferential aspect of Mrs. L.'s comments, to which she responds by saying that she does not feel like being in therapy, because she does not want to be any more intimate with anyone than she has already become in treatment. The therapist views this as an oblique reference to her spontaneous comment of the session before, and seeks to make the connection between that comment and her present desire to withdraw. She responds by talking

might have increased your feeling of vulnerability.

**P:** If I talk to you, I can't hide. I don't think there is any way of continuing in this process without going beyond that point I don't want to go beyond. It just seems to be built into the process, just by being here and the way you conduct the sessions, it's going to happen. I don't know what that point is or why I don't want to go beyond it. I feel at risk. There is some part of me I don't want to know about, hear about. In the last two days I've examined my skull. What is my anxiety about? What is all this feeling about? I've come up with nothing. I know I'm very unhappy with myself in certain areas, especially the way I'm handling health issues, but I just don't know. . . .

almost ingenuously about her fear of intimacy, her sense of vulnerability with people, and in particular in treatment.

**T:** You come here and find that you are exposing yourself, and it is not what you expected.

**P:** (slightly teary) I don't like it. Before this, the only person I've revealed myself to is my husband and even with him, I limit how much of me I let him know. I never even as a child had friends I could reveal myself to. I convinced myself I didn't want it. *Last time—unexpected to me—I just outright said "I just don't want to change." It just came out. That was on a really deep level.* I don't want anyone telling me how I should be. Those people are encroaching, pushing me toward being something else. And those people are to be avoided, stymied in

The therapist mirrors Mrs. L.'s sense of exposure and vulnerability. She responds with affect. Her comment, "I never even as a child had friends I could reveal myself to," reflects an almost universal experience of schizoids. If the therapist takes an initial history, this aspect may not show up as clearly as it does during later stages of treatment. However, schizoid adults tend to have had difficulty with relationships all their lives. Commonly, as children they either did not have close friends or had one main friend at a given time. Often there is a history of having lost this friend due to a family relocation or some other interruption. Even as an adult, the patient may wonder what went wrong with

some way. There are two things that stand out about that comment last week: Number one, that it was such a surprise to me and, number two, that I would say it, that I would come out and say that I'm happy with the way I am, and if I had my way I'd be left alone. If I had my way, my husband wouldn't want me to change, and you wouldn't. I'd probably stay just the way I am. I may not be evolved in many ways, but I'm comfortable with the way I've worked out my life.

an important childhood friendship.

In this segment she focuses for the first time sharply on the spontaneous remark of the session before that has heightened her sense of vulnerability and triggered her distancing defense.

**T:** You think that I want you to change?

**P:** Well, maybe not you, but that's what this process is about really. Isn't it?

**T:** So you feel ambivalent about being here, because you are comfortable with the way you are, and just the fact that you are coming here implies that you are intending some sort of change. The fact that you don't want to change is something you would not feel safe to say to anyone. You were feeling safe here and you allowed yourself to be spontaneous and that popped out, and this has alarmed you.

Her allusion to the therapist's wanting to change her brings a request for clarification from him. For her to characterize the therapist as working against her is an obvious attempt to distance, which his clarifying question interrupts.

Although the outcome of this intervention seems to be positive, an example of a better intervention might have been, "You felt closer to me last week when you shared yourself spontaneously, and now you are attempting to restore a safer distance by thinking of me as working against you." The therapist actually says something akin to this shortly afterwards; however he does not link the patient's sense of vulnerability to her attempt at distancing. These patients are surprisingly unconscious about their distancing and what has triggered it. In treatment, they find it very helpful in understanding themselves when their oscillation between approaching and distancing is pointed out to them.

In general it tends not to be helpful

to intervene in ways that push the schizoid patient. The therapist's actual intervention here pushes the patient to give up her distorted characterization of the therapist and interrupts her attempt to restore a comfortable distance. Control is a major issue in the schizoid patient's life because without it the schizoid patient cannot feel safe. If the therapist pushes the patient at all, the schizoid patient experiences it as an attempt to control her, and she is likely to respond by feeling unsafe and distancing.

**P:** Uh huh. It's not just that I don't want anyone else to hear it, it's that I don't even want to hear it myself, because once I hear myself say it out loud, I can't deny it; then, I feel like I have to do something about it. Ideally, I should be able to stuff it—to never know it was there. If I was really good I'd be eagerly addressing rough edges to patch them up so I wouldn't see it, like a drunk who doesn't want to know she is. But you are right. I feel safer with you than I would with anybody, because of your technique. You don't judge. But I wouldn't care if you were some kind of saint, I still don't want to get into this stuff—I don't want to change. But if I come here, it seems like I can't not get into it. I say to myself, "I'm paying for it, let's not waste my time."

In the patient's next comments we see again the schizoid patient's characteristic oscillation between approaching and distancing. She makes several open, honest comments about her need to deny her extreme sense of fear and vulnerability; in doing so she is again opening up slightly more to the therapist. Among these comments is her expression of her lack of awareness of her own feelings and how threatening these are to her. Then she makes a directly contactful comment about feeling safer with the therapist than she would with anyone, and immediately begins to distance by attributing the sense of safety to his technique rather than to a gradually deepening sense of trust of the therapist as a person. Again in an attempt to restore a comfortable distance, she pushes him away with the comment, "I'm paying for it, let's not waste my time." This is not the devaluing attack of a narcissistic patient, but the poignant struggle of the schizoid to find a place which is neither too close nor too distant.

**T:** It's a paradoxical situation. You don't want to reveal yourself but you find that you continue to come here and you do end up revealing yourself.

**P:** Right. I delude myself into thinking I could be the one who could come here and explore my problems pretty much as an exercise—talk about them theoretically, intellectually—look at a few discrete problems without bringing my insides into the picture. That's an adaptation that I felt like has worked for me in the past. The truth is that it's my greatest enemy in relationships, and that has been really the only problem I've had in my life. Even with my parents, the relationship was basically intellectual—I didn't really let them know what was inside of me. My whole life, all my relationships with people have been characterized by not letting them get near me.

**T:** And characterized by a fear of those people.

**P:** Right. What they'll think of me, what they'll do to me. Boy, that's exactly right. Every possibility I've ever had for a relationship has frightened me, especially authority figures. Some of them haven't hurt me but I've still feared them as if they would. Boy, that hurts. A guy once said to me "I don't know what it is, but there is something wrong with you." He was the first guy who got at a personal level. In his eyes I was sick. And during that period of time I certainly didn't

Again the therapist mirrors Mrs. L.'s characteristically schizoid dilemma, her oscillation between wanting to be distant and safe, and yet wanting to maintain the connection. The patient responds with more exploration of her sense of isolation, her inability to let anyone get close to her. The therapist reminds her that the need for distance comes from her fear; Mrs. L. responds to this comment by expanding upon the point. There is an openness and ingenuousness about her description of her disconnectedness from people that is also characteristic of schizoid patients. Once they have begun to feel trusting and willing to be open with the therapist, they can say some very honest and tragically sad things with only a trace of teariness because of their ability to distance from their feelings. Nevertheless, the listener cannot help but be moved and see through their minimal show of emotion to the deep well of feeling beneath it.

think I was doing anything strange or odd—just being me. But you know I'm not aware of how much distance I put between myself and others. There is a range, but even my closest is still far away. I can really stay distant or I can open up a little—that's the range.

**T:** You navigate between two dangers. If you lose contact you'll *vaporize* and if you get too close you'll be—

**P:** *Swallowed up or obliterated.*

**T:** So you found a way to adapt; you've attempted to chart a course that is safe. You try to maintain a ritualized contact or a structured contact with people that enables you to feel reasonably stable and anchored in the universe, but is emotionally distant enough that you don't feel the threat of getting too close.

**P:** Yes, it's safe but uncomfortable. I really think it's weird that I find it so difficult to sit down and have a conversation with even a friend I've known five years or more. If I thought of all the people I could enjoy a one-on-one five minute conversation with, there are not more than four or five. Even with my brother we'd be superficial most of the time. An intimate conversation could not be sustained for more than an hour. Even with my best friend, we could have a conversation for an hour but couldn't talk about anything really significant for an hour. There have been times I have really thought I was inca-

The therapist responds by again summarizing the characteristic schizoid dilemma. As repetitive as this may seem, it is necessary. One must keep in mind that this dilemma defines the schizoid patient's lifelong struggle. She is consumed with this struggle daily. Although so many of her actions are motivated by the schizoid dilemma, surprisingly she has probably rarely been aware of this motivation. These patients usually find it enormously clarifying to realize the pervasiveness of this struggle in them.

The therapist's use of the term *vaporize* is taken from the patient's own use of this word in a previous session. The patient adds the other half of this dangerous balancing act; either she loses contact and is "vaporized" or she gets too close and is "swallowed up or obliterated." This kind of intense feeling of danger is part of every schizoid patient's daily existence; it is not merely dramatization on Mrs. L.'s part. With every schizoid patient, when trust is established in the therapeutic relationship, these kinds of poignant descriptors emerge.

The therapist continues his summarizing comment, which is a bit long winded but does serve to bring

pable of having a friend. I'd have to say, "Yes, I don't have any friends," because with a friend I believe you should be able to have a personal conversation for some duration. The last person I really felt comfortable with was my brother's ex-wife who was eight years older than I am. I did feel comfortable having conversations with her. I guess, when I think about that it's as clear to me as it is to anyone else; I think to myself, *"You stupid so and so, you really do need to change." But I guess what I really feel is that I need to but I don't want to.* I get this negative feeling. It's just more comfortable to stay at a superficial level with people. I can talk about a project, a vacation, their work, my work, but please don't talk about us as human beings. I don't want people asking me a lot of personal questions and I don't draw it out of them either because I don't like it when they carry on. My husband has said one problem is I observed that my mother was extremely feeling oriented and I was repulsed by it and modeled my life in opposition. I really don't know what about it I found repulsive, but it is true I am repulsed by it. (A short discussion follows of the patient's experiences with her parents and her determination not to end up the way they did.)

the patient's dilemma further into focus.

The patient now launches into a lengthy, apparently meaningful exploration of her difficulties with intimacy. The focus of the session returns to the initial subject, the patient's ambivalence about change. Again she says that she needs to change. "I need to but I don't want to." She is in treatment in spite of herself. She has a deep sense of her isolation and her need for treatment; however the idea of change is terrifying. In particular the idea of intimacy is terrifying.

This conflict takes her into an apparently productive exploration of the historical basis of her repulsion to feelings.

**T:** We're out of time today.

**P:** OK. I don't feel worse for having hurt a little. I don't feel any better, but I did touch the hurt a

At the end of the session she essentially says, "That hurt, but not too bad." Then she reiterates an inner

little today. I still don't know what's behind the curtain that I don't want to go through. There is a fear that it's dark and awful and the me that's in there is really disgraceful.

sense of herself that there must be something at the core of her being that is too "disgraceful" for her to even let herself know about.

**The Schizoid Dilemma**

As demonstrated in the previous transcript, the schizoid individual is constantly walking a fine line between two devastating dangers. If he becomes too distant from people, he believes he will disintegrate, dissolve into oblivion, vaporize, be lost. If he gets too close to someone, he is afraid of being co-opted, used, swallowed up, devoured, totally appropriated. Various patients have put it in different ways:

Cast off, a dust bowl in the corner of the universe.

I stayed home today sick. Being alone is as traumatic for me as being with somebody. . . . depressed about being in the quiet of the house. . . . I feel like a lost person, unconnected. I was really looking forward to therapy tonight, to be back in connection with someone. When I'm with people I fantasize about being alone; when I'm alone I feel lost.

I hate that feeling, the feeling of being sent away, pushed away. (pause, slight tears) Not wanted. It's almost like dying. (very teary) Like I'll never come back, like I'm away from everything and can't get back. It's just a terrible feeling. There is no purpose to it. There isn't anyone there, I'm just all alone. (long pause) I don't know what there is to say about it. (very teary) I feel like everything I'm doing is to keep that feeling away. It's a feeling of nothingness, having no substance. I don't want anyone to know about it. It's a feeling too that it will never end. There is nothing I can do, nothing to change it. I get away for little periods and there it is again. My marriage, work, church are all geared to get past this.

Although I think it's irrational, I nevertheless expect to be attacked. If someone attacks me my fear is of annihilation, oblivion, not death but nonexistence. I'm going to turn into vapor.

Get too close and you'll be swallowed up or obliterated.

> For me, connection to people is like a mine field; like it's going to explode in my face any minute, it is so loaded. But at least here I can talk about it; this is the only place I can talk about it.
>
> With relationships you have to be careful; they're like being next to a giant circular saw—one false step and it's all over.

The schizoid's struggle to find a safe path between these two dangers contributes to the unique character of his treatment. Other patients with personality disorders struggle to get a handle on material that they have been avoiding or denying. When they do not know what to talk about in treatment, it is usually because they are not aware of relevant material, despite its abundance. When a schizoid patient claims to have nothing to talk about, it usually means that he does not feel safe talking about any of the many things that he knows are relevant. Often, if the therapist is able to address something in a session that has made the patient uncomfortable, the schizoid patient can relax and resume meaningful exploration of his issues. Whereas the borderline and narcissistic patients usually come into treatment thinking that the problem resides outside themselves, the schizoid can often dispassionately talk about his social shortcomings as a root of his problems.

## HARRY GUNTRIP

Guntrip was an English psychiatrist, a contemporary of Melanie Klein, who identified and elucidated the inner dynamics of the schizoid personality. In many books and articles on the subject, he described in vivid detail the schizoid individual's struggle.

### Etiology of the Schizoid Disorder

According to Guntrip (1968), the etiology of this condition is in infantile deprivation, a caregiver (mother) who is unresponsive to the infant's physical and emotional needs. In particular he identifies three types of deprivation: "*tantalizing refusal* by those responsible for the infant to satisfy his need for love, *impingement* of a hostile aggressive object or situation that arouses direct fear of an overpowering outer world, and evokes withdrawal as a flight into the inner world, and *rejection and neglect*, nonrecognition or desertion, by the outer world, [what Winnicott called a] *'deficiency disease'* " (p. 75). He describes the infant as experiencing hunger to be life threatening because of a lack of confidence that the infant's cries will ever be noticed and responded to. Consequently, whenever the breast is withdrawn, the infant feels completely cut off from sustenance, and when the breast is finally offered again, the infant's impulse is to completely devour it, for fear of losing it again. The impulse to devour the breast leads to a fear of destroying the object if it comes too close, and in doing this destroying his universe, his context for existence. At the same time the infant projects these feelings onto the object and fears that he himself will be devoured, swallowed up.

This then translates into the schizoid dilemma, fear of having no human connection and, at the same time, fear of being too close. Guntrip describes the "in and out programme" (p. 36) in which the schizoid person yearns for closeness and then, if some additional closeness is achieved, becomes scared and pulls away. Then he feels cut off, disconnected, and begins to yearn for closeness again, and the process repeats. The "schizoid compromise" is to find a "half-way-house position, neither in nor out" (p. 61).

The issue of closeness and distance pervades the schizoid patient's life. The closer he feels to someone the more he experiences the need to allow that person to dominate him in order to minimize the devastating possibilities of conflict, attack, and rejection. Any increase in closeness or involvement represents loss of autonomy and freedom while any decrease raises the specter of rejection and exile. One patient put it like this:

> External controls make things predictable. That is what I seek. Yes. I give over control, there is no question about that. . . . The sense of giving over control when I get close to another individual is very strong. If I'm relating and I keep control of myself it will mean say, "No," which will mean in my terms anger and attack and abandonment, so to avoid those feelings I give myself over lock, stock, and barrel. I'm becoming more aware of that now. I avoid that by not having anything to do with anybody. I pull away.

Much of Guntrip's theory may be a bit too complex and involved to lend itself to immediate practical use. His description of the schizoid self and object split parts, for instance, involves two levels of splitting.[3] Guntrip's writings do, however, provide a sensitive portrayal of the schizoid patient's plight and valuable insight into the inner experience of these patients.

## TREATMENT OF THE SCHIZOID DISORDER

### Ralph Klein

Ralph Klein is a psychiatrist who has done extensive clinical work with schizoid patients. He has produced a number of very practical and useful principles for their treatment. Most of the clinical material in this chapter is based on Klein's contributions,[4] his sensitivity to the schizoid struggle, and his practical application of theory in treatment.

### Etiology of the Schizoid Disorder

As I understand his thinking, Klein is in basic agreement with Guntrip about the etiology of the schizoid condition. However, he views this condition as originating at any point during early development, rather than the extremely early period referred to by Guntrip. Naturally the earlier the origins of the condition in a particular person, the more severe (lower level) the condition that is likely to result. Klein sees Mahler's rapprochement period as a likely time for the schizoid condition to take hold, the same period as is credited with the beginnings of borderline conditions.

### Safety—the Schizoid Patient's Paramount Concern

The first and ongoing objective in the treatment of the schizoid patient is to understand him. In order to make this possible, the therapist must help the patient to experience the therapeutic environment as safe so

[3]The first level of splitting is between a libidinal unit and an antilibidinal unit, and the second an internal splitting of the libidinal unit that he describes as serving to protect the libidinal self and object from being attacked and destroyed from within the patient himself by the antilibidinal (sadistic, attacking) internal object representation.

[4]Ralph Klein is the clinical director of the Masterson Institute in New York City. For the most part, his theoretical orientation is very similar to Guntrip's; however he has made very helpful and practical contributions in the area of treatment.

that the patient feels free to reveal himself to the therapist. Since the schizoid's dominant feeling is his extreme fear, the therapist often makes special allowances for the schizoid patient to facilitate his feeling safe. These include allowing the patient to exercise a much greater degree of control of the parameters of treatment than would be appropriate with other patients. Klein recommends under certain conditions allowing the patient to dictate the frequency of visits, the direction of discussion, and even the positioning of the furniture in which the therapist and patient sit.

He indicates that although he never accepts gifts from other patients, he often will accept a gift from a schizoid when it represents the patient's being vulnerable and making an outreach to the therapist that he might not be able to make in a more direct way. A patient might offer the therapist a poem, a drawing, or some other form of personal expression. With schizoid patients especially, these kinds of indirect statements are not unusual. It is also common for schizoid patients to request an every-other-week treatment schedule, something that can work for the schizoid patient but is not usually advisable for patients who do not rely so extensively on distancing defenses. To reduce the possibility that the patient will feel threatened or intruded upon, Klein recommends softening interventions by making them a little more tentative than one otherwise would. For instance, "I wonder if this might be. . . ."

## The In and Out Programme

The therapist pays careful attention throughout the treatment process to even subtle variations in relative distance between therapist and patient and also between the patient and other significant people in his life (the in and out programme). In sessions, these are expressed by changes in a myriad of phenomena including level of affect, degree of personalness of information shared, silences, responsiveness, spontaneity, expressiveness, and directness with which patient relates to therapist. Through these indicators, the therapist can sense the patient's relative level of comfort with the therapist so that the therapist can guess when something has threatened the patient or made him feel unsafe. Also, when the therapist notices an unexpected change in relative distance, either increased or decreased, between therapist and patient, the therapist can predict with some accuracy that the patient will become threatened and defend. The therapist continually interprets the patient's adjustments in relative distance by describing the schizoid dilemma; he cannot allow himself to get too close or too distant from others. This process of carefully tracking the patient's subtle shifts in relative closeness, in degree of affective expressiveness, in quality of presence, is the core of Klein's approach to the treatment of these patients.

Schizoid patients are so sensitive to variations in relative distance that just about any change in the therapist's routine is likely to be noticed and evaluated by the patient in terms of its meaning with respect to relative distance, what the therapist appears to be feeling toward the patient, and ramifications with respect to safety for the patient. These variations include vacations, changes in fee, appointment time, level of alertness of the therapist, therapist's style of dress, therapist's style of intervention, and any change in the physical furnishings of the therapist's office. This is why the positioning of furniture can be important to the schizoid patient, especially if the chairs are a few inches closer to each other than usual or further apart than usual. For the schizoid patient, control of information is an important method of maintaining a safe distance. For this reason, interpretations that indicate that the therapist knows more about the schizoid patient than the patient expected her to know can be very threatening.

Klein points out that whereas with borderline patients the primary focus of the therapist's interventions is what the patient is doing outside of treatment and with narcissistic patients the primary focus is on what occurs during the treatment hour, the treatment of a schizoid patient requires that the focus be balanced. The ultimate yardstick for gauging the schizoid patient's progress in treatment is his increasing ability to feel safe enough to take risks in interpersonal relationships both inside and outside of the treatment room.

As the therapeutic focus is divided between the transference and the patient's life outside of treatment, the in and out programme should be evidenced through risk-taking in both the patient's outside life and within the transference. Sometimes the patient becomes increasingly close to the therapist while continuing to distance from everyone else in his life. In this case the relationship with the therapist is probably being used defensively to allow the patient to experience a sense of being anchored or connected to another person without needing to take risks with people outside of treatment. On the other hand, if the patient's movement seems to appear exclusively in the outside world, there is probably something that has occurred within the transference that has frightened the patient and that the patient has been unwilling or unable to process with the therapist.

### The Schizoid Triad

The therapist can attune himself more finely to the patient by tracking the schizoid triad, a schizoid version of the triad identified by Masterson for patients with personality disorders. For each of the personality disorders, the triad takes the form of movement toward supporting the self, followed by dysphoric affect, followed by defense. In the case of the schizoid, as Masterson and Klein view it, the movement toward the self is exhibited as an attempt at experiencing feelings, closeness, or spontaneity, and is followed by a dysphoric affect that is predominantly fear of being attacked or swallowed up, but is also fear of harming or offending the object and causing it to withdraw. Both fears exist simultaneously. The defense is almost always distancing, sometimes including withdrawal into fantasies of intimacy. By tracking the triad, the therapist can increase his ability to tune in to and understand the patient, and through the therapist's consequent interpretations the patient feels understood and consequently more trusting of the therapist, and becomes increasingly aware of her underlying painful feelings. As with the other personality disorders, the more aware the patient is of her underlying pain, the less satisfied she will be with her current form of adaptation to life.

## SCHIZOID SPLITTING

### Object Relations Units of the Schizoid Disorder

Like the other personality disorders, self and object splitting characterizes the schizoid structure. Unlike the borderline and narcissistic forms of splitting, the schizoid character has no really positive object relations unit. There is a negative object relations unit consisting of a sadistic, depriving, intrusive, viciously attacking object and a self that is vacant, exiled, or vaporized. These are linked to affects of aloneness, alienation, anger, fear, and anxiety. The object relations unit resulting from positive or libidinal splitting is known as the master/slave unit. Because the schizoid has not had the benefit of an experience of contact and trust in infancy, the most positive relationship that he can manage is one in which he is not being attacked. He accomplishes this by assuming a part self representation of a trapped, helpless, completely compliant person relating to a another person (part object) whom he perceives of as rigid, easily offended, and extremely controlling. These slave and master representations are linked to affects of fear, anxiety, obsessive caution, and control.

Just as the higher level borderline patient tends to favor clinging over distancing defenses and the lower level borderline tends more to distance, the defense used by the schizoid tends to vary, depending on his level. The higher level schizoid perceives the master/slave unit ambivalently, an acceptable alternative to exile, but one in which he sacrifices his autonomy and much of his self-esteem in return for security and some sense of relatedness. He prefers this to the more distancing alternative. The lower level schizoid relies more heavily on distancing and fantasized relationships. He experiences the master/slave unit as more threatening, a complete appropriation of the self; Klein describes it using the image of the movie *Invasion of the Body Snatchers* in which pods from outer space gradually take over people's identities.

The lack of a truly positive split may explain why a therapist who understands the schizoid personality is so apt to be touched by her plight. The narcissist has a grandiose self representation in which she defends against her underlying sense of worthlessness by feeling omnipotence and an inflated sense of self-importance. The borderline has a rewarding self representation in which she defends against an underlying feeling of abandonment and is able to feel loved and appreciated by clinging, appending herself to the object. The schizoid, however, is unable to defend effectively enough to produce a euphoric state; the best she can hope for is to feel reasonably safe from attack while maintaining some sense of relatedness to another human being, which keeps her from disappearing into cosmic isolation.

## Countertransference

The therapist's countertransference to the schizoid patient often arises out of the therapist's acceptance of the patient's projection of the master component of the master/slave unit. The therapist begins to be impatient and attempts to move the patient along. This is experienced by the patient as an attempt to control her. Occasionally, the patient can also take on the master part of the split and project the slave part onto the therapist. In this situation the patient becomes very controlling and demanding, and the therapist feels controlled. Most commonly, however, in response to the emotional wall erected by the patient between herself and the therapist, the therapist becomes bored and uninvolved with the patient. This lack of involvement can become extreme to the point that therapists have been known to nod off in a session with a schizoid patient.

## The Schizoid Compromise

Neither of the object relations units available to the lower level schizoid is acceptable to him; in Klein's terminology, the schizoid is either in exile or in jail. If he lives in the master/slave object relations unit, he is careful to make no waves and he perceives others as tyrants who will not tolerate the slightest insubordination. He gives up any hope of expressing or even experiencing himself. The alternative to the master/slave relationship is complete self-reliance and isolation as a protection against the vicious, attacking, tyrannical object; an exile from the world of relationships. Self-reliance taken to an extreme carries with it a sense of having no relatedness to anchor the schizoid person, no tether to keep the person from drifting in space into total isolation and oblivion. One might think of the scene from the movie *2001—A Space Odyssey* in which the astronaut's lifeline to the spaceship is cut and he is catapulted off into the infinite nothingness of space.

## The Role of Fantasy

Especially for the lower level schizoid, fantasy serves as his tenuous tether to the world of relatedness. To make the schizoid's isolation tolerable, he maintains an extensive and rich fantasy life in which he is involved in intimate relationships or in which he holds a prominent social position that allows him to be easily related to other people. Because of its vital importance, this fantasy life will remain hidden from others, including the therapist, and may not emerge in all its richness until well into the treatment process. It is a far more prominent feature for the lower level schizoid who finds both object relations units to be intolerable than it is for the higher level schizoid who can adapt to a master/slave existence.

One common avenue for fantasy is romantic novels and films. Just as these can stimulate imagined relationships, real life interactions can also become the kernel of relationship fantasies. What may be for the other person a polite or superficial exchange can be magnified in significance and depth by the schizoid. Therapists are often surprised to learn well into the treatment process that a schizoid patient has felt intensely personally involved with them, and that the patient has assumed all along that the intensity of involvement was mutual. Naturally, to abruptly deprive him of that belief would be deeply hurtful and serve no constructive purpose.

Another example of how a schizoid can create an internal substitute for relatedness is by feeling connected to God or spirituality. Besides the clear guidelines for life and the sense of belonging to a group that religion can provide, spiritual devotion offers the possibility of intimate and sometimes intense experiences of relatedness to spirit, a relationship that can be emotional and yet safe.

An interesting twist to the fantasy of relatedness is the elaborate fantasies of suicide that schizoid patients often create. These fantasies can be especially misleading for the therapist because they often involve a detailed plan of execution although without a specific time planned. Therapists who have been schooled to become alarmed when the patient relates a suicide plan that includes a specific method are likely to be in a state of perpetual alarm with some schizoid patients. Schizoid individuals continually perseverate, fantasize, and plan. As just described, if they are depressed and experiencing themselves in exile, they will use fantasy as a lifeline out of exile to relatedness. These fantasies can include elaborate suicide plans that have been obsessed about and thought through to the last detail.

## Case Example—the Role of Fantasy

Mr. M. is an example of a lower level schizoid who relied on fantasy to help him live with his extreme isolation. He was a young man who had few social contacts in his life. He worked, as do many middle to lower level schizoid individuals, at a civil service job where his income was secure, and he was not called upon extensively to relate to other people. He would go to work in the morning and then come home in the evening and remain in his bedroom looking at pornographic photographs of women. The schizoid's fantasy life can often focus on sex, either as a formula for connectedness or as a sadomasochistic projection of the master/slave unit. Mr. M. engaged in these fantasies to the exclusion of meaningful relationships in the real world.

He entered treatment shortly after a problem developed at work between him and his direct supervisor. As a result of this conflict he felt that the supervisor was attempting to get rid of him, and he began behaving in a withdrawn way that appeared paranoid and somewhat bizarre to his co-workers. Eventually a human resources worker suggested that he go to an E.A.P. (employee assistance program) counselor who referred him to treatment. His main motivation for pursuing treatment was the fear of losing his job. He hoped in treatment to learn what he could do to appease his supervisor and other people at work and regain a sense of security.

At first his therapist misjudged Mr. M.'s difficulties in relating to others. She suggested to him that he could not overcome his difficulties with people if he continued to hide out at home and avoid people. In the session that followed she was pleased to hear from Mr. M. that he had ventured outside of his home one evening and gone for a walk during which he had been tempted to approach a young woman who was showing interest in him. Encouraged by Mr. M.'s initial responsiveness, the therapist challenged his use of pornography, saying that he was using it defensively to avoid facing the world and improving his life. In response to these comments, Mr. M. canceled his next two sessions, each with several days' notice and a plausible excuse. In terms of the object relations units, Mr. M. responded initially with the compliance of the master/slave unit. His temptation to approach the woman he had seen during his walk was probably no more than a fantasy he had nurtured about approaching the woman. When the therapist challenged his use of pornography to embellish his fantasies, Mr. M. felt misunderstood and attacked. His response was to go into exile, canceling his next two sessions. In general, the schizoid's use of fantasy, although defensive, is so absolutely essential to the schizoid compromise that for the therapist to interpret its function before the patient has developed an ability to create true relationships with real people is overwhelmingly threatening for the patient.

After obtaining consultation about the case, Mr. M.'s therapist began to interpret his massive fear of attack and his use of pornography and fantasy as his only semblance of a relationship with another person. Mr. M. resumed regular attendance in treatment, and over time gradually reduced his dependence on pornography as he was able to develop a stable and safe relationship with the therapist. He gradually began to take risks both within and outside of treatment, tentatively forming minimal relationships on the outside. After six years of treatment once a week, Mr. M. is still slowly emerging from his fantasy cocoon.

### Master/Slave Unit

Because it is so prominent in virtually all the schizoid patient's relationships, including her relationship with a therapist, the master/slave unit must be thoroughly understood and recognized by the clinician. The schizoid individual cannot be in a relationship without immediately taking the slave role; for her there is no alternative way to *relate*. The more involved in the relationship she becomes, the more intense the slave role becomes for her. The slave role can range from painfully obvious to the observer, to insidiously subtle, going undetected for years by even a very skilled and experienced clinician.

The patient's experience of enslavement is very deep. One patient compared her experience in the master/slave unit to the Israelites' experience of bondage in Egypt. Later in the session the therapist made use of this allusion:

**P:** The context started becoming very uncomfortable for me and it seemed more than innocent to him. I felt trapped and held (physically) and I wound up avoiding him and not seeing him again as the only way out. If I did see him by chance I would be very uncomfortable.

**T:** The Israelites again. You are either in slavery or wandering forty years in the desert.

**P:** Yes, at least I'm consistent. (teary)

## CLINICAL EXAMPLE—SCHIZOID SPLITTING AND THE IN AND OUT PROGRAMME

In the following session with a schizoid patient, Mr. N., the therapist explores the two parts of his split representations of his wife, and then attempts to make the patient aware of this splitting process. The master/slave unit clearly shows itself throughout the session in Mr. N.'s description of his life, and to some degree in the transference.

**P:** I've been mulling over how I feel. I've been able this week to stuff this down pretty good so it's not been on my mind a lot—I've been able to get it out of my consciousness. . . . But I'm not sure that that's a wonderful thing, because I've had some sleep disturbance and I think it was because I was ignoring a problem. Therapy has been depressing and I think it will continue to be if it goes on for a while.

I tried to put names on my feelings. A principal element is I feel badgered and beat up by my wife. This relationship is a negative to my peace of mind. She bullies me, badgers me. She is taking advantage of a sense that I will not desert her. So I feel manipulated and used. There are actually two feelings. The first is being disquieted. The second is feeling manipulated because I believe she takes advantage of my loyalty. So I feel trapped, hopeless, and I despair of resources. That combination of feelings is very disturbing to me. I feel the typical solutions are unavailable to me by my own choice and my ethical system and my commitment to my wife. If I did actually leave her, I fear that my sense of integrity, of my whole being, would be compromised. I can't run away from it and I can't fix it. I feel really boxed in.

The patient begins with an allusion to his ambivalence about focusing on painful material, and consequently about therapy in general, although this is clearly a patient who is committed to treatment. He is upset because he feels badgered and bullied by his wife. As he describes it, one is likely to think of his wife as an insensitive tyrant, but we must remember that we are seeing her through the eyes of someone who only knows two types of relationships, one in which he slavishly complies and the other in which he is mercilessly tyrannized. In the case of this patient, he would probably be content with a relationship in which he lets his wife lead and he complies. However, he perceives his wife as also attacking him which may make the slave role of the master/slave relationship unbearable. Because he feels attacked, he considers the possibility of leaving this situation which would otherwise be secure and safe for him.

His reference to his integrity being compromised seems also to be characteristic of many schizoid patients. They often get themselves into situations in which they feel tyrannized and they do not take action on their own behalf because they believe such action will compromise their integrity.

In most cases, integrity to those patients represents the opposite of culpability. The young child who has been abused over a period of time usually blames himself; since he was so severely punished, he feels that he must have done something wrong.

Similarly, when the schizoid encounters tyranny or exile he feels a sense of badness, culpability, or guilt. In contrast, if he can maintain harmony through the slave role, he has a sense of peacefulness and order. Similarly, it is unacceptable for the schizoid to fail to obey and consequently cause the object to become upset; the experience of causing someone else pain is experienced as a loss of integrity. He refers to his ability to properly conform and maintain a peaceful settled state as maintaining his integrity; integrity is a haven from disorder, guilt, and conflict.

Schizoids often attempt to maintain their sense of integrity in ways that are clearly destructive to themselves.

In this case, Mr. N. feels that by leaving his wife he would become thoroughly reprehensible and bad. It is not clear whether this expectation comes from a belief that she will attack him for leaving or an anticipation of his wife being deeply hurt by his leaving and his feeling responsible for causing her pain.

I feel frightened in those times when the relationship is tense, that the outcome will ultimately be the end of the relationship, which means the end of life as I know it. I'm relatively comfortable in the relationship, so when it's sour I feel it will end, and with an emotional upheaval that I wonder if I can stand. I wonder if I can live the rest of my days in isolation from my wife and family. So when it comes to considering these things I think, "No, I will not live that way."

The thought of leaving a relationship is a drastic and terrifying idea for the schizoid patient, as he describes eloquently in this session. He describes his wife's role as the person who manages his relationships with his children, arranges to see them, and makes the phone calls. He believes that without her to do that he will become even further isolated from them than he already is. His description of his friends is typical of some schizoid personalities; he has many acquaintances, but none of these relationships are personal.

**T:** Do you think of it as living the rest of your days in isolation from all people?

**P:** No, I don't think of it that way. The kids wouldn't want to stop seeing me but my wife is the social director. Without her I'd be further separated from the children. I'd have to change my ways and do what she now does for me. Right now, I coast. I would find it difficult to make it all happen myself, arrange to see the kids, make the phone calls. I find it difficult to be separated from anybody else who is a blood relative but I find it more difficult to actually be close to them, so I couldn't fall back on that. There is nobody else. There are a lot of business acquaintances—none are close personal friends. All my close personal friends are through my wife. I would be cut off from them.

The point is I fear that—a mind blinding fear when that possibility is reasonably real. Even when I consider packing up and leaving it scares the daylights out of me. (pause) Those feelings are too frequently a disturbance to my normal mood. As a businessman I need to relax and recharge my batteries at home to be as effective as I can be.

T: You seem to have made a shift here. You were talking about the impact on you personally of a separation and then you began to talk about its effect on you as a businessman.

The patient again comes back to his fear, a "mind blinding" fear of the possibility of his marriage ending. At this point he begins to defend by focusing on the effect of this possibility on his business career. One might think of this as a playing out of the "in and out programme," in which he has revealed himself and his feelings to the point that he is now feeling too exposed, and he then reins himself in by shifting his focus to his business life. The significance of this shift is placed in clear relief when considered in light of his comments immediately preceding this shift. He acknowledges that his business relationships are not personal, and then he shifts his focus from the effects on him personally of losing his marriage to the effects on his business career. The therapist then acknowledges this shift. Considering that the patient has been working very well on his own up until this point, it is probably premature for the therapist to jump in immediately with this comment. It would be better for her to wait and see if the patient brings himself back.

**P:** (slight laugh) I know I tend to be logical when other people wouldn't. So when I think of the effects of all this I think of it getting in my way of being successful.

**T:** I imagine that the discussion of your personal concerns felt too close to home, so you chose a focus that still related to the effects of all this but was not so close. I assume that you think of your business success as less personal than your happiness.

**P:** True. I'm not happy. The most important thing is to correct that. I can be in the middle of something and then boom, the whole combination of emotions. . . . I don't think I should be treated this way. I feel I'm being harmed, taken advantage of, misunderstood. She interprets me to myself without listening to me. "You feel this way or that way." She doesn't have the foggiest notion of how I feel. I feel she picks a fight, accuses me of being a failure. A fight develops and I feel like an innocent bystander. But that misunderstanding is really frustrating. Every day an action or state of mind is the basis for

The patient does not quite get the point of the therapist's intervention, and the therapist clarifies, this time explicitly identifying the process through a mirroring interpretation. From the patient's response, the therapist's intervention appears not to have been interruptive, and may in fact have helped the patient return to a more personal exploration of his concerns. He again describes his beleaguered state with his wife, ending with, "I'm less willing to avoid the fight, more willing to slug it out." Expressing the idea of slugging it out scares him and he retreats with a question to the therapist about whether she and his wife's therapist would recommend couples therapy. When the therapist does not answer immediately, he continues by evaluating his question himself, and apparently coming to a negative conclusion. It is unclear whether he might have taken the therapist's hesitation as a negative response and attempted to please her by coming to a negative conclusion himself.

picking a fight and what she faults me for is usually not even what I meant. I'm getting a shorter and shorter fuse. I'm less willing to avoid the fight, more willing to slug it out. My wife and I have questions for you and Theresa—are we candidates for couples therapy rather than individual? (pause) There are a lot of things I can say to you that I can't say in front of her. When I think about it, also, the timing wouldn't be great; I feel that we broke new ground last week.

**T:** I agree.

**P:** (talks more about the incident) . . . and she misunderstood me deliberately.

**T:** Did you try to clarify the misunderstanding with her?

**P:** No, I thought of a lot of things I might say but I didn't think I'd get anywhere with any of them.

**T:** You feel so embattled and threatened that you feel you dare not say anything to her directly, so all your negotiations concerning the relationship take place internally.

**P:** I can see how I've caused problems. Last week I came in angry because I felt she (describes incident). . . . I felt innocent. I would have a lot of trouble sharing my reaction. . . . She attacks my self, what I think about myself. . . . She can say something so casually that can be so hurtful. Last week I made a fool out of myself. I made a foolish statement and she corrected it. She could have let it go but she painted it as it was. It

The patient goes back to a discussion about his wife's treatment of him, concluding that she misunderstood him deliberately. The therapist ignores this assumption on the part of the patient that he knows his wife's intentions, and instead interprets the patient's use of fantasy and internal dialogue to maintain a sense of relatedness, pointing out that his fear leads him to keep his dialogue inside himself. At this point the transcript is sketchy, indicating that the patient's response to the intervention is to describe another incident in which he is also afraid to engage his wife outwardly. Again, in what sounds like a schizoid distortion of reality, he says "She attacks my self, what I think about myself." It is interesting to note that in this incident the injury sounds more narcissistic than schizoid.

devastated me. Not only did I judge myself but she did.

**T:** How do you know she did?

**P:** I asked her.

**T:** You did?

**P:** Yes, I said, "Do you know that what you said was mean?" She said, "Yes, I know." She gave me no mercy. So I thought to myself, "Okay, call it like you see it. I know the rules." But you know, I go way out of my way to not embarrass her. It is sad for me that she isn't able to be kinder to me. Underneath it all she was probably mad at me.

**T:** My guess is that when she said it you tried to hide how very deeply painful her remark was for you. I imagine that she knew it would sting a little, but I doubt if she could know how deeply hurt you would be, or if she ever found out.

**P:** Oh, very, very painful, self-obliterating. For that moment. I became a nonentity. It's interesting. When she said she meant what she said, that made me feel like a nonperson also.

**T:** When you feel something that strongly it's hard to imagine that someone else could not know how you feel. To you, it's the universe at that moment.

**P:** Right. I'm certain she knows what I'm feeling. It's like she and I are welded in my psyche. Like her conduct and mine are one and the same. You're right, I just assume that she must know what I'm feeling, but I'm so good at hiding it, how would she know? I

The therapist now makes a series of three interventions intended to clarify what actually happened between the patient and his wife; the therapist asks two questions and offers a clarifying comment speculating that his wife is probably not aware of how painful to him their interactions are. Again, Mr. N. does not respond to the clarifying aspect of the therapist's comment, but instead responds to the mirroring aspect; the patient expands upon the therapist's allusion to the deep pain that the patient feels. Assuming that the patient did not take in and acknowledge the therapist's clarification because he felt somewhat criticized by it, she now normalizes her comment by interpreting to the patient why he does not realize that his wife is unaware of the depth of his feeling. This time the patient's response is markedly different, taking in and expanding upon the therapist's interpretation. Again, some of his comments about being "welded in my psyche," "welded at the hip," and that "her conduct and mine are one and the same" are comments that sound more narcissistic than schizoid; however, schizoid patients usually have some narcissistic defenses. This welded quality, he explains, has to do with fearing separation, which probably in this case means expulsion.

felt she shouldn't have said it. I felt sorrowful for her conduct, in my own self, like we are welded at the hip. I probably feel too responsible for my wife. I don't know. . . . I guess I fear separation. Not isolation but separation from her.

I must fear that inordinately. We can have a three-hour evening session in which we don't communicate. By the end of that three-hour period I'm feeling lonely, cut off, disturbed. I can go away for seven days and feel no worse.

The comment that follows about feeling cut off is an interesting one. It probably describes what it means to him when she is not responsive to him. He is saying that the feeling of exclusion that he feels is complete, and that it could not be worse if he were completely away from her.

**T:** What are you saying about that?

**P:** I don't know. I don't know if that's normal or not. The antidote is a few minutes of friendly dialogue, physical touching, some endearing words. It just takes a few moments and I'm okay. That's got to be a major reason why I fear losing her, why I tolerate having a part of me ripped off, gone, why I let her call the shots.

At this point the patient shifts again. The therapist's interpretation of his belief that his wife must know what he feels has led him to focus his attention on what his wife thinks and feels. He has expanded on this theme for several minutes. Now he turns his attention to the benefits he receives from being with her and feeling connected to her. He talks about the profound effect any kindness from her produces on him, and concludes essentially that for these bits of kindness he is willing to accept the master/slave relationship that they have created.

**T:** What you've said is confusing to me. On the one hand you portrayed her as a vicious, attacking person who is trying to devastate you and from whom you want to get away, and now you describe her as someone who is soothing and important to you. It's hard to imagine that she can be both of these people.

The therapist's next intervention may appear at first to be a bit confrontive. It would probably not be recommended by Masterson or Klein, but is more along the lines that Kernberg lays out (Kernberg et al. 1989). The therapist points out the patient's object splitting with respect to his wife. There are many clinicians who would find this therapist's level of activity to

**P:** Both are true. She does seem to move back and forth with no predictability. I don't know who I'll come home to, a shrew or a person who is so soothing to me. But I heard something in what you said that bothers me. I don't want to escape from her. I want her to be more of the time soothing.

**T:** And you feel trapped.

**P:** I do! (slight laugh)

**T:** When you're with her and it's comforting to be around her, it's hard for you to think of her as the person who attacks you and with whom you feel trapped. She's one or the other in your mind, in the way you hold her.

**P:** As a mental characterization, it's either day or night. She acts the one way or the other.

I'm arguing with you! I do think that it's she who is changing from one moment to the next, not just the way I think of her.

**T:** You were thinking that she wanted to hurt you with her comment, but then when we talked about it you saw that she probably didn't realize how you felt. That's a case where you were viewing her as all black, and she may not have intended her remark to have the devastating impact on you that it did.

**P:** You're right. And the gray is probably more accurate. I perceive the polar extreme and probably cause it. (gives an appropriate example) I'll try to remember when emotions flare and I feel—try to remember she's

be too high, believing that schizoid patients usually have the capacity to do a lot of their own work in treatment, and do not require very much activity from the therapist. In the transcript, the patient, who is still in the more positive part of his object splitting, has difficulty relating to the therapist's characterization of the patient's wife as someone he wants to get away from. The therapist reminds him of the word "trapped," which he has used many times in reference to his feelings with her. He acknowledges feeling trapped. The therapist now reflects to the patient that it is hard for him to think of his wife in both ways at one time. He responds by indicating that *she* changes back and forth unpredictably.

He makes a point of letting the therapist know that he is disagreeing with her. In this transcript, there is very little evidence of the in and out programme with respect to the therapist. Here the in and out program is evidenced with respect to the wife, even in the varying ways he talks about her. The trust level between the therapist and patient appears to be fairly solid during the period of the transcript, with the patient being consistently open in his exploration of his feelings about his situation with his wife. When he makes a point of telling the therapist that he is disagreeing with her, he is displaying a clear trust of the therapist that she will not crush him for disagreeing with her. This "in" movement should be kept in mind when considering the

probably not intending so much hurt. It really does help. Something you said earlier in these sessions helped me spot when I've been going into a tailspin of depression, and I've been able to use it. One time she got on me about something or other and I felt that sinking begin and I couldn't stand it so I took my crossword puzzle and left the room. But I recognized what was happening and I made myself come back to deal with her eyeball to eyeball. It worked. It stopped the slide.

patient's response to the therapist's next comment. The therapist reminds him that his wife's behavior, as described earlier in the session, was not as heinous as he had originally perceived it, suggesting that there is distortion in his perception of her. He readily agrees with the therapist, and goes on to give an additional example that corroborates this perspective. Without the corroborating example that seems to suggest the likelihood of a true integration of the therapist's intervention, the patient's response would be suspect. Having just made an "in" move, the patient would be expected to make an "out" move, which would lead one to expect that the patient's ready agreement is merely compliance. The schizoid patient's ability to slip into the slave role with the therapist should never be underestimated.

**P:** Any suggestions for spotting this black and white stuff?

**T:** You feel so deeply hurt at times that it is hard to imagine that the person who hurt you might not have intended the hurt to the degree that you feel it, and you fear further attacks, so at those times it is difficult for you to do anything but shut down and withdraw completely. In the example you just gave, you overcame that fear and risked engaging her again. I know that that must have been very difficult for you to do.

**P:** I was pleased with myself—I felt that it took courage.

**T:** It's time to stop for today.

There is further question about the meaning of the patient's comments when the patient ends his next comment with, "Any suggestions for spotting this black and white stuff?" Schizoid patients do not tend to ask for advice unless they are emphasizing their slave position, or they have developed enough of a sense of trust that they can tolerate receiving advice without perceiving it as an attempt to control them. With this patient either possibility might be true. When the patient is really seeking advice, he is sometimes interested in obtaining information, since these patients are normally lacking in social skills and information, or he wants reassurance that the therapist is present, has not gone away. In this latter case it is usually enough for the therapist to make a comment like, "What do you see as the options?" In the above transcript the therapist merely reflects to the patient that she understands that he has just described something that involved taking a risk and was for him an accomplishment. It appears from his reaction that this response satisfied him.

## DIFFERENTIAL DIAGNOSIS BETWEEN SCHIZOID DISORDER AND DISSOCIATIVE DISORDER

Patients with lower level schizoid disorders and those with dissociative disorders have much in common. Their diagnoses may overlap and can be difficult to tell apart, since both patients usually have backgrounds that include a severely intrusive parent or parents leading to a defensive withdrawal and cutting off of affect on the part of the victim. For the patient with a dissociative disorder, this withdrawal takes the predominant form of dissociation that may include development of multiple personalities. For the schizoid patient, the withdrawal takes the form of cutting off of emotions and avoidance of interpersonal relationships and situations that might stimulate emotion. For both patients, there is an intense distrust of others; however in dissociative disorders and posttrauma cases, the distrust is usually limited to certain kinds of situations or relationships. A woman with a history of sexual abuse by her father that caused her to dissociate, for instance, might mistrust men but feel comfortable with women. The schizoid patient's distrust of relationships will be more pervasive, often including some degree of paranoia. The schizoid fears intimacy of any sort because it will lead to domination and attack. The schizoid's defense of trying to stay out of harm's way by playing a slave-like role in relationships (or less commonly playing a master or tyrant role) is not dissociative, nor is his withdrawal into fantasy. While in the slave role, he is usually aware of what he is doing and why, although his perception of the situation as being dangerous is usually distorted. While in fantasy, he is well aware that the real world far from matches his fantasized life. However, some distortion often enters into his perception of casual relationships that he may imagine as being far more meaningful to the other person than they actually are.

Dissociative disorders and posttrauma cases vary, depending in part on what point in the patient's life trauma occurred. If it began in infancy with a primary caregiver and continued for some time, it is unlikely that the patient would have been able to develop whole object relations; in other words the patient is likely to utilize primitive self and object splitting as well as dissociation as a primary defense. In these cases, the patient will present with a dual diagnosis of some form of personality disorder together with the dissociative disorder. The later in life the trauma has occurred, the narrower the impact is likely to be on object relations.

A form of treatment commonly used to treat dissociative disorders is hypnosis. The memories blocked off through disassociation are usually very difficult to access through the processes available in normal talk therapies. Conversely, hypnosis is not usually recommended for the treatment of schizoid disorders because of their difficulties with loss of control. It is naturally, then, very important for the clinician to be able to distinguish between these two conditions.

## CONCLUSION

The schizoid patient can at once be the easiest to relate to of all the personality disorders and the hardest. His sensitivity and the poignancy of his life emerge immediately once he begins to feel safe in treatment, and a therapist cannot help but be moved by his plight. Yet the schizoid can shut down in an instant at the slightest hint of danger. The task of recognizing the patient's defensive withdrawal when it occurs and discovering what the patient is responding to can be challenging for even the most skilled and experienced of clinicians. The treatment process is usually painstakingly slow, with many schizoid patients beginning treatment by coming once a week or even once every other week, and staying in treatment for six to ten years. If the therapist questions the value to the patient of this slow-moving treatment, she should remember that however distant the relationship between therapist and patient appears to the therapist, it is probably for this patient by far the most meaningful relationship that he has and he is probably moving as fast in treatment as he dares.

# Part III

# 6

# Differential Diagnosis

*He's a real nowhere man*
*sitting in his nowhere land.*
*making all his nowhere plans for nobody.*

*He's as blind as he can be*
*Just sees what he wants to see*
*Nowhere man can you see me at all.*

*Nowhere man please listen*
*you don't know what you're missin'*
*Nowhere man*
*The world is at your command.*

*Doesn't have a point of view*
*Knows not where he's going to*
*Isn't he a bit like you and me?*

*Nowhere man don't worry.*
*Take your time, don't hurry.*
*Leave it all*
*'til somebody else lends you a hand.*[1]

The song asks, “Isn’t he a bit like you and me?” Well, maybe a bit, but we get the clear impression from these lyrics that this is a fairly disturbed person, this Nowhere Man. He is obviously a lost soul. We can safely assume that there is a personality disorder present here, but what kind of personality disorder?

The diagnostic process is extremely delicate. It is not enough simply to keep in mind the descriptions of the various diagnostic categories and try to match a patient to one of the descriptions. Unfortunately, many patients do not seem to fit neatly into any of the categories. Part of one diagnosis fits the patient, while the other part of that diagnosis doesn’t. Part of another diagnosis also fits. The therapist often sits in the session vacillating from one diagnosis to another, looking for some definitive indication.

Some clinicians solve this practical problem by questioning the entire concept of diagnosis, characterizing it as a dehumanizing process of forcing patients into rigid categories that distort the patient’s individual qualities. Humanistic therapists often take the point of view that diagnosis is a medically-oriented technique that has no place in an empathic therapy process. They contend that it is only necessary for the therapist to remain open and attuned to a patient, regardless of the patient’s psychological makeup, and that the qualities that Carl Rogers identified of congruence, empathy, and unconditional positive regard are necessary and sufficient for effective therapy with any patient.

While this contention may or may not be true, it is indisputable that the more fully a therapist understands a patient, the more effective the therapy can be. To this end, it is advantageous for a therapist to be sensitive to nuances of the patient’s meaning that might not be apparent from the patient’s articulations. If diagnosis can be accurately performed, it will yield a plethora of additional information about the patient. It will sensitize the therapist to aspects of the patient that the therapist might otherwise miss. It will enable the therapist to understand the patient more deeply. Whether a therapist dehumanizes the patient in the process of thinking about him diagnostically is a function of the therapist’s own style, not an inherent quality of diagnostic thinking. The careful attention that a therapist pays to the patient’s underlying meanings is central to the diagnostic process; it is intended as a way of listening to the patient, not as a substitute for listening to him.

Kohutian therapists make only a rudimentary diagnosis. They differentiate personality disorders from neuroses and psychoses, but do not take the logical next step of dividing their very broad category of "narcissists"[2] into useful diagnostic subcategories.[3] As a result, they may use the same techniques to treat all of the patients who fall within this broad category. Instead of thinking diagnostically, they think about the level and type of developmental arrest of the patient, and use this information to formulate expectations and strategies for treatment. Even with this approach, the Kohutian therapist would still, it seems, be interested in any additional information available to provide a deeper understanding of these patients. The refining of this broad category into the three subcategories presented in this book provides important new information and makes it possible to treat these patients more effectively.

Another common objection to diagnosis is that it narrows the focus of the therapist's view of the patient. If the diagnostic categories are few, the entire diagnostic approach can appear reductionistic. This is certainly a valid concern, especially if there is a rigidity about the manner in which diagnosis is applied. If, once diagnosed, a patient is assumed to belong in a particular designated category from which there is no escape and with which comes a variety of additional attributions, including a complex story about how the patient probably became this way, the diagnosis is likely to distort rather than enhance the therapist's understanding of the patient. If, however, the diagnostic process is treated as a way of organizing some of the myriad complex communications presented by the patient, it can be used as a tool to alert the therapist to aspects of the patient's thoughts and feelings that may not have been otherwise apparent. As such, diagnosis becomes a process that is not focused on a goal, the final diagnosis, but is ongoing, continuing throughout the treatment.

It is beyond the scope of this book to discuss whether the diagnostic categories presented here are legitimate and stable attributes of

---

[2]Greenberg and Mitchell (1983) state, "Nevertheless, the clinical examples of 'schizoids' presented by British authors such as Guntrip bear a striking resemblance to the clinical examples of 'narcissistic personality disorders' discussed by American authors such as Kohut" (p. 385).

[3]Kohut recognizes some diagnostic categories of personality disorders other than "narcissist" but these additional categories combined include only a small percentage of personality-disordered patients. The category he refers to as borderline, for instance, includes only the very low level borderline patient who has so great a structural deficit that he requires help from the therapist in structuring his daily life. Kohut does not attempt to break down the very broad category of "narcissist" (Meissner 1986, p. 405).

patients. Empirically, therapists find that the use of these categories is helpful; however most experienced therapists find that the diagnoses of some patients seem to change well into the course of the treatment. From a practical point of view it is irrelevant whether this change occurs because the original diagnosis was incorrect, because the categories themselves are artificial and overly restrictive, because the patient changed during treatment, or because the patient simply doesn't fit into any one category. All that matters, practically speaking, is that therapists can expect that diagnoses may change, and that an approach to treatment that seemed to be appropriate and successful with a given patient may eventually become inappropriate or less than optimal.

Most therapists who rely heavily on the diagnostic process report that patients can briefly shift beyond their diagnostic category and demonstrate capacities that would not normally be expected of them. A narcissistic patient, for instance, who is not object related may appear briefly to succeed in relating to the therapist as a whole object or he may briefly begin addressing material that is characteristically schizoid. It is important for the therapist to have the flexibility to recognize these shifts when they occur so that the therapist can respond appropriately.

While many clinicians resist categorization of patients, others attempt highly refined characterization. The revised third edition of the *Diagnostic and Statistical Manual of Mental Disorders* of the American Psychiatric Association, *DSM-III-R*, provides standardized descriptions of diagnostic categories. It divides the category of "personality disorders" into eleven subcategories, but suggests that patients often fit into more than one category.[4] This book uses a smaller number of categories that are of practical value in that they not only suggest subtle information about the patient but also point to an approach to the treatment for each category of patients that is tailored to the needs of those patients. The antisocial disorder is one that is not treated extensively in this book because there appears to be no effective psychotherapeutic treatment for this condition.

---

[4]On the second page of the section on Personality Disorders, the *DSM-III-R* suggests, ". . . many individuals exhibit features that are not limited to a single Personality Disorder. In this manual diagnoses of more than one Personality Disorder should be made if the individual meets the criteria for more than one."

There is a rough correspondence between the other ten categories and the three broad categories presented here. The *DSM-III-R*'s categories of paranoid, compulsive, and narcissistic personality disorders tend to be closest to the narcissistic personality disorders described in this book. The *DSM-III-R*'s categories of dependent and borderline personality disorders tend to be closest to the borderline personality disorder described in this book; and the *DSM-III-R*'s categories of schizotypal, avoidant, and schizoid personality disorders tend to be closest to what this book refers to as a schizoid personality disorder. The *DSM-III-R* categories of passive-aggressive and histrionic overlap both the borderline personality disorder and the narcissistic personality disorder.

The *DSM-III-R* is an important tool in enabling psychological professionals to organize their thinking about patients' symptoms and to provide a common language for communicating about patients. For this purpose, however, it must restrict its scope to relatively objectively observable behaviors. While a patient's observable behaviors are essential in diagnosing him, his more subjective motivations, feelings, attitudes, and defensive system are also very important. Different patients can present the same behaviors but with different motivations requiring a different treatment approach. Consequently, the *DSM-III-R* symptom orientation prevents it from also being treatment oriented; it does not suggest treatment approaches.

The process of differential diagnosis presented in this chapter is intended to address the problems the clinician actually encounters in diagnosing patients. Chapters 3, 4, and 5 of this book present detailed discussions of each of the three main subcategories of personality disorders; borderline, narcissist, and schizoid. The descriptions of these will be summarized in this chapter. The next step, however, will be to explore the problems the clinician encounters when patients do not appear to fit neatly into any of the categories described, or when some aspect of the patient's behavior seems inconsistent with the patient's apparent diagnosis.

As indicated in the introduction, the diagnostic categories used in this book follow those of Masterson. It is assumed that the reader is familiar with the characteristics of psychosis, and able to recognize psychosis in patients. The focus here will be on differentiating patients with personality disorders from neurotics, and in determining whether a personality disorder is narcissistic, borderline, or schizoid. It is also assumed that the reader has read about the general characteristics and treatment of these personality disorders in the previous chapters on the borderline, narcissistic, and schizoid patients.

The ambiguities of behavior and language make the task of diagnosis a complex one; the therapist must determine the patient's underlying feelings and motives in order to make an accurate diagnosis. Since the therapist cannot go inside patients' heads, he or she must make use of all the available information that patients present. The therapist can begin by considering patients' own accounts of what they feel, what motivates them, and how they think about themselves. In addition, the therapist can look at the patient's presenting problem, examine the patient's history, and analyze the patient's defenses. Finally, the therapist can attempt to construct a model of the patient's self and object representations. (See Chapters 3, 4, and 5 for detailed discussions of the split self and object representations of each diagnostic category.)

**Forming an Initial Diagnostic Impression**

Since all this information is not immediately available when a patient enters therapy, the therapist must start by sorting through whatever information is available about the patient and forming a hypothesis, a working diagnosis. In the beginning the therapist may be unable to settle upon one diagnosis to work from, so he may want to entertain a pair of possible diagnoses. The therapist then proceeds to work with the patient using this hypothesis, and continues to evaluate the patient's responses to see if they are consistent with the working diagnosis. In testing his diagnosis, the therapist is constantly asking the question, "What do these words and actions mean *to the patient*?" In this way the diagnostic process itself helps the therapist to increase his sensitivity to the inner meanings that the patient draws from his experience.

If a particular response seems inconsistent with the working diagnosis, the therapist must try either to understand this response in a way that is consistent with the working diagnosis, or reevaluate the working diagnosis. For example, a patient who appears to be a narcissist in most respects, but lacks apparent grandiosity and talks about the importance of his relationship with his wife, represents a diagnostic problem, because narcissists tend to be grandiose and not object oriented. What does it mean when this patient says that his wife is "important?" If she is important for her beauty as a trophy, a symbol of the patient's power and success or a source of adulation, then this attitude would be consistent with what would be expected of a narcissist. The therapist must also consider whether the patient actually lacks grandiosity or is perhaps only hiding it as would a closet narcissist. (See Chapter 4 for a full discussion of this phenomenon.)

## NEUROSIS VS. PERSONALITY DISORDER

### Neurosis

Humanistic growth-oriented therapy works well with patients who can continue to function day to day while struggling with painful historically based feelings. For these patients the therapist's help in deepening or intensifying their experience of memories and feelings facilitates their learning about themselves. While exploring these memories and feelings, these patients can maintain their relationships, perform adequately at their jobs, and handle the everyday problems that arise in their lives. They have relatively healthy defenses like humor, repression, displacement, suppression, intellectualization, and reaction formation, which allow them to control the amount of affect-laden material that surfaces, so that they are not overwhelmed.

Sessions with these patients are characterized by an ongoing exploration of the behaviors and feelings that they see in their lives that do not make sense to them. They will come into a session still concerned about questions that were left unanswered in the session before, and report about recent experiences that will shed new light on these questions. Between sessions, the patient often thinks about the therapy. If a therapist is able to help him or her identify an example of irrational behavior that is destructive, the patient will usually react with surprise and curiosity. The patient will be interested in further exploring the topic, and, if successful, the exploration that follows will bring up dreams, memories, and affect, of which the patient was previously unaware. There is a sense that the therapist and the patient are partners in an exploratory process, that a therapeutic alliance exists between therapist and patient. These are relatively healthy neurotic patients.

The issues that bring neurotics to therapy often have to do with their level of happiness or fulfillment. They may have ambivalences, anxieties, or fears that they would like to understand and control. They have repressed feelings that need to be given expression. They may have problems in letting go in relationships, or experiencing satisfying sexual relations. They may be attempting to clarify their life goals or values. They commonly have issues associated with competition or guilt. These issues are likely to be different with respect to the way they relate to men from the way they relate to women.[5] They are generally able to realistically assess their own strengths and weaknesses, and those of others. If they enter therapy complaining of a difficulty in functioning or controlling themselves, it is usually limited to one or two areas of their lives.

Since neurotics repress psychological material that is too painful to experience directly, the therapy process for neurotics is intended to uncover this material. The process centers around the exploration of these patients' unconscious minds.

### Personality Disorders

There are other patients, however, like those with the personality disorders described in the previous chapters, for whom the above description is far from the case. These patients find the memories activated by therapy to be overwhelmingly painful, so they are rarely able to sustain a spontaneous exploration of these memories with appropriate affect. If they do press themselves to explore issues related to affect-laden memories, they will often be unable to manage the feelings that these memories bring up. After a therapy session in which these memories have been stimulated, personality disordered patients may become anxious or depressed. They defend against these feelings with avoidance, denial, clinging, splitting, and other relatively immature and maladaptive defenses. Increased reliance on these defenses hinders their ability to function in day to day activities and in particular in intimate relationships.

The defenses that patients with personality disorders use tend to involve acting out of dysphoric feeling. These patients' ability to contain painful affect is far more limited than the neurotic's. In fact, in a therapy session, patients with personality disorders tend in the

[5]Kernberg's *Borderline Conditions and Pathological Narcissism* (pp. 12-21) offers an excellent and concise discussion of differential diagnosis between personality disorders and neurotics.

beginning of treatment to be almost continually in defense. The defenses they use are also more destructive than those of neurotics.

The complaints that bring patients with personality disorders to therapy are usually related to the destructive impact of their defenses. Rather than a concern for maximizing their fulfillment in life, these patients are concerned more concretely with getting through life. They maintain a distorted perception of themselves and others in order to mask the more painful aspects of reality. They have difficulty with relationships for the same reason that they have difficulty with therapy; relationships touch upon feelings that can be overwhelmingly painful for them. They can have problems with performing consistently at work, at home, and in every area of their lives, especially in relationships. Rather than attempting to refine their lives, patients with personality disorders are usually trying to keep their lives together.

With these patients, there is little or no sense that the therapist and patient are partners in an exploratory process. Instead, these patients enter therapy with unrealistic fantasies about therapy. They have a "black box" view of therapy, expecting the therapist to magically repair them. They may view the therapist as someone who will nurture them, criticize them, fix them, direct them, make decisions for them, or tell them what they need to know about themselves or about others; they do not expect the therapist to neutrally facilitate as they explore and learn about themselves. They usually do not attempt to answer uncomfortable questions that arise during their therapy. Instead, they await direction from the therapist as to what they should talk about. Often they will forget from one session to the next what they have been talking about. It is common for these patients frequently to forget their reason for being in therapy, asking the therapist to remind them. Through treatment, however, these patients can begin to appear more and more like neurotic patients, working increasingly more consistently in treatment.

## TYPES OF PERSONALITY DISORDERS

This chapter focuses primarily on differential diagnosis among personality disorders, beginning with a summary of the characteristics of borderline, narcissistic, and schizoid patients.

**Borderline**

Borderline patients are characterized by the borderline split, discussed in detail in Chapter 3. They see the world as black or white, bad or good. When the world seems good, they will do whatever they can to maintain that view of the world. They avoid activities that might threaten to destroy this view, including decision making, engaging in conflict, or self-assertion, all of which tend to bring up feelings of independence and isolation. Borderline patients may cling to demeaning relationships rather than face the loss involved in a separation. They may cast about for someone else's advice, questioning the value of their own feelings and opinions. They may wait until it's too late to make a decision, for fear that the decision they make would turn out wrong or not be approved of. They are likely to abandon a friendship or quit a good job rather than risk the unrealistic possibility that they might be abandoned or fired.

Their therapy sessions are initially characterized by attempts to shift the responsibility for their treatment to the therapist. Rather than explore important questions that they may have raised themselves, they will tend to move on to a new subject as soon as these questions are posed. Alternatively, they may simply pause and wait for the therapist to say something that they can react to, or ask the therapist a question so that they need not continue in their own exploration. With these patients, identification of an irrational behavior that is destructive will primarily produce anxiety in the patient, rather than curiosity. Because their ability to contain painful affect is extremely limited, they are more inclined at these times to change the subject than to want to explore it.

They see the therapist as a nurturing person whose purpose is to make them feel good, not a person who will help them explore uncomfortable areas in themselves. Another way of saying this is that these patients see the therapist as the indulgent, clinging parent rather than the parent who promotes autonomy and independence. They engage in regressive helpless behavior to force the therapist to take over for them. (See Chapter 2 for a discussion of transference acting out of helplessness.) When they are not viewing the therapist as the indulgent nurturing parent, they view him as the critical, unloving parent. The therapist's countertransference reaction is often to feel different than the mean parent figures the patient talks about, and to want to nurture or rescue the patient.

**Narcissist**

Narcissists are characterized by their inability to recognize other people as whole and separate from themselves. They live in a world of cosmic isolation in which there is no one else but themselves; yet they are unaware of needing closeness with another person. Because the pain of their isolation is so deep, they protect themselves with an impenetrable wall, a barrier against any outside input that might touch them emotionally and open them to feeling this intense pain. Two major components of their wall are self-sufficiency and grandiosity. Behind the grandiosity is a person who feels empty, worthless, or incompetent. Their need to protect themselves from feeling these feelings is of utmost importance to them. Narcissistic patients will become critical or devaluing or withdraw entirely from relationships rather than feel exposed to being wounded emotionally. They remain aloof from any intimate involvement rather than risk the vulnerability that comes with opening up to another person. They take dangerous and unnecessary risks, rather than open themselves to the reality of their own imperfections and mortality. They are likely to abandon an artistic calling for which they truly have talent rather than face the inevitable minority of critics who find even minor fault with their work. Even the possibility of positive change is threatening to them, because it suggests that they may not have been perfect before the change.

In the therapy session, they are either struggling with the feelings of humiliation or failure, or they have difficulty defining their reason for coming to therapy. To point to a problem that may have brought them to therapy is to be self-critical and consequently wounding. Even in therapy they attempt to maintain the grandiose self-image of a person without faults who can do no wrong. The more subtle closet narcissists may feign humility and emphasize their weaknesses so convincingly that it takes a trained ear to detect the underlying grandiose self who privately knows that these weaknesses are merely an illusion, and who looks forward to the day when the world will recognize the superior human being underneath who patiently awaits discovery.

The therapist's countertransference experience with the narcissist often involves anger, helplessness, grogginess, envy, shame, or grandiosity. Since these patients have ironclad defenses against emotional contact, their affect is usually fairly flat; the therapy session can feel like an emotional desert, and the therapist may continually need to struggle to stay alert. On the other hand, narcissists can be glib and entertaining, creating the illusion of making contact. Frequently, they are initially out of touch with themselves or too concerned with the possibility of making a mistake to risk choosing a topic to discuss in therapy. They cast the therapist in the role of the authority and rule maker, and attempt to get the therapist to point to a direction of exploration. They expect the same perfection from the therapist that they expect from themselves, and they tend to compare themselves with the therapist and compete. If the therapist makes a mistake, the narcissistic patient can be brutal. What appears to be a relationship or alliance between therapist and patient can dissolve instantly; even after two or three years of therapy, the narcissist can react to an inadvertent wound and quit therapy without ever looking back. Therapists may be left feeling inadequate and inept. On the other hand, it may be so important for these patients to maintain their fantasy of the therapist's perfection, that they may respond to the therapist's mistakes by distorting their own reality. (See Chapter 4, the section on idealizing transferences, for an explanation of this phenomenon.) When this happens, the therapist often gets the impression that her conduct of the therapy with this patient has been flawless, and the therapist's own grandiosity is likely to flower.

### Schizoid

Schizoid patients yearn for a relationship, but the possible injury associated with even slight emotional contact is more than they are willing to bear. They are continually faced with the dual fears of both isolation and engulfment. There is no comfortable direction for them to turn. Afraid of direct contact, they attempt to express their locked-in emotions through artistic expression, or they retreat to the safe haven of intellectual thoughts and pursuits. Control is an obsession in their lives because they cannot risk the emotional upheavals that might result from a situation that gets out of control. For some, most of their feeling of relatedness comes from their fantasies. They weigh carefully everything that they say or that is said to them, replaying conversations over and over in their heads. Their concern about hidden meanings and implications of what has been said can take on a quality of paranoia. Since their interactions are few, they will obsess about even simple polite exchanges.

They often come into therapy with the express purpose of learning how to be in a relationship. They become extremely uncomfortable when confronted, and can withdraw from therapy if it becomes overwhelmingly uncomfortable. Contrary to the stereotype of the schizoid, they often appear somewhat emotional. Their eyes may water easily, and this can create an inaccurate expectation in the observer of an impending flood of emotion. It is, however, only the observer who expects this flood of emotion; the patient may even be unaware of the connection between this frequent teariness and the underlying feeling.

Schizoid patients often bring the therapist a series of concrete expressions of their feelings. Their minds and imaginations are extremely active, for it is only in their minds that they can hold relationships. Consequently, their fantasized relationships with people, including their therapist, can be extraordinarily exaggerated in intensity. They commonly believe their relationships to be far more significant to the other person than they actually are. If the therapist is not adequately attuned to the patient, the therapist can wonder why this person continues to come to therapy and what she might be getting from coming, while to the schizoid patient this therapeutic relationship is the most significant relationship that he or she has ever had. This significance may never be directly communicated to the therapist.

## PRACTICAL PROBLEMS IN DIAGNOSIS

The foregoing descriptions of the various diagnostic categories may appear dissimilar, but the task of distinguishing between these diagnostic categories is far from simple. Patients do not generally present themselves in a manner completely consistent with any of the above descriptions. Patients' symptomatic behaviors, the way they use words, their intentional and unintentional concealment of data, and the ambiguities present in all the diagnostic indicators make the process of diagnosis delicate and often tentative.

### Difficulty with Diagnosis Based on Behavior

The same response can be displayed by patients with a variety of character structures, as illustrated by the upset that people feel at the ending of a relationship. If the upset arises from a sense of loss and abandonment, there is a possibility that the patient might be borderline or neurotic. The neurotic is likely to mourn the loss, to think about the aspects of the relationship that he misses, and to feel sad and perhaps alone. Rather than mourn the loss, borderlines are likely to try to fill the void in some way or otherwise defend against feeling their sadness or aloneness. They may be upset for some time, but they are unlikely to deal with the feelings of loss directly. On the other hand, if the upset arises more out of a sense of failure without a real feeling of loss, there is more of a likelihood that the patient is narcissistic. The narcissist might feel like a failure for not being able to sustain a relationship, or the narcissist might feel humiliation and deflation at having been spurned. Specifically, because the narcissist does not fully recognize other people as unique and separate from himself, he is not missing the relatedness to another person as much as he is feeling deflated by the loss. Still another possibility is that the patient's upset arises out of the dashing of a fantasy of intimacy and involvement that was never shared by the other person; in this case, there is more of a possibility that the patient is schizoid. For a behavior to be useful diagnostically, the therapist must understand the meaning of that behavior to the patient.

### Ambiguity of Language

Each of the four patient categories in the above example might use some of the same words and phrases to describe their upset; "difficulty sleeping," "can't get it out of my mind," "a feeling of betrayal," "shock," "depression." This illustrates a very important principle which, although obvious, is often forgotten: different patients use the same words to mean quite different things. There is often a tendency for a therapist to assume that when patients use words, the words have the same meaning as when the therapist uses them. In the above example of loss of a relationship, the schizoid, the borderline, and the narcissist would use the word "depressed" to describe how they feel. The schizoid uses it usually to describe a decreased sense of relatedness in his life. The borderline uses it to mean sad, hopeless, alone, rejected. The narcissist, on the other hand, might use it to mean deflated, humiliated, and empty. If the therapist responds to the narcissist's depression by saying, "You really miss her, don't you?" the therapist will miss the point, and the narcissist will experience an empathic failure, an indication that the therapist does not understand him. If the therapist has any question about the patient's diagnosis or use of words, it is best for the therapist to ask him about the meaning of words.

Other feelings that are beyond the narcissist's capacity are love and guilt. Narcissists live in the same culture as everyone else, so they use the same language, but the words they use reflect a distinctive experience. When they feel loved, for instance, they are talking about feeling understood, a oneness with another person. When they love someone, again they refer to a oneness with the other person, a sense of the other person as an extension of themselves, a reflection of their own perfection. They also often use the word *love* to mean passion. When they talk about guilt they are referring to a feeling of having failed; having done something for which they might be criticized. Borderline patients use the word *love* to refer to nurturing. When someone takes care of them or takes over for them they feel loved. If they use the word *guilt*, they are likely to be referring to feeling that they've been bad and that someone is angry at them. When the schizoid uses the word *love*, he is talking about a feeling of relatedness, which in many cases is synonymous for him with being dominated. The word *guilt* for the schizoid patient refers to a sense of having stepped out of line and created the possibility of being attacked.

Similarly the feelings of affection and loneliness can have different meanings. Affection is an expression of love and loneliness describes the absence of affection. For the borderline patient, love means togetherness, nurturing, and taking care of someone. For the narcissistic patient, it means understanding, mirroring, admiration, or idealization. For the schizoid, if affection is expressed by someone, he doesn't trust it and it makes him uncomfortable. The only love or affection within the range of his experiences arises when he feels acknowledged by someone or related to.

Fear of rejection is another term that can have multiple meanings. Usually it is the borderline patient who is concerned about rejection, because it is linked to underlying dysphoric feeling. The narcissist, however, may refer to fear of rejection when he is concerned about the wound he feels when someone fails to adequately mirror him. Rather than loss of a relationship, he fears the loss of the mirroring function. The schizoid who fears rejection fears the loss of relatedness, which is so horrible to him as to be unthinkable; he is afraid of disintegration, obliteration, ceasing to exist.

## Hidden Pathology

For a variety of reasons, patients can conceal their true pathology from the therapist. Part of the nature of the closet narcissist is that she hides her grandiosity. (See Chapter 4 for a full explanation of this phenomenon.) Sometimes the true pathology is revealed only after several years of therapy, considerably complicating initial diagnosis. The borderline may initially use narcissistic defenses and appear to be a narcissist; then, when the narcissistic defenses have been addressed in treatment, the borderline diagnosis becomes clear. A patient may comply so effectively with the therapist's expectations that the patient's diagnosis is obscured. Patients who have been in therapy and gotten control over some of their defenses, and patients who have been in twelve-step programs can also be difficult to diagnose, because they can look and sound much healthier than they actually are. Then, when their defenses are put under the increased strain of surfacing historical pain from a real life adversity or from therapeutic exploration, these defenses are overwhelmed and begin to fail, and the patient's underlying structure again reveals itself. The schizoid patient usually makes conscious decisions to withhold aspects of her pathology from the therapist; her automatic assumption of the slave role in her relationship with the therapist causes her to avoid exposing issues that she perceives as potentially upsetting to the therapist or that she fears will leave her unacceptably vulnerable. The schizoid patient's intense use of fantasy to create a sense of relatedness is often only discussed after many years of treatment.

## INITIAL DIAGNOSIS—ESTABLISHING A WORKING HYPOTHESIS

When a patient first comes to therapy, the therapist evaluates the patient's grasp of reality, the patient's ego functioning, the patient's object relations, and the nature of the initial transference relationship to determine the level of the patient's psychological health. If patients' perceptions of reality are extremely distorted, their ego functioning poor, their object relations immature, and they seriously distort their perception of the therapist, they are likely to have a severe disorder, a psychosis. If these phenomena are less extreme, they are likely to fall into the personality disorder category. Within that category, the more extreme person is referred to as low level, while the less extreme person is referred to as high level, which is distinct from the mainly neurotic patient who is very high level. The patient's grasp of reality is reflected in the way he tells his story. As the therapist listens to the story, the therapist gets a sense of the accuracy of the patient's perception of himself, his perception of others, and especially his perception of the therapist. A psychotic patient, for instance, might report, "I am very popular. Some very important people have shown an interest in me lately. I think they are considering inviting me to run for president. No one has come out and said anything yet, but I can tell that there are things happening." In contrast, a neurotic would describe his status fairly realistically: "I am very popular, although there are some guys at work who give me a hard time. I don't know why they do it; they must know that their comments don't feel good to me. They joke about how short I am. It doesn't bother me enough to do something about it. I'm afraid if I said something to them, it would make everyone uncomfortable." A patient with a personality disorder in the same situation might say, "I am very popular. Everyone thinks I'm a nice guy. The guys at work make fun of me because I'm so short, but it doesn't bother me, and they don't mean any harm by it. One guy gets pretty mean at times. He's sort of the ring leader. I could say something, I guess, but I don't want to create waves and make everyone uncomfortable." In comparison to the neurotic patient, the patient with a personality disorder distorts reality, as indicated by the inconsistencies in his description. He denies that he minds the comments that his co-workers make, but talks about wanting to stop them. He talks about how nice a guy everyone thinks he is, but that some co-workers make fun of him. Although he refers to one of them as a ring leader, there is a second instance of denial in his failure to acknowledge that these co-workers might be aware that they are being hurtful to him.

In addition to the patient's grasp of reality, the therapist hears about how the patient relates to others, how mature his relationships have been, and to what degree he has been able to sustain emotional intimacy. The therapist determines whether the patient is able to see himself and others as whole people, without splitting. (See Chapter 1 for a detailed discussion of the phenomenon of splitting.) As the patient talks about his accomplishments and his problems, the therapist pays attention to the patient's level of functioning and ego strength. Finally, the therapist takes note of the nature of the relationship that develops between himself and the patient. The neurotic patient is able to relate to the therapist fairly realistically as someone whose job it is to support the patient's self-activation; the patient with a personality disorder relates to the therapist primarily as a partial person whose function is to fill a particular need. The psychotic patient distorts the relationship even further. All of these factors indicate to the therapist whether the patient is likely to have a personality disorder, a neurosis, or a psychosis.

Once the therapist rules out the possibility of psychosis, he initially takes cues about the kind of interventions to use with the patient from the way in which the patient relates to him. Borderline patients tend to engage the therapist intensely, even in a first interview, and the therapist feels tugged at for nurturing. Narcissistic patients can also engage intensely with the therapist, but they do it more from the position of judging, evaluating, and demanding of the therapist or of idealizing the therapist. On the other hand, a narcissistic patient can be so self-involved that he leaves little opportunity for the therapist to comment, and the therapist feels superfluous or invisible. Schizoid patients seem very interested in the therapist, but maintain an emotional separateness as well. To a lesser degree, all of the above descriptions can also be true of neurotic patients. The way patients relate to therapists normally reflects the way they engage in relationships in general. The more object related the patient, the more stable the therapeutic relationship is likely to be, and so the more likely he will be able to handle frank or confrontive feedback. Thus, the patient's manner becomes the therapist's initial guide in relating to him, and, with nonpsychotic patients, it constitutes the basis of the therapist's initial diagnostic hypothesis.

As more information about the presenting problem, history, and primary defenses emerges, the therapist formulates a firmer working hypothesis of the patient's diagnosis. Initially, with sketchy information, there can be little subtlety brought to this process. Patients with issues relating to loss or helplessness tend to appear borderline, while patients who seem very independent and have vague presenting problems or issues around perfection or failure tend to appear to be narcissistic. Those whose issues revolve around relatedness seem schizoid.

Although all patients with personality disorders can display a wide range of defenses, the types of defenses common to lower level patients are predominantly distancing, while those of higher level patients are predominantly clinging. Distancing defenses include avoidance, denial, intellectualization, devaluing, and withdrawal, while clinging defenses include clinging, externalization, compliance, and the acting out of helplessness. Some defenses can be employed either in the service of clinging or distancing.[6]

## DIAGNOSIS BY INTERVENTION

A common method of distinguishing between borderline and narcissistic patients in the beginning stages of treatment is to make an intervention and see if it works. Since narcissists tend to respond to interpretation and borderlines to confrontation,[7] one might assume that this litmus test might yield important diagnostic information, and often it does. However, a single intervention is not a good diagnostic test. Since patients often do not respond to an intervention the first time it is made, especially if this intervention represents a shift from a previous style of interventions, it is often necessary to make a series of consistent interventions to yield diagnostic information. This method is much more efficient with new patients than with patients who have already developed a relationship with the therapist.

Nevertheless, under the best of conditions, this information can be misleading. For instance, a narcissist will be likely to respond to an accurate interpretation. A narcissist is unlikely, however, to respond to an inaccurate interpretation, unless the narcissist has developed an idealizing transference and is trying to find a way to undo the

[6]Most theorists view narcissistic patients as higher level than borderline patients because of their higher level of functioning in the business world. Kohut supports this view, claiming that the narcissist's idealization and grandiosity are actually undeveloped forms of healthy adult functions. Masterson alone describes narcissists as more primitive than borderlines. He sees the narcissist's idealization and grandiosity as pathological defenses, and observes that narcissists are markedly less object related and their defenses are more primitive than borderlines, indicating a lower level of psychological development. Although narcissists do function more effectively and advance in areas like business that do not require emotional sensitivity, Masterson asserts that they do this in the service of their grandiose defense, rather than as true activation (Kernberg 1975, pp. 16–18). Most theorists also think of schizoid personality disorders as more primitive than borderline or narcissistic disorders. Guntrip, however, clearly indicates that the schizoid style is found in emotionally high functioning as well as low functioning people.

[7]Confrontation with borderlines and interpretation of narcissists are discussed in Chapters 3 and 4 respectively, and Chapter 7 contains an extensive discussion of both confrontation and interpretation.

therapist's mistake. In fact, it is somewhat indicative of a narcissist if the patient responds to an interpretation by becoming cold and withdrawn. This would indicate that the interpretation was faulty, and the patient is a narcissist who expected perfect mirroring and was wounded or disappointed by the inaccuracy of the interpretation.

A borderline's response to interpretation may be positive and productive, especially if the borderline is high level or the interpretation comes at a time in the treatment when the borderline is already fairly self-directed. On the other hand, a borderline can take an interpretation as an indication that the therapist is willing to do some of the patient's work. If the patient already has a problem activating himself, the interpretation is likely to cause him to become more passive or to hang back and wait for the therapist to do more. To recognize this passivity, the therapist needs to look for a drop in the quality of material the patient is presenting in the session. Typical examples of passivity occur when the patient asks the therapist a question, brings up problems without making any attempt to solve or even explore them, changes subjects before fully exploring them, or chitchats in session. The patient may even become silent, complaining, "I don't know what to talk about." This silence is distinguishable from that of the narcissist because it is a pleading, helpless silence while the narcissist's is a cold, punishing, or challenging silence.

What then might one conclude if the patient responds well to confrontation? For example, suppose the therapist humorously remarks, "I notice that three times now you've brought up the question of how you are going to respond to your wife's ultimatum that either you stop drinking or she'll leave, and each time you changed the subject. Are you intending to avoid the subject until your wife makes your decision unnecessary?" A schizoid patient is not likely to respond well to confrontation because he or she will interpret it as an attempt to coerce or control. The narcissist too responds poorly to confrontation; he usually interprets it as criticism, feels wounded, and withdraws. If the confrontation continues over time, the narcissistic patient is likely to become increasingly resentful and can leave therapy. This, however, is not always the case. A narcissist with an idealizing transference may respond to an accurate confrontation by feeling seen and understood, and so the confrontation becomes further evidence of the competence of the therapist and additional reason to idealize the therapist. The idealizing response to the above confrontation might be, "Old eagle-eye over here never lets me get away with anything. I guess you are right. I am hoping the problem will go away on its own." The therapist will notice over time, however, that this patient will not integrate these confrontations; he will not continue to see his avoidant behavior as destructive. While in the slave role, the schizoid patient might easily appear to respond well to confrontation, sometimes for years. Perhaps the most diagnostic response to confrontation would be deep affect. In this event, the therapist can be reasonably confident that the patient is borderline and has heard the confrontation and integrated it, giving rise to the deep feeling response. In fact, if a patient is being treated as borderline but never responds to confrontation with affect, there is reason to question the diagnosis.

On the other hand, although borderline patients are capable of responding well to confrontation, for several reasons they may not. The therapist's confrontation may be inaccurate. It may concentrate on a relatively insignificant defense, missing the major one. It may be part of a shotgun approach in which the therapist is confronting a variety of defenses, leaving the patient confused and feeling criticized. The confrontation might be delivered without empathy or it may carry countertransferential material. Even if the confrontation is well focused, empathic, and consistent, the patient may perceive it as critical. If this occurs, and the therapist does not clarify the noncritical intent of the intervention, the confrontation will fail. Any of these could be reasons for a confrontation to miss the mark. In addition, confrontations may be ignored by the patient if the patient thinks that by ignoring them they will go away. Therapists who have had a history of being warm, friendly, and nurturing with a patient can reasonably be expected by the patient to be tenuous in their confrontations; these therapists are likely to back off, rather than be perceived as a nagging, judgmental parent.

Another situation in which a patient may not find it necessary to respond to confrontation is if the patient's environment takes care of all the patient's needs and makes it unnecessary for the patient to do anything for herself. If, for instance, the patient has figured out how to get her parents, her grandparents, and the welfare system all to support her quite comfortably, it is likely that being helpless and dependent on others may feel ego syntonic to that patient despite the cost to her this dependency entails in self-esteem. It may be hard for the therapist to convince that patient that this behavior is destructive, and that the good feeling that comes from supporting one's own actions feels better than the good feeling of having one's needs catered to.

Similarly, it will be hard for a patient who has attached to a newborn baby or a "sugar daddy" to allow abandonment depression to come to the surface, when it is so easy, at any moment, to feel attached to this other person, and not feel alone. To this patient, there is little motivation to endure in therapy the painful process of pursuing a separate sense of self.

Still another reason why a borderline patient might not respond to confrontation, even if it is accurate, is that he or she may be viewing the therapist as a critical withdrawing parent (WORU). In this case, the confrontation, no matter how well constructed, will be perceived as a criticism, and the meaning to the patient of the confrontation will not be examined. Often in such situations, however, the delivery of the confrontation is influenced by the therapist's countertransference. If the therapist feels at all critical or annoyed with the patient, this feeling is likely to leak into the intervention, and the patient will notice it, giving the patient evidence that his or her view of the therapist as a withdrawing, withholding parent is accurate.

## DIAGNOSTIC IMPLICATIONS OF PRECIPITATING EVENTS AND PRESENTING PROBLEMS

The presenting problem and particular event that caused a patient to seek treatment sometimes suggests a possible diagnosis.

Borderlines usually come to therapy feeling anxious, lost, overwhelmed, sad, or depressed. There is often a precipitating event like a loss, separation, uncharacteristic success, or important decision to make, but the borderline may have defended so thoroughly against the immediate feelings produced by that event, that he or she is not fully aware of the relevance of the event to his or her decision to seek treatment. Examples of common precipitating events are divorce, separation, moving to a new geographical area, graduating from school, moving out of parents' house, losing a job, being promoted to a new job with added responsibilities, physical disability, children about to leave home, or marital conflict. If there is a separation after a long-term relationship, it is usually the borderline's partner who has left. If the borderline patient has done the leaving, it is often by jumping into another relationship in order to avoid being alone in anticipation of the partner leaving. Often the purpose of therapy for the borderline patient is to develop a relationship with the therapist to make easing out of a present destructive relationship less painful.

Schizoids come to therapy in an attempt to escape their isolation. They can sometimes say that explicitly. There may be a precipitating event like a breakup of a relationship that makes them feel out of control. They may have been sent to therapy by a "master" in the form of a boss or spouse. They are likely to appear extremely controlled, and often have extensive intellectual explanations for the events in their lives. There is often elaborate suicidal ideation, although they may not choose at first to share it with the therapist. They devote intense energy to fantasy and may offer the therapist a piece of writing or art work that expresses what they are unable to express directly.

Narcissists frequently seek therapy after a significant life failure. A failure or any other event that punctures the narcissist's grandiosity stimulates the underlying feelings of emptiness and worthlessness that the narcissist defends against so aggressively. Typical failures are loss of a job, being passed over for promotion, financial problems, marital conflict, separation, divorce, aging, or an interruption in narcissistic supplies. If the failure is massive enough, it will overwhelm the narcissist's defenses and pierce his armor, causing fragmentation, or a loss of sense of wholeness or cohesion. In this deflated state the narcissist is no longer able to maintain his grandiosity and swings to the other extreme, feeling worthless, invisible, and incompetent. In this state he can come to a therapist in the hope of remedying his defects. The presenting problem, then, may be depression, suicidal feelings, or a disintegrating marriage or career. Sometimes a narcissist is referred to therapy by the courts, often after an offense in which the offender does not consider the harm to the victim, as in certain sex offenses, wife beating, and drunk driving. Older narcissists have better prognoses than younger ones in general, because the defect of aging is one that never goes away, leaving the narcissist with no escape but to look at what is so disturbing internally about aging.

On the other hand, the narcissist may come to a therapist to certify that he really has no problem. The presenting problem may be a disintegrating marriage or career, or simply that his boss or spouse thought it was necessary. If the therapist pushes for some indication of what the patient himself perceives as a problem, the patient feels attacked. The patient believes that the various problems are all due to his spouse's defects, or his employees' stupidity, or his boss's unreasonableness.

A presenting problem of difficulty feeling close to people is more typical of a neurotic or a schizoid than of a borderline or narcissist. The neurotic presenting this problem is referring to inhibitions about the expression of feelings and difficulties with anxiety resulting from attempts to achieve intimacy. Schizoid patients presenting this problem are presenting the classical schizoid dilemma: they want contact with people, but closeness terrifies them (Guntrip 1968).

Narcissists and borderlines can also present with a difficulty in feeling close to people. The narcissist is likely to frame his difficulty as a problem he is having with his spouse, who does not understand him. He might also say that he really has no problem with intimacy, but that he's come to therapy because his spouse says he has one, and so he's come to therapy to verify that he is not flawed. He sees people as serving a function in his life. The resulting dehumanization of people precludes true intimacy. Intimacy is not something that the narcissist usually seeks. He will tend not to notice a lack of it or consider that lack a problem unless he perceives a defect or failure in his inability to sustain a marriage.

Borderlines complaining of a difficulty with closeness would be referring to the way they interrupt relationships as they get close to someone by becoming frightened that the person will reject them. To avoid the rejection, they reject the other person first, or they provoke a conflict that leads to distancing in the relationship. They might also describe how they chase partners away by their clinging behavior or, if they have less self-awareness about their clinging, they might complain that although they make attempts at intimacy, their partners seem to pull away.

As indicated earlier in this chapter, a presenting problem of depression is possible for any of the three personality disorders. The therapist must evaluate the nature and origin of this depression.

Borderlines commonly complain of feeling overwhelmed; this is usually an expression of helplessness, an attempt to be taken care of, which is an expression of the wish for reunion. It is a very unlikely presenting problem of a narcissist unless precipitated by a major loss of confidence and disintegration of the grandiose defense. It would be equally uncharacteristic for a schizoid, who might be more fearful of a loss of control resulting from difficulty setting limits and dealing with conflict.

**Lack of Presenting Problem**

Narcissists are more likely than borderline or schizoid patients to come to therapy without a self-avowed presenting problem. There are, however, other factors that can lead to this phenomenon. Someone who utilizes denial as a primary defense, like a substance abuser or a codependent, may come to therapy claiming that the problem is how to deal with a spouse, parent, child, or co-worker. Also, some borderlines will come to therapy after a significant loss and have very little sense of the precipitating event. All they will be able to talk about initially will be their symptoms, and these may sound very general, like, "I've recently been depressed."

## DIAGNOSTIC IMPLICATIONS OF PERSONAL HISTORY

A history is obviously very useful diagnostically in distinguishing between neurotic conditions and personality disorders. The history provides an indication of ego strength, of the patient's ability to handle major and minor emotional trauma, and of how the patient defends against the affect involved in painful situations. It also indicates the degree of emotional trauma in a patient's past, revealing the kind of psychic damage that has been done. As the history is related, the therapist gets a sense of whether areas of the patient's past are being omitted, denied, or distorted. Neurotic patients are likely to omit parts of their history or relate screen memories, memories that carry manageable affect but describe events from an aspect of the history where there are repressed memories that are deeply affect laden. Patients with a personality disorder will usually distort painful areas of their history, deny their significance, avoid talking about them, relate these portions of the history with inappropriate affect, or have virtually no memory about large blocks of time in their past. Perhaps most importantly, a personal history can indicate whether or not there is substance abuse or other nonpsychological impediments to treatment present. Before treatment gets under way in the wrong direction, it is a good idea to take a formal history, including questions about alcohol and drug use early on in treatment.

The history is also useful, however, in differentiating between the various personality disorders. In the history of a borderline patient, for instance, the therapist is likely to notice that symptoms emerge at times when the patient makes major moves, experiences loss, makes important life choices, or takes independent action. Common events that can produce symptoms include times when the family moved from one home to another, when a friend or family member moved away, when the patient started in a new school, especially junior high school or college, and any separations, divorces, or deaths. Symptoms include all of the typical borderline symptoms as well as other behavior that by itself might not be considered symptomatic. For instance, if a borderline moves away from home to go to college, he or she may be likely to do poorly in college, often becoming depressed, and skipping classes, or becoming helpless and finding someone to cling to and be taken care of by. The history of a borderline patient is also likely to include descriptions of the acting out of borderline defenses, like clinging, distancing, and splitting. This information is helpful to the clinician as an indication of what kind of defenses to look for during treatment.

With narcissists, the history is usually skimpy, but often reveals early responses to failure or the possibility of failure, the need for perfection, and the detachment from real relationships. The narcissist typically has one or more narcissistic parents. The narcissist functions as a mirroring selfobject for those parents, valued only for what he or she can do to support the parents' grandiose self-image. This is played out in an enormous need on the part of the child to meet his or her parents' unrealistic expectations. Because of their discomfort with flaws, narcissists describe their childhoods as reasonably healthy and see their parents as having been adequate or good parents. If there was an undeniable problem in their childhood, they pass it off as typical of the problems that all people have.

The history of schizoid patients is usually marked by neglectful, depriving, or extremely intrusive parents. The parents' invasiveness and deprivation produce a feeling in this patient that he can never feel safe, that he is always in danger of attack; at the same time he feels utterly isolated, lacking the validation that comes with a sense of connection to another human being. The patient often reports a feeling of being different from other people, of being on the outside of society looking in. The schizoid patient is not likely to report a very full history unless it is reported without affective connections. He or she normally reports having grown up with very few or no friends. If the schizoid talks about having had a good friend, there is likely to be a pattern of finding a friend and then holding on to that friend as long as possible, not making new friends until the previous friendship has ended. Unlike other personality disorders, the schizoid patient often remembers many of the details of his or her history, but is unwilling to share that history with the therapist until he or she feels safe enough to do so.

Both borderlines and narcissists have difficulty making constructive life choices. Neither is in touch with his or her inner concerns, preferences, and aspirations. In addition, making choices for a borderline is an individuative act, and so stimulates abandonment depression. For narcissists, making choices exposes them to the possibility of making a mistake, and the consequent embarrassment or humiliation. Borderlines passively tend to back into decisions, while narcissists either avoid decisions that are based on personal preference or make decisions in order to further unrealistic grandiose goals based on an inflated appraisal of their abilities. It is useful when taking a patient's history to pay attention to those times in the patient's life when a major decision or self-activation was required, to see how the patient defended against the emotional stress brought on by these situations. This information is not only helpful diagnostically, but helps the clinician to predict how the patient will respond in treatment.

## Typical History of a Borderline Patient

Mrs. P. is 26 years old. She grew up in an alcoholic home. Her parents fought frequently and on occasions her father abused her mother physically. Both parents drank, but Mrs. P.'s father drank far more than her mother. Her father was in the military, which required the family to move frequently from one geographic area to another. As a result, Mrs. P. claims that she never remained in any school for more than two years. She says that she had plenty of friends and was well liked, but learned not to get too close to any of them because she knew she would soon move away from them. She was active in 4-H clubs, Girl Scouts, and later a sorority. Her mother "lived for her," being overprotective, and constantly wanting to be involved in all of Mrs. P.'s activities. Her father was rigid and distant, and not at home very much. She never felt close to him.

When Mrs. P. was 9 years old, her father and mother separated for the third time. A year later they were divorced. Mrs. P. continued to live with her mother. Her mother became extremely agitated and nearly required hospitalization. Mrs. P. took care of her. Her mother remarried six months after the divorce.

Mrs. P. never got along with her stepfather, who also had a drinking problem. When Mrs. P. was 13 years old her stepfather molested her. She dealt with this problem by trying to stay away from home at friends' houses as much as possible. At 15, she began going out with a 19-year-old boy, and moved in with him six months later. Her reason originally for not telling her mother what her stepfather had done is that she felt as though she had somehow been to blame, and she was afraid her mother would be angry at her for letting it happen. Now, at age 26, she has been divorced once after a three-year marriage, and has been married to her second husband for three years.

During the past four years she has been attending the local community college, accumulating credits toward an AA degree. She has accumulated more credits than are necessary, but has been unable to decide on a major subject, so she has not received the degree. She is still on good terms with her mother and visits her at least once a week. When she sees her stepfather, she is cordial and distant. She has never told her mother about the molestation because she does not want to be responsible for the breakup of her mother's marriage, which she assumes would occur.

Frequent family moves do not create personality disorders, but they often aggravate an incipient personality disorder by creating a series of losses, causing the person to avoid meaningful relationships and emotionally isolating the person. If the parents are dysfunctional, the increased dependency on the family that these moves cause makes the disorder more severe. It is generally believed that borderline disorders occur as a result of a person's experience as a young child during the rapprochement subphase of the period of separation and individuation (Mahler 1975). Although Mahler places this subphase at the fifteenth through the twenty-fourth month of life, some other theorists place the critical period for the etiology of the borderline condition as early as 6 months of age. Traumatic losses experienced after that period deepen the condition and lower the prognosis for successful treatment.

In the case of Mrs. P., one might conjecture that her parents' unstable relationship, the alcohol abuse, and the apparent emotional difficulties of her mother caused the original borderline condition. The subsequent loss of her father, the successive family moves, and the stepfather's abuse added to the severity of the condition. On the positive side, her ability to attend community college classes and complete them indicates that Mrs. P.'s ability to function is not entirely disabled.

Some of the information in the history suggests the possibility of a schizoid diagnosis as well as borderline, such as her decision not to get too close to any of her friends when growing up and her distant relationship with her father. However, schizoid patients are usually socially inept whereas Mrs. P. was well liked as a child and joined a variety of social organizations. In addition, Mrs. P.'s mother also appears to be a clinging borderline, which is common for borderline patients and very unlikely for a schizoid patient.

Attending a college that is close to home, difficulty deciding on a major or on a career, and neglecting to take the final steps to complete a degree that one has worked hard for are all typical borderline behaviors. Although for most people going to school is a form of activation, for most personality disorders it is a way to avoid venturing out into the world. It is a safe environment where they can get approval from teachers and parents by studying and doing well on tests. Rather than have to look inside for a sense of self and self-worth, they can get a clear outside indicator of worth by the grades they get.

Mrs. P.'s response to the molestation is not uncommon as an initial response among nonborderline and borderline patients alike. She feels bad about herself and projects that her mother will also think she is bad. She defends against the dysphoric feelings about herself and the experience by clinging in a typically borderline fashion. She avoids addressing the problem and finds friends and eventually a boy friend to whom she can turn. She continues to cling to her mother and continues to avoid dealing with her relationship with her stepfather. Her reason for not addressing the stepfather is a variation of the original reason: she believes that if she is open about what happened, there will be a bad result, and she will be responsible, and therefore bad.

## Typical History of a Narcissist

Mr. Q. is 42 years old. He came to therapy because his wife threatened to divorce him if he did not. He has been married for eight years and has two children. He is especially attached to the older, his son, of whom he is very proud. Mr. Q. physically struck his wife a week before entering therapy. He had acted very threatening in the past, but this was the first time he had actually struck her in the five years since he had stopped drinking. Five years ago he had decided that his drinking was a problem, and so one day he abruptly stopped. He hasn't had a drink since that day. He has gone to one AA meeting, but felt he couldn't relate to the people there, and anyway, he knew he could stop without AA. He has considered the consequences of a divorce and found them undesirable, especially the dividing of his assets, loss of his children, and loss of his home.

Mr. Q.'s memory of his childhood is extremely sketchy. He does not remember any specific events or interactions involving his mother or father, except one time that he was caught stealing from the local candy store, and his father was notified. His father was furious and beat him with a stick, leaving him with bruises, including one on his face. The one other thing he recalls from early childhood is that he was a good student and his father was very proud of him. He remembers more from his late teen years, which he spent hanging out with his friends and playing tennis, a sport at which he excelled. He does not remember any excessive drinking on the part of his mother or father, but he does have a memory during late teens of his father's alcohol consumption increasing to the point of frequently drinking himself to sleep. Although he cannot actually remember his childhood, he believes that his parents were good parents, and that his childhood was happy and relatively uneventful.

Mr. Q. does not feel that he has any problems that he is not already handling. He is concerned that he lost control and struck his wife, but is certain that it will not happen again. He is unsure how therapy can be of help to him, but he would like to preserve his marriage, so he is willing give therapy a try.

An extremely sketchy memory of childhood is common for personality disorders, but especially so for narcissists. The ability to quit a highly addictive behavior like drug or alcohol abuse completely merely by making the decision to do so is a quality that one would not find in borderlines, but might find in narcissists. Narcissists are sometimes able to do this because they come to a point where they perceive the addictive behavior both as a flaw and as an indication that they are not in complete control of themselves, two intolerable conditions. Mr. Q. is typically unconcerned about his relationship with his wife. His concerns are about three things that offer him narcissistic supplies: his wealth, his home, and his son, whom he sees as an extension of himself.

## Typical History of a Schizoid Patient

Mr. R. is 44 years old. He is coming to therapy because he feels dead inside and does not feel close to anyone, including his wife and two children. His wife also feels that he could benefit from some therapy. He describes a childhood of painful isolation. His father was often gone from the house, and when he was present he was ineffectual. His mother was extremely unreasonable and demanding. Her behavior was bizarre in some ways and when Mr. R. was 12 years old his mother's behavior became so strange that she was institutionalized. After that, she was recurrently institutionalized for short periods. He does not remember feeling close to either his father or his mother. He recalls his mother's behavior being so erratic that he never knew when she would be approving of him and when she would be critical of him or punitive. His father was apparently unwilling or unable to intervene to protect him. His paternal grandmother, of whom he felt very fond, died when he was 8.

Mr. R.'s memory of his childhood is reasonably detailed. However, he recalls the incidents without affect, even incidents that seem certain to have been traumatic or otherwise emotional for him. He had an older brother and a younger sister. He remembers making a good friend when he was 5, but his friend moved away several years later. He remembers then having another good friend for several years, but something happened in that relationship and one day this friend simply stopped speaking to or associating with him. Mr. R. has never understood what caused that relationship to end so abruptly. After that he did not have any friends for the duration of grade school, and even in high school his friendships were basically perfunctory and activity oriented. The only people he felt close to were his family members.

In high school he was a good student in mathematics and the sciences. However, he still kept to himself and devoted much of his time to reading. He did not date. He went to college to study engineering. A girl friend of his younger sister became interested in him and they began a friendship. After several years, he began to date her and eventually married her. He describes her presently as extremely demanding and unreasonable but to him the thought of leaving her or even resisting her demands is unthinkable. Nevertheless, he is extremely self-sufficient and does not like to depend on anyone. In his work as an engineer he feels similarly uncomfortable with his boss, from whom he continually fears reprimand. His work is meticulous and his boss says he is very pleased with Mr. R., but Mr. R. distrusts his boss's praise and remains continually anxious at work.

Although Mr. R.'s primary reason for coming to therapy may have been his wife's suggestion, some higher level schizoid individuals do seek treatment themselves. Neither of Mr. R.'s parents was close to him; it is very common with these patients that at least one parent is extremely intrusive and critical, and the other is absent, uninterested, or negligent. Some very high level schizoid patients have parents who are not intrusive but merely unable to bond; they might have been schizoid themselves, or a sickness, physical or mental condition in the parent or the child might have interfered with their connection. For whatever reason, schizoid patients were unable to bond adequately with either caretaker and consequently grew up feeling cut off from their feelings, extremely isolated, and distrustful of closeness to another person.

They do not have strong social skills and in childhood they lack strong friendships other than possibly one good friend at any given time to whom they are extremely loyal. Even as adults, their strongest relationships are often with members of their family of origin. As are many of even their most casual relationships, these relationships are likely to be of the master/slave type and can be sadistic. Many schizoid adults remain unmarried and are sexually inactive, although they may fantasize frequently or obsess about sex as they do about all forms of relating to people. If they are sexually active, their sexual relations are likely to reflect the master/slave unit and may be sadomasochistic. Their home life and work life again reflect the master/slave unit if indeed they live or work with other people. Often they do not. At work they tend to be meticulous; nevertheless, they typically fear criticism from authority. They usually stay at the same job for long periods of time and are likely to turn down promotions that might destabilize their secure position or involve a greater degree of interaction with other workers.

## DIAGNOSTIC IMPLICATIONS OF SPLIT SELF AND OBJECT REPRESENTATIONS

The borderline condition is known for its good and bad split self and object representations. (See Chapter 3.) It is also true, however, that narcissistic disorders and schizoid disorders have split self and object representations. It is theoretically useful, therefore, to examine the self and object representations in the diagnostic process. In practice, however, early in the therapy process it is very difficult to discern accurately the patient's self and object representations, so that this analysis tends to be more useful in confirming a preliminary diagnosis than in formulating one.

The negative split self and objects of the various personality disorders are often not easy to distinguish without a deep understanding of the patient. However, the positive split self and objects are more easily distinguishable. The borderline's good part-self representation is of someone who is loved and lovable and good. In order to maintain this part-self representation, the borderline is compliant and helpless. This behavior contrasts with the narcissist, who may be compliant when mirroring an idealized selfobject, but does not tend to play a helpless role. Helplessness is an extremely painful feeling for narcissists because it makes them feel vulnerable to attack and humiliation. When the narcissist, in the "positive" pole of his split, is grandiose and possibly devaluing, he is easily distinguishable from the borderline.

The schizoid patient experiences safety, connectedness, and a sense of control in the positive part-self representation. Schizoids do not tend to play a helpless role either. For the schizoid to be helpless would mean a loss of control that would be unbearable. The schizoid who engages in relationships does, however, often appear to be compliant while playing out the slave role in the master/slave unit, which for him is the positive object relations unit. This compliance is in time distinguishable from that of the borderline in that for the schizoid it represents submission, complete domination for which there is no alternative but terribly painful exile. The schizoid sometimes appears initially to be a bit grandiose, but this grandiosity is paper thin and distinguishable from the narcissist's grandiosity, which is pervasive and extremely resilient.

One relatively easy distinction to spot is the way borderline personalities and narcissistic personalities respond to success. For the borderline personality success usually stimulates the negative object relations unit, so that he becomes anxious and expects something bad to happen to him. For the narcissistic personality, especially in the early stages of treatment, successes are usually part of an attempt to bolster his grandiosity. Rather than produce anxiety, success for the narcissistic personality usually produces elation. For the schizoid, success often means change, which can create new vulnerability; it is therefore often viewed with caution.

## DIAGNOSTIC INFORMATION IN COUNTERTRANSFERENCE

Countertransference results from psychological material emerging in the patient that stimulates the therapist's own unresolved psychological material. If uncontrolled, countertransference can subvert a therapeutic process; if identified and controlled, however, it can yield useful diagnostic and therapeutic information.

### Therapist Feeling Responsible for the Patient

A common form of countertransference is the sense of responsibility that therapists sometimes feel for their patients. Therapists who become directive with patients often begin to feel responsible for what happens to the patient as a result of the therapist's direction. With a borderline patient, the therapist's excessive feeling of responsibility is likely to be a response to messages of helplessness and hopelessness from the patient. If the therapist takes on the patient's problems and feels responsible for solving them for the patient, the therapist is likely to feel like the patient, overwhelmed, frustrated, and helpless. With a schizoid patient, a therapist can sometimes feel intensely responsible for the patient as a result of inadvertently assuming the patient's projection of the master role in the master/slave unit.

### Therapist Feeling Like a Tyrant

Assuming that the therapist has maintained therapeutic neutrality, if the therapist begins to feel like an ogre or tyrant in response to the patient's suffering and withdrawal, there is a good chance that the therapist has accepted a schizoid patient's negative part-object projection. As has been pointed out repeatedly in this book, the borderline split causes the borderline patient periodically to see the therapist as withdrawing, attacking, or critical, which the therapist can internalize as feeling harsh and unreasonable. However, this feeling is less extreme than what the therapist of a schizoid patient would tend to feel. The therapist's countertransference response may be to wonder if the therapeutic interventions have not perhaps been too critical, abrasive, or judgmental. The therapist may wonder if the pain that the patient is experiencing is really necessary; the therapist questions if perhaps he is pushing the patient too hard.

With a borderline patient, when the therapist accepts the negative projection, he or she feels a pull to say something nurturing or reassuring to the patient to convey the message, "I'm really not all that bad, am I?" Since this message is a response to cues from the patient, it unfortunately subtly validates the projection and the patient's expectation of emotional rescue by the therapist. If the therapist identifies the negative projections, it is usually effective for the therapist to clarify the patient's response by exploring with the patient why the therapist's neutral interventions sound critical to the patient. The patient's negative projection, however, is not always obvious, often taking the form of the patient discussing some third person who is very withholding or attacking. As the patient describes this person, the therapist thinks, "I would never be like that. I'm such an understanding and giving person." Upon thinking this, the therapist finds himself or herself spontaneously making an understanding, nurturing comment to the patient, thereby gratifying the patient's unspoken demand that the therapist make the patient feel good. Masterson refers to this as the therapist "stepping into the rewarding unit." (See Chapter 3 for more detail.) This unspoken demand usually comes at a time when the patient has begun to struggle with difficult therapeutic material that is naturally creating anxiety. By gratifying the patient's demand, the therapist steers him away from that material and the anxiety that accompanies it.

Although narcissists can also project a critical quality onto the therapist, it is different than the countertransference response elicited by the borderline or schizoid patient. The therapist of the narcissist is more likely to feel guilty about injuring the patient, to feel as though he has made a clinical error; the patient's rigid and intensely self-critical standards of perfection are often taken on by the therapist who then feels remorse for the slightest misjudgment or faulty perception.

### Therapist Feeling Groggy or Distancing

A therapist can feel groggy or withdrawn as a countertransference response. For instance, the therapist can feel this way as the borderline patient's abandonment depression begins to surface if the therapist has unresolved abandonment issues. If the therapist has unresolved narcissistic vulnerability, he might respond to narcissistic patients' devaluation or disengaged style by himself disengaging and becoming bored or sleepy. If the patient is schizoid and the therapist has unresolved schizoid issues, the therapist might respond to the patient's protective distancing with her own protective distancing, becoming groggy or otherwise uninvolved.

### Therapist Feeling Particularly Engaged with the Patient

Since narcissistic patients view others as extensions of themselves, they do not normally acknowledge the therapist as a separate and unique individual. Consequently, the therapist can feel somewhat invisible in a session with a narcissist. The patient might, for instance, talk on and on about recent events in her life without any affect and without any interest in obtaining input from the therapist. When she does not engage the therapist other than possibly in a demanding sort of way, the therapist can tend to feel bored or uninvolved.

The exception to this is the narcissist who develops an idealizing transference to the therapist. In that case the therapist may feel engaged, acknowledged, or charmed by the patient, because the patient is so finely tuned to the therapist or is even singing the praises of the therapist. If the therapist responds to this praise or cultivates it, the patient will continue it in lieu of personal introspection. As much as the therapist would like to believe that this is one of the few areas where the patient's perceptions are penetrating, sharp, and undistorted, the therapist should remind himself that the patient is responding only to his own image of a perfect therapist, and not to the person. If the therapist recognizes the patient's praise as part of an idealizing transference, the therapist will need to exercise restraint in not allowing himself to resonate to the patient's idealization.

This phenomenon of a sense of closeness between therapist and patient can also, of course, come from genuine relatedness. However, in the initial stages of the therapy of a narcissist, this patient is not interested in or capable of genuine relatedness. With a higher level borderline patient, however, a certain amount of genuine relatedness is possible. However, when a borderline patient would rather focus on the therapist than he would on himself, he is using the relationship defensively rather than attempting to make genuine contact. Especially if the borderline patient sees the therapist as someone who will take over for him and take care of him, the borderline patient will bond to the therapist. This bonding will take on a different quality than that of the idealizing narcissist or the neurotic, as reflected by the effect of the therapist's interventions. With the narcissist, this good feeling that the patient gets from feeling close to the therapist is likely to be exhibited through some form of expansive behavior ranging from further display of grandiosity to genuine activation. With the borderline patient, however, this good feeling is likely to take on a soothing effect in which the patient becomes more passive, dependent on, and clinging to the therapist.

For the neurotic, this good feeling is likely to produce a little of each of the two previous effects, but primarily the good feeling will translate into intimacy, and so will produce anxiety or discomfort in the patient, which the patient is likely to bring up and discuss in the therapy.

Surprisingly, this sense of closeness can also appear in therapeutic relationships with schizoid patients. It arises in the therapist out of a combination of empathic response to the patient and the patient behaving as though the relationship is close, without actually engaging the therapist emotionally. The key here is the uniform lack of emotional intensity in the sessions, and the patient's attitude toward the therapist assuming a closeness that does not correspond with the therapist's experience in the relationship. The good feeling that the patient gets usually translates into the patient experiencing his slave role more intensely. However, as the relationship develops, the therapist can feel extremely engaged as the patient's ingenuous vulnerability becomes very apparent, allowing the therapist a glimpse of some of his enormous emotional importance to the patient.

### Therapist Feeling Helpless or Inadequate

A therapist tends to feel helpless or inadequate when assaulted by a borderline patient as part of a projective identification or projection of the negative part-object onto the therapist. This tends to be a hot anger. A narcissist can produce feelings of helplessness or inadequacy in the therapist by a simple supercilious frown, a raised eyebrow, an offhand comment, or a more overt behavior like lateness to sessions, termination of treatment, or criticism of the therapy. He or she tends to be cold and precise, and the result is devaluation more than heat. Often these attacks are especially painful to the therapist because the narcissist has been carefully scrutinizing the therapist and has identified the therapist's vulnerabilities. Schizoid patients can also produce feelings of helplessness in a therapist as a result of their need to control and their frequent power struggles with the therapist. In all of the above situations, the therapist may not be aware of feeling helpless or inadequate. Instead, he or she may be conscious of feelings ranging from irritation to a desire to punish the patient.

## DIAGNOSTIC IMPLICATIONS OF DEFENSES

Analysis of defenses can be useful in diagnosis, but it can also be confusing. As emphasized in Chapter 2 of this book, it is important for the therapist to understand the patient's use of defenses and the particular painful feelings that the patient is defending against.

## Variations in the Triad

The borderline, narcissist, and schizoid triads have been described in detail in previous chapters. Tracking these triads yields excellent diagnostic information. The borderline defends in response to abandonment depression stimulated by loss or activation. The narcissist defends against emotional injury resulting from puncturing of the grandiose self or exposure of the defective self, whereas the schizoid defends against threats to safety resulting from loss of control, sudden changes in relative distance, attack, or the fear of rejection. Each defends in his or her own characteristic way.

### Avoidance

Avoidance is a good example because it is commonly used by borderline patients, narcissistic patients, schizoid patients, and neurotic patients. The borderline uses avoidance to escape looking at an uncomfortable question or to otherwise avoid facing an uncomfortable situation. The narcissist uses avoidance to protect himself from potentially deflating subjects or experiences. The schizoid uses it to preserve a feeling of safety, and the neurotic uses it to avoid discomfort. For all of these patients, the avoidant behavior looks the same, but for each the motivation is slightly different.

### Withdrawal

There are two forms of withdrawal—one to punish and defend from attack, and the other to defend from engulfment. The first form describes the narcissist's use of withdrawal, while both forms describe the borderline and schizoid patient's use of it. Withdrawal is particularly prominent for lower level borderline patients, although the borderline's use of withdrawal tends not to be as cold and unfeeling as that of the narcissist.

### Clinging

Clinging is most typical of borderlines. The narcissist engages in relationships in order to obtain narcissistic supplies: admiration, money, sex, and power. If a narcissist appears to cling to an old relationship, it may be an attempt to avoid the failure or humiliation involved in an ending. The borderline clings to avoid the abandonment feelings connected with separation. The schizoid clings to old relationships because however unpleasant they are, they still provide relatedness, and the alternative to relatedness is unthinkable.

### Compliance

Compliance is typical of borderlines, narcissists, and schizoids. The borderline complies to win attention and love. In complying, the closet narcissist is repeating the childhood role of providing a mirroring selfobject function to narcissistic parents. (See Chapter 4 for detailed discussions of the closet narcissist and the mirroring selfobject.) In addition, sometimes the closet narcissist complies to avoid conflict or criticism. The schizoid complies as part of a passive response to conflict, in order to maintain a safe, stable environment.

### Devaluation

Devaluation is most typical of the narcissist. For many reasons, however, the borderline can also devalue. Sometimes it is to provoke the therapist to become more active. Sometimes it is in the service of projective identification where the patient identifies with the aggressor, getting to feel powerful, like the historical parent, by making the therapist feel small and helpless. Sometimes it is an expression of anger. The narcissist's devaluation, on the other hand, tends to be more intense and biting. Its purpose is to write the other person off, make the other person disappear. It arises in sessions when the therapist inadvertently wounds the patient, usually by imperfect mirroring or by interfering with the patient's idealization of the therapist. The patient, who has identified with the therapist, now sees the therapist as imperfect, and must write the therapist off in order to prevent the identification with the therapist from reflecting negatively upon the patient. The schizoid patient can become angry and critical only when she has given up on the relationship, when the master/slave unit has given way to exile. In the master/slave relationship, the schizoid can take the master role but then she tends to be more controlling than critical and devaluing.

### Manic Defense

The manic defense for narcissists is all pervasive. It is a way of life. It supports their grandiosity and helps them to avoid feeling. For the borderline patient, the manic defense usually appears for a specific purpose, to defend against a particular feeling that is surfacing. If it appears it is usually short-lived. For the schizoid, business is a pervasive defense to avoid feeling and substitute for relatedness.

### Grandiose Defense

Grandiosity is the hallmark of the narcissist; however a borderline can also display grandiosity. When the borderline displays it, it has a different quality than when the narcissist does. With the narcissist, the grandiosity is ubiquitous and uninterrupted. The borderline, on the other hand, may have periods of grandiosity, interspersed with periods of self-doubt or questioning. Often, what appears to be grandiosity is in fact a weak grandiose defense, or an intensified sense of well-being resulting from being taken care of by someone in grandiose style. While the narcissist's grandiose defense is ironclad and fiercely protected, the borderline's grandiose defense is thin and can be easily dropped. Schizoids, too, can display grandiosity; they also often display other narcissistic defenses during the initial stage of treatment and they also exhibit grandiosity in the form of grandiose fantasies. These fantasies usually include a way in which they will be enormously successful and relate to others from that position. The fantasy provides a vision of a safe position of authority, as well as a structured, controlled way of relating to others. So, the schizoid's grandiose fantasies tend to be different from the fantasies of a narcissist in that the schizoid's fantasies are more object-oriented.

### Humor

Humor is a very mature defense used by neurotics and other fairly healthy character structures. Humor, however, can also be used in the service of an avoidance defense. Although narcissists can sometimes be dry and humorless, tending to be injured by facetious remarks, others can be charming and funny, and use entertainment as a distraction. Borderlines, too, can use humor to avoid, but not as commonly as do narcissistic disorders.

### Independence Defense

Independence in a patient is hard to evaluate. On the one hand individuation is healthy, but independence can be taken to an extreme, and used as a way to avoid the vulnerability of interdependence in relationships. This form of protection is typical of narcissists, who cannot tolerate dependency. It is also not unusual for lower level borderlines as a form of distancing, and for borderlines who have been in a therapy process or a twelve-step program. These latter are delicate cases, because these patients will often feel proud of their new-found self-sufficiency. A schizoid patient also often appears to display an independence defense. If the therapist challenges this defense instead of interpreting the schizoid patient's need for safety, the patient is likely to become frightened and withdraw.

## CONCLUSION

The difficult part of diagnosis is making sense out of apparent contradictions that would otherwise cast doubt upon the diagnosis. The patient who is diagnosed as a borderline but appears to be grandiose and devaluing may be a borderline patient who is identifying with the aggressor in projective identification. The patient who is diagnosed as a narcissist but obsesses over the loss of a relationship may be a narcissist who feels insulted at the thought that someone might not want to be with him. The patient who appears to be schizoid but produces some affect in sessions or clings to a spouse may in fact be schizoid. In each case it is the task of the clinician to formulate a diagnosis based upon an understanding of the underlying meaning and significance to the patient's actions and expressions. In this context, the diagnostic process is of greater importance to treatment than the diagnosis itself.

Ultimately, the questions that the therapist is asking when trying to understand the patient are, "What is this patient's underlying view of self and object, and what is the underlying affect? How does the patient defend against the underlying painful affect, and what is the patient's present capacity for introspection and real self experience? What is the meaning of the patient's behavior and expressions?" These are, of course, also the essential questions involved in the process of differential diagnosis described in this chapter. Whether or not a clinician uses the particular categories of diagnosis that have been emphasized in this book, his or her understanding of the patient's view of the world can be enhanced by an active ongoing attempt to organize the information that the patient presents; diagnosis is one method of doing this.

# 7

# Interventions

Recently, I observed a 3-year-old boy hold his teddy bear over the railing on the upstairs landing of the waiting room in my office and say, "Look, mommy." I'm sure his mother knew exactly what this meant, but she asked, "What are you doing?" He said tauntingly, "I'm going to drop it." She said, "You know mommy doesn't want you to drop things over the railing; it could hit someone." He had a big grin and he almost sang, "I a-a-am." There was a silence as his mother calculated her next move while trying not to appear amused. "I'm going to do i-i-it," he sang. His eyes sparkled. She decided to interpret, "Sweetheart, I know you want to play with mommy." That fell flat, so she added, "You know when you want to play with mommy you can just ask mommy to play with you." He sang, "Here I go-o-o." She switched to confrontation. "If you drop that, I'm not going to give it back to you until we get in the car." He dropped the teddy bear over the side, laughed, and taunted, "I did it!"

Although this was obviously not a clinical situation, it reminded me of a crucial point about treatment: sometimes the patient and the therapist are playing two different games with two different sets of rules. The mother was trying to reason with her son, to offer him a better approach to getting what he wanted. He was having a fine old time already, and wasn't interested in her logic; besides that, he knew that her logic was part of her game. She was trying to alter the situation by reasoning with him; he was enjoying her predicament, and the power he was able to exercise in putting her in it.

The analogy between this interaction and the psychotherapy situation is a close one. For example, a 28-year-old woman who is receiving disability payments for work-related stress and is also receiving financial support from her parents comes into treatment complaining of low self-esteem and stress. In the first session, she explains her financial situation and asks for a reduced fee. This patient has established a way of life in which she is reenforced in her expectation that she will be taken care of by others. Although she herself might agree that this way of life undermines her sense of self-esteem, she is very comfortable with it and it makes her anxious to even consider giving it up.

Here is a situation in which the patient's maladaptive dependent behavior, a defense against the emotional stress of separation and individuation, is at least partly ego syntonic, despite the patient's intellectual questioning of the behavior. To interpret to this patient that she feels inadequate because all her life she has been reenforced in the belief that she cannot support herself would be as effective as the mother explaining to her son that he would have more fun if he asked her directly to play with him. Like most dependent borderline patients, this patient is not complaining about being dependent; she is very comfortable with that. She views it as a way to receive love. Her reason for entering treatment is that her low self-esteem and her stress make her uncomfortable; she hopes that psychotherapy can make her more comfortable. She is not expecting a therapist to provoke anxiety in her by telling her that there is a problem with her life-style; she is coming to therapy to feel good. She does not realize that there is a difference between feeling better and getting better.

Although this phenomenon seems to be especially true for borderline patients, it is often true for narcissistic and schizoid patients as well that the patient's purpose in being in treatment is not the same as the therapist's purpose. Borderline patients tend to come into treatment to be taken care of and feel loved; they expect treatment to be consistent with the other people and institutions in their lives that they cling to in the hope of being nurtured and approved of. Narcissistic patients enter treatment usually because their defenses have failed them and they are feeling deflated and defective. They may hope that therapy will provide them with a key that will correct the problem and allow them to go back to their pursuit of perfection, or they may hope that the therapist will agree with them that it is other people who are at fault and responsible for the problems. Schizoid patients view psychotherapy as a dominant/submissive relationship that is reasonably safe and will provide them with a needed connection to the world. Schizoid patients' dominant emotion is usually fear; as they listen to the therapist's intervention they may be assessing how the therapist feels toward them, trying to understand what the therapist wants from them, and figuring out how they can avoid incurring his wrath.

Because patients come to treatment with a wide variety of agendas, they respond to different types and styles of intervention. In this chapter, a range of interventions will be described and illustrated including confrontation, exploratory interventions, mirroring interventions, clarifications, and interpretations.

## CONFRONTATION

Written material about confrontation is often misunderstood because of the unpleasant connotations associated with the word *confrontation* and because when a reader takes the words of a confrontation from a printed page without hearing the therapist's tone of voice or having a sense of the nature of the relationship between therapist and patient, the confrontation is likely to sound critical and rejecting. According to the traditional analytic definition, a confrontation is an intervention that points out a particular phenomenon relating to the patient about which the patient was conscious or nearly conscious but of which he is not presently aware; it is not inherently critical, harsh, or rejecting. Its purpose is to bring a pattern of thought, feeling, or behavior to the patient's attention so that it can be explored and further understood. Forcefulness or aggressiveness on the part of the therapist can be involved in confrontation, although they are discouraged by many clinicians who use confrontation.

A confrontation may imply no judgment about the phenomenon it calls attention to, merely that the phenomenon occurs and that it would be useful to explore, although often there is an understanding by the therapist and the patient that the therapist considers this phenomenon undesirable in some way. Typically, a confrontation has the effect of directing the patient's attention to the particular phenomenon, after which the patient discovers something about the phenomenon either by himself or with the help of a clarification, interpretation, or further confrontation from the therapist. Although most definitions of confrontation agree with the above definition, they seem to vary slightly as to what kinds of phenomena a confrontation demonstrates to the patient. There seem to be two main categories of confrontable phenomena, one including transference phenomena and the other including defense or resistance.

## The Need for Strong Confrontation

With a maladaptive defense the purpose of confrontation is often to make that defense ego dystonic to the patient. When mild confrontation does not accomplish this purpose, a stronger form of confrontation is eventually needed. This is well illustrated by the 28-year-old woman described earlier in this chapter who is being supported by disability payments and a stipend from her parents. As was pointed out, this patient's motivation for change is minimal. Unless the therapist intervenes fairly actively, I do not believe that this patient is likely to take it upon herself to question her life-style, and without questioning her life-style, this patient's investment in her clinging defenses will make therapeutic progress unlikely.

Without strong confrontation on the part of the therapist, this patient's prognosis is not good. A scenario that is repeated over and over in many psychotherapy offices is that the dependent patient thrives in therapy and becomes very attached to her therapist over a period of a year or two until the patient's outside dependency, which has not been effectively addressed in the treatment, causes her to terminate treatment. In the example of the 28-year-old woman, for instance, the patient might respond to the treatment by splitting between the therapist and her parents, when, as a result of her therapy, she feels supported in standing up for herself in a conflict with her parents, they decide that her therapy is causing problems, and threaten to cut off her stipend unless she terminates treatment. She believes that she needs the stipend so she feels that she has no choice but to terminate treatment.

Interpretations will probably go nowhere with this patient, even if she finds them to be interesting or enlightening; her investment in her dependent way of life is simply too great. Mild confrontations that merely point out the behavior of this patient should be tried but will probably also be unlikely to overcome her strong motivation to maintain her dependent life-style. If these are indeed ineffective with this patient, and if the therapist agrees that the patient's dependent life-style prevents her from exploring her own internal strengths or developing a sense of autonomy, then it would appear to make sense for the therapist to use stronger confrontation. One possibility for stronger confrontation is one that points out directly to the patient the undesirable consequences of the behavior; I refer to this as a *sharp* confrontation. Sharp confrontations sometimes also express the consequences of a behavior in a way that jars the patient and calls her attention to the gravity of the situation. A yet stronger possibility for confrontation is to use a consistent series of confrontations, a confrontive posture, or a confrontive *style* that will continually bring the central issue into focus, even when the patient repeatedly attempts to avoid or deny it. A series of confrontations can be strengthened further by punctuating the series occasionally with a sharp confrontation.

There are many other situations in which mild confrontations may not be effective and it will probably be necessary for the therapist to use stronger confrontation. If, for example, the patient is constantly running about chaotically putting out fires in her life, there is no time for introspection. If her brain is swimming in drugs or alcohol, she may not be able to accomplish the most basic task of getting herself to therapy sessions on a regular basis, and if she does she will probably not be ready to face her inner conflicts. If she relies heavily on escape mechanisms when confronted with stressful situations, she may not be available emotionally or physically for treatment.

## Confrontation as an Infrequent Intervention

There is a very different quality to confrontation when it is used on rare occasions during an otherwise interpretive approach to treatment than to confrontation that comprises the central characteristic of a style of treatment. When an isolated confrontation is used at a strategic time, it may appear anomalous to the patient, and the patient may not understand the reason for the interruption in the therapist's otherwise interpretive style, but in most cases the anomalous aspect of it serves to alert the patient to the fact that there is something especially important that the therapist is pointing out. Hopefully the patient ends up feeling appreciative that the therapist cared enough to make the extra effort involved in the confrontation.

Although the use of an occasional confrontation is often purposeful and planned, it can also be spontaneous. Often there is a certain amount of countertransferential feeling involved on the part of a therapist with an otherwise interpretive approach to treatment when he spontaneously chooses to make an exception and confront the patient. The therapist may feel irritated or anxious, or it may be too painful for the therapist to stand by passively while the patient considers the possibility of acting out in a self-destructive way. Although communicating these feelings may be unintentional, it is possible that the therapist's show of a limited amount of spontaneity and emotion, in these cases, may also have a facilitating effect on the treatment[1] in that it indicates to the patient that the therapist has feelings about the treatment and in particular about the patient, that the patient matters to the therapist.

When the therapist is being unintentionally spontaneous and out of role, the patient obtains a glimpse of the person in the room with him, and these fortuitous glimpses can help the patient evaluate whether the therapist can indeed be trusted. Especially for the patient whose spontaneous behavior in childhood provoked his caretakers and resulted in painful reprisal, fear of how the therapist will react when feeling provoked cannot be easily dismissed. When this patient sees the therapist in an unguarded or off-balance moment, a time when the therapist is not calm and in control, or a time when the therapist feels personally embarrassed, pressured, or threatened, the patient may get a sense of the therapist's personal integrity. In resolving these awkward and vulnerable moments, the therapist may either defend at the expense of the patient, possibly by denial or avoidance, or introspect and attempt to address the event directly and honestly. The patient legitimately seeks to reassure himself that the therapist's apparent nonjudgmental caring and professional objectivity will not disappear when the patient becomes more himself in a way that the therapist may not welcome.

## Confrontation as a Style

When confrontation is used as the predominant intervention in a consistent style of treatment or when it is used repeatedly to accomplish a specific therapeutic objective, it has a far greater influence on

[1]In "The Meanings of Confrontation" (Adler and Myerson 1973) Paul Myerson suggests, "Is the therapist's irritation itself, in the context of his overall concern and involvement even when he is unaware of his annoyance, the crucial quality that reaches some patients and affects them favorably? Is it the therapist's irritation that convinces these patients that he is real, truly involved, and interested in his welfare?" (p. 36).

the patient's perception of the therapist and ultimately of himself. Whatever impression the patient gets of the therapist is reinforced over and over with each confrontation. Instead of viewing the confrontation as incidental to the therapist's style and of the therapist's personality, repeated confrontation comes to be viewed as representative of the therapist's style and of the therapist. Negative transference is far more likely to arise; the therapist's style of confrontation has a significantly greater impact on the therapist/patient relationship.

Even when confrontations are being used in sequence or as the basis of a style of intervention, it should not be assumed that the therapist is constantly intervening. On the contrary, the therapist may be a bit active when there is severe acting out on the part of the patient, but for the most part the therapist is attentively listening, just as he would be if he were using a nonconfrontive style of intervention. Unless there is good reason to believe that the patient is in defense and will not of his own accord bring himself back to the issues that concern him, there is no reason for the therapist to interrupt the patient's work by intervening, and there is especially no reason to confront.

## Use of Physical Cues

Although not often thought of as confrontive, the process of bringing the patient's body language to his attention is a mild confrontation when the patient is not fully aware of the phenomenon that the therapist is pointing out or when the patient is aware of it and the intervention calls attention to the patient's resistance to feelings associated with the phenomenon. Most therapists consider this to be an extremely effective intervention, especially when it enables the patient to recognize an affective response that was not being addressed. Changes in gloss or moisture in the patient's eyes, sighs, facial expressions, and shifting of body position are some of the most commonly noticed cues. However, there are innumerable others including shifts in voice quality, skin tone, hand position, and depth or frequency of breathing. This type of intervention helps the patient to become aware of his genuine response to what is being discussed; it often opens a small window to the patient's inner affective self.

## Certainty in Confrontations

One aspect of confrontation that strongly influences how it will be received by the patient is the certainty with which the therapist presents the confrontation. Some therapists tend to confront in a manner that implies that there can be no question about the accuracy of their observations and conclusions. Whereas the therapist may be certain of his observations, the significance he ascribes to them reflects his estimation of the patient's feelings or motives. These therapists may justify their point of view by arguing that if, in the process of confronting, they appear to have any doubt about their positions, the patient will seize upon that doubt as a way to discount the confrontation. Greenson (1967), on the other hand, when he discusses confrontation, states on a number of occasions that he never acts as if he is sure about the truth of an assertion he makes in a confrontation, because he can never be absolutely sure about what goes on in a patient's head. Instead, Greenson qualifies what he says with phrases like "it seems to me" or "this evidence would seem to indicate."

I adhere to the latter point of view. I believe that it is presumptuous of the therapist to assume that he knows what is going on in the patient's head. The stakes are high; if the therapist acts certain of his point of view and he happens to be wrong, he can damage the patient who is already having a very difficult time getting in touch with his insides and determining which of his thoughts and feelings really belong to him. In addition, the therapist's certainty about the patient's inner thoughts and feelings demeans the patient and conveys a message that the therapist is unrealistically powerful and omniscient, while the patient is consequently relatively powerless.

For the borderline patient especially, this message is ironic because the purpose of confronting the borderline patient is to empower him by interrupting his acting out and denial. As it becomes increasingly difficult for him to continue to put off addressing the meaningful conflicts and issues he faces, he begins to take control of his life. The appearance of certainty in confrontations also affects narcissistic and schizoid patients. These patients see the therapist as unrealistically powerful. The narcissistic patient tends to idealize him and try to find a way to believe his assertions, while the schizoid tends to become frightened of him and comply, while going further into hiding and feeling a greater need for protection. In this way, if a therapist has misdiagnosed a narcissistic or schizoid patient as borderline and proceeds to confront him, an overly confident style of confrontation can lead to further confusion in the diagnosis and misdirected treatment based on what appears to be the patient's integration of the confrontations.

The schizoid patient who complies may be difficult to recognize because his true responses are almost completely guarded and hidden from the therapist. With these patients, the therapist must watch for the slightest indication of negative transference, because they will carefully attempt to avoid revealing their disagreement, dissatisfaction, or fear. For instance, the schizoid patient may be offering a hint that a confrontation was inaccurate when he comments about his past belief about the subject of the confrontation and how wrong it apparently was. The narcissist's idealizing response leads to a behavior that is similar to compliance, but with a different motivation. The narcissistic patient's idealization leads him to mirror the therapist and want to be like the therapist. Consequently the patient alters his behavior to be consistent with the therapist's attitudes, not because he wants to placate, but because being like the therapist gives him a sense of specialness and well-being.

This type of confrontation seems to be especially offensive to self psychotherapists, who, in fact, tend not to be supporters of any type of confrontation. Wolf (1988) makes the point that the effect of the therapist's taking a position of certainty with respect to the patient's inner thoughts, feelings, or motivations is to risk duplicating what may have been the pathological childhood experience of the patient; if the patient's reality was different than the parents' realities, the patient's reality was labelled wrong and the parents' realities were right. Stolorow, Brandchaft and Atwood (1987) make a strong case against this type of confrontation as well. They cite as an illustration of an inappropriate confrontation an example of confrontation offered by Kernberg (1975) to patients who reject a series of the therapist's confrontations; Kernberg suggests that the therapist "point out to the patient that he is treating the analyst as if he wished to make him feel defeated and impotent" (p. 247). These authors ask how the patient could respond otherwise if in fact the therapist's confrontations did not fit the patient. For the therapist then to assert to the patient that he is rejecting the therapist's confrontations in order to make the therapist feel impotent would be to add one more confusing, misdirected, and perhaps damaging confrontation to those that had come before.

### Determining the Impact of Confrontation

Necessary to the effective use of confrontation in any context, but especially as a style of treatment, is the therapist's ability to determine if the patient is actually integrating the confrontation or if, instead, the patient is complying or idealizing. In practice, this is very difficult and is probably not always possible. With borderline patients the theory would indicate that if confrontation successfully challenges the patient's maladaptive defenses, the underlying affect should begin to surface, usually in the form of depression, or the extinguished defense should be replaced with another. Thus, when the therapist believes that he has effectively gotten through to the patient and that the patient has made increased efforts to control some significant form of acting out, the therapist should be able to verify this belief by observing a shift in the patient's defenses or in the patient's affect.

Sometimes these observations are relatively easy to make; at other times, however, they can be complicated. The patient who experiences the therapist's confrontation as critical can feel abandoned by the therapist, especially if the therapist's confrontive style represents a shift from a previous nonconfrontive style. In this case the patient's depression will not be an indication at all of integration of the confrontation. The patient who has learned to emote as part of her repertoire of compliant responses can produce the false appearance of experiencing depression. A patient can make life changes that seem to indicate therapeutic progress but are in the service of defensive compliance. Finally, a patient can become deceptive about a particular form of acting out in order not to incur the therapist's displeasure, so that the therapist believes that the patient is no longer acting out in this way. The patient who has stopped talking about this aspect of his life begins to focus on other aspects where there are predictably other forms of defensive acting out, leading the therapist to believe that the defenses that were confronted have been eliminated and have been replaced by these new defenses.

## The Need for a Collaborative Style

It should be apparent from the foregoing discussion that there are many drawbacks and pitfalls to a confrontive style of treatment. Many of these concerns can be ameliorated or eliminated if the therapist approaches confrontation in a collaborative way; that is, the therapist points out what he is seeing and hearing that does not make sense. Then he asks the patient how the patient makes sense out of these observations, or tells the patient what seems to be the apparent implication of these observations and asks the patient how she sees it. With this approach, the therapist is expressing himself in a direct, genuine, and caring way, and the patient is more likely to see him that way. The therapist is not assuming any special powers of perception or reasoning. He is merely stating the obvious and perhaps puzzling about the apparent contradictions with the patient. No matter how human the therapist's approach to confrontation, there is no way to escape the possibility that the patient might respond with compliance that may go undetected. The more genuine and undogmatic the therapist, however, the more possibility there will be for a dialogue to continue between therapist and patient in which the patient's true responses to the therapist's interventions will become clear.

Because of the many real and potential drawbacks to confrontation, many therapists, including analysts and self psychologists who use a neutral approach to treatment, avoid confrontation. Some therapists reserve confrontation for only the most extreme cases of acting out, believing that in addition to confrontation being experienced by the patient as direction from the therapist, the patient often feels intimidated. As an alternative, these therapists propose that if collaborative nonconfrontational interventions are used to establish an atmosphere in treatment in which the patient feels safe and supported, the patient will be able to relinquish his defenses including his acting out, and confrontation will not be necessary. This position contrasts starkly with the opinion of Kernberg, Masterson, Adler, Buie, and some others who recommend the initial use of a confrontive *style* with borderline patients in general.[2] They believe that nothing but confrontation will be effective because these patients will perceive interpretation as a way in which the therapist thinks for the patient, and it is essential for these patients to relinquish their belief that the way for them to be loved is by getting other people to take care of them. Another argument for confrontation of dependent borderline patients is illustrated by the 28-year-old woman described at the beginning of this chapter; her dependency is so ego syntonic for her that it is not likely to become a central focus of her exploration unless the therapist directs her attention to it and points out the negative consequences involved in it.

[2]It should be remembered that these clinicians are referring to somewhat different groups of patients when they use the term *borderline*.

## Sharp Confrontations

Patients will often have conflicting feelings about maladaptive defensive behavior even before it is addressed in treatment, although their denial may be so strong that they do not entertain this conflict for more than a moment at a time. In the best of all situations for a sharp confrontation, the patient already *knows* that it is in his interests to cease his acting-out behavior even if he does not *feel capable* of controlling it, so that sharp confrontation amounts to the therapist adding the weight of her healthy observing ego onto the side of the patient's healthy observing ego in the patient's internal conflict about the acting out. Hopefully the patient can use the strength of the therapist's healthy ego to help him do what he is already struggling to be able to do himself.

It is helpful in structuring a sharp confrontation for the therapist to remind patients of their own internal conflict before the therapist takes a side. An example of a sharp confrontation that is intended to shock the patient as well as point out the consequences of her behavior would be: "You have talked about how hard it is for you to feel like an adult in the world when, at 28 years of age, you are still receiving an allowance from your parents; yet, you are afraid that you cannot make it on your own so you make no attempts at breaking away. As long as you maintain this childlike dependency, however, how do you foresee your self-esteem or self-confidence appreciably improving; at this rate, it seems to me that you'll still be struggling with the same feeling of inadequacy when you're fifty." Assuming that the patient herself is conflicted about her dependency upon her parents, this intervention will have a sobering effect, conveying to the patient the seriousness and immediacy of the issue. If the therapeutic relationship is well established and sharp confrontations have been rare, the patient should hopefully also be able to take from this intervention the message that the therapist is concerned and cares about what happens to the patient.

## The Effect of Sharp Confrontation

Sharp confrontation results in a variety of possible reactions from the patient. The desired response is that the patient recognize the need and purpose of the confrontation and explore the pattern that has been confronted. Sometimes, however, the patient feels intimidated and complies in an attempt to pacify the therapist. Sometimes the patient feels "bad" and complies in an attempt to gain the therapist's approval. Sometimes the patient is so involved in the transferential feelings elicited by the confrontation that he is unavailable to examine the issue being addressed. In order to avoid impeding the progress of the treatment, it is very important that the therapist remain attuned to the patient and accurately assess the patient's ability to utilize sharp confrontation.

Confrontation has on occasion been discussed using the story of the farmer who sells a burro to another farmer. The seller tells the buyer that the burro is a fine animal who will carry heavy loads long distances and will pull farm implements. The seller demonstrates, commanding, "Pull," and the burro responds immediately to this command. When the buyer arrives home with the animal, however, he finds that when he says, "Pull," nothing happens; the burro will not budge. He takes the animal back to the seller who analyzes the problem and explains to the buyer that he is not going about it in the proper way. He demonstrates by commanding, "Pull"; when the burro does not respond, he takes a large stick and breaks it over the burro's head. This time when the farmer says, "Pull" the burro pulls. The seller turns to the buyer and explains, "You see, before you tell him what you want him to do, you have to get his attention."

The issue with respect to sharp confrontation is whether, as some therapists assert, its effect is to get the patient's attention, or whether its effect is also to cause the patient to feel intimidated or at least pressured. I think it is clear that if sharp confrontation is used, in addition to the anxiety that is produced for the patient by bringing an uncomfortable issue to the patient's attention, there will also be anxiety, often a very large amount of anxiety, produced by the fact that the confrontation is coming from the therapist who is presumably a looming figure in the patient's life.

The desired impact of sharp confrontation is that the patient will see the logic in what the therapist is saying, feel understood and cared about by the therapist, and give the issue the gravity that it deserves. Often, however, the patient will be overwhelmed by his anxiety and defend against it by either concealing from the therapist his acting out or, as just discussed, by responding compliantly. If the patient responds to sharp confrontation by hiding his acting-out behavior from the therapist, the treatment will be significantly affected. The patient will perceive a barrier between himself and the therapist and the therapist may not have available the necessary information to process this material in treatment.

Although these defensive responses are problematic, when taken in the context of the severely destructive forms of acting-out behavior that constitute some of the alternatives, there are some patients and some situations for which compliance is not necessarily a bad thing. If severely destructive acting out is interrupted, even as a result of hospitalization, medication, or compliance out of a feeling of intimidation, there is at least a possibility that the patient will become available to be treated in more neutral psychotherapeutic ways. If after sharp confrontation the therapist returns to a more neutral tone, the impact on the therapeutic relationship of the therapist's confrontations will need to be understood and effectively addressed in the treatment.

When the urgency of the patient's acting out is not so great as to leave the therapist no choice, the timing of sharp confrontation is very important. An ill-timed confrontation can bring up so much negative transference that the positive aspects of the message are entirely missed by the patient. It is preferable for the relationship between therapist and patient to be secure and for the patient to be reasonably convinced of the positive intentions of the therapist at the time of a sharp confrontation. In addition, the issue being addressed should be sufficiently identified that there is not disagreement between therapist and patient about what the patient is doing that the therapist considers to be maladaptive.

## CLINICAL EXAMPLE—CONSISTENT CONFRONTATION

The following is an example of the use of a moderate confrontive style of treatment. The therapist addresses Miss S.'s propensity to act out at work, identifying her splitting and challenging her tendency to avoid situations that make her feel uncomfortable.

**P:** I'm falling apart at the edges. . . . (describes an unpleasant interaction with another employee earlier in the week)

It made me feel really low. I lack confidence. . . . Anybody

Miss S. begins the session by describing her difficulties at work, as she has on several previous occasions. She describes how fragile she feels and how much pressure she feels, which she attributes to her job. The

who is strongly critical has more effect on me right now. I feel really vulnerable. I don't want to have to decide anything. I'm sick of it. When I'm feeling this way at work, I feel like my bad feelings about myself stay with me all the time, even when I'm not at work. It's hard for me to let go of the pressure and the tension. There is constant pressure there, a continuous oppressive climate.

therapist decides to intervene in order to obtain more information about the patient's externalization of the pressure she feels.

**T:** Where is the pressure for you?

**P:** I have too much to do so I can't get involved with anything to the degree I need to. My control is very tenuous. I think that something has got to go wrong when I'm hurrying everything I do, and then I'll be blamed. I'll be responsible, told that it's my fault.

**T:** You used to like your job. What changed?

**P:** I'm feeling the pressure more these days. There has always been more of a cushion in terms of the amount of time that management allowed for something to get done. I don't know if that has changed now, or if it's just my perception of the attitude of management that has changed. I think there is a possibility that they might take away some of my accounts where there are problems.

I think they think of the problems as being a result of me not doing the job well enough, although no one has pointed a finger or blamed anybody. My boss gets upset whenever anything goes wrong, and I feel I'm going to get blamed.

He first asks about the nature of the pressure the patient feels on the job. Then, getting a sense Miss S. is primarily suffering as a result of her fear of blame from her boss whom she has never previously cast in such a negative light, the therapist makes a mildly confrontive comment drawing the patient's attention to how her feelings about the job have swung from positive to very negative; in other words, he points out how she is splitting.

Her response to this confrontation is to say that the work load has increased. She acknowledges, however, that the change may be just in her perception of management's attitude.

**T:** Do you remember when your feelings about work changed?

**P:** Yes. I think my feelings changed last August after that incident when George (her boss) was angry about my losing the Porter account. It's made me feel like I'm responsible for any problem that could come up. I feel like he's still annoyed at me. Every day I go into work thinking how nice it would be to not have to do this. It's been a miserable four or five months. There isn't anything positive coming from him. It's been cold, businesslike and unpleasant for me.

I really don't know what more he wants from me. There's a limit to what one human being can do; I can tell myself that, but I still feel bad about myself so much of the time. I feel rotten, lousy. I reach a point where I feel I can't do it anymore, that I have to get away.

The therapist attempts to clarify the nature of the problem by asking her when it began. She recalls that it dates back to an incident that occurred with her supervisor after which her feelings about work changed. Her supervisor was critical of her and yelled at her, and now she is afraid that if something else goes wrong she will be blamed again; she experiences this as a pressure. Her response to this incident has apparently been to feel bad about herself, rotten, lousy; she feels overwhelmed and wants to escape.

**T:** It sounds like after he criticized you for losing that one account, you have felt that he is looking for the opportunity to criticize your work. Before, you thought he supported you and you felt good about yourself; now, you think he's looking for ways to find fault with your work, and you feel bad about yourself. Has he actually done anything since then that would give you reason to believe that he feels so negative about your work?

**P:** Well, not exactly, but he never has a good word to say about me, and I know he's capable of it

The therapist again confronts her splitting defense by reminding her that, although the boss was only critical of her one time, she now believes that he doesn't like any of her work. The therapist asks her if there is any further basis for this belief.

She responds by offering some evidence that the boss is indeed unhappy with her. At this point the patient has not accepted the idea that through the mechanism of splitting she has taken a single event with her boss and transformed it into a wholesale indictment of her work and of her worth as a human being. She is still viewing her "rotten" feeling as a

because I've heard him tell other people that he liked their work. My yearly review is coming up in three months and I think it will be a poor one. There's a chance that it will be "performs adequately" but I think there's a good possibility that it will be pretty critical. I think he might even be waiting for an excuse to get rid of me. By then we'll know whether or not we lost the airline account.

**T:** You say that you don't know what he wants from you. I'm curious why you haven't talked to him about how he feels about your work rather than wait until June to find out.

**P:** I've thought about it, but if he is feeling about me the way I think he is, I don't think I want to hear it. It would make my job even more miserable, knowing that he doesn't appreciate my efforts and that he probably wants to get rid of me. The way it is now, I'm doing the best I can and we'll see what happens.

**T:** Do you think there is something wrong with your work?

**P:** No, not really. I'm sure some people could do a better job, but I think I'm doing an adequate job. He just gets upset when he gets flak. If something goes wrong, he's going to get flak from his boss and then he blames me. I know it's not all my fault. There's so much more involved than what

product of her boss's attitude, rather than as a result of her own internal processes.

When she indicates that she does not know what the boss wants from her, and she is going to wait three months for her review to find out where she stands with him, her acting out of avoidance becomes more apparent. The therapist shifts the focus of his confrontation to her avoidance.

In this intervention, the therapist makes it clear that, although Miss S. has been suffering with her beliefs about her boss, she has done nothing to find out what she can do to alter his impression of her, if in fact his view is negative. The therapist questions why she has chosen not to talk to her boss directly.

Again her avoidance is evident from her response. She would rather put off hearing the bad news. There is also denial indicated here when she says she is doing the best that she can. The therapist could have addressed this directly by asking, "How do you know you are doing the best you can if you don't know what he wants from you?"

Instead, the therapist does some reality checking; he asks whether perhaps the patient is aware of something that she is doing that would cause the boss to want to get rid of her. His concern, given the avoidance and denial that is already evidenced, is that she may be acting out more severely than she has so far revealed. He wants to know what she is doing at work that would cause the

I do. I just do a small part, but I feel terrible.

**T:** You're saying that you feel terrible at work because you think your boss is unhappy with your work and is going to blame you for anything that goes wrong, and you anticipate that it is very possible that something will be going wrong with the airline account, and yet you don't talk to him about the situation. You would rather put off hearing the bad news until there isn't anything that you can do about it.

**P:** Well, the idea of hearing that he is unhappy with me and doesn't recognize how hard I'm working to pull it out—I would just hate hearing that. It would make me want to quit now before he has a chance to fire me. And I don't want to ask him whether there's anything else I can do because I'm afraid he'll ask me to put in more hours and I'm already putting in too many. If I don't offer him the opportunity to ask, I won't have to deal with either giving in to him and suffering more or finding a way to say "no" to him without making him more angry with me than he already is.

**T:** It seems to me that the way you are handling this situation with your boss is consistent with the way you handle many similar situations in your life. It is so painful for you to hear that your boss is disappointed in you that

boss to want to get rid of her, if indeed he does. Her response to his question is to deny that her work merits the negative attitude that she thinks her boss has.

The therapist now returns to confronting Miss S.'s avoidance. This confrontation is the most direct yet; however she does not take it in. Instead she makes a further case for avoidance, describing how talking to her boss about the situation would create an unpleasant situation that she wants to avoid; in particular she does not want to have to engage her boss in a direct conversation about her personal limits and how she might be able to address some of his needs without compromising her own.

In this transcript the therapist is relatively active, intervening frequently to focus the patient's attention on her avoidance. It is possible that without the therapist's interventions, the patient would have begun to question for herself why she does not take a more active role in resolving her problem at work. The therapist's experience from previous sessions in which this problem arose, however, was that the patient avoided exploring this question just as she avoids other problems in her life. For this reason the therapist chooses to pursue a relatively active course in this session.

Now the therapist sharpens the confrontation still further. He explains that it is important for her to look at the way she is handling this situation because it is consistent with a larger pattern. Then he mirrors the painful aspect for her of setting limits

you put off finding out how he actually feels, and in the process you lose any opportunity you might have had to find out specifically what his concerns are and to work out a solution with him. In putting off hearing about his disappointment you leave yourself feeling depressed and bad about yourself every day at work and you also ensure, if he is in fact disappointed with you, that he will stay disappointed.

**P:** It is interesting, isn't it, how I set myself up for that. It is true of my relationship with George, but other people too. God, it just struck me that that might be affecting my ability to be intimate with Jeff (her boyfriend). I never think of myself as having disappointed him but I think I'm afraid I have, and I bet that's one of the reasons that I'm afraid to get close and I expect him to leave me. I can see how it happens all the time with my friends. I did it again just the other day. The company is sponsoring an evening of theater. Jeff has no interest in theater, but one of my friends from work asked me if I wanted to go with her. I said, "sure." But then another friend asked me to go with her. I didn't want to disappoint her so I said I would, and I figured somehow I would arrange for the three of us to sit together. I know that these two friends aren't that fond of each other and really wanted to go with me, and I should have explained the situation; I wasn't or disappointing another person, and points out the price she pays for her avoidance, namely that she increases the likelihood that she will in fact disappoint the person and she perpetuates her fear and depression.

This time she takes in the confrontation and integrates it, as evidenced by her identifying this pattern in several other relationships and pointing out for herself the negative outcome that it produces. She closes the session by accurately indicating the importance of whether during the coming week she takes action based upon the insight she has gained. Although she makes this comment with respect to the situation with her boss, what she does about the theater situation with her two friends will also be telling.

From Miss S.'s response to the final intervention in this session, it is apparent that her avoidant behavior pattern has for the moment become ego dystonic. Because of the personality-disordered patient's ability to deny or split off an unpleasant reality, a defense which for now has come to be seen as "bad" can within a matter of minutes, hours, or days again be seen as "good." Each time a maladaptive defense is successfully addressed, however, the patient has a broader base of understanding about its maladaptive character, so that it becomes easier and easier for it to be seen by the patient as ego dystonic.

honest because I didn't want to disappoint her. Now I'm dreading the evening out because I know it's inevitable that they'll both be disappointed.

**T:** Our time is up.

**P:** Well, I can see that it makes sense for me to talk to George this week. We'll see if I do it.

In the series of confrontive interventions used in this session, the therapist begins with very mild ones and gradually sharpens them as the patient resists recognizing the implications of her behavior. Because the interventions are attuned to the patient and help her to view her behavior patterns more clearly, she does not experience them as harsh or critical. She struggles to maintain her denial about the consequences of her behavior, but eventually she lets go of the denial and examines her avoidant behavior pattern realistically.

## SOME FACTORS AFFECTING THE USE OF CONFRONTATION

Some of the factors a clinician might consider before using a confrontation are the alternative interventions available, the urgency of the situation, the patient's past responses to confrontation, the diagnosis and the degree of object relatedness of the patient. In addition, the therapist might consider:

*Patient's Observing Ego*: What is the amount of observing ego the patient has at his disposal to be able to make use of the confrontation? Higher level borderline patients have more observing ego than lower level borderline patients and are more able to use the information in the confrontation to explore their own behavior. Borderline patients tend to have more observing ego than do narcissistic patients.

*Stage of Treatment*: Confrontation at the outset of a therapeutic relationship is risky. The patient has little experience on which to base an assumption of the therapist's good will. The therapist has relatively little information about the patient and is less able to anticipate the patient's response to confrontation. Further on in treatment the therapist knows far more about the patient and the therapeutic relationship is more established and stable. Still further on in treatment, the patient's acting out diminishes to the point that milder interventions are usually effective and confrontation is rarely necessary.

Confrontations in the earlier phase of treatment tend to address the patient's acting out, so their focus is primarily on the patient's interaction with his environment outside of treatment. As the patient's acting out is controlled, the focus of interventions tends to turn toward the patient's resistance to internal exploration and to the transference. These interventions will be much softer. If confrontation is used, it will usually be followed with clarification and interpretation.

*Potential for Stimulation of More Severe Acting Out or Defensive Behavior*: If the patient is already projecting onto the therapist a punitive attacking object representation, confrontation may intensify that projection without allowing an opportunity for the patient to take in the information involved.

*Potential for Compliance*: What is the likelihood that the patient will translate the confrontation into an invitation to comply? If the therapist can anticipate that the patient will attempt to respond compliantly, the therapist can structure the confrontations as neutrally as possible. For instance, to confront the patient's splitting the therapist might simply identify the swing from one polarity to the other: "Are you aware that your boss's comment was only critical of the speed of your work, and yet his comment seems to have darkened your whole view of yourself; you've forgotten about all of the things you do well."

*Countertransference*: How much of a part in the decision to confront is being played by the therapist's countertransference? Typical countertransference issues affecting this decision are the therapist's reluctance to confront because of his wish to continue to play the role of the "good" nurturing caregiver, the therapist's aggressive response to feelings of irritation and helplessness arising from the patient's complaints about or attacks on the therapist, and the therapist's desire to have a well-behaved patient leading the therapist to encourage compliance (Adler and Buie 1973).

*Centricity of Theme*: Is the issue that the therapist intends to confront of central importance to the treatment? An issue is worth confronting only when it is a predominant factor that is in the way of the patient's progress. By tracking a patient's defenses a therapist places himself in a better position to evaluate which defenses are most likely to interfere with the treatment process.

### Fundamental Therapeutic Qualities

In confrontations, as in all therapeutic interventions, the underlying assumption is that the therapist is able to remain genuine. The three attributes of an effective therapist that were stated originally by Rogers in the 1960s are as important now as they were then, namely, that successful psychotherapy requires a therapist who is congruent, empathic, and has unconditional positive regard for the patient. While these principles are taught to every beginning therapist, their meaning is often distorted over time. In the interest of completeness, they are restated here:

*Congruence*: The therapist's message to the patient must be as internally consistent as possible. If the therapist is expressing surprise, for instance, the qualities of his or her voice should reflect surprise. If, on the other hand, the therapist is making a neutral observation and he or she appears to be irritated, the patient will become confused or distrustful. Congruence should arise naturally out of direct, sincere communication.

*Empathy*: The therapist should have a sense of what the patient is experiencing. A necessary element to empathy is understanding. Empathy is often confused with nurturing, which is not neutral and has the potential of encouraging a patient to compliantly cling to the therapist. Especially with a patient who has a personality disorder, nurturing often does not mean the same thing to the patient who is receiving it as it does to the therapist who is giving it.

*Unconditional Positive Regard*: This term refers to the therapist's neutral acceptance of the patient without judgment. It does not imply expressions of support, caring, or encouragement, which are often confused with unconditional positive regard.

## GRADATIONS OF CONFRONTATION

In order to illustrate the nuances of variation in interventions from sharp confrontations through simple confrontations to soft mirroring confrontations, a short excerpt of transcript of a 32-year-old single woman will be presented here along with a variety of interventions ranging from quite sharp to very soft. Some of these interventions are better than others but all are included here for the purpose of illustrating the range of possibilities.

> Miss T.: So I spent the whole weekend looking at cars; new ones, old ones, domestic, foreign, blue, white. And I don't feel any closer to a decision than I did two weeks ago. I read *Consumer Reports* and the foreign cars seem to be more reliable but my parents always drove Chevrolets and Fords; I don't want to feel like a traitor. Really what I want is a new car because I know it will be reliable, but first of all I don't have enough money for a new car, and the idea of spending all that money on myself seems selfish anyway. I keep thinking that my neighbors will say, "Where does she come off spending that much money on a new car, when her house is the scourge of the block. Why doesn't she spend some of that money to paint her house?" They don't seem to be complaining about their own new cars, and honestly, my paint is in better condition than a few others on the block. But I have really had it with cars that break down every two weeks. I guess I could borrow the money against the equity in the house. And then I could get the new one that I drove yesterday and liked. John (a friend) warned me that the technology on new cars is changing so quickly that it will probably be obsolete in a few years. He says I should buy a used one and wait a few years before looking at new ones. When he bought his, it was the end of the model year and they were having all those clearance sales. Maybe he would be willing to take a look at the one I liked yesterday and tell me what he thinks.

The above patient is probably a borderline disorder, a dependent type. She struggles with the decision of what car to buy, and is preoccupied with how other people will react to her decision. Even when considering the purchase of a new car, the specifications of which are standard and easily available, she needs a male friend to take a look at it with her and give his approval. With some imagination, one can also consider the possibility that this patient is closet narcissistic, that she is anxious about making a decision for herself because it would represent an expression of her inner self and would expose her to potential criticism from neighbors, family, or friends. She might also feel anxious because she thinks of the idea of owning a new car as exhibiting her hidden (closet narcissistic) grandiosity. Although this patient does not sound neurotic, she might be a predominantly neurotic person who is experiencing a particularly stressful period of life at the time she makes this statement, and consequently feels especially unsure of herself and in need of reassurance. Her concerns over the reactions of her family, her neighbors, and John, all of whom have new cars, could represent an element of competitiveness.

Presumably the therapist treating this patient has additional information on which to base his assessment of the meaning of the patient's comments. Depending on his assessment, as well as the factors discussed in the previous section, including the therapist's own style and the point in treatment in which this statement occurs, the therapist could intervene in many different ways. Responding with attentive silence is of course an attractive possibility. Silence can be confrontive or it can simply provide the patient with the space she needs either to process the material she has brought up or to provide more material on which the therapist can more firmly base his intervention. In the excerpt from Miss T. there is no compelling reason at this point for the therapist to respond other than to provide material for this chapter. If the therapist were to intervene at this point, however, the following are but a few possibilities, beginning with the sharpest confrontations and then gradually moving to softer interventions:

### Examples of Confrontation

**T:** *You just finished saying that you liked the car. What difference does it make if John likes it? Is it going to be your car or his?*

Short but not sweet, this intervention contains a bit of humor to make it more palatable. It assumes that the patient has enough resilience and observing ego and is sufficiently object related to consider the message contained in the confrontation, rather than to simply hear it as a criticism. Most therapists would reserve this kind of intervention for a patient who has been in treatment long enough to establish a fairly secure relationship with the therapist and who has been impervious to other more mild forms of confrontation.

Some therapists, however, like Dr. Berger in *Ordinary People*, would use an intervention like this almost at the outset of treatment with a wide variety of patients from neurotic to narcissistic; it conveys a message that treatment is going to involve frankness on the part of the therapist as well as the patient, and it cultivates in the patient an idealization of the therapist for his confident, self-assured, almost cocky manner.

**T:** *You know that he is usually critical of you. Why do you turn to him for reassurance?*

This confrontation addresses the dependent aspect of the relationship of the patient with John. It ignores the patient's larger difficulties with decision making and her excessive concern with other people's opinions, which is the source of her need for reassurance. Because confrontations like this can easily be interpreted by the patient as criticisms, they would only be useful with a patient who has a stable relationship with the therapist. However, a series of this type of intervention with any type of patient is likely to produce a perception of the therapist as an attacking object, and, if the patient is schizoid or borderline, a strong possibility of a compliant relationship with the therapist. Normally this strong a comment would be reserved for very destructive acting out, not for an issue like dependency as it relates to purchasing a car.

**T:** *It seems that every time you begin to feel insecure about your ability to make decisions, you turn to someone like John to help you with the decision. The ultimate effect, however, is that you let him make the decision and then you are even more insecure about your own decision making ability.*

This confrontation is softer than the previous ones, although it might be more effective. It points out the pattern of behavior and the price that the patient pays for it. It still has the narrowness of the previous intervention in that it addresses only one aspect of the defensive behavior that the patient has exhibited, and it is still harsher than is often necessary.

**T:** *You have been raising three children on your own while you supported yourself and earned a degree at the same time; you are obviously very capable. It doesn't make sense to me that when it comes to making this decision about what car to buy, you act as though your opinion is only worthwhile if other people agree with it.*

This intervention has the advantage of realistically pointing out a strength that the patient possesses while at the same time confronting the way the patient is treating herself. It would still be reserved, I think, for situations in which milder confrontations had not proved effective in interrupting a steady stream of dependent behavior in which the patient undermines her self-confidence and self-esteem.

**T:** *A moment ago you began to explore some of the possible solutions to your problem, and then you shifted the focus to John. You have come here because* *of your concern about your inability to face up to problems when they arise in your life, and I have noticed here on many occasions that when you begin to try to solve a problem, you tend to turn your attention instead to someone else. You don't keep your attention on a problem long enough to give yourself a chance to decide how you want to approach it.*

This confrontation has both softness and effectiveness. It is slightly broader than the previous confrontation in that it addresses the patient's difficulty with thinking through a problem, which encompasses her difficulty making decisions for herself. This confrontation would be considerably softer without the last sentence. However, it would be less likely to be effective. One strength of this type of intervention is that it ties the patient's behavior in the session to the problem for which she originally sought treatment; this is a useful technique for making a behavior or defense ego dystonic to the patient.

**T:** *It sounds like you are not sure whether it is more important to satisfy yourself in your choice of cars or to make other people happy.*

This confrontation addresses the same issue as the previous one in a somewhat gentler style. The behavior is not explicitly labeled as problematic, but the implication is clear. There is, however, nothing in this confrontation that really communicates to the patient *why* this behavior is problematic; a patient would need to be high level to make use of this confrontation.

**T:** *I notice that you keep shifting back and forth between your own thoughts and feelings and your concern about what others think—your parents, your neighbors, John. What comes up for you when you address your own thoughts and feelings that makes you shift?*

This intervention is similar to the previous intervention; however this one takes the emphasis further off pointing out the maladaptive nature of the behavior and instead attempts to help the patient focus on the internal process that gives rise to her behavior. This intervention is a hybrid of a confrontation and an exploratory intervention; it is considerably softer than a direct confrontation, and could be used with a wider variety of patients. It opens up the possibility that in exploring her internal process the patient will discover for herself the price she pays for neglecting her own opinions, or she may describe aspects of her internal process that provide an easy opportunity for the therapist to help her to see the price she pays.

**T:** *When you talk about choosing a car and you bring up your concerns about other people's reactions, I am reminded of your decision not to go to college because your father thought that girls shouldn't be educated.*

The purpose of a confrontation is often to cause a maladaptive defense to become ego dystonic. Just as interpretations can be especially elegant and effective when they connect a present feeling and behavior pattern to a similar past one, a confrontation can do this too. In the above confrontation, the therapist links a past behavior that is already ego dystonic for the patient to a similar present one that appears to be ego syntonic. This type of confrontation would be chosen by the therapist over many others if the historical connection were available. It is especially useful because the therapist avoids being in the position of inviting defensiveness by being the outside person pointing out a problem with the patient's behavior. This intervention would be most appropriate for a high level patient, unless the patient's negative feelings about the historical choice she had made were quite strong, in which case a similar conclusion about the present behavior would be difficult for her to avoid, even for a lower level patient.

**T:** *It seems hard for you to make this decision. Perhaps you are confusing yourself by trying to guess what everyone else will think.*

This confrontation begins with a mirroring comment that softens it and helps the patient to feel that the therapist is attuned to her. As with an interpretation, any effective confrontation should leave the patient feeling understood by the therapist. If the patient feels unfairly criticized or misunderstood, the confrontation has missed its mark and must be processed further. The above confrontation clearly suggests that the patient's pattern of focusing on the object is counterproductive; however, this intervention is one that is likely to be understood and accepted by a wide range of patients. It could still sound critical to a narcissist, however, because it focuses on a weakness or defect.

The weakness of this confrontation is that it says very little. It suggests that trying to guess what everyone else will think interferes with making a decision, but it does not focus the patient's attention on her own internal process. This intervention is more like a suggestion with respect to technique for decision making.

### Confrontive Sequences

A confrontive sequence is a way of softening an otherwise sharp confrontation. It involves first a mild confrontation identifying the behavior that is to be addressed. Many of the interventions just described accomplish this purpose. After the patient has responded to this confrontation, the therapist can use a follow-up comment if necessary to point out the maladaptive aspect of the behavior. This approach has many advantages, especially when the focus of the confrontation is one that has not been the focus of previous confrontations:

1. It gives the patient the opportunity to focus on the area of behavior that the therapist is focusing on so that the eventual more sharp confrontation does not feel abrupt to the patient.
2. It allows the patient the opportunity to explore the initial confrontation, so that the follow-up may become unnecessary.
3. It allows the therapist and patient to agree on the behavior that is being observed and confronted, so that the impact of the more sharp confrontation is not lost in the patient's denial that the behavior even occurs.
4. It allows the sharp portion of the confrontation to be shortened so that it can have maximal impact.

*Examples of Confrontive Sequences*

**T:** *Perhaps this is one more example of how scary it is for you to take a stand that might result in disapproval from others—in this case the disapproval from your parents, your neighbors, or John.*
**P:** (elaborates)
**T:** *It sounds like in the process of avoiding their disapproval you lose yourself.*

or alternatively

**T:** *So in the process of pleasing others it becomes increasingly difficult to know and identify your own preferences and make the right choices for you.*

*Mild Confrontation*

**T:** *Buying a new car can be exciting and pleasurable, but for you it seems to be fraught with anxiety. How do you understand that?*

Narcissistic patients might feel criticized, hearing this comment as pointing out their defects; however, this comment would probably be useful if the patient were borderline. This intervention includes a mirroring component and has a collaborative quality. The therapist who uses it is not trying to make a point other than that there seems to be something the patient can learn about herself from the degree to which she becomes anxious in trying to make this decision.

**T:** *It sounds like this decision means more to you than simply choosing transportation.*

This intervention also contains a mirroring component as well as a shade of the quality of a confrontation in that it directs the patient's attention to her inordinate amount of concern about this decision. Her struggle to make the right decision is actually a defense against experiencing her fear of the individuation involved in making the decision. Attuned as it is to the patient's current experience, this intervention would probably be inoffensive to almost any patient.

## Mirroring Interventions

Mirroring interventions acknowledge a feeling, or in some cases an attitude, of which the patient is either already aware or approaching awareness. Sometimes the feeling that is acknowledged is just out of the patient's awareness. These interventions differ from confrontations in that confrontations are designed to turn the patient's attention to something of which he was not presently aware; confrontations steer the patient into a new course of investigation. Mirroring interventions, on the other hand, are intended to be solely empathic, supporting the patient in the direction that he is already investigating. Mirroring interventions have a range of effects:

1. They help the patient feel more connected to the therapist by reassuring the patient that the therapist understands what the patient is feeling.
2. They help the patient to develop a vocabulary and to describe his internal experience.
3. They help the patient to think about his internal experience.
4. They help the patient to feel accepted by the therapist.

5. They help the patient to develop a sense of sameness with respect to the therapist.

*Example of Mirroring Intervention*

**T:** *It sounds like you are really struggling with this decision.*

This is a simple mirroring comment that encourages the patient to disclose more about her thoughts and feelings. The patient's defenses are not addressed and her feelings, which are being defended against, are not sharply brought into focus, so there is not a sense that this intervention will lead to a follow-up interpretation of the patient's defenses.

## Exploratory Interventions

Exploratory interventions are interventions in which the therapist poses a question that elicits information from the patient. These interventions are not challenging; they pertain to the material currently being discussed by the patient. In addition to helping the therapist to clarify her understanding of what the patient is talking about, these questions often help the patient to clarify for himself what he thinks or feels about this material. They also convey a message to the patient that the therapist is listening and is interested in what the patient has to say.

**T:** *What will it mean to you if John doesn't like it?*

This intervention elicits information about the significance to the patient of the event that she is trying to avoid, and it does so in a way that is fairly neutral. In so doing, it requires the patient to turn inward and introspect.

**T:** *How has it been for you to struggle with this decision making process?*

This is in the "how does it feel?" category. Although patients with lower level disorders can become frustrated with questions about their feelings, many higher level patients can respond well to them, especially if the patient exhibits a physical indication that there is some feeling surfacing. In the case of the above patient, there seems to be so little referencing of internal feeling states that it is unlikely that she has much access to feelings. If the therapist knows that this patient is normally able to check inside herself and talk about what she feels, this intervention might be very useful. If a patient's primary difficulty, however, is with *containing feelings* so that they not interfere with her ability to *think* through problems, the therapist should be careful about directing the patient toward her feelings.

**T:** *What are your concerns about the possibility of buying a car that John does not approve of?*

An intervention like this invites the patient to provide additional information about her thoughts and feelings against which she is defending. It is useful for collecting new information and especially for creating a common pool of data between the therapist and patient that can then be drawn upon in a follow-up intervention that may be either confrontive or interpretive. In many cases this type of question leads the patient herself to interpret the motivation for her defensive behavior or to focus on the maladaptive aspect of the defense.

## INTERPRETATION

Interpretations explain to the patient why a particular occurrence happens. Phenomena that are interpreted tend to be already the focus of the patient's attention; otherwise the intervention would have a confrontive component. *Nongenetic* or *process* interpretations explain a phenomenon in terms of the patient's immediate or recent experience. For example, "I wonder if you didn't start thinking about quitting because you felt hurt that your friend received recognition and you didn't, so you thought you could spare yourself further hurt by quitting." *Genetic* interpretations explain the phenomenon in terms of material from the patient's early personal history. For example, "I wonder if you didn't start thinking about quitting because you felt hurt that your friend received recognition and you didn't, and you felt it was hopeless for you to ever get recognition, just like it felt hopeless for you when your father favored your brother." *Transference* interpretations are interpretations that relate to the therapist/patient relationship; they may be genetic or not.

In Greenson's classic book on psychoanalysis (1967), he describes the interplay of three interventions: confrontation, clarification, and interpretation as they are used in analyzing resistance and in analyzing transference. In his model, the therapist listens to the patient and uses confrontation to make the patient aware of a particular behavior or feeling. Then he uses clarification to describe more fully the phenomenon in question; this may include when the phenomenon occurs or how it occurs. Interpretation is then employed to explain why the phenomenon occurs. The principle is that before a pattern can be interpreted the patient must agree that the pattern really exists. As the pattern is more fully identified and observed, the patient can often supply the interpretation himself as to why it occurs.

Some analysts who do not use confrontation prefer to use a confrontive type of interpretation. For instance, "Last week you talked about how your father dominated the conversation in your family, disregarding other people's needs. Then you began today by telling me about a dream in which you are angry when a strange man tries to take away your food. Now you are saying that you forgot to pay your bill, even after I reminded you to do so. It seems to me that you are angry about my asking to be paid because you believe that, like your father and the strange man, I am disregarding your needs and only concerned about my own." In this intervention the therapist is confronting the patient's anger and the patient's acting out; however the therapist's intervention is in the form of an interpretation of the reasons for the patient's anger.

Many of the factors that are considered during the formulation of a confrontation are also considered during the formulation of an interpretation: the objective, whether the interpretation will result in new insight for the patient, whether without the interpretation the patient is likely to arrive at the same insight himself, the patient's past responses to interpretation, the strength of the relationship between therapist and patient, and the diagnosis. Additional factors include:

*Countertransferences*: Typical countertransference responses are: to feel threatened by the patient's individuative behavior and want to use interpretation as a way to maintain the patient's dependency upon the therapist; to want to be seen as the good, nurturing caretaker; to use interpretation as a way to intellectualize or distance from a patient who is becoming uncomfortably open and vulnerable; to use interpretation to impress the patient with the therapist's power or expertise, especially when the therapist is feeling helpless, useless, or inadequate as part of a projective identification; or to use interpretation as a way to reinforce a feeling of attunement that feeds the therapist's need for merger with the patient.

*Stage of Treatment*: For most clinicians, the early stage of treatment is one in which the patient develops a deepening sense of connection or selfobject transference with the therapist, and the therapist learns about the patient; the therapist usually does not attempt to make any deeply meaningful interventions. With narcissistic patients who have great difficulty feeling connected to the therapist or identifying their own inner experiences, early interpretations tend to center around the patient's experience within the therapeutic environment. The patient typically does not have ready access to his emotional experience outside of the immediate therapy hour, so that interpretations of outside experiences do not tend to be very productive, and often lead to the patient feeling criticized. With patients like borderlines, whose observing ego is sufficient to permit them to evaluate the impact of their behavior, early interventions center around their activities outside of treatment because in this context it is easiest to point out the self-defeating aspects of the defensive behaviors that have been for them ego syntonic. For the therapist to focus too heavily on these patients' experiences that have occurred with the therapist within the treatment hour would have the effect of intensifying these patients' hopes of developing an intense relationship and clinging to the therapist, hopes that are initially overwhelming and distracting for them.

In later stages of treatment, interpretations focus on helping the patient to understand his feelings and thoughts in the context of his experience of himself and his history. There is then a reasonable sense of common purpose between the therapist and patient; the patient is receptive to the therapist's explanations and has a context with which to understand the therapist's role in the patient's self-exploration. As the patient becomes aware of deep yearnings, the therapist and the therapy become a focal point for the patient's historically based expectations; the therapist's interventions must be more and more finely attuned to the patient, or the patient's fragile emerging self may be injured and retreat. Interpretations in particular must be attuned to the patient's own questions, rather than the therapist's theory or interests.

*Potential to Stimulate Passivity*: Interpretation can interrupt a patient's own individuative efforts at answering his own questions. It should only be used if the patient is not on course in coming up with his own explanations.

*Likelihood of Stimulating Defense*: Just as confrontations that penetrate the patient's defenses too abruptly stimulate increased defensive activity in the patient, so do interpretations that penetrate the patient's defenses before the patient is ready. Many narcissistic patients do not want insights at the outset of treatment because insights represent to these patients their failure to have been performing perfectly and in particular to have perfectly understood themselves. This type of interpretation tends to stimulate in these patients a grandiose defensive response to compensate for the injury caused by the intervention. On the other end of the spectrum of patients, dependent patients may react to interpretation by increasing their clinging behavior.

## Examples of Interpretation

**T:** *It sounds like choosing a car is a weighty decision for you. I imagine that that is because the car will be an expression of yourself, your own preferences. Making such a public statement feels exposing to you, makes you feel vulnerable, so you want to first make sure that other people like John won't judge you for it.*

This is a mirroring interpretation that assumes that the patient's defensive structure is primarily narcissistic (closet). It mirrors the patient's feeling of vulnerability from the exposure that results from making a public choice for herself, and then interprets her concern about other people's opinions (John's in particular) as a defense against this feeling. Its purpose is to make the patient feel understood and supported and at the same time make her aware of the link between her feeling response and her defense without labeling either. The emphasis is on the mirroring component of the intervention and the therapist's understanding of the patient; there is no attempt made to point out the maladaptive nature of the defense.

Mirroring interpretations are an excellent way to help a narcissist to become aware of the way she defends. They tend not to injure the patient if they are empathic and accurate. The drawback to this type of intervention is that if it is used frequently it intensifies the treatment and makes it very painful for the patient, elevating the risk that the patient will feel overwhelmed by the feelings that are surfacing and discontinue treatment. This risk can be minimized if the therapist takes care to ensure that these interventions are attuned to the patient and nonconfrontive, that the feeling and defensive behavior that are being focused on and linked by mirroring interpretations are already the focus of the patient's own exploration. With fragmenting narcissists for whom the likelihood is that after a short period of treatment they will reconstitute their grandiose selves and no longer feel the need for treatment, this kind of intervention offers the possibility of helping them see their genuine need for treatment so that even after they have ceased to fragment there is a possibility that they might remain involved in treatment.

Mirroring interpretations were developed by Masterson for use in the treatment of narcissistic and schizoid disorders. If this type of intervention were to be used with a borderline patient, the therapist would need to monitor the patient carefully to see if she responds to the therapist's level of activity by becoming increasingly passive and expecting the therapist to do a substantial amount of her thinking for her. An extremely positive sign would be for the patient to take an interpretation like this and expand upon it, bringing it up at future times when the same kind of defense is at work. A negative sign would be for the patient to respond to this intervention by tossing the ball back to the therapist and acting helpless, saying, "You're right, I do use other people that way because I hate to feel like I'm on my own. So, what are some things I could do to change that?"

**T:** *You seem to be anxious about other people's reactions. I imagine that you are afraid they will feel injured and will attack you like your father did whenever you disregarded his opinion.*

This interpretation utilizes some genetic material and attempts to explain the patient's considerable concern about what other people think about her decision. This explanation could relate to a borderline or a closet narcissistic patient. It has a mirroring component, and could be converted to a mirroring interpretation by adding an explanation of the patient's defense, how she turns to John for reassurance as a way of managing her anxiety.

In general, it is important to hold back on deep genetic interpretations until the therapeutic alliance has developed to the point that the patient is receptive to this depth of material. Premature introduction of deep material, material that is not approaching consciousness, will stimulate the patient to intellectualize about the material and make it affectively less accessible. As in the above example, however, interpretations referencing historical material of which the patient is already aware can be useful far earlier in the treatment as long as they do not stimulate new defense by penetrating to an emotional level that is deeper than the patient is ready to go.

### Clarification

**T:** *It seems that you have no difficulty making decisions that are based on objective criteria; it's the subjective ones in which you are making a statement of your own taste that are such a struggle for you.*

This comment helps the patient to understand the nature of the problem with decision making by differentiating between decisions that are and are not difficult for the patient. It has the quality of a collaboration between therapist and patient in understanding the problem, and would only be used after the patient's attention has already turned to her difficulty with decision making, but before the pattern of her difficulty has been identified clearly enough to interpret.

## TRANSFERENCE INTERVENTIONS

It is apparent from the level of Miss T.'s discussion that she has only been in treatment for a short time. Her focus is outside of herself; not only is she continually distracted by thoughts of what other people might think, but the issue itself that she focuses on is her problem with buying a car rather than her internal difficulty with activation. This type of external focus is typical of the early stages of treatment for all personality disorders. An early objective for the therapist is to help the patient to redefine the problem and locate it within herself so that she can work with it through introspection. During the initial stage of therapy, the therapist's interventions focus on the aspects of the patient's character and defenses that constitute the greatest impediment to working in an introspective way in treatment.

With the borderline, the therapist focuses initially on the patient's acting out, which threatens to destabilize her life or maintain the chaotic state it is already in. Although the patient's acting out will occur during the treatment hour, it will usually be difficult to demonstrate convincingly to the patient the maladaptive aspect of this behavior unless it can be linked to similar acting out outside of treatment, the destructive results of which cannot be denied. For instance, the patient finds reasons at the end of sessions to delay leaving. While this can be addressed within the treatment hour, it will probably be difficult for the patient to grasp in any deep sense why it is not in his interest to soak up every minute of the therapist's time that he can, unless this clinging behavior is linked to clinging behavior outside of treatment, behavior that causes the patient to feel like a helpless appendage of the person she clings to.

With the narcissist, the therapist focuses first on the patient's sensitivity to narcissistic injury and his tendency to protect himself by devaluing other people and distancing. Not only is the narcissist's response to injury by far the most common reason for the premature termination of treatment, but it is also the pathway into a genuine discussion of his feelings of vulnerability. Since the narcissistic patient is usually not aware of his painful feelings, it is generally more productive to talk about his injuries as they occur in treatment and are fresh than to try to reconstruct the patient's experience of an injury that has occurred outside of treatment. With a schizoid patient, the focus of interventions is evenly divided between the patient's concerns about control and safety within and outside of the session.

As treatment progresses and the patient's focus turns inward, the kinds of interventions that the therapist makes become less dependent on diagnosis. There is less acting out to confront and, independent of diagnosis, the therapist and patient are engaged in a basically collaborative exploration of the patient's internal experience. Only when the personality-disordered patient seems to have gotten a reasonably secure hold over his impulses to act out and his other maladaptive defenses is it prudent for the therapist to draw additional attention to the patient's more intense transference feelings toward the therapist. This intensification of the patient's transference feelings will lead to deeper affect against which the patient will attempt to defend; if the defenses the patient turns to are destructive, the progress of the treatment is arrested as the therapist will need to go back to earlier types of interventions until these defenses have again been brought under control.

In the excerpt from Miss T., it did not make sense in the early stage of treatment that she was in to focus on her transference feelings. In the following transcript excerpt, however, Mr. U., a 39-year-old man, is further along in his treatment than was Miss T. It is atypical in that Mr. U. is in a very escalated state emotionally when he makes his comments. In strong language, he blames the depression that he has been feeling on the therapist and the treatment. The more advanced stage of his treatment makes this excerpt a useful one to demonstrate some transference-oriented interventions. It is also an interesting excerpt to look at because in it the patient is intensely critical of both the therapy and the therapist, and a typical therapist's countertransference response would probably be to want to confront him. As is often the case in these situations, this patient would probably respond better to interpretation than to confrontation; however several confrontations are presented and discussed.

**Mr. U.:** I'm just talked out. I think I'm coming Mondays and Fridays to fill your schedule out. So yes, I guess that is a lack of trust. A while ago you said I was doing all these other things as a way of avoiding my painful feelings, and I bought that and the result is that I end up coming here and beating myself up and leaving here feeling like shit and angry. I don't want to do that anymore. So, I'm not coming on Fridays anymore. And I definitely do have a question about what goes on here. That's real. I've been coming to see you off and on for many years and if what I see happening is "progress," I don't want it. I don't want to make "progress" where I come here and beat myself up and feel like shit. I know that you feel I have to get into all this shit to get through it, but I don't see this working.

This patient's attitude is not unusual. He characterizes the emotional pain he is feeling as arising from the treatment rather than from within himself. He is angry at the therapist for being inept and uncaring, and believes that he is being encouraged to suffer as an end in itself. He believes that by cutting back on treatment he can solve the problem. This approach is reminiscent of the Roman emperor who, when he received an adverse message from one of his generals, would have the messenger beheaded. Patients can forget that they are in treatment because they have a problem. In most cases it is the defense against what this patient refers to as his "shit" that originally gave rise to the problem. The choice for Mr. U. is not between feeling the pain or killing the messenger; it is between feeling the pain or living with the problem and its accompanying negative self-image and dysphoric affect.

## Confrontation

**T:** *This sounds like another case of "if you don't like the message, kill the messenger."*

or

**T:** *You are sounding like you believe that the treatment puts those painful feelings in you, that if you cut back on treatment the painful feelings will go away.*

These types of confrontation do not seem to be necessary in this situation. They are relatively harsh and invite the patient to become more combative. If the above excerpt were to have occurred early in treatment, some therapists could probably justify the use of confrontation, but I believe that the use of confrontation in response to this patient would very probably be an example of acting out of countertransference by the therapist. The focus of the patient's comments are on his painful experience of the therapy and the therapist, and the therapist's response should focus on the patient's transference.

## Transference Interpretations

**T:** *In some respects you seem to perceive the situation here as a replication of your situation growing up, when you got the message, "Be tough and endure it. You're on your own."*

Although the therapist does not explicitly say, "You have these feelings because of your situation growing up," this statement is implied. The particular wording chosen by the therapist is intended to remind the patient of a specific historical context in which he felt that he received the message that he had to be tough and endure the pain because no one would be there to help him out.

Making this type of historical connection is generally very effective. In this case it helps the patient to change his focus from his external environment to his internal dynamics; it presents a historical explanation that strikes an emotional chord and replaces the patient's transference acting out and externalization. This type of intervention is only effective if it recalls a specific historical situation or event, if the historical situation or feelings that it recalls are really closely related to the current transference acting out, and if the intervention comes at a time when the patient is emotionally available to consider it.

**T:** *Last session you referred to "this longing that I've never had this close to the surface before." I think as this longing gets closer to the surface it is increasingly frustrating and painful for you that you can't get the nurturing from me that you didn't get from your mom. You feel hopeless about treatment and you think of the feelings of closeness to me as the source of these painful feelings, so you attempt to find relief by distancing from me and cutting back on treatment.*

An intervention like this cuts through the defensive barrier the patient is attempting to erect through his criticism of the therapy and the therapist. It not only connects in an empathic way to the deeper feelings that the patient is struggling with, but it explains the defensive nature of the patient's behavior in a way that invites the patient to explore his resistance. The therapist assumes that the patient's threat to act out his frustration and feelings of hopelessness by cutting back the frequency of sessions is impulsive and made for effect rather than a decision that has been made with conviction. His threat is viewed by the therapist as a narcissistic defense.

A transference intervention like this is only appropriate well into an ongoing treatment process when the patient has been able to acknowledge the importance of therapy to him, the patient's defenses are thin, and the emerging self is close to the surface. Unless an interpretation like this is accurate and attuned to the patient, it will cause the patient to feel more alienated from the therapist.

**T:** *Last session we were talking about commitment, how you become increasingly scared that you might be betrayed by me as you come closer to feeling committed to investing yourself in this (therapy) process. I wonder if there isn't a connection between the fear we were talking about and your decision today to cut back on treatment.*

Again, by interpreting the defensive nature of the patient's upset, the therapist invites him to explore the underlying conflict. As with the previous intervention, this type of intervention is only effective when the therapeutic relationship is well established and the patient's defenses are thin. This intervention might be chosen over the previous one if the therapist believes that the patient's threat to cut back on treatment represents a choice that he is seriously considering, rather than an impulsive expression of his discontent. Although the central issues in the patient's comment are safety and distance, which sound schizoid, this patient's fear would be consistent with a narcissistic disorder as well, and his flamboyant style of expression fits more for a narcissist than a schizoid.

**T:** *(Attentive silence)*

One option for the therapist is to remain silent and see if the patient is able to work out some of his confusion himself. Especially when the patient is attempting to provoke the therapist into making an aggressive comment that can feed the patient's fury and help the patient distance, silence can be both a prudent and effective intervention as long as it is not used to punish or withdraw from the patient.

### Transference Confrontation

**T:** *Do you think I'm encouraging you to "beat yourself up?"*

or

**T:** *What is it like for you to come session after session to a therapist who you believe cares nothing about you, who you think sees you as a way to keep his appointment book full?*

Either of these two transference confrontations might be useful with this patient, especially in a phase of treatment when the patient's feelings about the therapist are relatively unexplored. Each of these interventions encourages the patient to examine his hostile feelings toward the therapist.

### Mirroring Interventions

**T:** *You sound angry.*

or

**T:** *It sounds like you see me as uncaring, seeing you only to fill out my schedule, and that I have been treating you all these years with an approach that is ineffective. I assume that you must be very angry at me.*

These mirroring interventions would have the effect of calming the patient down by helping him to feel understood by the therapist. They would be especially useful if the patient's upset were the result of a narcissistic injury in which the patient did not feel understood by the therapist. A mirroring intervention tends to encourage or repair the patient's mirror transference. If, however, the patient does not perceive himself as angry, these interventions would be experienced by the patient as transference confrontations.

## EXPLORATORY AND EDUCATIONAL INTERVENTIONS

Exploratory interventions are those in which the therapist attempts to clarify the patient's meaning or broaden the patient's understanding by requesting further information. Educational interventions involve the therapist's compensating for a deficit in the patient's past experience by providing information about an area of life in which the patient is naive or uninformed. Both interventions can be relatively neutral and very useful.

### Exploratory Interventions

**T:** *I understand that you feel very bad when you leave here, and it sounds like you are saying that you feel bad about yourself, but I'm not clear exactly what the bad feelings are.*

or

**T:** *Do you think of me as encouraging you to suffer as an end in itself?*

In each of these interventions, the therapist attempts to clarify more precisely the meaning of what the patient is saying. Information-gathering questions like these, if they express a true interest in what the patient is saying, help the patient to clarify his own thoughts. This type of intervention is also useful when the therapist feels on the spot and needs time to think about the patient's comment and decide on a more incisive intervention.

**T:** *You are saying that you are distrustful of me. I wonder if there is anything I may have done earlier this session or last session to further disappoint you.*

Especially with a narcissistic patient who is being critical of the therapy or with a schizoid patient who is withdrawing, it is often helpful for the therapist to ask if the patient knows what happened to cause him to feel injured or unsafe. Even if the patient is unable to supply this information, the question buys time for the therapist to try to remember the sequence of events that might have led to the injury. A similar question would be to ask when in particular the patient began to feel this way. These questions would not be used when the therapist thinks he understands how the patient was injured, and they also run the risk of fueling the flames when the patient feels that the therapist should know what he did wrong and should be apologizing.

**Educational Interventions**

Patients often make faulty decisions because they do not have adequate information. In addition to the emotional scars left by parental shortfalls there is also a lack of parental modeling and education in the practical and social skills required for success in our complex modern society. Almost all therapists I have spoken with intuitively recognize the need for the therapist, in a fairly neutral, informational way, to directly help the patient to make up some of these deficiencies. The patient who experiments with physical or emotional intimacy after a lifetime of fearful abstinence would no doubt benefit from an occasional comment clarifying an area in which she might otherwise end up having a discouraging experience. The patient who enters a formal educational program after believing that such an endeavor was beyond him might find it very difficult to understand the educational culture in which he will be required to perform; a small amount of guidance in the form of information about what is really expected of students and how experienced students tend to deal with institutional requirements can make the difference between a successful experience for the patient or an experience that supports his original feelings of inadequacy.

In the area of alcohol abuse education is a very powerful intervention. Very few alcoholics are aware of the physical and emotional consequences of alcohol addiction, and almost all are in denial about the relationship consequences. Once a therapist has established that a problem exists, an educational intervention can be more effective than other more direct confrontations, and it does not create an adversarial relationship between therapist and patient. If necessary, it can be followed by direct confrontation.

## ALCOHOL INTERVENTIONS IN "NEUTRAL" PSYCHOTHERAPY

### General Psychotherapy and Alcoholism

Alcoholism is a problem that is present in virtually every psychotherapy practice. It is very important that psychotherapists have information about it. Approximately 10 percent of the general population in this country who drink are either problem drinkers or alcoholics (Metzger 1988), and the percentage that applies to the part of the population seeking psychotherapy treatment is far higher. Despite the prevalence of the problem and the profound effect it has on clinical effectiveness, it is rarely discussed in those books about psychotherapeutic treatment that are not exclusively devoted to the problem of alcohol abuse or addiction.

Two reasons authors of general psychotherapy books rarely discuss alcoholism may be either that they, like many other therapists, do not recognize the importance of this area of treatment or that they do not feel that they have sufficient expertise in this area and are concerned about inaccuracies. A large percentage of psychotherapists fails to recognize alcohol abuse as a serious problem when it appears in treatment, even when the patient specifically identifies it as a concern (Brown 1985). Many of those who recognize it either lack adequate information about it and its treatment, or believe it does not require any special attention.

Authors' decisions to omit information about alcoholism treatment from general texts may have to do with the enormous seriousness and intensity with which recovering alcoholics and alcohol treatment professionals approach the subject of alcoholism and its treatment. Because of the life and death significance of this issue, those professionals who specialize in alcoholism treatment react strongly to inaccuracies or omissions in literature that could be misleading on this subject. In addition, any attempt to deal with the subject of alcoholism treatment in a section of a larger book will necessarily omit important aspects of the subject; at best enough information can be presented to make readers aware of the nature of some of the phenomena involved and to motivate readers to pursue additional information in more specialized books on the subject. As a result, most authors who are not themselves experts in this area probably believe that it is safer to leave the writing about this subject to those who specialize in alcoholism treatment. This practice is unfortunate. There is a barrier between general psychotherapists and most alcohol treatment professionals that probably has some of its origins in the relatively poor track record of psychotherapists in dealing with alcohol related issues[3] and the consequent distrust in the AA community of psychotherapy. The current paucity of information and expertise in the general psychotherapy community about alcohol abuse and treatment makes it unlikely that this situation will change in the near future. The practice of omitting discussions of alcoholism treatment in general texts on psychotherapy does not help. If psychotherapists were to encounter information about alcoholism in general texts, instead of needing specifically to seek information on this subject from specialized texts, perhaps many more therapists would have at least the fundamental information about alcohol related problems, their impacts, and their treatment.

## Alcoholism and Personality Disorders

Because they rely on relatively primitive defenses, people with personality disorders often develop addictive patterns of behavior and many become physically addicted to alcohol or drugs. Therapists must take into account both the psychological component of the behavior patterns of these patients and the physiological component because the latter can impact significantly on the patient's thought and memory capacities. The injuries to self-esteem caused by these patients' inability to control their use of alcohol or drugs, combined with the effect of their addiction on their ability to function, tend to render introspective psychotherapy ineffective.

With his splitting defense, an addicted patient with a personality disorder tends to develop a split between the "bad" people who stimulate his anxiety by confronting him with reality and the "good" people who collaborate with him in his denial of the damage he is doing to himself by his addiction. Psychologically, the drug or alcohol functions as a permissive parent that comforts and soothes the patient by helping him to put his problems aside. The alcoholic refers to alcohol as his friend, just as he does his drinking buddies. The addicted

[3]One study of AA members found that of those who had experienced psychotherapy prior to abstinence, only 16 percent found it very helpful as compared to 64 percent who found psychotherapy very helpful after abstinence (Brown 1977).

patient is likely to split between that friend or permissive parent and anyone, like the therapist, family member, or employer, who the patient perceives as trying to take that parent away.

Consequently, there are additional complications to the treatment of personality-disordered patients who are impaired by substance abuse or addiction. The therapist cannot treat the apparently defensive behavior of drinking, for instance, as simple avoidance even when the drinking obviously is used in the defensive service of avoidance. The therapist must understand the physiological and social components of alcoholism in order to understand the patient. The therapist must understand the physical limitations of the patient who is actively drinking in order to help him to gain control over his drinking, which means for the alcoholic to stop drinking entirely. Until the drinking is arrested and a significant period of sobriety is maintained, there can be no sustained, deep, painful introspection.

## The Need for Directive Treatment

Whether or not a patient has a personality disorder, the abuse of alcohol or other substances can represent a barrier to treatment, especially if it is not addressed by the patient during treatment. The treatment of substance abuse seems to represent a major stumbling block for the therapist who attempts to maintain therapeutic neutrality; many therapists do not treat substance abuse as a separate and significant problem, and hope it will be resolved during the course of their normal approach to treatment. Substance abuse is a tenacious problem with unique obstacles to successful treatment, and unless it is specifically addressed it will ultimately undermine any treatment.

Just as the clinician is forced to play a directive role in helping to provide structure for patients with very low level disorders because otherwise the chaotic state of their lives would obstruct therapeutic progress, the clinician must, on occasion, intervene forcefully in the destructive and self-defeating behavior of the alcohol- or drug-addicted patient, depending on the patient's motivation, the level of his physical impairment, his level of functioning, and the stage of his addiction. The disruptive effect to treatment of such a problem should not be underestimated (i.e., denied). As long as the patient continues to rely actively on alcohol or drugs as an instant escape from painful affect and uncomfortable situations, he will use this mechanism to avoid the difficult issues that he would otherwise be confronting in treatment, so any attempt at traditional psychotherapy will have limited success until the addictive behavior is under control.

The problem, as I understand it, for most clinicians is that they feel if they become actively involved in addressing the substance abuse, they will be abandoning the neutral therapeutic process and will ultimately lose the patient, because he will either become actively involved in a program for the treatment of substance abuse, or, more commonly, he will avoid the issue by quitting treatment entirely. In addition, many clinicians find it exceedingly difficult to make the transition smoothly from a neutral to a directive stance and then even more difficult later to return to a neutral way of working. It is possible, however, to confront substance abuse in a mild but consistent way that will not interfere with the neutral therapeutic relationship any more than other mild confrontations. When the patient does face her drinking problem and enters a program like AA there will be a period of time in which her discoveries concerning her alcoholism will be more important to her than her psychotherapy, and appropriately so; however, if a firm therapeutic relationship has already been established, this does not usually mean that psychotherapy must entirely stop during this period. Eventually, after a year or two, the patient will take a renewed interest in psychotherapy as her interest focuses on the historical and psychological aspects of her addiction and her feelings about herself. Preferably, if the alcohol problem were identified and addressed soon after treatment began, the patient could suspend treatment and focus her energy on dealing with her alcohol problem through a professional or self-help program, returning to treatment later, when she is capable of making good use of it.

### Indications of a Possible Alcohol Problem

Stories abound of patients with alcohol abuse problems who were unsuccessfully treated for years by clinicians because the subject of substance abuse was not addressed or even mentioned in treatment. The subject may not be mentioned because part of the abuse problem is denial, so the therapist or the patient either denies that the problem is important enough to bring up in treatment or that there is a problem at all; he is also motivated not to bring up the problem because he is so dependent on the substance psychologically and often physically that he will not take the risk that calling attention to the abuse might force him to address it and prevent him from continuing to use the substance.

In order for substance abuse to become a focus of treatment in a timely way, it is often necessary for the therapist himself to call attention to the problem. The first step for the therapist is to discover that the problem exists. This can happen through a few direct questions during a discussion of personal and family history, but often the essential information is not revealed because the patient is denying the problem. More often it happens as a result of the therapist noticing signs that point to the possibility of a substance abuse problem. In addition to the more obvious indications like somatic complaints[4] associated with alcohol consumption, drunk driving arrests and alcohol related problems at home or on the job, some hints of a possible alcohol abuse problem are:

1. frequent mention of alcohol, bars, or drinking in various contexts that may seem innocuous when considered separately,
2. mention of having a drink to calm down or to prepare for a social encounter,
3. mention of having a headache or hangover in the morning from partying the night before,
4. comments about increasing difficulty remembering things,
5. the existence of a codependent pattern of behavior; this usually indicates a substance abuse problem among one or more family members, and sometimes a problem with the patient himself,
6. at least one close relative, including parents and grandparents, or ex-spouse who is an alcoholic,
7. mention of friends or offspring abusing alcohol,
8. rapid mood changes after drinking,
9. indication of an unusually high tolerance to alcohol, and
10. the patient talking about the amount that he drinks and how he controls it.

## CLINICAL EXAMPLE—CONFRONTING ALCOHOLISM

Almost all professionals in the field of substance abuse treatment use a directive approach to treatment. They view alcoholism as a life and

[4]Among the many possible somatic complaints associated with alcoholism are weight gain, upset stomachs, insomnia, liver problems, diabetes, headaches, and difficulties with memory.

death issue and one that must be attended to as quickly and effectively as possible. From their perspective, insight-oriented psychotherapy is appropriate only after the patient has achieved sobriety. They question any clinician who does not take up the issue of alcohol use with the patient early in treatment and pursue it consistently when there is reason to suspect that a problem exists.

Most psychotherapists who specialize in long-term treatment do not pursue alcohol abuse with this degree of concern or persistence. They tend to try to work within the approaches with which they are familiar, and many do not notice or address the issue of alcoholism. Many, in fact, have personal motivation to deny the seriousness of alcoholism because they or someone close to them uses alcohol abusively. Others who do not deny its seriousness are unaware of some of the typical ways in which alcoholism eludes or undermines treatment. The therapist who treats Miss V. in the following clinical example is such a therapist.

**Miss V.**

This clinical example was chosen for inclusion here because in many ways the patient and the treatment closely resemble a non-alcohol-related treatment that might be conducted by a therapist who practices a primarily neutral approach to treatment, and it illustrates a very common error that neutral therapists make in attempting to maintain neutrality while treating an alcoholic patient. Miss V. was referred by a physician for treatment of depression related to problems at work. There was no indication of an alcohol-related problem in the referral. The therapist did not take a formal history and in particular did not ask questions related to the patient's personal and family history with respect to alcohol consumption. The patient, like many alcoholic patients, attempted to conceal her abuse of alcohol, and the subject of excessive drinking did not come up until the forty-fifth session of weekly treatment. During that time the therapist treated Miss V. as a closet narcissist who had fragmented as a result of failure at work and the realization that her youth had disappeared and she had not achieved the heights to which she had aspired. After the therapist recognized Miss V.'s alcohol problem, he unfortunately let it slip into the background. Eventually, however, he used confrontation to address Miss V.'s alcohol-related denial. Although the therapist's clinical errors and omissions with respect to alcohol caused Miss V.'s treatment to be considerably slower and less effective than it could have otherwise been, it was ultimately successful in helping Miss V. to address a twenty-five-year-old alcohol problem and to make other significant personal progress. For therapists who have experienced difficulty integrating into their clinical work a more focused approach to the treatment of alcohol-related problems, this example may be helpful.

With many alcoholics and problem drinkers the patient is herself somewhat concerned about her habit and offers the therapist hints that there may be a problem, although she can be expected to distort the extent of the problem. During her first year of weekly treatment, Miss V. made several references to social drinking that the therapist did not notice. Any reference to drinking can be an opening for the therapist to explore more fully the role of alcohol in a patient's life. She made her first reference to excessive drinking in her forty-fifth session; she referred to getting extremely drunk once and "slobbering." When her therapist inquired about the frequency for her of this type of experience, she responded deceptively, claiming that she did not drink regularly and that this type of experience was very rare. A therapist should expect that a problem drinker is likely to conceal the extent of her habit. During the next twenty sessions, she made two more references to excessive drinking; one was that a friend chided her about being an excessive drinker, and the other was about having to get drunk with a particular man in order to have sex with him and having a hangover the next day. Equally telling were two references during this same period to not drinking excessively on particular occasions. Although these comments did not point conclusively to a drinking problem, especially since the patient made a point of saying that she was a very moderate drinker, the therapist was alerted that there was very probably an alcohol problem. In each case the therapist pointed out the discrepancy between Miss V.'s characterization of her drinking as very moderate and the incidents that she was describing.

At this time a more thorough alcohol evaluation was needed, along with a discussion about the nature and consequences of alcohol abuse. Instead, however, this therapist instead attempted to maintain his neutral stance. Whether or not they are part of a formal personal history-taking process, alcohol evaluations are not severe departures from the traditional neutral stance any more than are suicide assessments. If he is uncomfortable with his own skills in this area, a therapist can send a patient to a specialist for an alcohol evaluation. Most therapists would not hesitate to have a patient evaluated by a physician for a medical condition that might be affecting her psychotherapy; the same should be true of an alcoholism evaluation.

## Denial and Avoidance

In the seventy-first and seventy-second sessions, the patient made reference to not drinking for a week, "because I thought it would make me depressed," and how easy it had been to stop, another indication that there was some question in the patient's mind about how much control she had over her drinking. These last comments were noteworthy also because they were the first indication that Miss V. was questioning her drinking habit. The therapist asked how much information Miss V. had about alcohol and its effects; Miss V., like most alcohol abusers and addicts, had almost none. The therapist provided her with some information at this time, although clearly not enough. Then he explored Miss V.'s tolerance to alcohol by asking about her history with respect to the quantity she had been drinking and its effect on her. She informed him that the quantity had been stable at one or two drinks a night for many years. Knowing the likelihood that this information was inaccurate, the therapist should have explored this subject further.

For almost a full year after this, the subject of alcohol did not come up again in Miss V.'s therapy. Given the extensive indications already available to the therapist that Miss V. had a drinking problem, he should not have let the subject of the patient's drinking fade away. A confrontation that minimally breaks neutrality would have been to comment on the disappearance of this subject from the treatment and ask the patient what thoughts she might have about that. As long as the therapist keeps the subject of alcohol consumption active by occasionally making reference to it if the patient has not brought it up for a period of time, the patient will have difficulty dismissing the subject and denying its importance.

At the point in treatment when the patient first acknowledges a potential problem with her drinking, many experts in the treatment of alcoholism would advocate tenaciously confronting the patient about her drinking until her denial and deceptions have been abandoned. In many cases this is an effective approach; if the patient can let go of her denial and begin to look at the seriousness of her problem she can begin to learn more about it and recognize the pervasiveness of its effects. In some cases, however, the patient will continue to distort the information and deny the existence of a problem. In Miss V.'s case, the bits of evidence that the therapist had of a few drunken experiences and some concern about drinking too much are enough to form a reasonably secure hypothesis for the therapist about the patient's problem with alcohol, but not enough to prove anything to a patient who is determined to resist admitting that she has a problem.

One possibility would be for the therapist to ask questions about the details and history of the patient's drinking habits and those of her parents. The more information the therapist collects, the better will be the therapist's position to point out the evidence that her drinking constitutes a serious problem for her. As long as this questioning process does not become dogmatic, it can also have the beneficial effect of focusing attention on the seriousness of the issue. On the other hand, for the therapist to ask specific alcohol-related questions represents in itself a confrontation, which, if the therapist does not remain attuned to the patient, may place the patient in an adversarial role with respect to the therapist. Another alternative for the therapist would be to offer the patient some sobering information about alcoholism. The therapist should, however, track the patient's responses and try to avoid provoking the patient into further denial and deception.

## Treatment While the Patient Is Still Drinking

What can be accomplished therapeutically during the period that the patient is in treatment and actively drinking? The patient cannot be expected to sustain any significant levels of dysphoric affect because these will be dissipated through drinking. Insight therapy that gives rise to internal conflicts will be avoided, and the patient's memory problems are likely to interfere with session-to-session continuity or deepening of insights. If the therapist does not confront the alcohol problem actively, the patient will probably continue to drink. The problem will not go away, and it will come up again and again, each time giving the therapist a more secure platform from which to confront it.

It is in the patient's interest, however, for the therapist to address the problem as soon as she is able to. If drinking is continuing during the period of treatment it can reach a more advanced and destructive stage while the therapist is waiting for a particularly propitious time to address it. It is also possible, if the patient believes that the therapist does not understand the drinking problem or is not taking it seriously enough, that the patient will get discouraged and leave treatment. A strong argument for taking a formal history, including questions about alcohol use, at the outset of treatment is that not only will the therapist have access to information that will permit him to effectively confront a patient with a drinking problem, but the problem will become apparent from the beginning of treatment before the treatment has taken another direction and valuable time has been lost.

Although a rapid identification and treatment of the drinking problem is clearly most desirable, frequently it does not occur. During the period prior to addressing the alcoholism, however, some therapeutic progress can be achieved. In Miss V.'s case, during the period that she was actively drinking, there was an idealization of the therapist and a sense of increased personal security and ego strength that Miss V. was able to take from her relationship with the therapist, despite her active drinking. These selfobject functions enabled her to take risks in her life that she had previously been unable to take. She had a talent for painting and had had some formal training but had never exhibited or sold her work. During the early portion of her treatment she began to talk about the possibility of finding a gallery that would exhibit her work and she explored her avoidance of this threatening possibility. Eventually she controlled her impulse to avoid and summoned enough courage to approach a gallery that ultimately agreed to take her work. She also overcame her social awkwardness and joined several organizations that got her out of her apartment at night. These initially frightening experiences in group social situations ultimately contributed to the confidence that allowed her to face an AA meeting. At work, she took the difficult step of successfully applying for a promotion. In other words, with many patients, the selfobject transference that they develop with the therapist and the exploration of their avoidance can be very helpful, even when these patients are still actively drinking. In addition, the building of ego strength and confidence that takes place during this period enhances the patient's ability eventually to confront the alcohol addiction and the avoidance and denial related to it. Without the ultimate confrontation of the drinking problem, however, these gains would be lost. Once the patient has achieved sobriety, she can explore the deeper emotional issues that trouble her.

Since denial and avoidance are typical defenses that go along with alcohol abuse, the therapist must be careful in how he approaches the subject of alcohol use and abuse. If the therapist gets too far ahead of the patient by labeling the patient's drinking as destructive and out of control before the patient is close to doing the same, the patient may feel badgered and begin concealing the problem from the therapist. The therapist must be attuned to the patient's own ambivalence about the problem and gently support the patient's healthy observing ego.

In response to one of Miss V.'s early comments, the therapist inquired in a matter-of-fact way about how often Miss V. has had this type of experience with alcohol. She distorted the truth, saying it was rare. Just the asking of that question was a mild confrontation and was perceived by Miss V. as mildly threatening; however, it probably did serve to support Miss V.'s own questioning about the level of her drinking. When dealing with a problem as serious as alcoholism, confrontation is necessary, even if it is perceived as mildly threatening by the patient. In the case of Miss V., more confrontation would have been preferable to the delay that arose from not confronting her denial of her alcohol problem.

## Confrontation of the Drinking Problem

During the year in which the alcohol problem was not addressed or admitted to, the therapist focused many of his interventions on Miss V.'s use of denial and avoidance in other areas of her life and, from his perspective, the treatment was still appearing to progress adequately. When the subject of alcohol came up again in the one-hundred-ninth week, alcohol was again being viewed negatively by the patient. Unintentionally adding further evidence concerning the extensiveness of the problem, she commented on buying some clothes and how her charge cards were lower than ever partly because she was not spending money on alcohol.

From this comment one might guess that during that past year Miss V. was making attempts at cutting back her drinking in order to convince herself that she had not lost control over it. Later on in treatment she revealed that during this period she had indeed cut back several times, only to return each time to her previous level. At night, she had been reading self-help books about alcoholism in the hope of gaining insights from them about her drinking, but, as she admitted after becoming fully abstinent, she was not sure if it was the reading of the books that was putting her to sleep at night or if it was the drinks she had while she was reading them.

Almost each of the next eight sessions contained some reference to alcohol in a negative light. Several of these were references to stopping, like, "I've also quit drinking again." Her denial was weakening. The therapist's part in this process was to interpret the defensive role of her drinking and to provide information about the connection between drinking and some of the symptoms Miss V. was reporting like depression, difficulty with memory, and sleep disturbance. Again, at this point the therapist could easily have taken a more active role by exploring with the patient more of the details about her experience with drinking and by informing her about the process of becoming addicted and some of the indications of danger.

## Attempts to Control the Drinking

In session one hundred seventeen Miss V. said, "I'm depressed and sleeping a lot. It's not serious. And I'm not going to start drinking again; it's not even an issue." The following session began:

| | |
|---|---|
| **P:** I got drunk this week on vodka before I realized it.<br>**T:** Considering your determination last week not to drink, it must be very disappointing to you to see more evidence that you aren't in control of your drinking. | The therapist responds to Miss V.'s admission of having gotten drunk by mirroring her disappointment and at the same time underscoring the apparent implication that her drinking habit is out of control; this is a mild confrontation of the patient's denial about her lack of control of her drinking. |
| **P:** Well, it was my third night to myself that week and I guess I panicked. There wasn't anything wrong; nothing in particular had happened. | Miss V.'s response does not acknowledge this implication, but instead goes on to attempt to deny that the episode has any particular meaning. |
| **T:** So what do you think was going on for you?<br>**P:** I don't know. I was alone, but it's not as if I mind being alone. I really am good company for myself. I've been so busy lately that I didn't have time home alone, so Friday, Saturday, and Tuesday I was alone, but I don't see that as a problem. Somehow I had too much vodka. | The therapist reasserts that the episode does have meaning by asking what she thinks was going on, implying that the episode does indeed have some significance. This intervention is weak, because it allows Miss V. to avoid the issue of whether she really can control her drinking. Miss V. claims to not understand where the drinking incident came from. |
| **T:** Well, I wonder if it didn't have to do with your change of attitude toward the gallery.<br>**P:** That certainly did change this Saturday. They really don't carry other work at the same level of artistic expression as my stuff. The artists they carry don't have the history and training that I do. | The therapist suggests that it may have had to do with a disappointment Miss V. suffered in relation to a gallery. Miss V. elaborates on the disappointment but does not comment on its relationship to the drinking. |
| **T:** When you first started exhibiting there you were very pleased to be invited and you were proud to be | The therapist then interprets the drinking on Tuesday night as a defense against the narcissistic injury |

associated with that group. When you realized that their quality was not what you had thought, it was very disappointing to you, a loss of your sense of kinship with them, a loss of some of the good feeling about yourself that you got from being associated with them, almost a loss of a part of yourself.

**P:** That's exactly on the mark there. . . . takes the luster off.

**T:** So I would think that it was not just that you were alone Tuesday night, but you had just had this very painful loss that you attempted to insulate yourself from by drinking.

**P:** Well, that certainly fits; Tuesday evening was the time that I had planned to begin work on a new piece to exhibit there. . . .

that Miss V. suffered with respect to the gallery. This makes sense to Miss V., as indicated by her comment and the additional corroborating information that she supplies. This could have been an excellent time for the therapist to reintroduce the question of whether Miss V. can indeed control her drinking.

Alcohol consumption can be both a physical addiction and a defense. To treat it as one of many defenses, ignoring the physiologically addictive aspect, would be harmful to the patient. The physical addiction can only be dealt with by permanent abstinence. But, even when an alcoholic stops drinking, the psychological patterns and defenses that develop either before or during the addiction remain intact until addressed through some type of program or treatment. Hence the term *dry* or *dry drunk* refers to an alcoholic who has merely stopped drinking, while *sober* refers to an alcoholic who is in the process of recovery. Interpreting the defensive way in which alcohol is used usually helps the patient to recognize that his drinking is not merely a relaxing habit or a refreshing break, but it is being used as self-medication and follows a pattern that adversely affects other aspects of his life.

Early in the next session, Miss V. volunteered, "I've also quit drinking again." It was now becoming apparent to Miss V. that she used drinking defensively to ward off painful feelings about herself, and that her attempts at stopping were not effective. However, she was not yet willing to acknowledge that her drinking was out of control. This would have been an excellent time for the therapist to focus on Miss V.'s resistance to facing her drinking problem. He might have asked her what it would mean to her if she were to recognize that she was an alcoholic (Brown 1985). He could have helped her explore other underlying issues. For an alcoholic, it is extremely difficult to accept the fact that short of abstinence it is not possible for her to control her drinking, but her acceptance of this fact is absolutely necessary to her recovery.

If it had been undeniably apparent that this patient's drinking was affecting her work or her home life, the therapist could more easily have confronted her drinking at this time, especially since further delay would mean more deterioration to her situation at home and at work. But, largely due to the therapist's failure to systematically obtain more information about Miss V.'s drinking habits, the acknowledged ill effects of her drinking at this point were only depression and sleep disturbance, both of which the patient attributed to causes other than alcohol.

When a similar clinical situation arose a short time later, the therapist did decide to intervene more actively. Miss V. had talked about consuming a large amount of hard liquor. The therapist pointed out that this seemed to contradict her earlier belief that her tolerance to alcohol had not appreciably changed, and she grudgingly accepted his assertion that her tolerance had increased. He explained that this was an indication of an addictive process, and then explained the physiological effect of alcohol on the body, how addiction occurs, and the fact that it is a degenerative, irreversible process. The session ended with a meaningful exchange:

**P:** (long pause) What a long strange trip this has been. This conversation today has gotten my attention in a way that few have in my life. Well, it's enough to say that I've quit, and I think I can do it over the long term, and it's a good thing we talked about it . . . . because I think for the first time I have a long-term plan for my life and it doesn't include being sick like that. It's funny. I saw H. today. We had a supervision meeting. I think my boss was envious of my comfortable relationship with H. He watched us real carefully. (more about this incident) . . . .

Here it is clear that the patient wants to stop drinking; however her digression into talking about the incident with H. is an indication that her defensive avoidance still has the upper hand in her internal conflict.

(Nearly the end of the session)

**T:** You mentioned that you are not sure for how long you intend to

Rather than address the avoidant defense, the therapist recognizes that

quit drinking. I know you've made several other brief attempts to quit. Are you intentionally leaving the time frame vague so that it won't feel like a failure to you if you resume drinking?

**P:** That may be true. I will think about that during the week.

(End of session)

the frank discussion about the effects of alcohol has jarred Miss V. and uses this opportunity to apply some pressure in the form of an interpretive confrontation that addresses her resistance to really testing herself to see if she has control over her drinking. Again the therapist is mildly confronting the patient's denial of her difficulty with controlling her drinking.

It is common for alcoholics to declare that they are going to cut back or stop drinking for a while. These declarations, when they fail, can be effective in demonstating the drinker's lack of control if they are specific, for instance a limit of two drinks a day or complete abstinence for a certain length of time, like three or six months. Without specificity, however, when the patient abondons her resolve, it is easy for her to convince herself that she has achieved her goals or that she is making a choice to resume drinking. Once the patient is questioning her control over her drinking, it is useful for the therapist to challenge the meaningfulness of vague intentions to cut back or stop. A commitment to control drinking for a limited time, however, should not be thought of as a test. Some patients will succeed in temporarily abstaining in order to reenforce their denial, while others will conceal their failure from the therapist. In addition, it can be more important how the drinker manages to stop drinking during this period than it is whether she is able to stop. If the patient is able to stop drinking, but is obsessed with thoughts about alcohol during the period in which she is not drinking, she is verifying that she has a problem.

### The Following Session

**P:** I've decided that I will reevaluate the effects of not drinking after a year.

### Five Weeks Later

**P:** I had a first drink. . . . The guy made such a big deal out of me and was so hospitable that I thought it would hurt his feelings if I didn't have one. After the first shot, it felt so good, I didn't care. Then they all felt great. I didn't feel like going to work today but I had to. I'd forgotten how confused I am when I have a hangover. Now I know I'm not going to drink again, period.

**T:** What makes you think you can control it? *(Again the therapist confronts the patient's denial about her ability to control her drinking.)*

**P:** I don't know. I've controlled smoking, and that was harder initially. But

I was probably more dependent on alcohol so it will be harder. *(In fact Miss V. had only temporarily quit smoking, as she had on many other occasions.)*

**T:** And you have a physical addiction to alcohol.

**P:** So why am I so confident? I don't have any choice but watch myself. It is definitely not what I want. I don't want to waste days and evenings of my life drinking or getting over a hangover. I thought there was not going to be a problem, but I don't have it under control. This is no nickel and dime situation; we're playing for a lot of marbles here.

**T:** True.

**P:** I have to admit, it was wonderful, though. I've never drunk that much in my life. But I know it's gone too far.

**T:** Have you considered attending AA?

**P:** I'm resistant to that. There's an AA chapter in the basement of . . . . I've sat in a little bit, hung around and listened. My reaction is that I don't want to be around that much religion.

**T:** The meetings vary in character. Most people have to try four or five before they find a meeting with the qualities they want.

**P:** I'm resisting. I say to myself that I don't have time. Hell, what do I have to do that's more important?

**T:** On most days there are meetings during lunch hour within walking distance of where you work.

**P:** Where do I get more information? I guess I can get their number from the phone book.

**T:** Yes.

**P:** . . . I'm sitting here developing such a case of shame. . . . Until now I could pass myself off as having a little problem with drinking. I can't say that anymore. I don't imagine the shame will last forever.

## The Following Session

**P:** When I left here last week, I called a friend who has been encouraging me to go to AA for a long time. She hasn't been heavy duty about it. . . . So I went to a meeting. I was real comfortable with these people. They publicly express things about stuff that I couldn't even express to myself or to you until this last year. In the first hour I decided I really was an alcoholic.

## Sobriety Achieved

Despite the mountain of evidence, Miss V. indicates that she was still not convinced of her addiction until she went to the AA meeting. From this point on Miss V. began attending AA regularly, daily during some periods. This began a new stage in her treatment. For about a year after she began attending AA, her psychotherapy treatment was of secondary importance to her in comparison to her work in AA and her sobriety. The psychological and physiological effects of withdrawal from alcohol represented more than enough of a challenge for her, and she had little interest in creating more pressure by delving deeper in her psychotherapy. In time, however, her discoveries in AA became less frequent and of less significance, and she began to take increasing interest in her psychotherapy treatment again, especially from the perspective of her addiction.

The treatment of an alcoholic certainly does not become simple once she has achieved sobriety; however it is far more straightforward than the treatment of an alcoholic who is still drinking. Especially during the initial period of abstinence, the patient and the therapist need to remain alert to stressors in the patient's life that can potentially trigger a relapse into drinking. In particular, initially the therapist must make sure that the therapy itself does not become a stressor that can lead the patient to feel overwhelmed and return to drinking.

Miss V. has now been sober for two years as of this writing, has recovered much of her alcohol-impaired short-term memory, and says she feels no temptation to return to drinking. She has acknowledged that she had been concealing from the therapist through omission and distortion a far more serious drinking problem than she had admitted. In the two years since she stopped drinking, she has continued in treatment, developed a romantic relationship with a man that is far more mature than any she had ever had previously, and handled the stress at work of two significant promotions without returning to alcohol.

This case illustrates the latitude available to the therapist. A therapist more experienced in treating problems with alcohol abuse would probably have been able to successfully challenge Miss V.'s denial of her alcohol problem in far less time than did this therapist. As long as the patient remains connected to the therapist and involved in the therapy, however, the drinking problem will not evaporate; the therapist will be given repeated opportunities to address it. Usually, if the therapist does not participate in the patient's denial, he can eventually address a substance abuse problem effectively even after missing many opportunities to do so.

## CONCLUSION

This book has presented some powerful clinical and conceptual tools for psychotherapists. By formulating a diagnostic hypothesis and evaluating the meaning of the patient's comments and behavior in the context of that hypothesis, the therapist can come closer to understanding the patient and empathizing with him. As the therapist becomes more attuned to the patient, the therapist can more effectively support the patient's basic struggle to find his real self and allow it to emerge. In the field of psychotherapy it is rare to find an approach that offers this degree of technical precision, strengthening the clinician's innate ability to intuit about the patient's inner struggle and to anticipate the course of the treatment. The techniques presented in this book, once they are mastered, should become common sense to the therapist and invisible to the patient. They should become part of the therapist's understanding of his own behavior as well as his patients'.

To balance the technical character of this book, it is fitting to end on a more human note. It must always be remembered that the curative component of any psychotherapy treatment has at its core the relationship between the therapist and the patient. Just as the therapist must impact on the patient, the patient must feel that he impacts on the therapist; the patient must feel that he matters. The therapist who is so polished that the patient cannot get under his skin will be limited in his impact on the patient. In the context of an otherwise carefully structured setting, it may be the therapist's mistakes, his occasional leaky countertransference, or his inability to be completely neutral that creates the most spontaneous and real interactions between the therapist and the patient, that convey to the patient the therapist's humanness and genuine concern. On the other hand, the therapist who lacks structure will be unable to create a safe enough environment for the patient to work as deeply as he otherwise might. Psychotherapeutic treatment must be a blend of clinical structure with human flexibility, therapeutic neutrality with genuine concern, and professional objectivity with a touch of explicit subjectivity.

# References

Adler, G., and Buie, D. H. (1973). The misuses of confrontation in psychotherapy of borderline cases. In *Confrontation in Psychotherapy*, ed. G. Adler and P. Myerson, pp. 147–162. New York: Science House.

Adler, G., and Myerson, P., eds. (1973). *Confrontation in Psychotherapy*. New York: Science House.

Breuer, J., and Freud, S. (1893-1895). Studies on hysteria. *Standard Edition* 2:268–270.

Brown, S. (1977). *Defining a process of recovery in alcoholism*. Doctoral Dissertation, California School of Professional Psychology, Berkeley, CA, April.

_____ (1985). *Treating the Alcoholic—A Developmental Model of Recovery*. New York: John Wiley & Sons.

Cashdan, S. (1988). *Object Relations Therapy*. New York: Norton Press.

Chessick, R. D. (1985). *Psychology of the Self and the Treatment of Narcissism*. New York: Jason Aronson.

Freud, S. (1894). The neuro-psychoses of defence. *Standard Edition* 3:43–68.

_____ (1914). Remembering, repeating and working through: further recommendations on the technique of psycho-analysis. *Standard Edition* 12:145–156.

_____ (1916). Some character-types met with in psycho-analytic work. *Standard Edition* 14:309–333.

_____ (1926). Inhibitions, symptoms and anxiety. *Standard Edition* 20:77–175.

Goldberg, A., ed. (1978). *The Psychology of the Self—A Casebook*. With H. Kohut. New York: International Universities Press.

Greenberg, J. R., and Mitchell, S. A. (1983). *Object Relations in Psychoanalytic Theory*. Cambridge, MA: Harvard University Press.

Greenson, R. R. (1967). *The Technique and Practice of Psychoanalysis*. New York: International Universities Press.

Guntrip, H. (1968). *Schizoid Phenomena Object-Relations and the Self*. London: Hogarth Press.

——— (1971). *Psychoanalytic Theory, Therapy, and the Self.* New York: Basic Books.

Haan, N. (1964). The relationship of ego functioning and intelligence to social status and social mobility. *Journal of Abnormal and Social Psychology* 69:594–605.

Hamilton, N. G. (1988). *Self and Others.* Northvale, NJ: Jason Aronson.

Kernberg, O. F. (1975). *Borderline Conditions and Pathological Narcissism.* New York: Jason Aronson.

Kernberg, O. F., Selzer, M. A., Koenigsberg, H. W., Carr, A. C., and Appelbaum, A. H. (1989). *Psychodynamic Psychotherapy of Borderline Patients.* New York: Basic Books.

Klein, M. (1975). *The Writings of Melanie Klein, Volume I—Love, Guilt, and Reparation and Other Works 1921-1945.* New York: Free Press.

Kohut, H. (1966). Forms and transformations of narcissism. *Journal of the American Psychoanalytic Association* 14:243–272. New York: International Universities Press.

——— (1968). The psychoanalytic treatment of narcissistic personality disorders. *Psychoanalytic Study of the Child* 23:86–113. New York: International Universities Press.

——— (1971). *The Analysis of the Self.* New York: International Universities Press.

——— (1977). *The Restoration of the Self.* New York: International Universities Press.

——— (1987). Narcissism as a resistance and as a driving force in psychoanalysis. In *Techniques of Working with Resistance,* ed. D. Milman and G. Goldman, pp. 167–178. Northvale, NJ: Jason Aronson.

Kohut, H., and Wolf, E. S. (1978). The disorders of the self and their treatment. *International Journal of Psycho-Analysis* 59:414–425.

Mahler, M. S. (1975). *The Psychological Birth of the Human Infant.* New York: Basic Books.

Masterson, J. F. (1976). *Psychotherapy of the Borderline Adult—A Developmental Approach.* New York: Brunner/Mazel.

——— (1981). *The Narcissistic and Borderline Disorders—An Integrated Developmental Approach.* New York: Brunner/Mazel.

——— (1983). *Countertransference and Psychotherapeutic Technique: Teaching Seminars on Psychology of the Borderline Adult.* New York: Brunner/Mazel.

Masterson, J. F., and Klein, R., eds. (1989). *Psychotherapy of the Disorders of the Self—The Masterson Approach.* New York: Brunner/Mazel.

Masterson, J. F., et al. (1991). *Comparing Psychoanalytic Psychotherapies: Developmental, Self and Object Relations; Self Psychology; Short Term Dynamic.* New York: Brunner/Mazel.

Meissner, W. W. (1959). Narcissistic personalities and borderline conditions: a differential diagnosis. *Journal of the American Psychoanalytic Association* 7:171–202. New York: International Universities Press.

Metzger, L. (1988). *From Denial to Recovery.* San Francisco: Jossey-Bass.

Ogden, T. H. (1979). On projective identification. *International Journal of Psycho-Analysis* 60:357–373.

Stern, D. (1985). *The Interpersonal World of the Infant.* New York: Basic Books.

Stolorow, R., Brandchaft, B., and Atwood, G. (1987). *Psychoanalytic Treatment—An Intersubjective Approach.* Hillsdale, NJ: The Analytic Press.

Vaillant, G. E. (1977). *Adaptation to Life.* Boston: Little, Brown.

Vaillant, G. E., and Drake, R. E. (1985). Maturity of ego defenses in relation to *DSM-III* Axis II personality disorder. *Archives of General Psychiatry* 42:597–601.

Wolf, E. (1988). *Treating the Self-Elements of Clinical Self Psychology.* New York: Guilford Press.

# Index